An Introduction to International Relations Theory

An Introduction to International Relations Theory

Perspectives and Themes

Third edition

Jill Steans, Lloyd Pettiford, Thomas Diez and Imad El-Anis

Routledge
Taylor & Francis Group

LONDON AND NEW YORK

First published 2001 by Pearson Education Limited
Second edition published 2005
Third edition published 2010

Published 2013 by Routledge
2 Park Square, Milton Park, Abingdon, Oxon OX14 4RN
711 Third Avenue, New York, NY 10017, USA

Routledge is an imprint of the Taylor & Francis Group, an informa business

ISBN 978-1-4082-0488-7 (pbk)

British Library Cataloguing-in-Publication Data
A catalogue record for this book is available from the British Library

Library of Congress Cataloging-in-Publication Data
Steans, Jill.
   An introduction to international relations theory : perspectives and themes / Jill Steans and Lloyd Pettiford with Thomas Diez and Imad El-Anis. -- 3rd ed.
         p. cm.
   Includes index.
   ISBN 978-1-4082-0488-7 (pbk.)
 I.   International relations--Textbooks.   I. Pettiford, Lloyd, 1966–
II.   Title.
   JZ1242.S74 2010
   327--dc22

2009046189

Typeset in 10/12 Times by 3

Contents

Preface   ix
Acknowledgements   x

Introduction   1

About this book   9
Perspectives and themes   12
Origins   13
Assumptions   14
Themes   16
Summary, criticisms, common misunderstandings and further reading   19
Criticisms   19
Common misunderstandings   20
Further reading   21

1 Liberalism   23

Introduction   23
Origins   26
Assumptions   31
Themes   32
Summary   48
Criticisms   49
Common misunderstandings   50
Further reading   51

2 Realism 53

Introduction 53
Origins 55
Assumptions 57
Themes 58
Summary 70
Criticisms 71
Common misunderstandings 73
Further reading 74

3 Structuralism 75

Introduction 75
Origins 76
Assumptions 85
Themes 86
Summary 99
Criticisms 100
Common misunderstandings 101
Further reading 102

4 Critical Theory 103

Introduction 103
Origins 107
Assumptions 115
Themes 116
Summary 126
Criticisms 126
Common misunderstandings 127
Further reading 128

5 Postmodernism 129

Introduction 129
Origins 134
Assumptions 142
Themes 143

Summary   151
Criticisms   152
Common misunderstandings   153
Further reading   154

6 Feminist perspectives   155

Introduction   155
Origins   157
Assumptions   165
Themes   165
Summary   180
Criticisms   180
Common misunderstandings   181
Further reading   182

7 Social constructivism   183

Introduction   183
Origins   184
Assumptions   187
Themes   192
Summary   200
Criticisms   201
Common misunderstandings   202
Further reading   202

8 Green perspectives   205

Introduction   205
Origins   212
Assumptions   217
Themes   217
Summary   228
Criticisms   228
Common misunderstandings   230
Further reading   230

Conclusions, key debates and new directions 231

Introduction 231
The post-positivist debate 232
Positivism and critiques of positivism in IR 232
Post-positivism in IR 240
The next stage in IR theory? 245
Further reading 247

Glossary of key or problem terms 249

Further reading 259

Index 273

Preface

It has been great to have the opportunity to produce a third edition of this text, this time with the full collaboration of Thomas Diez and Imad El Anis. Beyond them, all thanks offered in the first two editions still apply and we would also like to thank the publishers for patience in the face of unavoidable delays.

Lloyd Pettiford and Jill Steans (August 2009)

Acknowledgements

We are grateful to the following for permission to reproduce copyright material:

Figures

Figure 1.2 from *World Politics: Trend and Transformation*, 7th ed, St Martins (Kegley, C.W., and Wittkopf, E.R. 1999) p.310, Macmillan; Figure 2.1 from *World Politics: An Introduction to International Politics*, 2nd ed, Prentice Hall (Hocking, B and Smith, M 1995) p.75, Pearson Education; Figure 4.1 from *World Politics: Trend and Transformation*, 7th ed., St Martins (Kegley, C.W. and Wittkopf, E.R. 1999) p.163, Palgrave Macmillan; Figure 8.3 from *World Politics: An Introduction to International Relations*, 2nd ed., Prentice Hall (Hocking, B. and Smith, M. 1995) p.141, Pearson Education; Figure 8.4 from *World Politics: Trend and Transformation*, 7th ed., St Martins (Kegley, C.W. and Wittkopf, E.R. 1997) p.381, Palgrave Macmillan

Tables

Table 2.1 from *Global Politics: An Introduction*, Blackwell (Bretherton, C and Ponton, G 1996) 99.23-48, John Wiley & Sons; Table 3.1 from *Global Politics: An Introduction*, Blackwell (Bretherton, C and Ponton, G 1996) p.160, John Wiley & Sons

In some instances we have been unable to trace the owners of copyright material, and we would appreciate any information that would enable us to do so.

The publisher would like to thank the following for their kind permission to reproduce their photographs:

1 The Imperial War Museum picture library (Figure I.1). **2** Corbis: Bettmann (Figure I.2). **7** Corbis: Reuters (Figure I.3). **18** Corbis: Bettmann (Figure I.4). **46** Corbis: Chris Rainer (Figure 1.4). **78** Rex Features: Michael Charity (Figure 3.1). **91** Rex Features: Action Press (Figure 3.4). **110** Rex Features: Sipa (Figure 4.2). **119** Rex Features: Alistair MacDonald (Figure 4.3). **129** Corbis: Jose Fuste Raga (Figure 5.1). **137** Corbis: (Figure 5.2). **162** Getty Images: Lambert (Figure 6.2). **179** Corbis: Hulton-Deutsch Collection (Figure 6.3). **189** Rex Features: Sipa (Figure 7.1). **209** Corbis: Bettmann (Figure 8.1). **215** Rex Features: Tony Kyriacou (Figure 8.2). **224** Rex Features: DCY (Figure 8.5)

All other images © Pearson Education

Every effort has been made to trace the copyright holders and we apologise in advance for any unintentional omissions. We would be pleased to insert the appropriate acknowledgement in any subsequent edition of this publication.

Introduction

The story of the origins of International Relations usually begins with an account of the Great War (1914–18), a war so horrific that many people believed it was the war to end all wars. The destruction and devastation, the physical and economic effort expended on killing and the horrific slaughter of an entire generation (of predominantly young men) was on a scale few could have imagined before 1914. The study of International Relations grew out of the belief that war was the gravest problem facing humanity and that something must be done to ensure that there would be no more 'lost generations'.

The initial optimism that war could be prevented was short-lived. Just 20 years later the world was at war once again. In the wake of this Second World War, International Relations scholars continued to focus on the nature of international or inter-state relations, in their endeavours to understand the causes of war. In the aftermath of the conflict there were renewed efforts to organise the peace, with the birth of the United Nations in 1945. However, the mood of the time was rather less optimistic. The order which emerged after the Second World War was very different from the world of the 1920s and 1930s. Germany was almost completely destroyed by the war, and other European powers, like Britain and France, required major assistance packages to rebuild their shattered economies and

| **Figure I.1** | Soldiers 'going over the top' in the First World War |

Source: The Imperial War Museum picture library.

Figure I.2 The First World War was thought to be the 'war to end all wars' and inspired the creation of the discipline of International Relations. But nearly 100 years later and war is still very much a fact of life for many people around the globe.

Source: Bettmann/Corbis.

physical infrastructure. In contrast, the USA and USSR emerged from the war as 'superpowers', though the latter had suffered rather more than any other nation. In an age characterised by caution, if not cynicism, many scholars formed the view that the elimination of war was impossible and focused instead on how best to limit and contain conflict. As relations between the two military giants deteriorated in an atmosphere of suspicion and mistrust, and as awareness of the awesome destructive potential of nuclear weapons grew, politicians, military strategists and scholars alike turned their attention to the urgent need to maintain what became known as a 'balance of terror' between the USA and USSR, in order to prevent a Third World War and 'mutually assured destruction'.

HISTORICAL BOX

The Bomb

On 8 May 1945 the war in Europe had officially ended. At the time of the German surrender, it was generally believed that the allies would eventually triumph over Japan in the Pacific. Very little was left of the Japanese naval forces and the Japanese air force seemed to be on the point of collapse. However, Japan had proved to be a resilient and formidable opponent, and it was by no means assured that victory would come quickly. At 8.16 am on the morning of 6 August 1945 an American bomber nicknamed *Enola Gay* dropped the first atomic bomb on the Japanese city of Hiroshima. Three days later a second atomic bomb devastated the naval port of Nagasaki. The dramatic impact of the use of the bomb on people's perceptions of war is illustrated by the extract below. In the longer term, the impact of the bomb was to transform thinking about the nature and purpose of warfare, strategy and diplomacy, and open up an impassioned debate about both the morality and the efficacy of nuclear weapons.

> *The initial flash spawned a succession of calamities. First came heat. It lasted only an instant but was so intense that it melted roof tiles, fused the quartz crystals in the granite blocks, charred the exposed sides of telephone poles for almost two miles and incinerated near-by humans, so thoroughly that nothing remained except their shadows burnt into the asphalt pavements or stone walls.*
> (Extract from Fletcher Knebel and Charles Bailey, *No High Ground*, reproduced in Purnell's *History of the Twentieth Century*, London, Purnell Publications, 1968)

These events form the backdrop to the development of an academic discipline. However, much has changed since the Second World War. A key debate within contemporary international relations is whether the USA, which for so long has enjoyed a position of unrivalled influence in world affairs, has been eclipsed by Japan, the newly industrialised countries (mainly in South East Asia), and, perhaps even China, as we enter the 'Pacific Century'. However, this 'end of US hegemony' (dominance) thesis might appear unconvincing in the light of US military interventions in Afghanistan, Iraq and elsewhere in recent years. The language of human rights has become a global **discourse**, moving in to fill the ideological vacuum left by the end of the Cold War, empowering workers, women, indigenous peoples, ethnic minorities and other marginalised groups and arming them with a powerful vocabulary with which to articulate their grievances and demands; yet the human rights of individuals and specific groups across the world continue to be violated on a daily basis.

Discourse: the use of language to construct meanings. More specifically discourse refers to relatively 'bounded' areas of social knowledge (see Glossary).

Post-Cold War, the Soviet Union disintegrated, and ethnic and nationalist tensions re-emerged across this vast region of the world. Russian attempts to manage the difficult process of economic and political transition have been thwarted by ongoing conflict in the region and the failure – thus far – of the democratic project at home. Much of the European continent has enjoyed a period of unprecedented economic prosperity and has largely confronted the challenges of post-Cold War re-unification through recent waves of expansion. Yet the European Union has been accused of being a 'fortress', eager to stem the flow of poor, displaced people from North Africa, Bosnia and parts of the former Eastern bloc who are increasing seeking refuge in Western countries. The Middle East has emerged from a long period of colonial domination, but at the same time the rich oil reserves there mean that it remains of considerable strategic interest to the rest of the world, prompting intervention in the region's affairs, which can exacerbate existing tensions (increasingly complicated by the politics of water scarcity). The ongoing war in Iraq and the uncertainty and instability that attends post-war 'reconstruction' efforts similarly attests to ongoing and deeply entrenched conflicts in the region that also have an ethnic and religious dimension. Many parts of Latin America have been brutalised by a succession of military regimes which have plundered national resources and abused human rights in the name of national development. Africa has thrown off the yoke of formal colonialism, but continues to be dogged by problems of poverty and political instability, which in many African countries have been seriously exacerbated by the HIV/AIDS pandemic.

The inauguration of US President Barack Obama in January 2009 was followed by an initial wave of optimism (if not euphoria) that the US would provide a positive steer on many pressing problems from global climate change, to Arab/Israeli relations and the prospect of spreading and entrenching democracy across the African continent. Yet, Obama's inauguration followed in the wake of the most severe economic crisis to face the world since the Great Depression of the inter-war period, casting doubt on the prospects of a new and better world as we enter the second decade of the new millennium.

WORLD EXAMPLE BOX

The AIDS pandemic in Africa

At the end of 2007 it was estimated that some 22 million people in sub-Saharan Africa were living with HIV, with an additional 1.9 million people infected with HIV in that year alone. During 2008 HIV/AIDS claimed the lives of 1.5 million people in the region. While estimates vary, at least 11 million children have been orphaned as a consequence of the pandemic. The HIV/AIDS pandemic is a tragedy for African countries as well as individuals and families whose lives have been devastated by the disease. Life expectancy rates across the continent have fallen dramatically in recent years and continue to do so. Whilst a girl born in Britain today (July 2009) could expect to live beyond the year 2090, across Africa there are many millions who would not even make 2050.

Explanations for the scale of the problem are often rooted in the prevalence of certain cultural practices in Africa, as well as in gender inequalities and in the absence of committed political leadership and political will to combat the disease effectively. However, the HIV/AIDS pandemic has an international dimension. HIV/AIDS is a disease of poverty, since poverty profoundly affects the ability of individuals to secure adequate supplies of safe and nutritious food, to gain access to healthcare or to buy much needed medicines, all of which are crucial factors in combating AIDS. Moreover, a range of institutions and mechanisms of global governance shape the domestic policies of states over a range of issues and areas and these can have an adverse impact on public-health funding by reducing government spending on health and education.

Trade regimes dealing with intellectual property rights can also limit access to drugs that could alter the course of AIDS-related mortality in the developing world. The example of AIDS/HIV in Africa illustrates the complex inter-relationship between human security in individual societies and countries and the distribution of power and resources globally. It also points to how security/insecurity in the post-Cold War world cannot be viewed simply in terms of the absence of military threats, but also involves inequities in the distribution of power, income and resources among countries and specific social groups, and the impact that this has on the provision of education and primary health facilities for the poorest members of societies.

FILM BOX

Medecins Sans Frontières: *Invisibles*

This film (in fact made up of five short films) highlights a number of serious problems which are largely invisible, affecting as they do the poorest members of global society. Two of the films about Chagas disease and sleeping sickness highlight the ways in which the global pharmaceutical industry chases money in preference to cures.

Seek more information at: www.msf.org.uk

Today, the scourge of many different kinds of war and conflict continues to blight the lives of many of the world's peoples. However, it is no longer just the spectre of war that is perceived to threaten the peace, security and stability of the world. The agenda of world politics has changed radically: population has grown exponentially; poverty has increased dramatically; technology has advanced in rapid and unexpected ways; economic relations have become globalised to the extent that recession in one country can reverberate across the world, as the recent global economic crisis (2008–9) attests; sea levels have risen as a consequence of global warming, while pollution and the rapid and indiscriminate use of the world's natural resources threaten environmental catastrophe unless coordinated and effective action is taken.

There is no doubt that issues of culture, ethnicity, religion and identity have also re-emerged in recent years. Indeed, one of the most influential works published in the post-Cold War period is Samuel Huntington's thesis that the next great conflict would be along the lines of culture and civilisation, rather than ideology. Huntington's thesis has been very influential, yet there is much that could be disputed, not least Huntington's contention that people increasingly define their identity in ethnic and religious terms and that this does indeed now constitute the major 'fault line' in world politics. Huntington's thesis is seen in some quarters as simply an example of the 'Islamaphobia' that pervades discourse about security and 'threats' to the West in the wake of the September 11 attack on the World Trade Center in New York in 2001.

WORLD EXAMPLE BOX

The War on Terror

The 'War on Terror', launched by the US and its allies in the wake of the attack on the World Trade Center has served to elevate terrorism to the next great 'threat' to global security. There is nothing 'new' about terrorism. Unfortunately, it is a phenomenon that has long been a part of both national and international politics. The terrorist is seen to strike indiscriminately, seemingly making no distinction between 'legitimate' military and political targets and civilians. However, it is difficult in practice to differentiate terrorism from other forms of political violence. US government agencies are, in fact, inconsistent in the way they define terrorist and non-terrorists groups and action. Ultimately, it might be that 'terrorists', as opposed to 'freedom fighters', are those people who threaten or deploy force for a cause of which we do not approve. If no satisfactory legal definition for terrorism exists and it remains difficult to draw clear distinctions between the morality of terrorism as opposed to conventional warfare that involves civilian casualties and deaths, then we must ask how do some groups/agents/actions come to be defined as 'terrorist' and how this serves to legitimise certain kinds of violence – such as 'War on Terror' – as morally justified. This highlights that it is not only the concrete actions and dramatic events themselves occurring in international relations such as that which occurred in New York on September 11, but also the way in which we interpret certain acts and how discourses emerge on 'threats' to national and international security. The role of socially constructed meanings and ideas in international relations is discussed in greater depth in chapters 4, 5, 6 and 7.

Just what the changes sketched out above mean for the future of international relations is uncertain. For example, can international cooperation and dialogue help to engender the mutual respect and understanding necessary for people from different ethnic, cultural, religious and national communities to 'rub along' together? Or do we now live in a world where culture and religion really do constitute a fundamental fault line? Both tendencies – mutual tolerance and cohabitation, and suspicion, hostility and the perception of difference as a threat – seemingly co-exist in international relations.

It is not surprising, then, to discover that in recent years there have been challenges to a state-based, war-dominated understanding of the world. Just as International Relations in the earlier part of this century reflected the preoccupations and concerns of the time, the discipline has evolved and changed over time in response to what are perceived to be the urgent and pressing concerns of humanity today. What this means is that the student coming to the study of International Relations for the first time must not only grapple with the seemingly intractable problem of human conflict, but also develop an awareness of the changing nature of 'world order', the wide array of issues and concerns that have pushed their way onto the agenda of contemporary world affairs in recent years and also be receptive to the many voices clamouring to be heard. Contemporary international relations involve questions about the importance of the environment and economics, as well as war, peace and security. It means thinking about the needs, concerns and intrinsic value of different societies and cultures, as well as the actions and interests of the world's 'big players'. It means asking if we should think primarily in terms of globalisation and global processes, rather than a system or society of nation-states. Finally, at a time when many multinational corporations wield considerable power and influence over governments, should we continue to focus mainly on states (countries), or should we also include a range of other 'non-state actors'.

The study of International Relations (IR) also demands that we confront the question of the nature and purpose of human knowledge and understanding. Contemporary theoretical debates in IR focus on:

1. what can be said to exist, or what is real in international politics (an *ontological* question);
2. how can we understand the world and what is the status of the knowledge claims we make about the world (an *epistemological* question);
3. what methods we should adopt in our study (a *methodological* question).

To simplify somewhat: there are two major positions in contemporary IR theory – positivism and post-positivism. Positivists believe that we should endeavour – as far as possible – to study the world of international relations 'objectively' and dispassionately, in the same way that a physicist studies the physical world. Post-positivists contend that the scientific study of IR is not possible because our social position, values and so on influence the way we view the world and what we take to be the 'truth' of the world. This directs attention to the importance of social meanings, interpretations, ideologies and discourses on world affairs – in effect, the ideational dimension of the study of international relations.

Figure I.3 When is a terrorist not a terrorist? The answer might be 'when they are on our side'. From the perspective of these Afghans, the bombing of their country must look very much like terror.

Source: Reuters/Corbis.

CONCEPT BOX

Knowledge and understanding in IR

We all live on the same planet, but throughout history and across the globe people live and have lived very different kinds of lives; therefore, their ways of making sense of their world are quite different. Post-positivists of various hues believe that our understanding of the world is constructed through shared social meanings which invest actions and events with significance. The insight that people draw from specific experiences and shared understanding can be applied to different countries and cultures. Some feminists believe that women have very different ways of viewing the world and making sense of particular processes or events which are rooted in very different life experiences (see chapter 6). Karl Marx famously employed the term 'ideology' to describe the belief systems and world views of particular social classes, a view that continues to inform contemporary Critical Theory. Constructivists (see chapter 7) regard all knowledge as inherently social – knowledge is not 'out there' waiting to be discovered, but is actively constructed by people (subjects) endeavouring to make sense of the world. Post-structuralist thinkers (see chapter 5) argue that we can never completely grasp the essence or truth about the world; this is because we use language to invest our actions with meaning and to communicate with others, but language is 'unstable'; the meaning of words or terms – signifiers and symbols – is never fixed, but constantly shifting.

This raises the question of how we evaluate or rank different perspectives or views. Neo-liberal institutionalists (discussed in chapter 1) and neo-realists (chapter 2) believe that it is possible to distinguish between 'facts' and 'value' or 'truth' and 'ideology'. If it is not possible, however, then must we reconcile ourselves to the relativity of truth claims and also accept that competing world views are necessarily irreconcilable or incommensurable? This also raises questions about how power relations are implicated in 'knowledge claims'. That is to say, we have to consider whether certain explanations or stories about the world are accepted because they are intrinsically better, seemingly having a better purchase on 'reality', or because they are internally consistent, logical and so on, or whether our willingness to accept one interpretation of events (rather than another) is influenced by the status and power of the 'knower'. For example, universities as institutions confer special status on people – academics and students – as 'knowers'; we would generally accept that the views of people who have engaged in sustained study of world affairs are better informed and thus have a better purchase on 'truth' than the hypothetical 'man in the street'. However, those schooled in the study of International Relations draw upon a very specific intellectual heritage that excludes other 'ways of knowing' (as you read through this text, pay attention to how many works cited as 'authorative' are written by Western-based academics). Thus, cultural beliefs can be dismissed on the grounds of facts established by Western 'science', while 'women's knowledge' might be deemed to be founded in emotion and sentiment rather than reason, and so necessarily suspect. The nature of knowledge about the world of international relations and what we can claim in the name of knowledge is a core theme in many of the later chapters in this text.

Posing the question, 'why do we study international relations?', encourages us to reflect on whether we are hoping to effect positive changes, or whether we can do no more than gain a better understanding of intractable problems endemic to the human condition. Robert Cox, for example, made a famous distinction between problem-solving theories and critical theories. Problem-solving theories take the world 'as it is' and endeavour to think through problems and offer prudent advice to policy makers tasked with the challenge of negotiating the 'real world'. Critical theories, on the other hand, question the immutability of the present world order and see the purpose of theory as advancing the project of positive change (emancipation). While positivists are primarily interested in trying to discover generalisable 'laws' of IR, post-positivists tend to focus on the normative dimension of IR, focusing, perhaps, on questions of inequality, justice and rights. There has been a long tradition of normative theory in IR and, although we cannot cover areas like International Political Theory and International Ethics in depth in this text, we do draw your attention to the normative issues raised by various strands of IR theory at different points in the book.

Contemporary IR is a demanding subject for undergraduate study. First, the study of IR often assumes a fairly sound knowledge of international history and contemporary international affairs. Second, IR draws upon and blends many disciplines as well as considering a whole range of issues and ideas which, while they have a global context, are very different from the discipline's original concerns. Third, and perhaps most important, the student of IR today is faced with a much wider array of approaches than even ten years ago and the discipline is virtually unrecognisable from that of 20 or 30 years ago.

About this book

There are many fine introductions to International Relations but this one attempts to do something that other texts do not: provide a *first* introduction to the multitude of theoretical perspectives which have been brought to bear on international relations. Before we can begin to study international relations, we have to ask the question of what constitutes our field of study. That is, what actors, issues and processes do we regard as important or significant? The study of contemporary international relations is made even more challenging by the lack of consensus on these matters. A narrow definition of the subject might be that it is concerned with states (countries) and how they interact. This has the advantage of clearly identifying and limiting the subject matter and core concerns of the discipline, by concentrating on states as the central actors and limiting our study to how states conduct their relations with 'others', through foreign policy, diplomacy and war, for example.

However, this definition would not satisfy most IR scholars today, and would effectively exclude many issues and areas where new approaches and research agendas have generated fresh insights. A very broad definition of the subject might be that the discipline of International Relations is concerned with the human condition on a global scale. This definition has the virtue of being *relatively* inclusive (although this definition would raise objection from the increasing number of scholars influenced by ecological ethics – see chapter 8). It also demonstrates forcibly the value of International Relations as the only area of the social sciences which considers the world's peoples as a whole. On the other hand, it serves to blur the boundaries somewhat between the discipline of International Relations and other areas of the social and human sciences such as Politics, Sociology, Economics, History, Law and Geography. International Relations has always tended to be somewhat inter- (or at least multi-) disciplinary, including elements of Geography, Economics, History and Politics in particular.

Some scholars prefer to study the world by dividing it up geographically into clearly demarcated 'bounded spaces' such as nation-states and regions (for example Asia Pacific, Latin America, Eastern Europe). Some scholars make no real distinction between International Relations and Comparative Politics. Others argue that, increasingly, it is difficult to justify making such clear-cut distinctions between the international, the regional and the national and prefer to employ the looser terms 'world' or 'global' politics to describe their realm of study. Still another way of approaching the subject is to concentrate on 'issues' – for example, health, water, population, nuclear proliferation, trade and so on. There are also a number of distinctive sub-fields within International Relations such as Peace Studies, International Political Economy, Diplomatic History or Security Studies. As you can see, the range of issues, concerns and research orientations which can be incorporated into this field of study is, potentially, very wide indeed.

As well as deciding on *what* we are studying when we study International Relations, we also need to ask *how* we are to go about the task of understanding a complex world and, of course, why we are engaging in this activity in the first place. That is to say, what specific concerns and motivations inform and shape our activity? Once we begin to reflect on what we think is important or unimportant, significant or trivial, we are forced to ask a further question; on what basis do we make such judgements? For example, the call by some feminists (in the liberal and empiricist traditions) for research on the political, economic and social status of women around the world might be dismissed in some quarters as an indulgence or side issue. Feminists are, in turn, entitled to point out that women constitute over 50 per cent of the world's population and that the **marginalisation** of women and their lives is a consequence of the indifference and, perhaps, self-interest of the already powerful, who for the most part are men.

Marginalisation: the process whereby some issues or some people's lives are thought to be less important than others. The excluded or marginalised tend to be those with little economic or political power, at local, national and global levels.

Similarly, global warming might be regarded as an 'issue' in international relations which is slowly finding its way onto the agenda of international politics, but one which is at best a secondary concern for the world's great 'players' like the USA or Japan. However, global warming might be perceived as a pressing concern to people living in small island Pacific states, which are facing the threat of rising sea levels. In this case, global warming is likely to be viewed as a vital security concern.

'This is the very best island I know, and it's going to be drowned in the sea I think ...' Resident of Pacific Island, Tuvalu.

Moreover, the world is likely to look very different to a politician or career diplomat than it does from the point of view of a poor woman living in a heavily indebted country, or a coalminer whose livelihood has been effectively wiped out by the economic whirlwind of 'globalisation'. Clearly, the same world can be viewed from a number of perspectives or, indeed, we might say that there are 'many worlds'. It is not entirely surprising to find, therefore, that International Relations has grown into a diverse discipline with a number of quite distinctive approaches, which in turn focus on particular aspects of the world, raise certain issues and are driven by particular concerns. This means, of course, that in addition to the wide-ranging nature of the subject, the student must also confront the broad and diverse range of theoretical perspectives which have been brought to bear on aspects of international relations.

The perspectives in this book represent what might be said to be the well-established perspectives on International Relations, and also a number of critical and constructivist approaches that have gained currency in the field since the late 1980s. We are only too aware of the challenging nature of the subject and have tried to produce a book which steers a course between comprehensiveness, on the one hand, and accessibility, on the other. The major aim of the book is to provide an introduction to a number of theoretical perspectives. A theory is an attempt to explain something – an event or activity. For example, a theory might attempt to explain the cause of a war, or why and under what conditions states engage in cooperative trade strategies. A theory is thus a set of ideas, which are coherent, internally consistent and claim to have some purchase on the nature of the world and how it 'works'. A perspective is a particular representation of 'reality'. A theoretical perspective is, therefore, an attempt to construct a coherent explanation for a certain phenomenon, which in turn rests upon a wider belief system, or upon certain basic assumptions, about the nature of the world.

It is not unusual to find students who are rather sceptical of the value of theory, believing that much of what we observe in the world is 'common sense' or that we should simply concentrate on the 'facts'. Whatever their feelings, students of International Relations are increasingly expected to relate their work to theory in order to achieve the highest grades. This provides one justification for producing a book of this kind and a possible motive for buying it. Despite such pragmatic motives, it is important not to lose sight of why theory is important. You cannot assume that the 'facts' speak for themselves in some way and, as for so-called 'common sense', this can often be a 'smoke-screen' used to disguise an interested, particular or partial point of view. While this text is aimed at students new to the study of IR, an understanding of theory is the key to success at all levels of academic study. We hope that this text will provide students with the 'basic' upon which to build in future years.

REFLECTION BOX

The theory and practice of world politics

The relationship between theory and practice is complex and will be dealt with in some depth in later chapters. At this point, however, it is useful to consider the inter-relationship between how we understand and interpret the world and the consequences which this has for our actions.

Approaches to IR inspired by realism (chapter 2) often draw upon ideas about the essentially selfish nature of human beings. Moreover, since international relations are fundamentally anarchic (the international order lacks any central sovereign power or government), decisions and actions are taken in the context of uncertainty, where levels of trust are minimal. This is held to be a constant dilemma for states and, so, is a recurring theme in the International Relations literature. However, it is possible that starting out from these assumptions leads to certain types of behaviour and strategies that seemingly confirm and validate the realist world view. That is to say, our beliefs about the world serve to engender a 'self-fulfilling prophecy'. For example, suppose we are entrusted with ensuring that our country is secure from attack. We are in possession of weapons of mass destruction. However, this does not, in itself, guarantee our security, because other countries have a similar military capacity. We do not know for certain if these countries pose a real threat to us, but we cannot be sure that they do not. In such circumstances, a theory about the major processes and forces that motivate our behaviour and the behaviour of our potential adversaries is absolutely essential and, what is more, it is vital that we 'get it right'.

Suppose we believe that states are likely to behave aggressively, because this is 'human nature'. In such circumstances, we are likely to recommend a defence strategy that always enables our country to negotiate from a position of strength. The problem is, of course, that our action can then be interpreted as a form of aggression by our 'opponents'. In such circumstances, the relationship quickly degenerates into one of fear, mistrust and aggressive posturing. On the other hand, if our theory tells us that the real 'problem' is one of insecurity and mistrust, rather than real aggressive intent, our action will be very different. Rather than engaging in a build-up of arms, we might open up diplomatic relations, negotiate arms control treaties and suggest various verification procedures or confidence-building measures, which will help to strengthen the level of trust in the relationship.

We will not labour this point about the relationship between theory and practice here; suffice to say that it is important to recognise that theories might not so much describe an unproblematic world 'out there' as construct 'reality' in certain ways. This has consequences for how 'problems' are identified and events interpreted, and this, in turn, has important consequences for how we act. It is important, therefore, to have a basic grasp of theories and the practical consequences of adopting certain perspectives rather than others, at the very outset of study.

This book employs an approach which is more theoretically focused than many introductory texts. It is designed to help students cope with the theoretical deep-end of a rapidly changing discipline into which they will be thrown. This does not mean that students will be able to use this book without developing a general knowledge surrounding international affairs and a sense of the historical development of the practice of world politics. It is, accordingly, very much designed as a first introduction to the subject, aimed at first-level students in particular but also useful as a reference/source of clarification for all students. While, to some extent, we aim to encourage a degree of independent learning, this book is also designed to be used in conjunction with a programme of study. We hope, in particular, that it will allow you to make sense of unfamiliar terms which might emerge as part of that programme. To further assist you, we have included an extensive Glossary of key or problem terms at the end of the book and, where appropriate, we include brief definitions of key terms in grey panels in the text.

Perspectives and themes

In order to make the task of a comprehensive introduction manageable and to aid understanding, the discussion of theoretical perspectives is organised around a limited number of key themes. In putting together a book intended as a first introduction, we also recognise that the activity of theorising is a complex process and that the resulting theories are often rather complicated. The theoretical perspectives which you will encounter in this book frequently employ an unfamiliar vocabulary, or assume more knowledge than is useful to the beginner. Some introductory textbooks similarly might confuse the reader in their attempt to tell a story of International Relations which includes all possible caveats and nuances.

Perhaps an appropriate analogy for our efforts here is that they are somewhat akin to a teach-yourself language book. If you have ever tried to learn a language solely from a book, or even cassettes, you will realise that the real learning starts once you try to put your knowledge into practice. However, the initial stage of book-learning is very useful because it allows one to begin understanding and to start talking. Actual conversations will then introduce new vocabulary, often learned contextually, and one can also learn from mistakes that are made. International Relations theories have their own language, a specific vocabulary and a set of concepts, which are used to construct knowledge about the world. These theories could be said to be the difficult part of the language of International Relations and this book is designed to get you talking in this language.

As with a language (though the comparison is not exact) communication is the key. If you mistakenly learned 'Je voudrais *une* café' (rather than *un* café) this will not prevent communication; in time you will correct your error. Similarly, one does not need to understand or use the concept of a 'subjunctive' to begin learning or be understood in another language. Accordingly, we do not consider it a serious weakness, but rather a strength, that we seek to simplify International Relations so that you can begin to discuss it. Through discussion, misunderstandings will become apparent, ideas will develop and further reading will then become intelligible and, in turn, contribute to your deliberations. This book introduces a limited vocabulary and explains a limited set of ideas, organised around a selective set of themes. We are attempting to convey something of the diversity and scope of International Relations by offering you introductory chapters on a number of key perspectives. This is characterised by a degree of simplification: it does not claim to capture the full richness of its subject. This is because just as too much vocabulary, and therefore constant references to a dictionary, would likely discourage the language student, we are looking to explain International Relations, which has its own language, in a way that will be clearly understood and encourage the student's first steps. Where a specific vocabulary is introduced it is clearly explained.

A second major objective of the book is to equip you with the knowledge and skills necessary for further study. By the time you reach the end of the text, we hope that you will have a sense of the richness, complexity and, yes, difficulty of International Relations, but that you will also feel that you have learnt enough of the language and gained sufficient understanding of the basic assumptions and guiding ideas of each major approach to undertake more in-depth study with confidence. In the concluding chapter, we return to questions regarding the nature and purpose of theory, but address these questions in more detail.

In the first instance, we would suggest that you read the chapters in this book sequentially. The various boxes have been devised on the assumption that you will, for example, familiarise yourself with the fundamentals of liberalism, before moving on to digest the basics of realism. However, we also hope that, having read the text through once, you will then be able to dip into it from time to time, just as you would a language book, to remind yourself of key discussions or in order to be assured that you are employing a term in the correct context. When we learn even the basics of IR theories and attempt to engage in meaningful exchanges with others about the subject, we are drawing upon discourses about the world which have a distinctive language, which have a history, which draw upon particular intellectual traditions and which have been constructed in the context of specific interests and concerns.

At this stage, our objectives are to:

- introduce and clearly explain the vocabulary of theories;
- consider their specific intellectual origins;
- outline the basic assumptions of each in an easily accessible manner;
- show how these differing assumptions lead us to different views of the key concepts and themes of the discipline; and
- sketch some of the ways in which each can be criticised (though you should not assume from this that the authors *necessarily* agree with all the criticisms offered).

Origins

Chapters follow very similar structures. For the sake of clarity and simplicity, for the most part we discuss realism or Critical Theory, for example, as if it were a coherent and unified school of thought or perspective, when in fact most approaches – feminist, postmodern, social constructivist and so on – are characterised by their own internal debates and embrace different positions. Our justification in assuming a unified position and presenting feminism or realism or Critical Theory as a 'perspective' is that we do not want you to find your first encounter with IR to be unnecessarily frustrating or complicated. So, for example, we frequently speak of liberalism as if there were only one version, whereas in fact there are many different strands. You should be aware that not all of the texts which you will encounter can be neatly 'pigeon-holed' or labelled as, for example, 'Marxist' or 'postmodern'. Similarly social constructivism (chapter 7) is now recognised as a distinctive and, indeed, an increasingly influential approach in IR, but social constructivism can be viewed more as a continuum of positions ranging from rationalism to poststructuralism, rather than a singular perspective. Moreover, some strands of feminism can be aptly categorised as 'constructivist', whereas others, liberal feminism for example, are rationalist in orientation. We will elaborate on difficulties of categorisation and classification of theoretical approaches in the concluding chapter.

Another problem students encounter when endeavouring to negotiate a burgeoning IR literature is that approaches and perspectives may be referred to using a number of different names. Where appropriate, in the relevant chapters we shall draw your attention to different names and uses of terms. However, while essentially aiming to simplify theories, we also try to alert you to at least some nuances of each school of thought. This is best achieved by taking a brief look at the origins of the particular theoretical approach. This will also allow you to appreciate more fully the many 'strands' of feminist, or Green, thought and how they open up specific questions and areas of interest within the broader domain of International Relations.

Assumptions

All human action is based on certain fundamental beliefs about the nature of the world and the purpose of life. As Italian Marxist Antonio Gramsci famously held, all people are 'theorists'. In the course of our day-to-day lives we try to give our actions meaning by reflecting upon our particular motives for undertaking a course of action and what we aim to achieve. We will also, no doubt, weigh up the various obstacles to realising our objectives. However, for the most part our reflections will not extend to the fundamental assumptions we are making about the nature of the world and the purpose of human knowledge, preferring to leave the 'bigger questions' to the world's philosophers. In contrast, theorists devote a great deal of their time and intellectual capacities to pondering these same questions. Each perspective is built upon a number of assumptions about the nature of world problems and, relatedly, prescriptions for how to overcome them.

Realists, liberals and Marxists, for example, have developed their own distinctive approaches to studying International Relations, mapping out the field conceptually, identifying who they each consider to be the main '**actors**' and the big issues in international relations. While there will be some differences in the way certain basic ideas are applied to IR within each perspective, all liberals or realists, for example, share certain fundamental assumptions. These assumptions represent the liberal or realist points of departure in explaining the world. In each chapter we highlight some of the basic assumptions which underpin perspectives in International Relations. To help you, we have tried to keep the discussion of assumptions fairly simple in the first instance. We divide up our assumptions into a number of categories:

Actor: if the world is regarded as a stage then actors in international relations can be understood in much the same way as actors in a theatre. This notion of an 'actor' can be applied to entities that are recognised under international law, so in this sense states are actors, but not individuals. The notion of actor might also be used more loosely to describe entities which have influence or agency (see separate box); in this view actors might be states, multinational corporations, international organisations, NGOs, social movements, or in exceptional cases, influential individuals.

1. Perhaps the most basic assumption that each perspective makes concerns what constitutes human nature. The idea that we can identify an essential human 'nature' outside historical, cultural and social contexts is increasingly disputed within IR. Similarly, the idea that we can extrapolate the behaviour of entities like states from observable characteristics of human beings is also contested. However, we have decided to include debates about human nature and the relationship between human nature, human behaviour and state behaviour, because it has been influential in some strands of IR and, moreover, it is a simple but nevertheless useful way of comparing and contrasting perspectives. So, in each chapter we ask from this perspective: is human nature seen to be unchanging (immutable)? Or does behaviour vary according to the wider social and cultural context and over time? For example, critical perspectives argue that what we often take to be unalterable features of human nature actually describe human behaviour at a specific period in history. So, given current experience we might believe that people are 'by nature' materialistic and greedy. However, Critical Theorists argue that people are conditioned to behave in a self-interested manner and to accumulate material possessions in excess of their basic needs because capitalism is a divisive social system that generates conflict, competition and insecurity. It follows from this that human nature is not immutable or fixed, but changes in accordance with the social and political conditions of any given historical period.

2. We also highlight the basic assumption that each perspective makes about the main 'actors' and

'processes'. For example, realists argue that a central process of international relations is the exercise of power. States use whatever power they possess to advance or protect the national interest. So, in realist thought the state is a key actor and power is the main process while 'national interest' is a key concept. The liberal perspective highlights many actors, including states, non-governmental organisations (NGOs) and multinational corporations (MNCs), and stresses the fundamentally cooperative nature of international relations in a world which has become increasingly interdependent.

3. A third way of categorising or grouping certain approaches to IR is to look at the way in which they conceptualise and theorise the relationship between domestic societies/polities (the inside) and the international realm (the outside). We ask: from any given perspective, is there a clear separation between the 'domestic' and the 'international' realms? So, for example, traditional or classical realists see the state as a territorially and nationally 'bounded' community with distinctive boundaries. The domestic (inside) is very clearly demarcated from the international (outside). Greens, on the other hand, argue that focusing on the 'artificial' political and territorial boundaries which exist in the world (though not visible from space) detracts from the fundamentally interconnected and interdependent nature of all life (eco) systems on the planet.

4. Perspectives also help us understand the nature and purpose of human knowledge differently, so we might ask: does this perspective claim to be 'value free' or impartial? Does it claim to capture the essence of human behaviour – the mainsprings of human motivation – without reference to the ideational or discursive dimensions of human relationships? Relatedly, we ask whether this perspective points to universal laws, or makes universalist truth claims – that is, claims which apply to all people at all times?

5. We might also draw attention to the prescriptive implications of the perspective (what does it say *should* be done?). So, again, realists tend to have a very pessimistic view of the possibilities of creating a better world, and see 'theory' as essentially providing a guide to how states*men*, military leaders or diplomats should act in an insecure world. Their prescription, if they have one, is 'caution'. Liberals, Critical Theorists and feminists, on the other hand, argue that by gaining a better understanding of the human condition we are empowered to change it and frequently suggest how it should be changed.

6. Related to point 5, we will also occasionally touch upon the way in which each perspective views the relationship between constraints on behaviour and possibility of changes. We will ask: how does this perspective view the relationship between constraints on human action (structure) and possibilities for people to effect (bring about) changes in the existing 'order' and the way they live their lives (**agency**)? The prescriptive implications (in effect, recommendations) of a 'theory' might be revolutionary. That is, we might be forced to conclude that the only solution to the problems that beset humankind is fundamental change in the way societies – including societies of states – are organised, and a radical alteration in the way people behave. At the same time we might be forced to recognise that our action is constrained by the existence of concrete institutions and practices that support the existing order. This might lead us to conclude that, while change is possible and worth struggling for, in any historical period there will be certain limits on what can be achieved.

Agency: an actor (see separate box) is said to have agency when they are able to exert influence, or affect the outcome of any given process or event in some way. It is perhaps easiest to contrast 'agency' (*making* things happen) with the idea of 'structure' (the context in which things happen). For those people who believe that 'structure' is highly important in international relations, human agency is limited; actors are unable greatly to influence individual events or the general course of history, because they are constrained by the structure of the international system or world-system.

These assumptions are really the key to understanding the different types or schools of theory which exist within the broad domain of International Relations. We will not attempt to delve into questions of 'objectivity' or 'subjectivity' or 'universalism' or 'particularism' at this stage. This is some of the difficult language of theory and cannot be tackled until you have picked up the basic vocabulary. It is more appropriate to revisit these issues in the concluding chapter. Instead, we will confine ourselves to the less ambitious task of highlighting similarities and differences between perspectives as we work our way through the text and, from time to time, asking you to reflect on how certain interests and concerns have shaped each school of thought. At the same time, we hope that from time to time you will step 'outside' these particular debates and reflect upon the kinds of issues and concerns which are *neglected* by, say, realism, liberalism or structuralism. In this way you will become aware of the limitations as well as possibilities of 'explaining' and 'understanding' inherent in each perspective.

We would like you to be able to work your way through the various discussions of perspectives and themes, picking up the basic vocabulary as you go along, and getting a very general sense of the insights that they offer into, say, security or conflict. However, we also hope you will gain an understanding of the origins and assumptions of each, because this enables us to compare and contrast common and divergent underpinnings and so prepares the ground for more in-depth study. Reflections on the basic assumptions of different perspectives are encouraged from time to time.

In some sections of the text, however, you will be invited to consider similarities between different ways of thinking about the nature of security, or the problems of inequality and justice. Alternatively, you might be asked to consider the differing understanding of the relationship between the 'national' and 'international' realms offered by liberal or constructivist thinkers. In order to encourage reflection on these issues and upon key issues or debates, from time to time we will pose short questions in the text. You will also find a number of reflection-type questions scattered throughout this book in some of the reflection boxes such as that on p. 11.

Themes

We also discuss the particular insights which theories offer into various aspects of international relations. These discussions are organised around a set of specific themes: peace and security; the state and power; institutions and world order; identity and community; inequality and justice; and conflict and violence. The order in which we discuss these themes varies from chapter to chapter. In concentrating on certain key themes, we are not claiming that we have identified the 'essence' of international relations. The aim is rather to enable you to make quick and easy comparisons and contrasts between different approaches and so aid learning. However, we have selected the particular themes we have because they have preoccupied scholars in the past and continue to attract the sustained attention of International Relations scholars today. The degree to which we discuss certain themes in individual chapters varies. However, even though we have a relatively short discussion of peace and security in our chapter on structuralism, we are certainly not suggesting that a structuralist has nothing to say about this area. Rather, we are offering you an aid to study which identifies the dominant concerns of, in this instance, structuralist work in the field, which have shaped the way in which this particular perspective has emerged and developed within the context of International Relations. Inevitably, you are going to find 'grey areas' both in terms of intellectual orientation and key concerns.

Obviously, the various themes have been addressed at length by different thinkers at different times in the history of International Relations theory. From time to time, we will offer you short discussions of what we consider to be interesting and relevant discussions of human rights or peace which are drawn from some influential International Relations texts. Any discipline will have its classic or founding texts; these are works with which any student or scholar would be expected to have a certain level of familiarity. In occasionally presenting the key ideas of a particular text we are intimating that this text is regarded as one of those books and that you should look more into the ideas of a particular author. An author box looks like this:

AUTHOR BOX

David Ricardo (1772–1823)

Ricardo argued that individual countries had a comparative advantage in the production of certain kinds of goods and services. For reasons to do with their natural resource base or climate, perhaps, or because of the particular composition and skills of the workforce, some countries would always be able to produce certain types of goods more cheaply and efficiently than others. Ricardo argued that for this reason it made sense for countries to specialise in the production of certain goods and services and engage in trade with each other. Trade was to be positively encouraged because, even though not all individuals, groups and countries benefited equally, it was beneficial to everybody's overall welfare.

We do not intend to limit our discussion to key thinkers or texts that have shaped the development of IR as an academic discipline. This is because we recognise that students often learn more effectively through exposure to visual media like television or film. Moreover, film and other forms of mass media are themselves important social products that influence the way we think about the bigger questions concerning perhaps the morality of war or pacifism, the socioeconomic and cultural impacts of colonialism and so on. Occasionally then we will use a film or literary text to try to explain a central problem in IR, or to illustrate a particular idea or issue. A film box looks like this:

FILM BOX

Vietnam

The horrors of Vietnam, represented on the big screen through films such as *Platoon, Full Metal Jacket, Hamburger Hill* and *Born on the Fourth of July*, is the sort of thing that gets people interested in International Relations in the first place. As people study the discipline their initial reactions to war, for example, begin to change; this change is often fuelled by the way the films cause us to jump as each twig breaks in the forest. In fact, one of the big complaints of IR graduates is that a trip to the cinema is stripped of its innocent pleasure by all the questions which now spring to mind. For example, students of IR who have engaged with feminism might begin to question the way the war is presented and particularly about the representation of war and the 'celebration' of masculine traits in such films.

Many films about Vietnam (though not all) encourage us to identify with the 'hero' and not to ask political questions. Films often concentrate on the immediacy of specific conflicts and on individual heroes and villains. So, as the 'Gook' hordes emerge out of the forest darkness, faceless and indistinguishable, we instinctively feel for the poor GI. From the perspective of the Viet Cong, however, the GI is part of an invasionary force. US deaths (and MIAs) were a fraction of those suffered by a Vietnamese enemy fighting for the right to determine the future of their own country. IR students become aware that the USA, in its mass bombing and eco-logical destruction of Indo-China, was continuing where France had left off its colonial struggle. People become aware of US authors such as Noam Chomsky who has characterised US 'help' for South Vietnam as an invasion: an invasion to impose the will of the US over the likely outcome of democratic elections.

There are many subtle ways in which film and politics are interconnected. For example, it is not unknown for the US Pentagon to cooperate with film-makers (in terms of access to land and hardware, which is crucial to the production of many films), the price being a positive representation of US policy and conduct. Even some films with nothing to do with war might have an army recruitment booth appearing in the background. Of course, as our discussion above implies, people are not simply passive recipients of the messages that films aim to convey and, of course, one can easily point to examples of 'radical' war films that are deeply critical of, in this case, the USA. The point is that films can tell us much about international relations, but so can thinking about from whose point of view it is they are told and what assumptions about the world they are based on. Stories and representations of the world very often represent the perspectives of the powerful.

Finally, of course, 'themes' have emerged from perceived processes, tendencies or problems in the 'real world'. As we have alluded to above, the discipline of International Relations emerged in the wake of the First World War, when the need to understand the tragedy of human conflict, as a first step in creating a more stable and just world order, seemed urgent. Some scholars have been concerned with solving the immediate problem posed by nuclear weapons, or have been interested to discover patterns or cycles in world events. All assume, of course, that there is a real world 'out there'

Figure I.4   Thu Xuyn, S. Vietnam: Coughing Vietnamese women and children emerge from a hole from which they had been flushed by troopers of the 1st Cavalry using smoke and teargas while searching out Vietcong during operation 'Eagles Claw,' the latest phase of the central highlands campaign which started with Operation Masher.

Source: © Bettmann/Corbis: U1505657

which forms the object of their study. Whether there is a real world out there, or only differing representations and 'stories' about the world, is an interesting and important question which will be discussed at greater length in later chapters (especially chapter 5). At this stage we simply offer some examples of events which have been interpreted as significant and suggestive of particular trends or processes in international relations, or which have been offered up as illustrative of profound and certain 'truths' about the human condition. In so doing, we are trying to convey a sense of how theoretical discussions are inevitably shaped by context and historical circumstance. A world example box looks like this:

WORLD EXAMPLE BOX

The oil crisis

In 1973 the major oil-exporting countries decided that if they worked together they could control the supply and price of oil, by forming a cartel called OPEC. In this way, OPEC was able to charge oil consumers four times as much almost overnight. The effects were fuel shortages and panic. The oil crisis was significant for two reasons. First, it signalled the increasing importance of economics in IR. Second, both the immediate impact and aftermath of the oil crisis provided a powerful demonstration of just how vulnerable states could be even while their borders were policed, defended and secured. Clearly states existed in a world where the economy was becoming increasingly internationalised. In a situation of such interdependence states increasingly lacked control. The oil price rises of 1973 (and again in 1979) are just one reason why it became clear to some scholars that a concentration on military capabilities simply did not capture the full complexity of IR. The rise of economics also gave more weight to the claim that states were not the only actors of significance in international relations. So, whereas at the height of the Cold War in the 1950s and 1960s liberal approaches failed to make any serious inroads into the dominance of realism in the discipline, during the 1970s and 1980s the 'liberal' perspective, and more specifically liberal interdependence theory, became integrated into the IR mainstream.

Summary, criticisms, common misunderstandings and further reading

Each chapter will include a summary listing the main points made about each perspective. After such clarification, since International Relations is characterised by disagreement among scholars, each chapter looks at criticisms which might be offered of each perspective. To aid understanding, each chapter also includes a page box on common misunderstandings and also appropriate guidance on further reading; it is important to read the original works once you fully understand the basic ideas and assumptions which inform each distinctive approach. At the end of the book you will find a Glossary of key or problem terms which will include most of the words which are not readily apparent to a beginner in IR or the social sciences more generally. Finally, it is important to realise that the meanings generated by IR theories are conditioned by the specific context in which theoretical debates take shape. It is only by gaining a sense of how and why IR theories have evolved that we can fully appreciate the insights which they offer us.

Since we are primarily concerned to convey ideas, events, processes, practices and the way that these are understood and presented in IR, we have kept references in the text to a minimum. Where we have quoted from texts directly or closely followed a line of a particular argument or debate, our sources are acknowledged in the extended list of references at the end of this book. Otherwise, just a few key authors and influential works are listed in the further reading. This is not an uncontroversial approach and, in adopting it, we urge you to refer to more specialised readings once you have digested the basics. You will certainly need to do this in your essays and written assignments, since the parroting of textbooks and reproduction of 'second-hand' accounts will not suffice.

Earlier, we suggested that our efforts in this book are something akin to providing a teach-your-self language book. IR theory (presented herein through the device of theoretical perspectives) 'matters' because it provides us with a language, a vocabulary and a set of concepts through which we understand reality and frame our actions and prescriptions in international politics. Having explained the basic theoretical and conceptual underpinnings of IR and described the structure of this text, it is now time to get on with speaking the language of IR. The following chapter deals with the first of our major perspectives: Liberalism.

Common misunderstandings

1. *International Relations is International Politics.* International Politics is one aspect of International Relations. We might also talk of International Economics, World Sociology, International Cultural Studies and so on. IR has come to involve elements of all of these but has also evolved in its own particular way.
2. *International Relations and international relations.* Though it is not used by all writers in the field, this book employs a reasonably accepted system for talking about IR. Where we use the phrase 'International Relations', we are referring to an academic discipline – theory/study (we similarly capitalise other disciplines). Where we use 'international relations' (or 'International relations' at a sentence's start) we mean the *practice* of world politics. While 'IR' can be used as an abbreviation for either, we will use this where we need to refer to both International Relations and international relations simultaneously. This distinction will normally be evident by context, and you should not let this unduly affect the flow of your reading, but we mention it in the event that you become confused by our exact meaning.
3. *International Relations is current affairs.* Much of what we watch on the news has an international dimension; much of it makes judgements about what is 'good' or 'bad'. However, International Relations is more than simply what happens – it is about how we understand what happens and even how we (and that includes news programmes) come to define some international events as more worthy of coverage than others.
4. *International Relations has a clear definition.* It should be clear from the above that IR can be many different things to different people. Apart from the different emphases of the perspectives, however, it is often conventional to divide IR into 'International Relations' (the theory and the discipline itself) and international relations – the practice of world politics.
5. *Theory is a waste of time.* IR theory is difficult at times and may sometimes seem purely academic. However, as we noted above, the practice of world politics cannot be understood outside the various epistemological and ontological claims we make about the world, and these claims are at the heart of IR. Pragmatically, examiners are also looking for the level of sophistication of theoretical arguments and in terms of marks a little well-used theory can go a lot farther than a thousand parroted 'facts'.

Further reading

We hope that in choosing our introduction you have chosen wisely. But other introductions will offer different 'perspectives' and 'themes'. Here are a selection of those you might want to go to next, bearing in mind that several are available in other editions.

Baylis, J., Smith, S. and Owens, P. (eds) (2007), *Globalization and World Politics* (4th edn), Oxford: Oxford University Press.

Brown, C. (2005), *Understanding International Relations* (3rd edn), London: Macmillan.

Brown, C. and Sinley, K. (2009), *Understanding International Relations,* London: Palgrave.

Burchill, S. and Linklater, A. (2009), *Theories of International Relations* (4th edn), Basingstoke: Macmillan.

Dunne, T., Kurki, M. and Smith, S. (eds) (2009), *International Relations Theories: Discipline and Diversity,* Oxford: Oxford University Press.

Edkins, J. and Zehfus, M. (eds) (2008), *Global Politics,* London: Routledge.

Jackson, R. and Sorenson, G. (2006), *Introduction to International Relations: Theories and Approaches,* Oxford: Oxford University Press.

Kegley, C. and Wittkopf, E. (2001), *World Politics: Trends and Transformation* (8th edn), New York: St Martin's Press.

Mandaville, P. and Williams, A. (eds) (2003), *Meaning and International Relations,* London: Routledge.

McGowan, P.J., Cornelissen, S. and Nel, P. (2006), *Power, Wealth and Global Equity: An International Relations Textbook for Africa,* Juta Legal and Academic Publishers.

Weber, C. (2004), *IR Theory: A Critical Introduction,* London: Routledge.

1 Liberalism

Introduction

Liberal thought about the nature of international relations has a long tradition dating back to the eighteenth and nineteenth centuries. During these centuries liberal philosophers and political thinkers debated the difficulties of establishing just, orderly and peaceful relations between peoples. One of the most systematic and thoughtful accounts of the problems of world peace was produced by the German philosopher Immanuel Kant in 1795 in an essay entitled *Perpetual Peace*. Kantian thought has been profoundly influential in the development of liberalism in IR (see below).

However, solutions to the problem of war evaded even the most eminent of thinkers. In the nineteenth century, scholars contented themselves with merely describing historical events, and the study of international affairs was largely confined to the field of diplomatic history. In the wake of the destruction of the First World War, there was a sense of greater urgency to discover the means of preventing conflict. The senseless waste of life which characterised this conflict brought about a new determination that reason and cooperation must prevail.

While the conflict itself was horrific, International Relations scholars were initially quite optimistic about the possibilities of ending the misery of war. A new generation of scholars was deeply interested in schemes which would promote cooperative relations among states and allow the realisation of a just and peaceful international order, such as the fledgling League of Nations (see World Example Box, pp. 33–4). This liberal or *idealist* enterprise rested on the beliefs that people in general are inherently good and have no interest in prosecuting wars with one another. Furthermore, people suffer greatly as a consequence of war and thus desire dialogue over belligerence. Therefore, for idealists all that was needed to end war was respect for the rule of law and stable institutions which could provide some form of international order conducive to peace and security. The widespread anti-war sentiment within Europe and North America which existed in the 1920s seemed to provide the necessary widespread public support for such an enterprise to succeed.

During the late 1930s and following the Second World War, **idealism** fell out of favour for a long period of time, as realism (chapter 2) seemed to provide a better account of the power politics characteristic of the post-war era. The decline in the popularity of idealism was partly encouraged by the failure of The League of Nations to act as a forum for resolving differences peacefully and as a mechanism to prevent inter-state conflict. With the outbreak of a number of major conflicts in the inter-war period, the onset of economic nationalism as a result of the Great Depression and World War Two, it is not entirely surprising that a much more pessimistic view of world politics prevailed from the 1940s onwards. However, idealism dominated the academic study of International Relations between the First and Second World Wars with its basic faith in the potential for good in human beings and in the promise of the rule of law, democracy and human rights and continues to be influential within liberal IR theory today.

Idealism as used here is about a particular approach to International Relations and should not be confused with the notion of 'idealism' as describing say an unrealistic person. Further explanation in text.

There have been many innovations in liberal theory since the 1970s which are reflected in a number of distinctive strands of thought within liberalism. For example, idealism, pluralism, interdependence theory, transnationalism, **liberal internationalism**, liberal peace theory, neo-liberal institutionalism and world society approaches. In the 1970s a liberal literature on transnational relations and world society developed. So called 'liberal pluralists' pointed to the growing importance of multinational corporations (MNCs), non-governmental organisations (NGOs), pressure groups, and intergovernmental organizations (IGOs), as evidence that states were no longer the only significant actors in international relations. Liberal pluralists believed that power, influence and agency in world politics were now exercised by a range of different types of actors.

Liberal internationalism: the belief that political activity should be framed in terms of a universal human condition rather than in relation to the particularities of any given nation.

Furthermore, by the 1980s conflict was not the major process in international relations as, increasingly, cooperation in pursuit of mutual interests was a prominent feature of world politics. Terms much in vogue in contemporary International Relations literature (and in the media), such as 'globalisation' or 'multiculturalism', while not intrinsically liberal, have liberal adherents or interpretations and have received growing attention from liberal scholars. In more recent years liberals have made important contributions to the study of international relations in the areas of international order, institutions and processes of governance, human rights, democratisation, peace and economic integration.

In this chapter we aim to highlight the many and varied ways in which liberal thought has contributed to International Relations. We present liberalism as a coherent perspective or school of thought. Our justification for doing so is that, despite some differences in the 'versions' of liberalism, there are, nonetheless, prevailing and constant liberal principles and core assumptions. It is useful first to offer a few qualifications and clarifications. It is important not to lose sight of the fact that the term 'liberal' has been applied to the political beliefs of a wide variety of people. Liberals have views about the economic organisation of society, for instance; here we can detect a division in liberal thought between those on the political 'right' who believe that individual liberty must extend into the economic realm: that is, people must be free to buy and sell their labour and skills as well as goods and services in a free market which is subjected to minimal regulation. On the other hand, 'left-leaning' liberals recognise that the principles of political liberty and equality can actually be threatened by the concentration of economic power and wealth. This form of liberalism supports a much more interventionist role for the state in the regulation of the economy, in the interests of providing for basic human needs and extending opportunities to the less privileged. As we shall see below, these two strands of liberal thinking live on in neo-classical and Keynesian approaches to International Political Economy (IPE), which has developed as a discrete area of study within IR since the 1970s.

Liberalism, as an 'ism', is an approach to all forms of human organisation, whether of a political or economic nature, and it contains within it a social theory, philosophy and ideology. The result is that liberalism has something to say about all aspects of human life. In terms of liberal philosophy, liberalism is based upon a belief in the inherently good nature of all humans, the ultimate value of individual liberty and the possibility of human progress. Liberalism speaks the language of rationality, moral autonomy, human rights, democracy, opportunity and choice and is founded upon a commitment to principles of liberty and equality, justified in the name of individuality and rationality.

| Figure 1.1 | The relative growth in the number of international NGOs in the twentieth century. |

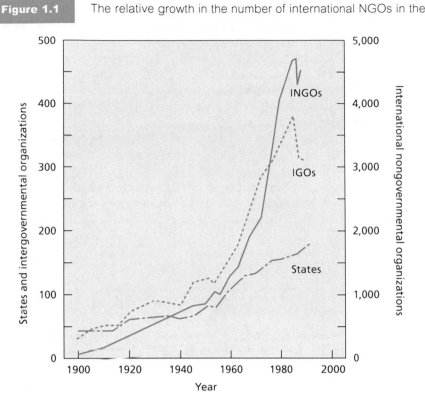

Original source: B.B. Hughes (1993), *International Futures*, Boulder, CO: Westview Press, p. 45.

Taken from: B. Russett and H. Starr (1996), *World Politics: The Menu for Choice*, 2nd edn, New York: W.H. Freeman, p. 66

Liberal pluralists see a complex web of interactions in International Relations that goes beyond the mere interaction of states.

Politically this translates into support for limited government and political pluralism. We will summarise the main assumptions of liberalism below. First, we need to consider further the historical and intellectual origins of liberal thought.

LITERATURE BOX

The Brandt Report

The report *North–South: A Programme for Survival*, published by The Brandt Commission in 1980, is an example of liberal internationalist sentiment and Keynesian economic philosophy in practice. The 'Brandt Report' outlined the many and varied ways in which economic interdependence had made all of the world's peoples vulnerable to economic recession and world economic crisis. Coming in the wake of the breakdown of the Bretton Woods economic system and, in some ways, anticipating the debt crisis and recession of the 1980s, it called for worldwide cooperation and active political intervention to protect the worst-hit countries and to revive the world economy.

> The suggestions of the Brandt Report are as relevant today, if not more so, than when they were originally suggested. The realisation that we now live in a world characterised by a single economic system has informed mainstream national economic policy around the world. The proliferation of bilateral and multilateral agreements aimed at liberalising trade and coordinating economic activity has picked up pace in the twenty-first century. The key influence in encouraging Free Trade Agreements (FTAs), integrated markets, single currencies and so on has been the assumption that economic growth and prosperity result from facilitating the operation of the single economic system and not resistance to it.
>
> The global financial crisis and subsequent recession, which are ongoing at the time of writing, offer another example of the complexities of what the Brandt Report discussed. The crisis and recession spread from one state to practically all states in approximately one year, demonstrating the economic interdependence that now exists in international relations. The responses to it have also taken on increasingly international or even global characteristics. The crisis has in effect legitimised the report and the responses to it have been influenced its suggestions.

Origins

In this section we will outline the main influences on liberal IR, which we have identified as Immanuel Kant, Adam Smith, David Ricardo, Jeremy Bentham, John Stuart Mill and John Maynard Keynes. For the sake of simplicity and clarity we have divided the origins of liberal thought into 'political' and 'economic' strands. We will then use these two broad divisions to contextualise the subsequent discussions of key themes within what we broadly term the 'liberal perspective' in International Relations. We hope that making this distinction between political and economic liberalism will help you find your way through a dense literature. However, you should be aware that inevitably there is some overlap between the economic and political strands of liberal thought.

In this section we begin with liberal idealism. In everyday usage the term 'idealist' is sometimes used in a negative, or pejorative sense, to describe a person who is considered unrealistic – a dreamer. However, it has a specific meaning in philosophy where it denotes certain beliefs about the nature of the world and the capacity of human beings for rational thought. Starting from the premise that the international system was something akin to an international 'state of nature' or 'war of all against all' (see chapter 2), Kant argued that perpetual peace cannot be realised in an unjust world. The only way that this state of affairs could be overcome would be for states to found a 'state of peace'. Kant did not envisage the founding of a world government, or even the pooling of sovereignty, but, rather, a looser federation of free states governed by the rule of law.

Kant did not see this state of affairs coming about fortuitously, or quickly. While the application of Kantian thought to international relations has been dismissed as 'utopian', it is important to note that Kant recognised that, in order to achieve a just world order, certain conditions were necessary, including the establishment of **republics**, as opposed to monarchies or dictatorships (and, perhaps, a near-universal commitment to liberal democracy). Indeed, Kant held that only civilised countries, those countries which were already governed by a system of law and in which people were free citizens rather than subjects, would feel impelled to leave the state of lawlessness that characterised the international state of nature. There has been some debate about how Kant saw the relationship between republics and other forms of polity. However, Kant is frequently interpreted as suggesting that countries where people were not free citizens, but rather subjected to the rule of a monarch, perhaps, or a dictator, were much more likely to be belligerent and warlike. If this was the case, logically it followed that a world federation would only be achieved when all states were republics. Just as Kant believed that a state of 'perpetual peace' would not be realised in the near future, contemporary liberals are under no illusions about the barriers to achieving justice and the rule of law under conditions of anarchy, but, like Kant, many insist that this is an ideal to be striven for.

> **Republic:** Traditionally this is a term used to describe a secular state in which there is a separation of powers in government and in which citizens are ruled by law and have some constitutional rights (in theory at least). However, in the contemporary world there are states which exist as (or claim to be) republics which are not, and do not claim to be, secular. An example of such a state is the Islamic Republic of Iran (simply Iran for short). The government of Iran does have a number of characteristics of traditional republics, such as popular elections, parliamentarians, political parties and a constitution. However, it also has branches of government which are not secular, but instead are directly concerned with religious matters. Furthermore, within the governing mechanisms in Iran exists an *ulema* (body of educated religious scholars and lawyers). The *ulema* are technically separate from the Iranian government and operate as 'advisors' or 'consultants' to it. Nevertheless, the *ulema*'s role often exceeds this official description to the extent that the final say on issues of governance is held by the upper echelons of the *ulema* itself.

Economic liberalism is rooted in an intellectual tradition stretching back to the works of Adam Smith and David Ricardo. (At this point, you might like to refer back to our brief discussion of Ricardo's work in the box in the introductory chapter). The key assumptions of nineteenth-century classical liberalism were that it is, in the long run, beneficial to all if markets are allowed to operate freely without state intervention and if countries are able to trade openly and freely with each other. This is because the market is seen as the most efficient means of organising human production and exchange, operating almost as if 'an invisible hand' were guiding and coordinating economic activity. If the free market is allowed to operate without government intervention, there will be the efficient division and distribution of labour and resources both within domestic economies and the international economic system. The result will be higher levels of wealth and production for all leading to the satisfaction of human needs and a higher quality of life.

Liberals also assume that human beings act rationally. In this usage, 'rationality' is evidenced by a person's ability to carefully weigh up the costs and benefits of any course of action. According to '**utilitarian**' thinkers like Bentham, people who are behaving rationally will always act to maximise their 'utility' or interest. If at first sight this appears to be entirely selfish behaviour rooted in a pessimistic view of human nature, liberals offer a moral justification for allowing such a state of affairs to continue. While individuals are essentially self-interested, collectively this type of behaviour is held to produce beneficial outcomes. According to Bentham we should base our judgements on what is 'right' or 'wrong', or 'good' or 'bad' on how far any action works to ensure the greatest happiness of the greatest number.

> **Utilitarianism:** A term often used in Liberalism and other approaches to IR referring to how the moral worth of a given action is determined. According to this concept, the value of any human action can be assessed according to the extent to which it contributes to the good of the community. An action has utility if it contributes to happiness, pleasure, progress and so on. Thus, donating money to charity can be deemed to be an action of high moral worth while simply buying a pair of shoes for yourself is not.

This does not mean that liberals see no role for the state in the economy. Liberals like Adam Smith accepted that the market would not necessarily produce much needed 'public goods' and that governments would need to provide them. States were also necessary, because they provided a regulatory framework – a legal system – to, among other things, enforce contracts and protect against corruption and unfair competition. However, classical liberalism held that it is in the best interests of all people, in the long term, if state intervention is kept to a minimum. According to liberals, the advantages of an unfettered free market are not only confined to the domestic economy. Free market economics generates a need for 'inputs', such as raw materials, into the production process and some of these have to be imported from abroad. Enterprises are also constantly seeking new markets for their goods and services. In this way, trade between states is encouraged. According to liberals, the advantages of trade are numerous. This is, of course, a very strong argument against economic protectionism, which, from a liberal perspective, is a consequence of states acting according to short-sighted and perverse conceptions of the 'national interest'. Left to itself, trade would prove to be mutually beneficial by, for example, bringing about interdependence among states and generating wealth, both of which would reduce the likelihood of conflict. This is because, in the case of the former, integration between states and people leads to shared interests and an increase in the costs of conflict. In the case of the latter, increasing wealth helps to satisfy human needs, and to an extent 'wants', thus reducing the need to attain these through conflict.

AUTHOR BOX

Francis Fukuyama

Kant's commitment to the pursuit of peace and the establishment of a just international order where states' actions are regulated by international law is widespread among liberals today. One of the most celebrated works on the end of the Cold War, Francis Fukuyama's *The End of History and the Last Man* (see Further reading) contained much which would have been familiar to Kant. Fukuyama's dramatic phrase 'end of history' is not intended to imply that we face some apocalyptic future. On the contrary, in simple terms, Fukuyama argues that human history *has* been driven by conflict and struggle over value systems and different ways to organise human societies. The driving force behind the Cold War was the ideological struggle between East and West, communism and capitalism. According to Fukuyama, the end of the Cold War saw the ultimate triumph of Western capitalism and liberal democracy. Liberal values are now widely accepted – if not widely practised – across the world and, since communism is seemingly discredited, there is no longer a credible alternative form of social, political and economic organisation. Fukuyama's thesis is an ironic twist on Marx's vision of communism as the highest form of human organisation and, thus, the ultimate end or destination of human history. (See chapter 3.)

It was noted above that nineteenth-century liberal economic theorists were against state intervention and regulation of the economy. However, for much of the twentieth century, liberals have been less hostile to state intervention. Indeed the economic order which emerged in the aftermath of the Second World War, in Western economies at least, saw the state playing a much greater role in directing the economic activity of private individuals and firms and providing welfare support for citizens – the so-called 'welfare state'. The actual influence of Keynes in the Bretton Woods negotiations held in the USA in 1944, which were held in order to establish a set of regimes, institutions and agreements negotiations has been disputed. However, Keynesian economic theory, which supported interventionist government policies to regulate what were basically free-market economies, formed the basis of the ideas which underpinned many Western economies in the post-Second World War period.

Figure 1.2   The increase in exports as a percentage of GDP since 1950.

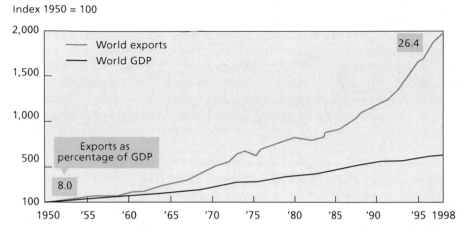

Original source: United Nations (1995 and 1999), *World Economic and Social Survey*, New York: United Nations, p. 35 and p. 2.

Taken from: C.W. Kegley and E.R. Wittkopf (1999), *World Politics: Trend and Transformation*, 7th edn, New York: St Martins, p. 310.

The aim of the Bretton Woods System (BWS) was to facilitate economic growth, development and trade by providing a stable framework for international economic activity. After the Second World War the prevailing wisdom was that the cause of the war was the economic collapse and world recession of the 1930s which created an unstable climate in which extreme nationalism flourished. It was believed that, when the economic climate was harsh, states immediately took action to protect their own economies. Typically, this involved measures to protect domestic markets, such as increasing tariffs. The knock-on effects of such 'selfish' behaviour were a slow-down in world trade and, eventually, international recession. The BWS was designed to create a framework in which it would be difficult for states to act in a self-interested way when the going got tough by, at one and the same time, discouraging protectionism and providing a helping hand to countries in temporary economic difficulties.

The BWS consisted of the International Bank for Reconstruction and Development (IBRD), the International Monetary Fund (IMF) and later the General Agreement on Tariffs and Trade (GATT), now the World Trade Organisation (WTO). In the first years of its existence, it was envisaged that the IBRD, more commonly known as the World Bank, would play an important role in distributing aid to the devastated economies of Western Europe. In more recent history the World Bank has served as a source of investment, aid and loans to the developing world. The International Monetary Fund was designed to ensure liquidity in the international economy. This means that, in effect, countries experiencing short-term balance of trade difficulties (effectively spending more than they were earning) could borrow money and so continue to trade effectively. In the longer term, if any individual country had an enduring – or structural – balance-of-payment deficit, the IMF could insist upon changes in domestic economic policy, including the devaluation of the currency, in return for fresh loans. The General Agreement in Tariffs and Trade (which came into being a few years after Bretton Woods and has since been superseded by the World Trade Organisation) was designed to bring about a gradual reduction in trade barriers around the world.

These institutions all played an important role in regulating the world economy. However, the linchpin of the system was the US dollar. The US dollar served as the major world trading currency.

The relative value of all of the other world currencies was fixed in relation to the US dollar. Since, in the post-war period, the US economy was easily the largest and most powerful economy in the world, it was believed that pegging all currencies to the US dollar would ensure confidence in the international economic system.

The BWS has been described as an economic order in which the broad principles of liberalism were 'embedded'. The system of multilateral institutions, fixed exchange rates, capital controls and trade regulation aimed to encourage the progressive liberalisation of trade among countries and to promote the principles of free-market economics internationally. However, none of these institutions or rules were incompatible with state intervention and the management of the domestic economy. This meant that, even while encouraging a large degree of free trade and open competition, states could pursue 'liberal welfare' or 'social democratic' goals, such as full employment and the provision of welfare goods.

In recent years neo-classical, or neo-liberal, economic theory has been highly influential in the theory and practice of development in countries of the so-called 'Third World'. The belief that the unfettered market ensured the most efficient allocation of resources, the best distribution of rewards, and the most effective means to foster economic growth continues to be widely held among élites at the International Monetary Fund, the World Bank and in many government overseas development agencies. Note that the use of 'neo-liberalism' (or neo-classical liberalism) in this context should be distinguished from 'neo-liberal institutionalism' discussed at greater length below. Neo-liberal or neo-classical economic theory has been used to justify structural adjustment programmes (SAPs) in the developing world, even though the social consequences may be very harsh indeed.

SAPs have been widely 'recommended' to Third World states by the IMF and the World Bank as an effective means of dealing with the related problems of poverty and indebtedness. The idea is that indebted states should try to export their way out of debt. As well as generating much needed foreign currency to service foreign debt, export-led growth strategies are held to encourage economic competitiveness, dynamism and growth which will eventually 'trickle down' to all sectors of society. At the same time developing countries are encouraged to cut back on welfare spending by the state, effectively privatising the provision of health and education services. It is argued that ultimately this will make economies more efficient. In the short term, however, 'spend less' means sacking government employees and slashing welfare budgets rather than buying medicines and building schools. Meanwhile 'earn more' can lead to wage reduction, chopping down forests, selling off assets to foreign firms at cut price rates and so on. In recent years SAPs have been heavily criticised by NGOs like Oxfam and Greenpeace as well as by former members of the World Bank. Consequently SAPs often include some notional safety net beyond which basic services and welfare goods should not be cut.

REFLECTION BOX

In this chapter we employ the term 'neo-liberal' in two very different usages with different meanings: neo-liberal institutionalism and neo-liberal (neo-classical) economics. You should be sure that you understand the differences between these two usages.

Just as there are distinct strands in economic liberalism, political liberalism is not all of one kind. Some liberals have applied the basic ideas of liberal thought as outlined above to their thinking about political community and obligation and to the nature and role of government. The insistence that individuals are the best judge of what is in their interests is a powerful argument against authoritarian (dictatorial) forms of government. Liberals generally argue for representative government based on democratic principles.

One of the most celebrated liberal thinkers of the nineteenth century, John Stuart Mill, argued that government was a necessary evil. That is to say, government was necessary in order to protect the liberty of individuals, but could become oppressive and tyrannical if its power was unchecked. For these reasons liberals generally argue for a 'separation of powers' and 'checks and balances' which ensure that no one political leader or arm of government can become dominant. This basic idea is the origin of political pluralism, which means the distribution or diffusion of power across a range of institutions or among a number of 'actors'. As we will see, so-called liberal pluralism has been very influential in International Relations, although the usage of the term 'pluralism' in this context is slightly different. We will return to this point later in the chapter.

In addition to the utilitarian conception of rationality, there is another strand of liberal thought which, while committed to the principle of liberty and wedded to notions of progress, has a rather different view of human autonomy and rationality. Rather than viewing rationality in means–ends or cost–benefit terms, the essence of 'reason' is seen to be the ability of human beings to understand moral principles. This strand of thought is associated particularly with Kant. For our purposes it is enough to say that liberals believe that the capacity to reason and to understand moral principles is universal, that is it is something which 'all' human beings possess. Collectively, these beliefs in human rationality, the possibility of progress, individual liberty and the dangers of unchecked power give rise to the liberal notion of universal human rights.

The various strands of liberal thought have contributed to the study of International Relations in many and varied ways. Below we will look at how liberals have viewed our key themes. But first, it is helpful to summarise briefly the core assumptions of liberalism.

Assumptions

The main points of the liberal world view or perspective can then be summarised thus:

1. Rationality and inherent good nature are the defining characteristics of human kind. Rationality can be used in two distinctive ways:
    - in instrumental terms, as the ability to articulate and pursue one's 'interests';
    - the ability to understand moral principles and live according to the rule of law.
2. While people rationally pursue their own interests, there is a potential harmony of interests between people.
3. Cooperation is possible and is in fact a central feature of all human relations, including international relations.
4. Liberalism challenges the distinction between the domestic and the international realm, claiming that multiple sets of relationships between people transcend national borders.
    - Government is necessary, but the centralisation of power is inherently bad.
    - Individual liberty is of supreme political importance.

From these basic propositions we can deduce or infer a number of other propositions which continue to inform liberal approaches to international relations. For example:

- If humans are inherently good and there is a harmony of interests between people, we might deduce that left to their own devices, people have no interest in prosecuting wars.
- If the centralisation of power is bad, political pluralism and democracy must be a superior form of political organisation.
- Because cooperation is possible, liberals believe it is thus possible to achieve positive changes in international relations.

- Similarly, liberals tend to emphasise the distribution of different forms of power (including military, economic, socio-cultural and intellectual forms) and influence among a range of actors, rather than focusing solely on the state.
- Furthermore, humans are important actors and possess agency to effect change.
- If reason is the defining characteristic of the human race, all people must have inalienable human rights.
- Liberalism is a universalist doctrine and so is committed to some notion of a universal community of humankind which transcends identification with, and membership of, the nation-state community.
- The liberal concepts of interdependence and world society suggest that in the contemporary world the boundaries between states are becoming increasingly permeable.

Themes

Peace and security

As we suggested earlier, liberalism is a paradigm which has a faith in the capacity of human beings to solve seemingly intractable problems through political action. The notion that human beings understand moral principles suggests that it is possible to transcend 'power politics' and govern relations between people (and indeed peoples) on the basis of legal norms, moral principles and according to what is 'right' and 'just'. However, liberalism should not be confused with pacifism. While some liberals might indeed be pacifists, it does not necessarily follow that a commitment to the peaceful resolution of disputes entails the rejection of the use of force whatever the circumstances. Clearly, even 'peace-loving' peoples and states could not be expected to forgo the right to use force in order to defend themselves from hostile aggression or, perhaps, if there was no other way to right a wrong.

AUTHOR BOX

Michael Doyle

Michael Doyle's work is particularly associated with democratic peace theory. The basic hypothesis of this theory is that, as states become more democratic, they become more peacefully inclined. The theory is based on a research project called the *Michigan Project* and on David Singer's work which documented in detail the incidence of wars since 1816. Researchers sought first to establish empirically how many wars had been fought by liberal states and against whom. On the basis of this they claimed to identify a trend: liberal states fought wars, but not with each other. Thus, they concluded, liberal states do not fight wars with each other. The implications of such a finding were that there existed in world politics a liberal 'zone of peace'. Moreover, democratisation along liberal lines was a recipe for peace. The prescriptive implication was that, in the interests of advancing world peace, foreign policies should include democratisation and human rights as central planks.

Democratic peace theory is sometimes held to be the closest IR has come to establishing a 'law' of international relations (in the scientific sense). However, it has been much criticised. First, the sample included republics as well as democracies and in some cases 30 per cent male suffrage was deemed enough to qualify as a 'democracy'. Doyle also excluded certain types of wars like civil wars. In terms of what statistics can tell us democratic peace theory can also be criticised. Even if we establish the existence of a liberal zone of peace, it may be that: a) the number of liberal states is quite small; and b) at the same time many states that are not democracies are also at peace with one another. So what, ultimately, can we read from the statistics? Today, variants of democratic peace theory exist which shift the emphasis towards understanding whether liberal democracy is 'war inhibiting'.

Peace and security are closely connected in liberal thought. The League of Nations (see box) was supposed to guarantee the security of states through a system which identified threats to 'peace and security' and allowed collective action to be taken against aggressive states, to deter or stop them. Clearly, since insecurity was itself a possible cause of war, a system of collective security would strengthen the international order and make peace more likely. The League of Nations also had an International Court to arbitrate disputes and so provide a peaceful means to resolve conflicts. Although the League of Nations foundered, the idea that an international organisation was needed to provide some sort of system of collective defence and a court of arbitration lived on in the United Nations, which was set up after the Second World War.

WORLD EXAMPLE BOX

The League of Nations

Prior to the First World War every country adhered to the view that governments were the legitimate representatives of sovereign states and that all sovereign states had the right to judge without question their own best interests and pursue these interests through an independently formulated foreign policy, through negotiation – diplomacy – and, when necessary, through military action. Moreover, among élites, the view prevailed that the 'national interest' and security concerns demanded that diplomatic relations be conducted in secret, and foreign policy be guarded from public scrutiny and criticism. The horrors of the First World War brought about a far-reaching change in attitudes among both political élites and influential sections of the public across the European continent. Even before the end of the war the principle of sovereignty was being subjected to critical challenges. A League of Nations Society was formed in London in 1915 and similar bodies sprang up in a number of European countries including France and even, briefly, Germany. In Britain the idea of forming a League of Nations won backing from across the political spectrum, as leaders joined together to argue for the formation of a new international system which would secure the peace, if necessary by the collective efforts of the 'peace-loving' powers.

The League of Nations was formed at the end of the First World War. The aims of the League were to provide a system of collective security and to deter aggressor states from pursuing their 'national interests' at the expense of their smaller, weaker neighbours. The basic idea which underpinned collective security was that, if any one member state fell victim to the aggression of a powerful neighbour, all members of the League would collectively join together in a determined attempt to deter or repel the aggressor. The idea was to make violence illegitimate as an option for states, and for other states to combine and oppose any state which used violence as a means for resolving its disputes in international relations. While it was recognised that this might ultimately require armed force, it was widely believed that 'world public opinion' would, in itself, prove to be a powerful deterrent to any would-be belligerent power. It was recognised that if the League was to be a success, the USA would need to end its period of 'isolation' and play a leading role in world affairs. Unfortunately, this was not to be. Although the US President Woodrow Wilson played a prominent role in the original conception and planning of the League, the US Senate refused to ratify the Covenant of the League of Nations, so preventing US membership. Thus, the League suffered a major moral and political blow almost before it got off the ground. Nevertheless, the League continued to function during the inter-war period, acting as an important forum for diplomacy by facilitating regular meetings between Heads of States. The League also gradually expanded its role in world affairs, setting up, among other things, a Permanent Court of International Justice to arbitrate international disputes.

However, although the existence of the League was, in itself, a powerful challenge to the view that states were exempt from public debate and criticism in their relations with other states, major powers were reluctant to refer their own disputes to the League. Similarly, action to achieve general disarmament was not successful. Indeed, by the late 1930s events in world politics had served to undermine the wave of optimism on which the League was born, as the behaviour of some states failed to live up to idealist expectations. In 1931 Japan attacked China, and the latter appealed to the League under Article 11. The League sent commissions and issued condemnations, but Japanese aggression was not punished. Italy invaded Abyssinia (Ethiopia) in an attempt to establish Italy as one of the great European imperial powers. This led to economic sanctions and protest by the League, but without the backing of military sanctions these were ineffective. In Germany in 1936 Hitler sent troops into the demilitarised zone of the Rhineland but referrals to the League, rather than resulting in resolute action, allowed Hitler to get away with a huge military and political gamble. Power politics appeared to be very much the order of the day and by the end of the decade, the world was at war once again.

Liberals have developed a distinctive 'peace theory'. Liberal peace theory returns to a familiar liberal theme that the people have no interest in war, in the sense that war is not in their interests. It follows from this that wars are frequently the result of aggression on the part of belligerent leaders or states pursuing a particular interest. Many liberal peace theorists are of the view that it is only when an end is put to tyranny around the globe and when universal liberal democracy and respect for human rights exist that international peace will prevail. In so far as democracy will also check the power of leaders and states, wars are likely to become less prevalent when, and if, democracy flourishes throughout the world. While, admittedly, there are different forms of democracy, democratic governments on the whole are representative of the people they govern and thus take on their characteristics. If humans are seen as inherently good, rational and have more interest in cooperation than conflict, liberals argue that democratic governments will be peaceful. A peaceful world order is also likely to be one in which human rights are respected and upheld.

WORLD EXAMPLE BOX

The United Nations

The United Nations (UN) was set up after the Dumbarton Oaks conference in 1944 in order to 'save successive generations from the scourge of war'. The conference was attended by only the USA and its wartime allies, including Britain and France, the Soviet Union, and China but, despite this limited representation, nearly all of the basic features of the new organisation were agreed at that meeting. The UN remained close to the spirit of the League of Nations in its stated objective of maintaining peace and security through the peaceful settlement of disputes and the promotion of trade and economic and social cooperation. The UN also added economic and social development and the promotion of human rights to its stated aims. However, while similar to the League in many respects, it was recognised that the founders of the UN must pay due regard to the failures of the League in order to ensure that the organisation did not duplicate the shortcomings and weaknesses of its predecessor. Above all, the new organisation had to be as universal as possible, and must include the membership of both the Soviet Union and the USA. It also needed 'teeth' in order to ensure effective action, rather than relying upon the force of 'world opinion' alone.

The two organisations were very similar in structure. Like the League, the UN had: an assembly, the General Assembly, which acted largely as a consultative body; a Court of Justice, located in The Hague; and a council (the Security Council) which formed the executive arm of the organisation. The UN also had a Secretariat headed by a Secretary-General, whose role included identifying and alerting the Security Council to 'threats to peace and security'.

Despite differences in ideology, the USA and Soviet Union were able to agree on most substantive issues to do with the structure and operation of the new organisation. However, they disagreed sharply over the structure and precise role of the Security Council. Eventually, these differences were resolved when it was agreed that the so-called 'big five' (the USA, the Soviet Union, China, France and the UK) would enjoy permanent representation on the Security Council and would have the right of veto over Security Council actions. Arguably, this concession to the realities of power politics was effectively to paralyse the Security Council, virtually preventing it from taking any effective action throughout the Cold War period.

In the light of the end of the ideological and political divisions following the end of the Cold War, it was hoped that the UN – and especially the Security Council – would finally be able to play an effective role in world affairs. Indeed, an enhanced role for the UN generally has been central to many visions of the post-Cold War 'new world order'. However, the post-Cold War record of the UN has been mixed. Attempts by the USA to legitimise intervention in Iraq in 2003 point to the continuing importance states place on 'good reputation' in ostensibly respecting international law and accepting that the Security Council has a role to play in international security. Yet, the seeming determination of the USA and allies to prosecute the war with Iraq *whatever* the eventual outcome of Security Council deliberations might suggest that power politics are very much back on the agenda of international relations.

In addition to the 'political' strand of liberal thought, 'economic liberalism' has similarly made a contribution to our understanding of peace. Along with the stress on moral reason and the capacity for good in human beings, after the First World War liberals were also advancing a notion of a 'harmony of interests' which would have been familiar to Adam Smith and David Ricardo. Liberal internationalism is based on the idea of a harmony of interests between the states and peoples of the world and, in good part, these mutual interests are rooted in the mutual benefits which arise from trade and economic integration. However, just as Smith recognised the need for certain 'public goods', liberals acknowledge that in order to have peace it is necessary to establish international institutions which can overcome the problem of anarchy and facilitate cooperation. We will return to the theme of cooperation, and the role of institutions in providing sound governance of international relations shortly. First, however, we need to draw out rather more explicitly how liberals have conceptualised and understood the state and power in international relations.

The State and power

Superficially, the liberal view of the nature of the state is similar to realism (see chapter 2), in so far as liberals accept that the defining characteristic of the state is sovereignty. Liberals would also agree with realists that the basic characteristics of the state are that it has a territory, a people and a government. Liberals regard the state as, at best, a 'necessary evil'. As can be inferred from the earlier discussion, liberals also make distinctions between different kinds of states. Authoritarian or tyrannical **regimes** whose power is unchecked are likely to be more belligerent, having little respect for human rights or regard for human suffering. In contrast, in liberal-democratic countries the state is held to be essentially a 'neutral arbiter' between competing interests in an open and pluralistic society. The state provides a framework (legal and political) in which it is possible to go about one's everyday business in the knowledge that one will be secure from harm, that contracts of all kinds will be upheld and that people will be able to pursue their varied aims and interests without restriction, providing that they do not, in consequence, harm others.

> The use of the word '**regime**' in IR should be distinguished from a regime in this specific context, meaning the rule of a particular leader or government, for example Saddam's regime. See the Glossary of key or problem terms for a full explanation.

This notion of the need to check the power of the state gives rise to the liberal concept of pluralism. In its original usage the term 'pluralism' referred to the belief in the need to distribute political power through several institutions, none of which is sovereign. Some liberals believe that the state to some extent reflects the interests and concerns of interest groups. In political systems dominated by parties this is to some extent inevitable. Moreover, there are also powerful élites within the government bureaucracy, the military and so on which might work to advance their own interests. However, liberals deny that the state reflects the interests of one, overwhelmingly dominant social class, or any one élite group. It is absolutely central to liberal thought that the state is seen as an autonomous body. In this context autonomy means that the state is fair and impartial, functioning as a neutral arbiter in disputes and policing the citizen body. This differs in fundamental ways from realist views, but also from structuralist and some feminist views, which you will encounter in chapters 2, 3 and 6.

Liberals are careful to distinguish between the state (which consists of the various arms of government, the police force, armed services and the law courts as well as a given territory and population) and **civil society**. Civil society refers to those areas of human life where individuals engage in collective action and activity, but which are outside the realm of state action or not directly within the purview or control of the state. So, for example, a vibrant civil society might be one in which people form associations like sports clubs or trade unions, or engage in social, cultural or 'independent' political activities, such as joining Greenpeace or Amnesty International.

> **Civil society:** civil society refers to those areas of human life where individuals engage in collective action and activity, but which are outside the realm of state action or not directly within the purview or control of the state.

Having said that state and (civil) society are clearly separated in liberal thought, liberals recognise that the state and civil society interact. The state provides a regulatory framework in which such activity takes place. For example, a 'social club' might be required to gain a licence to operate. The police might even monitor certain activities. Also, in a democracy at least, elements of civil society will try to actively influence the activities of the government – a central arm of the state.

Liberals argue that sovereign states are important, but they are not the only significant actors in

Figure 1.3   Where does a Ford car come from?

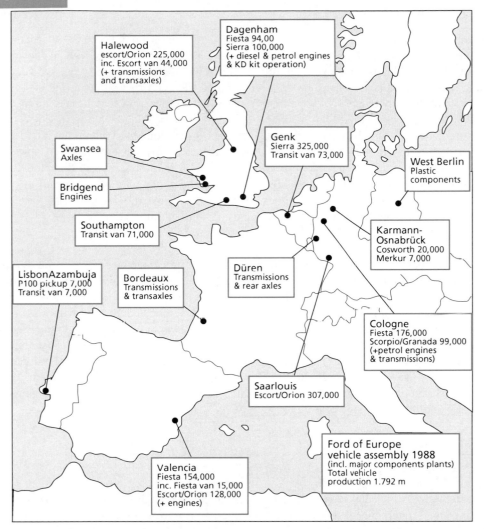

Original source: The *Financial Times*, 25 January 1989.

Taken from: B. Hocking and M. Smith (1995), *World Politics, An Introduction to International Policies*, 2nd edn, London: Prentice-Hall/Harvester Wheatsheaf, p. 101.

international relations. Just as the separation of powers implies that the essence of sovereignty is difficult to pin down or locate, contemporary liberals argue that the state can cede some elements of its sovereignty to other bodies, such as, for example, the United Nations or the European Union. Furthermore, actors such as multinational corporations (MNCs), international and regional institutions – for example, the United Nations, FIFA, the Organisation of African Unity – international non-governmental organisations (NGOs) like Greenpeace or Amnesty International, new social movements and even terrorist groups can also be said to be influential. Liberal pluralists were the first to significantly expand the purview of International Relations theory to 'actors' other than states and 'processes' other than foreign policy, war or diplomacy, which had dominated realist scholarship (see chapter 2).

The cobweb model

The analogy of a cobweb is often used to describe the plural complexity of international relations. The image which the cobweb model conveys is an intricate matrix with an enormous number of nodes (that is, points of intersection) which represent the way that the vast number of actors in international relations are connected to one another. From a liberal pluralist point of view, a multiplicity of actors interact in myriad ways. Liberals argue that these relationships are of different types and need not be characterised by conflict. Indeed, the spontaneous and voluntary nature of such linkages rather suggests that cooperation based on mutual interests is a major feature of international relations. Clearly, the cobweb model implies that power is widely diffused in international relations. However, one of the problems with this model and indeed, similar attempts by liberal pluralists to convey the complexity of actors and interactions in international relations is that it does not give us any sense of which 'threads' or nodes are most important or which 'actors' have the most power and influence.

Pluralism implies or denotes a diffusion of power. In liberal democracies power is held to reside with the people, in so far as the people are able to vote periodically to remove political leaders from office. However, the conception of 'people power' goes beyond the ability periodically to elect or remove governments from office. As we noted above, in a developed democracy with a strong civil society we might also expect to see people more actively involved in politics through their membership of social movements or support for the work of NGOs. In Western societies it is common for people who feel strongly about an issue to engage in lobbying activities designed to influence the decision-making process. Others prefer to work outside the formal structure of government, and take part in demonstrations. As the modern state has 'intervened' in more and more areas of human life, it has greatly facilitated this kind of politics.

Non-governmental organisations (NGOs)

The catch-all term 'NGO' covers an enormous range of organisations from what amount almost to huge international businesses on the one hand to local direct action groups on the other. Because of this, NGOs cover an enormous range in terms of the political spectrum and one cannot assume that working for an NGO implies a benign effect in terms of the world or a necessarily progressive contribution to that world. Some NGOs work so closely with governments that they can scarcely be described as independent entities and, indeed, are sometimes referred to by the paradoxical term GONGOs (governmental non-governmental organisations). Moreover, there are examples of corruption and misappropriation of funds in NGOs, casting doubt on whether they do always help those groups in civil society that they ostensibly represent. Nevertheless, there are many examples of NGOs, often larger ones but also smaller organisations too, which are able to operate independently of governments and 'big business'. Furthermore, their activities are often very effective and range from campaigns to raise awareness about certain issues, to high-tech research and development.

One of the best-known NGOs, Greenpeace, for example, operates on a global level and engages in numerous campaigns such as those aimed at bringing the issue of whaling to the public's attention. They also embark on 'missions' in the field, a good example of which are their operations aimed at disrupting actual whaling operations in the North Atlantic and Southern Oceans. Other groups seek to promote new technologies to reduce the negative environmental impacts human activities can have. For example, Friends of the Earth supports the development of technologies to replace aerosols.

Liberals take seriously the idea that people, sometimes individuals, but more usually acting collectively through pressure groups or institutions, can exert influence. In so far as power may be viewed as the capacity to act to advance an interest or to influence the outcome of an event or a decision, liberals believe that power is diffused across a range of institutions and among a variety of states and non-state actors. In International Relations the notion of 'pluralism' is not used so much to suggest the way power 'ought' to be checked and balanced, but rather as an empirical observation – it describes the way power is actually distributed in the international 'system'.

Liberal pluralists maintain that military power has become increasingly ineffective and so is no longer a reliable indicator of how powerful a state is in world politics. Power need not be conceptualised in simple zero-sum terms. On the contrary, power might be viewed in positive terms as the capacity to act collectively to realise a common 'good'. Moreover, the power which an 'actor' possesses may differ over time and according to the area under consideration. Liberal pluralists argue that it is impossible to quantify power simply in military terms. The economic wealth of countries such as Japan or many MNCs, such as Shell, IBM, Nissan and so on, is clearly a factor in understanding where power lies in international relations. Furthermore, 'actors' might also have more or less power depending on the issue area under consideration. For example, Norway is a relatively small country and does not play a particularly prominent role in organisations like the UN. However, as one of the major whaling states, Norway has tremendous influence in negotiations over the international ban on whaling.

Indeed, analysing the world according to different issue areas gives a very different, and perhaps comforting, impression of how power is distributed, compared to approaches such as realism. For example, in international negotiations over the dumping of toxic waste, developing countries – primarily the target for such waste – have been able significantly to affect negotiations and achieve global regulation of such activity.

Institutions and world order

As is evident from the earlier discussion, one of the ways in which liberalism has contributed to our understanding of international relations is through various works on the nature of institutions and world order. Obviously, the themes of cooperation and complex interdependence are strongly suggestive of how liberals see the regulatory and facilitating role played by institutions in international relations. In more recent years, neo-liberal institutionalists have developed a fairly sophisticated analysis of the nature of world order and the crucial role played by institutions and various regimes in regulating relations between states, as well as other actors. In this section we will discuss liberal ideas that have emerged in this context in more depth. First, however, we need to consider briefly an earlier school of thought, which, while not strictly speaking 'liberal', anticipated many arguments about the nature of interdependence and the need for institutions which were later developed by liberal IR theorists.

Like many ideas in International Relations, functionalism has its origins in another branch of the social sciences – Sociology. However, as the idea 'crossed the boundary' so to speak, its meaning changed somewhat. Functionalists argued that interaction among states in various spheres created problems which required cooperation to resolve; the most obvious examples being areas like telecommunications and postal services. The positive benefits, and mutual confidence, which arose from cooperation in any one area would likely 'spill over', encouraging cooperation in other more significant areas such as trade. Functionalists argued that integration was necessary because states were unable to cope with the effects of modernisation. International institutions were thought to be increasingly necessary as a complement to states, whose individual capabilities to deal with problems generated by new technologies were decreasing. Also, functionalists believed that, as the level of cooperation and integration increased, it would be more and more difficult for states to withdraw from the commitments they had entered into, since their people would be aware of the benefits achieved by cooperation. Such functional interaction would, in turn, have effects on international society, enhancing peace and making war so disruptive and costly that it would no longer be considered a 'rational' means for states to realise their aims and interests.

WORLD EXAMPLE BOX

The European Union

Ideas such as functionalism were clearly supported and encouraged by developments in the 'real world', such as European integration, which has today reached the stage of a European Union (EU). Indeed, the European Union provides an example of how functionalism can be seen as a prescription for how relations between states should be encouraged as well as an observation about perceived developments in the world of international politics and international economics. The EU is sometimes held up as an example of functionalist theory in practice. The European Communities (the European Atomic Energy Agency, the European Coal and Steel Community and the European Economic Community) were seen to be an effective way of achieving ongoing and extensive functional integration across a whole range of policy areas. Such integration would create a situation whereby national antagonism based on historical experience or competing interests, such as Franco-German border disputes, would no longer degenerate into outright conflict. War as a means to settle disputes would not only be disruptive and costly, but increasingly unfeasible since the economies of, in this case, France and Germany would be functionally integrated. From the earliest European agreements on tariff reductions and trade in certain areas, the European Community has developed through a combination of 'spill-over', functional integration and political will, to become a unified organisation – the European Union – with common rules and (almost) a common currency. Whereas war was once a regular feature of European international relations, few today expect EU member states to ever fight a war against each other again.

In the 1970s liberal pluralist perspectives began to contribute to our understanding of institutions and world order in international relations. It was clear that states were becoming more interdependent – more sensitive to, or even affected by, the actions of other 'types' of actor. In any given issue area in world politics the interaction of states and other actors was in need of, and in many cases subjected to, regulation according to a system of rules and practices (norms). This notion of interdependence continues to have resonance today. For example, many states and non-state actors have an input into the global debate over deforestation through conferences and other regular meetings. In liberal pluralist interdependence theory, politics is presented as a mutually beneficial process in which many actors seek to resolve problems in international relations. Furthermore, we are now living in a world where there are multiple linkages between, not just governments, but societies too. NGOs and élite groups are increasingly involved in forging links with like-minded individuals and groups in other countries, which bypass, or perhaps even subvert, state control. In addition, advances in technologies have made the boundaries of states increasingly permeable. For example, the development of nuclear weapons had profound implications for the security of state boundaries; periodic international recessions demonstrate the growing interconnected nature of economic activity across the globe, while, in more recent years, the growth of satellite television and the internet have demonstrated forcibly how quickly ideas and cultural 'artefacts' can travel around the world.

WORLD EXAMPLE BOX

The Global Financial Crisis

It is quite simply impossible to be unaware of, or even escape from discussions about, the global financial crisis which began in August 2007 in the United States and subsequently spread to the global financial system. Most people are aware that the crisis has led to economic downturns and recession in practically every country in the world and that it is 'bad news' for all of us. But what is it really all about? And what are the underlying causes of it?

The common explanation of the crisis starts with banking institutions in the United States engaging in large-scale lending to disadvantaged segments of society in the US market. The vast majority of this lending was in the form of mortgages to purchase housing. However, these 'sub-prime' mortgages were given to people who subsequently could not make the repayments to the banks. Panic in the general public that their deposits and savings would not be secure in their banks led to large-scale cash withdrawals and account closures right at a time when many banks did not have sufficient funds. Banks subsequently were forced to seek help from governments and international financial institutions for funds.

A knock-on-effect of the difficulties banks were faced with in terms of maintaining sufficient funds was that banks were increasingly reluctant to lend to each other and to businesses and individuals. This series of processes started in the United States but soon spread to banks and financial markets around the world. Within months states such as the UK, Germany and Japan were facing similar situations.

The health of the global economy is, in short, reliant upon the rapid flow of capital resources to maintain growth and stability. The slow-down in the flow of capital around the world as a result of essentially domestic processes in the United States and elsewhere has led to the global recession. There simply is not enough money flowing round the world to meet the demands for money in the forms of investments, loans and grants. While interdependence is demonstrated by the fact that a financial crisis in one state can lead to similar crises around the world, it is also demonstrated by the level of international cooperation which has taken place. States, international organisations, businesses and so on have sought to solve the problems causing the economic slowdown and to get the global economy back on track by cooperating with each other on issues of financial lending, tax rates, interest rates and economic policy.

In contemporary IR liberals continue to argue that interdependence compels states to cooperate much more extensively than they had done before. As we will see below, there is now an extensive neo-liberal institutionalist literature on the nature and functions of regimes and institutions in international relations. Moreover, modern states are incapable of meeting the complex and diverse needs of their citizens *without* cooperating with other states. International institutions and regimes become necessary to coordinate the ever-more-powerful forces of interdependence. Large and small states, developed and underdeveloped, are members of some or all of these institutions and all are said to benefit to some degree from cooperation. Although conflict is always present, institutions, or regimes, provide the fora for states to settle their differences without resorting to war.

In summary, for liberals cooperation is possible because the nature of twentieth-century science, technology and economics has produced interdependence between states, and other actors, such as non-governmental organisations, multinational corporations or international institutions. In some cases interdependence has forced states to give up some of their sovereignty and independence to international institutions, like the UN and EU. Increasingly, states are being required or compelled to engage in more intensive forms of cooperation which frequently give rise to regimes to regulate behaviour over a range of issues areas.

Whether or not liberals of all types accurately describe the nature and implications of interdependence is a moot point and one which we will return to in later chapters. However, there is no doubt that the number and types of regimes, treaties and institutions *has* multiplied rapidly in the past two decades. Furthermore, security considerations, defined as military defence, are consequently superseded by considerations of well-being, or welfare. In recent years liberal work on cooperation, regimes and institutions has been given a whole new lease of life with the development of neo-liberal institutionalism.

CONCEPT BOX

Neo-liberal institutionalism

One central question that has emerged in world politics since the early 1970s is: will international institutions and regimes survive in the wake of US 'hegemonic decline'? Since hegemony (in this context and usage) is a neo-realist concept, we will deal with this argument in more detail in the next chapter. However, the basic proposition advanced by neo-realist scholars was that international institutions depended upon the leadership or dominance of hegemonic states if they were to function effectively. In the absence of such leadership, they were likely to fail.

Neo-liberal institutionalists contested this thesis, arguing that successful cooperation was not solely dependent upon the existence of a hegemon, but rather on the number of players involved in negotiations and the perceived long-term benefits to be gained from cooperation, rather than just the short-term gains. In this view IR was not seen as fundamentally anarchic. States were seen as dominant actors, but since cooperation was rational and mutually beneficial, international organisations and regimes would endure over time, surviving the changing shifts in power and influence among major states.

Neo-liberalism is built upon the assumption that states need to develop strategies and forums for cooperation over a whole set of new issues and areas. The fundamental foreign-policy problem for any policy maker is to construct a policy that allows the state to gain the maximum benefit for its international exchanges while minimising the negative costs. If states were able to retreat into isolation or self-sufficiency whenever the costs of dealing with others became too great, there would be no reason to study the effect that interaction patterns have on world politics and states' behaviour. However, states simply cannot avoid engaging in relations with others. In the modern world **autarky** is not an option. Furthermore, while some members of the international system will experience far greater difficulties than others in either exploiting or coping with this interconnectedness, all will experience some sense of 'not being in control' of their own destiny. It is this combination of interconnectedness, plus loss of control, that is the hallmark of interdependence and leads states to seek cooperation with others.

The costs of interdependence can be grouped under two headings: sensitivity and vulnerability costs. Sensitivity costs refer to how quickly changes in one country bring about changes in another and the costs of those changes. For example, the USA is less sensitive than Japan to rising oil prices. Vulnerability costs refer to the disadvantages suffered by the state, even after it has changed its policies to try and cope with the actions of another state. The 'costs' and 'benefits' of cooperation are not necessarily distributed equally. The existence of asymmetries in costs and benefits allows some members to exercise relatively more power and influence than others in an interdependent world. However, since states are largely absolute gains maximisers, not relative gains maximisers, absolute gains matter as much as relative gains and cooperation is rational, given absolute gains assumptions.

Neo-liberal institutionalism is often described as a fundamentally different approach to IR from the neo-realism which you will meet in the next chapter. Indeed, one of the big debates in IR in the 1990s was the so-called 'neo-neo debate' in which the above arguments about costs and benefits, relative and absolute gains and short- and long-term conceptions of interest were played out. However, it is interesting to also note the similarities with neo-realism. As you will see, both neo-liberal institutionalism and neo-realism concentrate on states as actors. Moreover, both claim that the proper role of IR theory is to explore the conditions under which cooperation is possible and, moreover, that research in this area should be as scientifically rigorous as possible. For this reason neo-liberal institutionalism and neo-realism are sometimes described collectively as 'mainstream' approaches to IR, as opposed to the 'critical' theories we will meet later in this text.

Autarky: autarky means independent or self-sufficient. In the contemporary world Cuba – subject to a US economic blockade and constant political pressure – provides an albeit imperfect example of what might be described as 'enforced autarky'.

As we noted above, neo-liberal institutionalism is a rather state-centric approach to IR. However, liberals have also contributed to a growing debate about emerging forms of regional and global *governance*. The term 'governance' embraces collective processes of rule making, monitoring and implementation, conducted by diverse social actors and institutions at levels above and below the nation-state. Thus, governance refers not just to governmental institutions and policy making backed by formal authority, but also includes informal, non-governmental organisations operating within the public realm, that are increasingly involved in decision making and in the 'implementation and monitoring' of policy. Liberal approaches to governance are closer to the spirit of liberal pluralism in recognising the key role of NGOs, particularly their potential as agents of social change.

AUTHOR BOX

Richard Falk on 'Humane Governance'

Richard Falk has argued that the rise of international institutions and the forging of new policy networks between institutions, governments and civil society (particularly NGOs) mean that it is now possible to envisage possibilities for the 'humane governance' of international affairs. Globalisation – which encourages the rise of forms of governance beyond the nation-state – can potentially provide many beneficial opportunities for improving the material, social and cultural experience of peoples around the world. Within globalisation exists the potential for humane governance, if this is activated by the diverse democratic forces at play in international society. Falk believes the legitimacy of humane governance lies in: first, the growing acceptance among states that the world community can legitimately pass judgement on the internal

China as dictatorship not democracy

affairs of states – even if the legitimacy of direct intervention in the domestic affairs of a state might still be contested; second, states generally now take seriously their formal commitment to uphold human rights; third, the rise of a transnational, human-rights civil society. However, Falk also recognises that there are significant barriers to the realisation of humane governance which include: a prevalent anti-utopian mood in international relations; market forces which encourage greedy and self-interested behaviour and which now inform policy-forming arenas at all social levels of organisation, reinforcing neo-liberal economics and sapping the normative (see Glossary of key or problem terms) creativity of states by imposing the discipline of global capital on existing structures of governance; the assertiveness of non-Western civilisations which has challenged the assumption that Western normative projects deserve universal acceptance.

Inequality and justice

Traditionally liberals have concentrated on the importance of formal equality among people and equal rights. Idealists insisted that the rule of law and questions of justice and rights were absolutely central to international relations. We have also seen that liberals have been extremely active in promoting human-rights regimes through the United Nations and other inter-governmental organisations. The UN has been particularly important in promoting human rights as a legal obligation of states, clearly recognising that such rights should not be confined within national borders and establishing a range of international standards.

The original UN charter talks of 'the principle of equal rights and self-determination of peoples' and 'human rights and fundamental freedoms for all without distinction' (Articles 1 and 55). By late 1948 a UN Universal Declaration on Human Rights had been signed after much wrangling by communist states such as the USSR, religious states such as Saudi Arabia and by other states such as South Africa, who feared that they would be accused of violating the human rights of some of their people.

However, despite some initial resistance, the signing proved to be simply the beginning of a lengthy and ongoing process. Liberals stress the importance of civil and political rights. However, as more developing countries have become member states of the UN, the General Assembly has become more important in the development of human rights. In the 1960s, for instance, there were further declarations on civil and political rights and on economic, social and cultural rights. In more recent years, there have been significant conventions which cover the rights of minorities and indigenous peoples, the rights of the child, and the elimination of discrimination against women.

Some commentators argue that the gradual expansion of human-rights provisions has resulted in a situation where we now have a global consensus on human rights. However, it is important to note that many states have refused to ratify certain conventions and treaties. Moreover, the abuse of human rights is still widespread throughout the world despite the significant advances which have been made in international law.

WORLD EXAMPLE BOX

Slavery in the Modern World

The phenomenon known as 'slavery' is often associated with the past. The possession, ownership and use as labour against the will of the 'slave' by another human is usually seen as one of the more deplorable economic / political features of human history. In the modern world slavery is condemned as illegal, and most contemporary societies find it unacceptable. In terms of international law, slavery is classed as illegal and entirely contrary to UN declarations on human rights. Article 4 of the UN's Universal Declaration of Human Rights states that no person shall be held as a slave. Furthermore, slavery is entirely contrary to the liberal ideals of individual freedom, equality and opportunity and as such is opposed by all forms of liberal ideology.

However, contrary to popular belief, slavery is still very much a characteristic of the modern global economy. According to some organisations, such as The Anti-Slavery Society, in 2008 there were approximately 30 million slaves across all continents. It must be noted that, depending on the definition of slavery, this figure may be as high as 300 million. Many of these individuals work as forced labour in labour-intensive, low-technology manufacturing, natural resource extraction or as human resources in some service industries, for example in the sex industry. An example of how slave labour is still important in the global economy is that nearly 40 per cent of the world's cocoa bean supply which is used to make chocolate comes from slave labour in states such as Côte d'Ivoire.

A key problem is that information about the use of slave labour is not widely accessible and the voices of those who are or have been held as slaves are largely marginalised. However, there are increasing numbers of states, NGOs and other civil society movements which are tackling the problem of modern slavery through various means. For example, Anti-Slavery International (a UK-based NGO established in 1839) runs a number of anti-slavery campaigns around the world which include operations to raise awareness through the mass media, to pressure governments into action and provide support for freed slaves.

FILM BOX

Human rights and film

The theme of human rights is implicit or explicit in many films. Moreover, competing conceptions of rights often emerge in such films: for example, in the film *Killing Fields* about genocide in Cambodia. However, it must be noted that there are many competing conceptions and interpretations of what actually constitutes human rights. On the one hand human rights can be based upon notions of *individual* liberty and opportunity. While a competing view posits that the well-being of the *community* as a whole takes precedence over individual freedoms. With the latter, the well-being of the individual is directly linked to security, order and equity in the wider community.

Films such as *Paradise Now* (set in contemporary Palestine and Israel and focusing on the reasons for and preparation of a suicide bombing in Israel by two Palestinian men) portray the distinction between alternative views of human rights and freedoms. On the one hand there is the Israeli state which attempts to provide physical and psychological security for its population and, on the other, is occupied Palestine. The latter is not a recognised state and the Palestinian population have had the basic human rights of self-determination and freedom taken away from them as a result of the 1967 Arab–Israeli war and the subsequent Israeli occupation. The movie introduces the two main characters and offers a portrayal of their everyday lives and the hardships and humiliations they face as a result of the absence of freedom. As the story progresses, the men are encouraged to go on a suicide mission into Tel Aviv in Israel as a perceived means to achieving human rights for Palestinians through resistance to occupation. In essence, the movie represents the dichotomy of ensuring human rights for one population at the expense of the human rights of another.

Figure 1.4 The theory was to take Cambodia back to the 'Year Zero', i.e. start society again and get it right. In practice, this led to hundreds of thousands of deaths. Who said theory is not important?

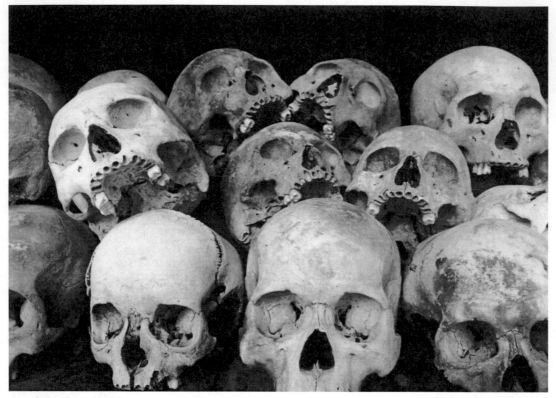

Source: Chris Rainer/Corbis.

In relation to concepts of justice and rights, the division between left-leaning and right-leaning liberals is of significance. Liberals on the right of the political spectrum have tended to concentrate on the importance of formal equality and equal opportunities – the right of each individual to be treated equally in the eyes of the law and an equal opportunity to participate in society or compete in the market place – rather than equality in outcomes. From this perspective, a 'free' and 'just' world is one in which everyone has the *opportunity* to succeed. Right-leaning liberals remain committed to the idea that the free market is the most effective means of realising the greatest happiness of the greatest number. Left to their own devices people will pursue their own interests, but in so doing will generate a dynamic society and vibrant economy and, in the long run, the benefits of this will be felt by all.

By contrast, left-leaning liberals have been more willing to countenance state intervention in the interests of addressing social inequality and barriers to genuine equal opportunities. Left-liberals recognise that in order to create a 'level playing field' it might be necessary to ensure that all people are educated and have a basic degree of social and economic security. The creation of a society in which genuine equal opportunity is possible requires, therefore, a degree of state intervention to provide education, healthcare and social security. However, by and large, liberals believe that it is better to 'tinker' with a liberal, free-market system to ameliorate its worst effects, than to risk individual liberty in the interests of absolute social and economic equality.

Identity and community

At first sight liberalism appears to have very little to say about issues of community and identity. After all, liberalism places supreme emphasis on the individual rather than the group. Indeed, critics of liberalism frequently argue that it presents a very 'atomistic' view of human society, in that people are presented as isolated beings who engage in relationships with others only when mutual interests suggest a beneficial outcome. The notion of community based on 'contract' in which the individual is seen to be protecting his or her independence or setting out his or her rights in opposition to their fellow citizens is central to classical liberal thought about the role of the state and the obligations owed to others.

However, contemporary liberalism does recognise the importance of issues of identity and community and their relevance to International Relations. In the first place, of course, liberals have offered a conception of community and identity which spans the entire planet and which defies the usual boundaries of state, nation, race, ethnicity, culture, class, gender and so on. This is the community of humankind, who possess inalienable human rights by virtue of the universal capacity for reasoned thought. Liberal pluralists have long expressed commitment towards a global society as a means by which the sovereign state system is transcended and more inclusive forms of community are realised. 'Global society' can be viewed in terms of a normative consensus bonding people together. In this view, people owe obligations to the 'people of the world' rather than simply to their fellow-citizens. Some commentators argue that forms of complex interdependence have resulted in the global spread of 'universal' values; for example, human rights (see above and box below) and democracy.

The growing significance of transnational politics and social movements in world politics also raises issues of identity and community. Transnationalism implies that people engage in numerous social interactions which tie people together across state boundaries. An alternative way of conceptualising global society is as a series of network-type, transnational relationships. In this view, technological innovations and increasing 'flows' such as media communications, technology and finance, bring in their wake the disintegration of previous forms of identity and attachment. The growing importance of transnational 'legitimised relationships' has been noted by liberals like Ferguson and Mansbach, who argue that, increasingly, human beings identify themselves in a variety of politically relevant ways, are enmeshed in a multitude of authoritative networks and have loyalties to a variety of authorities. Indeed, some liberals see an open and participatory politics emerging from transnational linkages across societies, which transcend the state.

WORLD EXAMPLE BOX

Multiculturalism and human rights

The principle that people have certain rights now meets with almost universal approval, yet arguments abound over the relative weights of different sorts of rights (economic or political for instance) and who they should apply to (individuals or specific groups). Many contemporary liberals concede that not only individuals but specific communities might also have rights which need to be recognised and protected. The rights of indigenous peoples to continue to enjoy a traditional way of life and of certain ethnic or religious minorities in societies across the world to celebrate their own unique expressions of identity and community are now both enshrined in international law, even if they are not always respected in practice. The dilemma for liberals is not in accepting the concept of difference or the right to be different, but in what to do when certain cultural practices or religious beliefs conflict directly with the individual's right to choose.

For example, we would expect liberals to support the right of a woman to defy customs and practices rooted in traditional or religious belief systems, in relation to, say, marriage or the family, if this was her choice. However, frequently, the position and role of women is absolutely crucial to the expression of group identity. In such circumstances, 'group' rights and the rights of the individual might be in tension. Liberal human rights scholars like Jack Donnelly have tried to find a way out of this dilemma by accepting a weak cultural relativist position, arguing that rights are universal, but different cultures may provide for rights through different means and so some variation in the way rights are implemented might be allowed. Thus, the notion of universal rights is retained, but some concessions are made to particular cultural differences which will affect the interpretation and implementation of the universal principles. Ultimately, liberals will usually argue that, where the various claims of culture and individual rights are in direct and obvious tension, individual rights should prevail.

REFLECTION BOX

Do social and cultural differences invalidate the liberal claim that all human beings have basic, inalienable human rights?

Conflict and violence

As demonstrated above, conflict and violence have been central concerns in liberal IR. We will not elaborate any further here; suffice to say that, in distinctive ways, liberals have seen themselves as activists in advancing the cause of peace. This liberal desire to see an end to conflict and violence has manifested itself in liberal peace theory and liberal prescriptions for peace and security. Liberals also see institutions as playing a central role in mediating and resolving conflict. Liberalism is sometimes dismissed as hopelessly utopian because of this strong desire to realise a less violent, less conflictual world. However, to reiterate, liberals do not see this occurring quickly or without political will and human effort.

Summary

1. Liberal thought has a long intellectual tradition. Early liberal thinking on international politics and peace was particularly influenced by the eighteenth-century German philosopher Immanuel Kant.
2. With regards to economics, liberal theories of the market are particularly associated with Adam Smith, David Ricardo and John Maynard Keynes.
3. There have been a number of distinctive ways in which liberal thought has been applied to IR: for example, liberal pluralism, world society, interdependence and neo-liberal institutionalism, as well as the related schools of functionalism and idealism.
4. Liberals are optimistic about human nature, because they believe that behaviour is largely the product of various interactions with our social environment.
5. Because of the above, liberals have faith in the possibilities of education, human progress and the establishment of fair and just institutions.

6. Liberals believe that the central characteristic of all human beings is rationality. This gives rise to notions of the intrinsic value of human life, the moral worth of the individual and the existence of inalienable human rights.
7. Liberals believe that the role of government should be limited, although there is some disagreement about just how far and to what ends the state should intervene in civil society.
8. In the international realm, liberals have faith in the possibility of cooperation, and suggest that all states can achieve their aims if they abandon the notion of self-help.
9. Liberals believe that not only states, but also NGOs, multinational corporations and institutions are important 'actors' in IR.

Criticisms

One set of criticisms centres around a fundamental contradiction between economic and political liberty. This criticism is centred on liberal support for the free market and the institutions of private property, both of which appear to be central to the liberal conception of freedom and choice. Critics argue that the operation of free markets and the private ownership of property and resources lead to the progressive concentration of wealth in fewer and fewer hands. This inevitably leads to a concentration of power among the wealthy, which in turn impinges greatly upon the liberty and meaningful choices available to poorer groups. Left-liberals have taken this criticism on board, and support a limited form of state intervention and welfarism in the interests of redistributing wealth. On the other hand, liberals on the right, often referred to as neo-liberals or neo-classical liberals, argue that state intervention is always a threat to individual liberty and justify the continuing operation of the free market on the grounds that it increases the overall level of wealth in society which then 'trickles down' to the poor. It is worth noting that there is little empirical evidence to support this contention.

The liberal view can, then, be reasonably criticised as simply providing a justification of the way things are; the observation that the 'liberal' system is of benefit to a very narrow section of humanity. For example, liberal pluralists generally provide a benevolent view of international institutions, MNCs and the whole liberal free-trade ethos which dominates today's international political economy.

In recent years there have been numerous attacks on the notions of **universalism** found in liberal thought. We will return to these in the chapters on Critical Theory, Feminism and Postmodernism. Briefly though, it has been argued that the characteristics held to be essentially 'human' are actually specific to a particular group of people at a particular period in history. So-called 'universalism' actually expresses the particular experience of dominant groups in the West, so the argument goes. Liberalism gives us a linear view of human progress and development. Again, this is because liberalism tends to universalise Western experience. In development theory, for example, liberals have suggested that poorer states are further 'behind' in the development process, but essentially on the same road and travelling in the same direction as richer, more developed countries. However, as we will see in chapter 3, it has been countered that much of the wealth of today's rich Western nations has been based historically on the exploitation of the natural resources and cheap labour of the global South. Green thinkers, who are discussed at greater length in chapter 8, also argue that liberal development strategies are resulting in environmental degradation, thus adding to the woes of already poor countries.

Universalism: the idea that politics can be guided by universally valid principles, rather than being conditioned by particular local conditions.

The pluralist view of international relations as a series of complex interactions between an enormous variety of actors is, at first sight, less contentious. However, it is disputed by realists, who, as we will see in the following chapter, argue for the continued primacy or dominance of the state in IR, and Marxists, who argue that a pluralist view misses the fundamental issue, which is inequality between various groups or *classes* at the international level.

In much the same way as most major perspectives in International Relations, liberalism can be said to be a Western paradigm. This is to say, the core assumptions of liberalism were formulated by early liberal scholars, such as those discussed above, who were exclusively from the West. While in contemporary International Relations students and scholars from all over the world and with very diverse interests can be classed as liberals or use liberalism in some form, they are essentially using a perspective which is founded on Western assumptions. Thus, liberalism has been criticised by some as being culturally specific as opposed to truly international.

Common misunderstandings

1. *Liberals believe that people are naturally good.* This is a somewhat simplified and rather old-fashioned view of liberalism. Certainly, liberals regard 'human nature' as malleable and are optimistic about the possibility of organising human life on a more just and harmonious basis. It is more accurate to say that liberals often believe human nature to be *inherently* good but not necessarily constant. Thus, human beings are *potentially* good.
2. *States are insignificant.* Certainly not. As we saw above, neo-liberal institutionalism is a state-centric approach to the study of institutions. Liberal pluralists have not sought to deny the state's role in IR, but simply to highlight that other actors also have roles, big and small.
3. *Cooperation means no conflict.* Far from it. Cooperation can be fostered by conflict. The liberal commitment to limited government is based on the belief that, left to themselves, people will act to further their own interests, which can create conflict. This necessitates a legal framework, but general spontaneity and freedom is the best way to create wealth and growth. Similarly, at the international level, if states' interests coincided exactly (in other words if they were harmonious) they would have no need to cooperate. Cooperation takes place in order to try and resolve conflicts (of interest). Cooperation is one way of resolving conflict.
4. *'Greenpeace should be involved in IR'.* Many students have the impression that acceptance of a liberal pluralist perspective automatically implies *promoting* the involvement in IR of non-state actors (such as Greenpeace). Liberal pluralists may argue that non-state actors *are* increasingly important in IR and even that this is a good thing, but theorists are concerned with how and why this is happening rather than (necessarily) directly sponsoring it.
5. *Liberal means tolerant and wishy-washy in a political sense.* Sometimes in common usage the term 'liberal' is used to mean progressive or left-leaning and is used in US politics particularly to contrast with 'conservative'. Liberal tolerance is paradoxical given its inherent universalism, and certainly not all view liberalism as politically progressive.

Further reading

Claude, I. (1956), *Swords into Plowshares: The Problems and Progress of International Organisation*, New York: Random House (an early liberal work that envisages a more peaceful, cooperative world).

Donnelly, J. (1993), *International Human Rights*, Boulder, CO: Westview Press (an excellent example of liberal thinking in IR on a core liberal concept).

Doyle, M. (1986), 'Liberalism and World Politics', *American Political Science Review*, Vol. 80, No. 4, pp. 1151–69 (sets out the relationship between liberalism, peace and international order).

Fukuyama, F. (1992), *The End of History and the Last Man*, New York: Free Press (at the time of publication, a highly influential text that presented a liberal vision of the post-Cold War international order).

Keohane, R. (1984), *After Hegemony: Cooperation and Discord in the World Political Economy*, Princeton, NJ: Princeton University Press (regarded as a key work in the development of what would eventually be called 'neo-liberal institutionalism').

Ohmae, K. (1999), *The Borderless World: Power and Strategy in the Interlinked Economy*, New York: Collins Business (here Ohmae describes the nature and level of integration and interdependence in the modern global economy and how this is leading to the decline in relevance of the state and the rising importance of other types of actors).

Rosecrance, R. (1987), *The Rise of the Trading State: Commerce and Conquest in the Modern World*, New York: Basic Books (in this key text from the twilight of the Cold War era Rosecrance argues that traditional preoccupation with conflict and security in international relations were obsolete as cooperation and globalisation altered the fundamental nature of the international environment).

2 Realism

Introduction

Realism is the most well-established theoretical perspective in International Relations. Indeed, it has been argued that realism has dominated International Relations to such a degree that students, and indeed scholars, have often lost sight of the fact that it is in fact one perspective amongst many. The result is that realism is often presented as if it were a 'commonsense' view of the world against which all other perspectives should be judged. We will return to this notion of realism as 'common sense' later in the book. At this juncture, it is enough to highlight that realism is one perspective in IR, not *the* perspective.

Realism has been represented using the idea of a billiard table in which the balls represent sovereign states (hence, the 'billiard ball model').

Realism is a complex and rich tradition of thought and you need to be aware of its nuances. Hans Bartelsen, for instance, has argued that realism is an area of debate rather than a single specific position. So, just as in a different context, 'Christian' implies a certain set of beliefs although there are variations within this belief system, so within realism we can identify classical and scientific versions, some realists who call themselves neo-realists or structural realists and so on. Differences and nuances aside, however, a number of texts and authors in International Relations have been collectively labelled as 'realist', because they share common assumptions and key ideas. In line with our desire to simplify somewhat as a first stage in understanding, in this chapter we will present realism as a coherent position or perspective in International Relations and for the sake of simplicity and clarity we concentrate on two versions of realism; classical (or traditional) realism and neo-realism.

Realism claims to be realistic in comparison with the utopianism of idealism, discussed at some length in chapter 1. Realists also claim to present more accurate analyses of international relations than advocates of other perspectives. Some of realism's major exponents have argued that their personal moral concerns or despair at the way the world is does not mean it is possible to change it. Some aspects of human behaviour are eternal through time and space. As we shall elaborate below, some realists argue that there are unchanging laws which regulate individual and state behaviour: states, like *men*, are by 'nature' self-interested and aggressive and will pursue their interests to the detriment of others and without regard to the constraints of law or morality.

Realists have traditionally held that the major problem of international relations was one of **anarchy**. Anarchy prevailed because, in international relations, there was no sovereign authority that could enforce the rule of law and ensure that 'wrongdoers' were punished. The League of Nations was a poor substitute for a truly sovereign power possessing a system of law and a military under the control of a single, sovereign government. However, realists went on to argue that it was impossible to set up a genuine world government, because states would not give up their sovereignty to an international body. Accordingly, realists argued that war could not be avoided completely. It is necessary, therefore, to accept the inevitability of war and pursue the necessary preparations for conflict. Only in this way can war be properly deterred, or at least managed.

> **Anarchy:** a condition in which there exists no centralised sovereign authority that enforces the rule of law. Realists are concerned with anarchy at the international level where there is no authority higher than the state.

After the Second World War realism emerged as accepted wisdom in International Relations because of the clear lessons that the conflict appeared to reiterate. Realists argued that the long history of world politics demonstrated that it was not an exercise in writing laws and treaties or in creating international organisations. Instead it was a struggle for power and security carried out under conditions of 'every country for itself'. By way of reference, they called themselves 'realists' and labelled the previously dominant approach 'idealism'. Realists argued that the focus of research in world politics should be on discovering the important forces that drive the relations between states. Realists believed that the pursuit of power and national interest were the major forces driving world politics. Focusing on these important forces, they argued, revealed that leaders had far less freedom to organise the world, and solve its problems, than proponents of idealism had originally suggested. Although realists accepted that laws and morality were a part of the workings of world politics, respect for law would only be achieved if it were backed by the threat of force. Realists also insisted that a state's primary obligation was to its own citizens, not to a rather abstract 'international community'.

AUTHOR BOX

Edward Hallett Carr

The reaction against idealism produced a number of very influential works in International Relations which mark the emergence of realism as the dominant world view in the post-Second World War period. One such work was E.H. Carr's *The Twenty Years' Crisis*, published in 1939. Carr is a central figure in the history of IR, whose continuing importance has been highlighted by recent attempts to (re)interpret this central work in the cause of (re)claiming Carr as a liberal, Marxist, English School scholar and even as a Critical Theorist. However, for a long period Carr has been identified with realism, because he produced a powerful critique of the core assumptions of idealism, arguing that the tragic events of the 1930s bore witness to the fragility of international institutions, the realities of the underlying struggle for power among states and the fallacy of a world public opinion supporting pacifism. Carr also rejected the normative underpinnings of idealism (a concern with questions of law, morality and justice) arguing instead for a 'science of international politics'.

Realists argued that, rather than concentrating on disarmament as a root to peace and security (a central objective of the League of Nations), states must, paradoxically, prepare for war. Realists believed that conflict was inevitable and so the best chance of avoiding war was to be strong in the face of real or potential aggression. Realists claimed that relying on reason to resolve the problem of war was utopian and ignored certain objective truths about world politics.

Although still in its infancy, even at this stage, International Relations theory was showing signs of what was to become a central characteristic; it 'evolved' through a series of debates. The Second

World War effectively settled the first great debate of International Relations in favour of the realists. The Cold War simply reinforced this view and allowed realism to continue to dominate International Relations scholarship throughout the 1950s and 1960s (see Concept Box, p. 56).

Neo-realism shares many core assumptions of traditional realism regarding the state, the problem of power and the pursuit of interests. However, neo-realists place more emphasis on the anarchic structure of the international system and the impact that the structure has on the behaviour of states as well as acknowledging, to a certain extent, the importance of non-state actors.

Origins

Although realism came to dominate the relatively young academic discipline of International Relations after the Second World War, it claims that what it is saying is not new and attributes its insights to a variety of sources. This section sketches the ideas of these writers who have either written on International Relations or had their ideas applied to it. The texts chosen here are not exhaustive but seek to make the basic point that realism makes a claim not just to validity across the globe (spatially) but throughout time (temporally) as well. To emphasise this point, realists are inclined to trace back their intellectual origins to over 2500 years ago and the writings of Thucydides or even beyond to ancient China and Sun Tzu.

AUTHOR BOX

Thucydides

The guiding ideas and the basic assumptions of realism are rooted in a tradition of thought dating back at least to the writings of Thucydides on the Peloponnesian wars, between the Greek city states of Athens and Sparta. Thucydides used the war to demonstrate how the logic of power politics (the pursuit of power and interest) characterised inter-state relations and conflict, rather than cooperation or action guided by higher moral principles.

It is sometimes argued that today's scholars and students of IR do not know any more about state behaviour than did Thucydides. His studies showed that the powerful did what they were able to and that the less powerful just had to accept it. Appeals to higher principles such as those by the people of Melos to the Athenians met with an iron fist, the fate of so many powerless peoples throughout the twentieth century.

The thoughts of Niccolo Machiavelli, a sixteenth-century Italian political thinker, and the seventeenth-century English philosopher Thomas Hobbes are also invoked to demonstrate how realism is supposedly founded on age-old wisdom. Machiavelli is famous, or perhaps notorious, for offering practical advice to the statesman which would ensure that they remained in power and achieved their objectives. He proposed a series of guides by which states' leaders might maximise their power. His advice included the instruction that promises must be broken when there is an interest to do so and that it is better to be feared than loved. These are two of the many reasons why Machiavelli is often accused of being an immoral thinker. The term 'Machiavellian' is used in common parlance to denote cynical and unprincipled behaviour, or used to describe people who act in a cunning and subtle manner, unscrupulously manipulating situations to their own advantage.

Perhaps, it is more accurate to describe Machiavelli's thought as amoral, rather than immoral, since he believed that moral or ethical behaviour was only possible under certain conditions of human existence and that the statesman had no real choice other than to act prudently and with due regard to the fragility of the political and social order. Although Machiavelli was not explicitly concerned with ethics or justice, it is clear that he regarded moral principles or justice as simply the stated preferences of the already powerful. There is no doubt that Machiavelli held an extremely dim view of human nature. Realists continue to argue there is no place for trust or sentiment in politics and point to Machiavelli's wisdom in elucidating this point.

The work of Thomas Hobbes has also been a key influence on realist thinkers. Hobbes is influential because he was among the first political thinkers to undertake a sustained discussion on the nature of secular (non-religious) power and authority.

CONCEPT BOX

An international 'state of nature'?

Hobbes 1588–1679 lived at a time of great social change and political instability. Perhaps, not surprisingly, therefore, one of his major preoccupations was the nature of political power, the basis of political order and, particularly, the origins of the state as the central, sovereign power. In order to explain the reasons and justification for the state and government, Hobbes posited the existence of a 'state of nature' in which all enjoyed freedom from restraint but in which, in consequence, life was 'nasty, brutish and short'. The conditions of life were unpleasant because it was man's nature to try and dominate and oppress others. For Hobbes, world politics was characterised by a war of all against all. Only mutual vulnerability (all men were vulnerable because they must of necessity sleep) and the desire for self-preservation allowed the setting-up of a sovereign body that would secure the conditions necessary for civilised life. However, while men might be persuaded to give up their natural liberty for the protection of the sovereign, the international realm would remain a war of all against all, since the conditions which forced men to give up their natural liberty for security in the 'state of nature' could never be realised in an international context. Put simply, states were not equally vulnerable to attack. Hobbes' classic work *Leviathan* remains one of the most influential writings on the nature of sovereignty and international anarchy. Indeed, international relations is sometimes likened to a 'state of nature'.

At times, Hobbes appears to evoke images which suggest religious influence and sympathies – inherent evil or wickedness, for example. However, his beliefs about the essentially selfish impulses of human beings were actually rooted in what he understood to be the insights of modern science. The extent to which we can discern scientific laws which help us to explain individual or social behaviour, or the extent to which the analogy of the individual in the state of nature can be made with the state in the international realm, is debatable. However, together, these two central assumptions provide realists with support for their argument about the need for states to behave selfishly in international relations. Such a view suggests that states are unified, purposive and rational actors in international relations in the way that individuals are in society. We might ask if this is an appropriate view. In order to help us decide whether these analogies are indeed appropriate and useful, we need to unpack the key assumptions of realism further.

Assumptions

While there are different variants of realism and, indeed, some subtle and intriguing differences between them, the perspective has some central assumptions which provide a common link. What is so important about these assumptions (or indeed any assumptions) is that, while realists argue that they are based on observations about the 'real world', it is interesting to note that our basic assumptions about the world actually inform our picture of reality. It follows, therefore, that different assumptions are likely to lead to very different world views. The extent to which realism helps to shape the very world it seeks to describe forms part of some more sophisticated critiques of realism which we will return to in later chapters (4 to 7 and the concluding chapter). So, what are the key ideas and assumptions which underpin realist thought? In summary the assumptions of realism are that:

- States are the key actors in international relations.
- Sovereignty, or independence and self-control, is the defining characteristic of the state.
- States are motivated by a drive for power, security and pursuit of the 'national interest'.
- States, like men, behave in a self-interested manner.
- The central problem in international relations is the condition of anarchy, which means the lack of a central sovereign authority at the global level to regulate relations between states.
- The aggressive intent of states, combined with the lack of world government, means that conflict is an unavoidable and ever-present reality of international relations.
- A semblance of order and security can be maintained by shifting alliances among states so preventing any one state from becoming overwhelmingly powerful and, thus, constituting a threat to the peace and security of others.
- International institutions and law play a role in international relations, but are only effective if backed by force or effective sanction.
- Power is the key to understanding international behaviour and state motivation. For realists the main form of power is military or physical power.
- Human nature can be said to be inherently selfish and constant. As a result, humans will act to further their own interests even to the detriment of others, which can often lead to conflict. Because human nature is unchanging, there is little prospect that this kind of behaviour will change.

The last point to be made here on the lack of centralised authority can be used to illustrate a key difference between traditional or classical realism and neo-realism (sometimes labelled 'structural' realism). To simplify, we might say that classical realism is an attempt to understand the world from the point of view of the statesman or diplomat who is forced to operate in an uncertain and dangerous world. Realism provides a guide to action based on the guiding principles of **realpolitik** in the interests of the preservation of the nation-state. Thus, realism focuses on states as actors and analyses international politics in terms of 'units' called states. On the other hand, neo-realism places more emphasis on the importance of the anarchic international system. Realism and neo-realism will be revisited in the conclusion; it is enough at this stage that you are aware of these key differences.

Realpolitik: a nineteenth-century German term popularised because of the way it seemed to capture the shrewd awareness – including the preparedness to use force where necessary – of Bismarck.

AUTHOR BOX

Kenneth Waltz

In a much-quoted work entitled *A Theory of International Politics* (1979) Waltz argued that: traditional realism contained significant deficiencies, notably that it was very 'agent centred', concentrating primarily on states. States constituted the main agents and units of analysis. Waltz claimed that any theory of international relations should be able to tell us something about both the units – states – and the system as a whole. While unit-level theories focused on agents such as individuals, or in the case of realism, states, system-level theories focused on the overall structure or system in which action took place. All systems were determined by organising principles, specific functions and the distribution of capabilities. The international order was unique in that while domestic orders were centralised and hierarchic, the international system was a realm of coordination and self-help. Moreover, while the units in domestic orders (citizens, for example) were subjected to law, the units in the international order (states) were at best interdependent, autonomous entities. International order was, therefore, mechanistic rather than organic. The international order was also anarchic.

Waltz argued that the system level had been neglected in IR theory, although it was clearly important in exerting pressures upon states from outside. Since we could potentially differentiate between externally generated and internally generated pressures, it would therefore be possible to identify the level at which crucial change occurs. It was possible that changes at unit level could affect the system as a whole, or conversely, changes at systems level could affect the unit (state) level. An example of a unit-level change affecting the system might be the collapse of the Soviet Union, which profoundly affected the global power structure. A change at the system level might occur if an alliance system collapses (in the absence of a clearly defined enemy), which in turn impacts on individual states.

Waltz's theory has been criticised on a number of grounds. However, it has proved a major influence on International Relations. Moreover, while in various ways Waltz's analytical distinction between 'system' and 'unit' levels could be criticised, his work was important in opening up questions about the appropriate level of analysis in IR and of structure and agency in the study of International Relations. Waltz's book was also something of a seminal text in the shift from traditional realism to the more 'scientific' claims or pretensions of neo-realism. This is a point that we take up and develop in the concluding chapter.

Themes

The state and power

Perhaps the core theme in realism is the centrality of the state. Indeed, states and inter-state relations constitute the very definition of the subject. The central characteristics of the modern state are that it has a defined territory and a government which is invested with sovereign authority and exercises power over a people. Some commentators add a fourth characteristic – recognition. Recognition means that the state's claims over that defined territory and its right to exercise sovereignty over its people are recognised by other states. Recognition can take many forms, but typically it involves opening up diplomatic relations or entering into treaty obligations with another state.

It follows from this that a central characteristic of the state is sovereignty. There are two types of sovereignty relating to states: internal sovereignty signifies the holding of authority within a given territory and over a given people; external sovereignty, meanwhile, involves being recognised by other states as legitimate in the sense of having the right to act independently in international affairs – that is, to make alliances, declare wars and so on. This conception of the state as the central actor which exercises power in particular ways has important consequences for how realists view the relationship between states and other 'actors' on the international stage. For example, multinational corporations (MNCs) are not regarded as independent or autonomous actors in the international economy, but seen rather as an extension of state power or an instrument of foreign policy. MNCs are not, then, held to be a significant economic and political force in their own right, exercising power and influence, but a measure and reflection of the power and might of particular states.

[handwritten margin note: Is this true? ? No!!]

CONCEPT BOX

What is a 'state'?

Despite the centrality of the concept of the 'state' in International Relations there are profound disagreements about, first, its nature and, second, its importance relative to other 'actors'. These differences will become apparent as we work our way through the text. There are other problems with the notion of the state as actor, or in conceiving of international relations as a system or society of independent, or autonomous, nation-states. It is not at all clear that a state does have to have a clearly defined territory in order to be a state. For example, the borders of the state of Israel are contested by many of its Arab neighbours. World leaders frequently meet with representatives of the Palestinian 'people', while some governments actually recognise the existence of a Palestinian state, although there is no clearly defined territory on the map which one could point to as 'the State of Palestine'.

For a very long period the USA and some other Western states refused to deal with the communist government of China and continued to recognise the exiled nationalist 'government' in Taiwan as the legitimate representative of the Chinese people. Moreover, there are numerous examples of states around the world where significant sections of the population clearly do not recognise the sovereign government as legitimate. The Irish nationalist (Republican) community in Northern Ireland is one such example. At first sight, these may appear to be isolated or exceptional cases, but in fact, there are large areas of the globe where boundaries are contested and dominant articulations of 'national interest' are challenged. Does this rather messier 'reality' render the realist concept of a system or society of bounded, unified and coherent state 'actors' somewhat problematic?

A second major theme in International Relations is that of **power**. Power can be regarded as an essentially contested concept – that is, one over which there are fundamental disagreements. Furthermore, it is a word which seems to be very similar to other words; words such as authority, influence and coercion. Realism has much to say on the concept of power in international relations. Realism does not claim to deal with all types of power, nor all types of power relationships, but it does claim to identify the fundamental essence of what constitutes power in international relations. Realists have been fairly careful to provide a clear definition of power, and show how it can be quantified and, crucially, who has it.

For realism, the essence of **power** is the ability to change behaviour/dominate and it often takes the form of military or physical power.

Table 2.1   Relative military and economic capability of nine major states

	Economic rank	GDP (2008) $US Billions	GNP per cap (2008)	Armed forces active personnel	Active divs	Combat aircraft*	Principal surface ships	Subs	Nuclear capability
USA	1	13,886.5	$46,040	1,650,500	15	5,371	137	104	YES
Japan	2	4,813.3	$37,670	237,000	13	540	62	22	NO
Germany	3	3,197.0	$38,860	367,300	8	611	12	40	NO
UK	4	2,608.5	$42,740	254,000	2	586	38	20	YES
France	5	2,447.1	$38,500	409,600	5	868	43	18	YES
China	6	3,120.9	$2,360	2,930,000	93	5,845	55	50	YES
Brazil	7	1,133.0	$5,910	336,000	8	272	21	4	NO
Russia	8	1,071.0	$7,560	1,714,000	106	3,342	161	185	YES
India	9	1,069.4	$950	1,265,000	37	864	25	15	YES

* Does not include helicopters

Original source for GDP and GNP per capita, World Bank (2008), *World Development Report 2009*, New York: Oxford University Press; source for military statistics, International Institute of Strategic Studies (1994), *The Military Balance 1994–95*, London: Brassey's.

Taken from: J. Vogler (1996), 'The structures of global politics', in C. Bretherton and G. Ponton (eds). *Global Politics: An Introduction*, Oxford: Blackwell, pp. 23–48 (Economic data up-dated). Realists would recognise the military component of power. How does this table comparing military statistics and economic indicators affect your understanding of power, if at all?

Some realists see power in stark, zero-sum terms. Individuals, like states, have power at the expense of others. Traditionally, realists have seen military capability as the essence of power, for fairly obvious reasons. The capacity to act militarily gives states the ability to repel attacks against themselves, and therefore to ensure their security. Or it enables them to launch attacks against others for specific ends. Realists have assumed that it is military capability that counts. It represents the 'bottom line'; the ultimate arbiter of international disputes. Power is both an end in itself and the means to an end in that it will deter outside attack or allow the acquisition of territory abroad.

In a world made up of independent states, force has been regarded as the ultimate arbiter in the settlement of differences. It follows from this that the potential for military capability, and hence power, depends on a number of factors such as size of population, abundance of natural resources, as well as geographical factors and the type of government of a given state.

— US today?

CONCEPT BOX

The balance of power

Realists have developed an analysis of how power is distributed in the international system. This idea is referred to as the 'balance of power'. A simple definition of the balance of power is that it is a mechanism which operates to prevent the dominance of any one state in the international system. The balance of power is sometimes viewed as a naturally occurring phenomenon, or a situation that comes about fortuitously. At other times it is suggested that it is a strategy consciously pursued by states. States engineer such balances to counter threats from other powerful states and so ensure their own survival. As we would expect, the balance of power is frequently measured in terms of military strength. For realists, the primary aim of the 'balance of power' is not to preserve peace but to preserve the security of (major) states, if necessary by means of war. The balance of power is about the closest realists ever come to outlining the conditions for a peaceful international order, in so far as peace is defined negatively as an absence of war.

In nineteenth-century Europe the situation was characterised by five or six roughly equal powers. These countries were quite successful at avoiding war, either by making alliances or because the most powerful state, Great Britain, would side one way or the other to act as a 'balancer' of power. Although the balance was seen as a good and beneficial thing, unfortunately the system of alliances which became 'set' in the early twentieth century – and which was ridiculed as 'deterrence' in the television show *Blackadder Goes Forth* – saw Europe ultimately embroiled in the First World War.

Although such ideas are easy to challenge by reference to many states in the modern world, a state is said to have power if it has a large population, abundant natural resources and a large area, mountainous terrain or other features making it hard to attack. There is, at times, an almost mathematical idea that adding and subtracting the strengths and weaknesses in these areas will lead to an accurate calculation of a state's power potential. In what has subsequently become an influential realist text in IR, *Politics Among Nations,* Hans Morgenthau engaged in an elaborate discussion of the sources of state power. However, in fact it is not easy to quantify power in this way. For example, population is not always a power blessing if such mouths cannot be fed.

? Frederick the Great also today

Population

The realist conception of power is challengeable in a very simple way if we look at population. Realists have assumed that large populations provide soldiers and are therefore elements of national power. If we look at China and the huge sacrifices it was able to absorb in, say, the Korean War (1950–53), then there is some evidence for such a case. However, for many countries today, including China, population size and growth is creating a range of problems. People are mouths to feed and brains to educate and place a great strain on resources. If we argue that power, even military power, must have an economic base, a large population is a big source of weakness for a country like Bangladesh.

As realists readily admit, in practice only putting power to the test in war can adequately resolve questions about the relative power of states and, even then, military power will not be decisive if there are reasons why it cannot or will not be used. For example, few doubt that the USA is a more formidable military power than Vietnam; however, the former was unable to defeat the latter in the particular conflict in which they were engaged in the 1960s and 1970s thanks to various factors such as the weight of US public opinion and differences in the leadership, tactics and morale of the two sides. In addition, the amount of power that a state can exert in any particular encounter may be specific to the issue or area under consideration. For example, collectively the states that make up the Organisation of Petroleum Exporting Countries (OPEC) have less 'military muscle' than the USA and some European countries, but they were able, collectively, to exert their will against the West and raise the price of oil dramatically in the early 1970s. As we will see in later chapters (particularly 3 to 7), there are many and varied ways of understanding power relations.

Conflict and violence

Conflict may be simply defined as disagreements which the parties involved seek to resolve to their own satisfaction. According to such a definition, conflict need not be violent and seems an inevitable part of human interaction, including as it does arguments over whether to visit the cinema or a football match, jealousy in relationships and so on. Human interaction it seems leads to disagreements. To realists, however, the conflict in which they are interested is the specific variety of inter-state conflict of a violent nature; most usually, but not always, wars.

The dominance of realism in International Relations after the Second World War can be explained in part by the Cold War, the period of history from the late 1940s to late 1980s. The causes of the Cold War continue to be hotly disputed. However, the initial cause of tensions was a series of bitter disagreements about the status of Germany after the Second World War. At the end of the war, the Soviet Union (USSR), the USA, France and Britain administered separate sections of occupied German territory. The Soviet Union and the Allies then began a series of meetings to negotiate over what would happen to Germany now that the war was over. To simplify somewhat, the Soviet Union believed it was important to ensure that Germany did not pose a threat to the Soviet Union in the future. They demanded that Germany be prevented from becoming a significant, economic and military power again. Furthermore, they believed that the Soviet Union was entitled to massive compensation for the war damage inflicted on it by Germany. On the other hand, the Allied Powers believed that the economic recovery of Germany was vital to the future prosperity of the European continent. Moreover, there is no doubt that the Allies also believed that a resurgent Germany would prevent the Soviet Union from becoming the dominant European power in the post-war period. Clearly, the peacetime aims of the two sides were incompatible.

The Cold War seemed to bear out the major contentions of realism, in that the division of Europe appeared to be a logical outcome of opposing interests over the post-Second World War security order in Europe. The 'problem' of Germany – a potential major power in the future – was 'solved' by its division. The superpowers' respective 'spheres of influence' were subsequently consolidated through alliance systems (NATO initially, and at a later date, the Warsaw Pact).

The Cold War is sometimes described as, fundamentally, a struggle about ideologies rather than interests. Realists, however, do not place much emphasis on ideas in IR. They would argue that the division of Europe was a logical outcome of power politics and irreconcilable interests and aims.

FILM BOX

The Cold War

The Cold War dominated International Relations, both in theory and practice, for nearly half a century. Consequently, it inevitably captured popular imagination in countless forms, including cinema. The anti-communist hysteria of the House Un-American Activities Committee and the pivotal role played by Senator Joseph McCarthy in identifying Soviet spies were at the heart of all aspects of American society in the aftermath of the Korean War. Coupled with the launch of Sputnik (the first satellite to be put into orbit, by the Soviets, in the late 1950s) this produced a wave of movies whose central theme was that the USA and the free world faced an imminent invasion. Much of this mood was captured allegorically in the popularity of science fiction B-movies such as *Invaders from Mars*, *It Came From Outer Space* and the classic *Invasion of the Body Snatchers* (1956). Although the director of the latter film, Don Siegel, denied that the film had a political message, many saw the film as either anti-communist or as a subtle critique of McCarthyism. The film recounts a tale of dehumanisation in which large seed pods from outer space appear in the Californian town of Santa Mira while its residents are asleep. The pods hatch identical replicas of the sleeping citizens who then murder the original inhabitants replacing them with zombie-like clones. The 'hero' of the movie, Dr Miles Bennel, valiantly struggles to stay awake so that the same fate does not befall him while struggling to warn the rest of the world of the fate that awaits them. His task is made more difficult by the fact that the new residents of the town do everything they can to prevent him.

For those who saw the movie as being anti-communist, the message was clear. The USA, indeed the whole free world, was in danger of being taken over by calculated emotionless communists who would enslave humanity. This enemy was omnipresent – you could not tell who was a communist, they could be anyone and everywhere. Consequently, America had to be ever vigilant and awake to the enemy both from outside and within. For those who saw the movie as anti-McCarthyite, the alien zombies were the anti-communist zealots who demanded an unquestioning loyalty to their ideology and would destroy all those who tried to stand in their way.

A final word has to be given to one of the best satires of the logic of 'deterrence' that dictated the nuclear strategy of the superpowers during the Cold War – Stanley Kubrick's 1963 film *Dr Strangelove*. In this film the Soviet Union has developed a doomsday machine that will automatically launch its nuclear weapons if the country is attacked. Unfortunately the USA does not find out about the machine's existence until too late. The film depicts a catalogue of communication failures between the President and his Soviet counterpart and between the President and his military chiefs, including the lone bomber that, having suffered the destruction of its communication system, flies into Soviet airspace to deliver the deadly payload that will trigger the doomsday machine. Coming as it did in the aftermath of the Cuban Missile Crisis, the film poignantly demonstrated and satirised the potential devastating cost of the destructive logic central to the superpower stand-off.

Realists limit their interest for the most part to the causes and nature of wars. There are differences of opinion as to where the focus should lie if we are talking about general rather than specific causes. Various scholars have argued for a concentration on the nature of human beings; others have suggested a focus on states themselves; and still others have preferred to pin the blame for conflict on the workings of the international system as a whole.

It is possible to argue for consideration to be given to all three points of view. The notion of 'three images' is associated particularly in an earlier work by Kenneth Waltz, his influential book *Man, the State and War*, first published in 1959. To simplify somewhat, Waltz's first image focuses on human nature as the root cause of war. This view suggests that as a species we are inherently greedy, aggressive, selfish and generally nasty. There is a good deal of evidence with which to support this claim but equally much to dispute it. The second image focuses on the state level, arguing that these are constructed in such a way that pursuit of national interest inevitably leads to nationalistic clashes with other states. The third image is that the structure of the international system itself leads to conflict by forcing states to act in a certain way.

WORLD EXAMPLE BOX

The Middle East

The Middle East is a region which has experienced considerable conflict in the twentieth century and indeed again in the early twenty-first. Though access to water is not usually the specifically cited cause of conflict, in very many cases analysts believe it underlies it. Israeli need for water, for instance, may be the most intractable reason for the failure to establish a lasting peace with the Palestinians. Water is a precious resource and becoming increasingly scarce as populations continue to expand. With rivers forming borders throughout the region, and usually flowing through more than one state, efforts to control water in one state (say through dam projects) may well lead to reduced supply in another. Such problems complicate inter-state relationships, including the Arab–Israeli and the Turkey–Syria–Iraq relationships.

More often realists look for concrete and specific causes of conflict – for instance, 'economic' arguments like trade wars. Some of the bloodiest conflicts of recent history have been over access to resources. We will expand upon how access to resources and environmental degradation might increase conflicts in chapter 8.

Peace and security

In realism, international relations by their very nature are characterised by conflict and competition. The existence of war is inevitable and ultimately unavoidable. International relations which are characterised by peace are therefore viewed, in a rather pessimistic (or realistic?) way, as being the exception as opposed to the norm. Peace is a condition where conflict and competition are absent, but will in time return. Thus, peace is not seen as an enduring condition nor is it seen as something which should be pursued in order to ensure security. This latter point results from the assumption that violent conflict will return. For realists in IR, security is a concept which relates to the state. A state is more or less secure to the extent that it can ensure its survival in the international system, generally through possessing sufficient power capabilities. With regard to security, instead of pursuing peace, realists concentrate on the conditions necessary to prevent war. Here, the relationship between power, security and conflict is of most importance.

Canada?

For realists security is about (state) survival. For those states, the majority, unable to guarantee their own safety through their own military forces, the balance of power represents a reasonable hope of being able to feel secure in international relations. Realists argue that, unlike in domestic politics (where governments are responsible for enforcing laws), in world politics there is no government to enforce laws and, as a result, each state has to provide for its own security. Self-preservation under such conditions demands that a state be able to protect itself, because it cannot rely upon help coming from other states. Policy makers, conclude realists, must therefore seek power for their country. To do otherwise, it is argued, would invite war and defeat, as another state or states would take advantage of this misjudgment. A key area of discussion in later realist work revolves around the dilemma of increasing one's own security at the expense of others'. Realists argue that creating institutions such as the League of Nations, which presupposes states have an interest in cooperation, was foolish and therefore bound to fail.

ANALOGY BOX

The stag/hare analogy

This analogy is sometimes used to illustrate the 'security dilemma' and problems of cooperation in international relations. The story involves a group of primitive hunters isolated on an island. They agree that if they can kill a stag they will have enough to feed all of them, but that to do this they must cooperate as it will require all their efforts to entrap and kill the animal. They set off to hunt the stag. Shortly afterwards one of the hunters sees a hare, which would certainly be enough to satisfy the hunger of an individual. In breaking off from the stag hunt to capture the hare the hunter ensures that he will satisfy his need for food. However, in so doing he effectively allows the stag to escape and the rest of the group are condemned to hunger. Cooperation among all the hunters could have led to an optimal solution where all were fed. However, the hunter faced a dilemma because he could not be sure that the group would catch the stag. Furthermore, he could not be sure that another member of the group would not break ranks in pursuit of the hare, in which case *he* would have gone hungry himself. In the context of this uncertainty, it was, therefore, rational to behave in a self-interested manner. The point of the stag/hare analogy is to illustrate that under conditions of uncertainty (i.e. anarchy) it is rational to act in a self-interested way. The tragedy of international relations is, therefore, that under conditions of anarchy even mutual interest does not guarantee cooperation and hence mutual gain.

Institutions and world order

Given the emphasis on the state, power, anarchy, conflict and security, it is not entirely surprising that throughout much of its history cooperation has been a secondary concern for realists. Broadly speaking, realism has tended to marginalise areas which are not the 'real stuff' of international relations, and therefore contends that international cooperation is significant only to the extent that it is engaged in *by* states for the benefit *of* states. Realism's basic assumptions involve the belief that, while much can interest us about the world, these should not sidetrack us from its essential features. In suggesting that certain facets of international relations are timeless, the traditional realist distinction has always been between the 'high politics' of foreign policy, diplomacy and war and the 'low politics' of economics. This means that the former has been regarded as much more important than the latter.

At first sight, then, a perspective based on assumptions concerning the sovereignty of states, the primacy of national interest and so on cannot have very much to say about international institutions.

To some extent, institutions have been something of a subsidiary theme in realist writings, but this does not mean that realists have no view on the character and role of institutions in international affairs. English School scholars like Hedley Bull (see chapter 7) have argued that supranational organisations such as the EU can be regarded as 'states in waiting'. In other words, they may acquire an identity of their own such that they become the citizen's highest source of loyalty. At such a point current states, such as Germany or France, become simply regions of a European state even if such a process might take a long time to come about.

In contrast, realists never lose sight of the central importance of states as the predominant actors of world politics. They believe that states only join international institutions and enter into cooperative arrangements when it suits them. Accordingly, such arrangements, alliances or cooperative agreements can be backed out of or broken, if and when they cease to be in the national interest, as easily as the hunter in the stag/hare analogy above left pursuit of the stag in order to catch a hare. Realists do not entirely neglect the study of the United Nations or the European Union, just as they do not deny that limited forms of cooperation occur and that international institutions might facilitate this to some degree. Nonetheless, the bottom line, to realists, is that international institutions are significant only to the extent that they allow states to pursue their own interests.

However, an important development in neo-realist thinking about the nature of institutions and international order has taken place not in International Relations theory as such but in the 'sister' discipline of International Political Economy (IPE). In this chapter we referred to neo-realism first in the context of the work of Waltz and his Theory of International Politics. However, within IPE a distinctly neo-realist perspective has evolved which is centrally concerned with problems of cooperation and the role of institutions in international relations, particularly in relation to the governance of the global economy. In the 1970s an initial recognition that economic interdependence between states was becoming more widespread and complex led scholars within the emerging discipline of IPE to ask how economic activity taking place across state boundaries could be coordinated effectively. Moreover, how could this increasingly complex international economic order be 'governed' in the absence of government?

CONCEPT BOX

International Political Economy (IPE)

This field of study is often seen as a sub-discipline of IR, but it can also be seen as a distinct discipline. Some scholars argue that IPE developed in the 1970s as a result of the limitations of traditional IR which, it was argued, focused too much on conflict, war and the state. IPE has developed into a field of study which considers a large range of issues and actors and sees politics and economics as being inseparable. The main areas of study have been the growth of the modern liberal order, development, modernisation, international trade, conflict and forms of power. A number of scholars were important in the development of IPE in the 1970s, including Susan Strange, Robert Cox and Robert Gilpin. They called for a revision of what issues, processes and actors were studied and how they were studied in IR. The result was a movement towards studying international political economy and 'low politics' *as well as* 'high politics'.

There is, however, a much richer and older tradition of IPE literature that pre-dates the 1970s rise of the discipline. Scholars such as Alexander Hamilton, Adam Smith, David Ricardo, Karl Marx and Friedrich Engels developed a rich body of literature on political economy and international relations. Within this earlier literature three broad paradigms or perspectives emerged: Liberalism, Marxism and Mercantilism. The first two of these developed into Liberalism and Structuralism as we have come to know them in IR. The latter is perhaps one of the precursors to Realism and was often termed Economic Nationalism. This school of thought informed much state policy in the late 1800s and early 1900s through to World War Two. The main premise of it was that economic power is the key to greater political and military power and states should seek to maximise their economic power through protection of domestic industries, increased exports and lower imports. This type of policy came to be known as 'beggar-thy-neighbour' and was seen as a cause of World War Two by liberals.

The point of departure for neo-realists in answering these questions was a fairly orthodox one: the problems generated by an essentially anarchic international system. However, in this specific context, neo-realists combined some fairly traditional realist ideas about power and the centrality of states in international relations, with certain liberal ideas about rationality and economic cooperation. We will not dwell on this here, but rather concentrate on how neo-realists have developed a view of 'governance' based on an analysis of the role played by dominant states in maintaining international economic order.

Neo-realists employed the concept of 'hegemony' to describe a situation in which one state is dominant in the international system. As we will see in chapter 4, the concept of **hegemony** is also central to some strands of Critical Theory. Critical Theorists use the concept of hegemony to talk about both dominant social forces and dominant ideas in IR. In neo-realism the emphasis, as one would expect, is on dominant states. Neo realists frequently cite two major phases of hegemonic domination (pax-Britannica and pax-Americana) which describe the periods of British dominance over the global economy in the nineteenth and early twentieth centuries and US domination in the post-Second World War period. Neo-realists typically argue that, when conditions of hegemony prevail, there is a much better chance that institutions will be established and/or function effectively. (There is a debate about this, however. See the Author Box below.) The hegemon is able to offer other member states positive inducements to cooperate, or conversely may impose certain sanctions on states that refuse to engage with other states cooperatively. It follows that in the absence of hegemony, institutions will be more fragile and less effective.

Hegemony is the dominance of a single power (e.g. Britain in the nineteenth century and the USA in the post-1945 period). It is employed to explain how international order is possible even in the context of 'anarchy'.

Neo-realists have found the concept of hegemony useful in explaining how an international economy based on fundamentally liberal principles and liberal economic practices could be secured in a world in which political authority was vested in nation states with competing interests and possibly mercantilist impulses. In the absence of an international 'public good' which would allow the international economy to run smoothly, the concept of hegemony was used to explain how a degree of regulation, or governance was possible. Neo-realists believe that states aim to maximise wealth and that this is best achieved by securing a broadly liberal, free-market international economy.

Attempts to fuse an analysis of the growth and expansion of a liberal international economy with an analysis of where power lies in the international state system gave rise to a theory of Hegemonic Stability. The idea of Hegemonic Stability was originally advanced by Charles Kindleberger to explain the collapse of the international monetary order in the early twentieth century and the economic depression that ensued from this. Hegemonic Stability Theory (HST) holds that there is always a proclivity towards instability in the international system, but this can be avoided if the dominant state assumes a leadership or hegemonic role. This role involves creating and upholding a system of rules which provide a secure basis for international order and cooperation under conditions of anarchy. In this way liberal values and norms could be fostered and upheld. Hegemonic powers are able to control finance, trade, and so on. The Bretton Woods System which comprised the General Agreement on Tariffs and Trade (GATT), the International Bank for Reconstruction and Development (World Bank) and the International Monetary Fund (IMF) is an example of international order founded upon US hegemony. It provided a system of rules, values and norms, based on liberal economic principles (see chapter 1) which broadly served the interests of the USA, although many other states were consenting partners in forging the post-Second World War international order.

AUTHOR BOX

Robert Keohane: *After Hegemony*

In the previous chapter we introduced you to a strand of liberalism in IR theory which has been labelled 'neo-liberal institutionalism'. Neo-liberal institutionalism endeavours to explain processes of cooperation and the role of international institutions in international relations. You will recall that neo-liberal institutionalists agree with neo-realists that anarchy is a 'problem', but they argue that the problem can be overcome without the existence of hegemonic states. In so doing neo-liberal institutionalism critiques many of the assumptions of neo-realism.

An important work on the way to the development of neo-liberal institutionalism was Robert Keohane's *After Hegemony*. Keohane argued that it was wrong to infer that cooperation was impossible without hegemony, since the condition of hegemony was not the only possible form or motive for cooperation. Hegemonic Stability Theory (HST) might be partially valid, but it was not sufficient for understanding the conditions under which cooperation took place. Cooperation seems to depend on: expectations; transaction costs; and conditions of uncertainty. All of these factors were affected by the existence of international regimes.

Keohane argued that, despite the fact that explicit, well-defined rules and procedures governing international monetary relations had practically vanished in the wake of the collapse of the Bretton Woods System (BWS), there had been continuity in the BWS regime principles, notably 'embedded liberalism' had persisted. Despite pressures facing trading regimes and dire warnings of the impending collapse of the system, in fact this has not occurred. Moreover, it was clear that changes in regimes and new patterns of cooperation that had emerged post-1971–73, were quite different from one issue area to another.

Keohane argued that one could possibly identify some causal links between US hegemonic decline and regime decline, but that this was not as direct and uncomplicated as HST suggested. Regime-eroding effects were to some extent counterbalanced by the value to governments of maintaining regimes (rules) that limited players' legitimate strategies and so reduced uncertainty. There was demand for regimes because they played a useful role in facilitating mutually beneficial agreements among states. Therefore, to understand processes of cooperation and the role of institutions or regimes, one must combine the insights of HST as a power theory with theories that stress the rationality and value of cooperation in itself and the functions performed by regimes in facilitating this.

Robert Gilpin, who is arguably the pre-eminent contemporary neo-realist IPE scholar, developed an analysis of US hegemony which rested on the premise that there was a direct relationship between US power and the stability of the international economic order. The Bretton Woods System eventually broke down because of a decline in the power and influence of the USA, a decline reflected in the switch to a regime of floating exchange rates from 1971. The USA could no longer maintain its currency at a high rate relative to its economic competitors. Gilpin argued that economic realities would eventually bring about an adjustment in the system and so the USA would eventually retreat from its commitment to the multilateralism of the Bretton Woods System as US foreign policy adjusted to harsh economic realities. This had obvious implications for the stability of the international economic and political order.

Identity and community

We will keep our discussion of realism and questions of identity and community rather brief since both have been somewhat taken for granted in realism rather than explicitly problematised or analysed. Realists argue that people identify first and foremost with the nation-state. That is to say, most people see themselves as British, or French or Canadian, rather than as members of the 'human race' or of an abstract 'international community'. For realists the only community of any significance in international relations is the nation-state. The state is also held to be of moral worth because it is the best form of political community that the human race has yet devised. Beyond the boundaries of the nation-state lies the realm of international anarchy where 'might makes right'.

There is a strong sense in realist writings that national security issues, particularly in times of war, offer a sense of shared political purpose. Therefore, it is meaningful to speak of an underlying national interest which governs state behaviour particularly in relations with 'foreigners'. The state must, of necessity, be concerned, first and foremost, with national security and the well-being of its own citizens. For this reason realists anticipate that migration and asylum seekers are likely to generate feelings of unease if not of outright hostility and nationalism among citizens and nationals of existing states. This is not because realists are personally indifferent to the plight of displaced people, but because they see fear of the 'foreign' as a core element of the insecurity inherent in international relations. Realists do not, however, endeavour to unpack the processes and practices involved in the construction of such identity groups and communities (this has, however, been an explicit concern of many other perspectives which we will meet later), but rather take the nation as dominant identity and community as a given in International Relations.

Inequality and justice

Realist arguments frequently make much of the dangers inherent in not accepting what we cannot change. Thus, for instance, they see great dangers for the international system in emphasising or prioritising social justice or human rights *in terms of the relationships between states*. Realists also emphasise the principle of sovereignty as the cornerstone of the international system. We outlined the realist critique of international law and problems of conducting relations between states on the basis of moral principles earlier and will not labour this point again. As is apparent from our earlier discussion, sovereignty bestows exclusive jurisdiction over a territory and people. To intervene in the affairs of other states is, then, to risk undermining the sovereign independence and autonomy of states. For this reason realists also argue that states have no grounds to comment on or criticise the domestic political, social or economic order of other states. States are relatively silent on the rights of other states' citizens and indeed should be. If all such issues were taken up by all states – that is, if internal sovereignty were not accepted – great instability might well result as states meddle in each others' affairs. Put another way: turning a blind eye is the lesser of two evils.

Thus, internationally, a state might regard itself as peaceful and democratic and so might therefore object to authoritarianism in Myanmar, communism in China or the death penalty in the USA but, ultimately, we have no 'right', either political or moral, to judge the actions of other states in regard to their own peoples. Indeed, ultimately this could lead to international conflict.

If at first sight realists appear to be giving a green light to dictatorship and oppression, they might argue in their defence that the principle of sovereignty protects the 'weak' to some extent. Whatever the realities of power and influence in the international system, sovereignty at least guarantees a certain formal equality among states. In contrast, English School scholars (see chapter 7) subscribe to the notion of an international society or society of states, pointing out that increasing respect for human rights is becoming an accepted norm of international society and might, in exceptional cases, form the basis for 'intervention'. Generally speaking, it is fair to say that most realists adhere to a view of sovereignty as the foundation of the international system and so place emphasis on the principle of domestic jurisdiction and non-intervention in the domestic affairs of another state.

FILM BOX

No End In Sight

The 2007 film *No End In Sight* is a documentary focusing on the years following the 2003 US-led invasion and occupation of Iraq. The film examines the interests and policy decisions which resulted in the war, occupation and subsequent *re-construction* efforts. It then explores the difficulties in pursuing and meeting these policy goals as well as looking at the problems that followed both in Iraq and elsewhere. Realists often argue that the domestic affairs of a sovereign state are, or should be, of no interest to other states. Furthermore, states should not interfere in the internal affairs of another state unless this directly adds to their power. There are often voices which call for intervention when there are forms of injustice, for example, if a population is governed and repressed by a dictatorship. However, realists would argue, that intervening in another state's domestic affairs in order to resolve injustices creates more problems than it solves.

One of the main reasons given by the Bush administration in the United States and the Blair government in the United Kingdom for invading Iraq was to *liberate* the Iraqi people from Saddam Hussein's government, which was authoritarian and responsible for violations of human rights and mass murder. While it is difficult to argue against the undesirability of the Hussein regime, realists would have suggested that the problem is for the Iraqis and not for the United States or United Kingdom to sort out. The civil war, ongoing military operations, continuous bombings, sectarian conflict, crime and instability that have followed the 2003 invasion and that are documented in *No End In Sight* certainly add some legitimacy to this realist claim. To draw an analogy with your own lives, you would almost certainly struggle unnecessarily if you tried to 'fix' every relationship you saw going wrong, tried to break up fights, chased burglars, went and knocked on the door of a household where you'd heard it rumoured that the children were poorly treated and so on and so forth; and if everyone were acting in a similar way – trying to resolve the problems of all – our day-to-day lives would be filled with confrontation.

Summary

1. Realism is just one perspective within IR not *the* perspective.
2. Realism is a label attached to certain ways of thinking – it is a broad school of thought. There are, however, a number of distinctive strands in realist thought.
3. Realism is sometimes referred to as 'power politics', the Hobbesian approach to International Relations or the 'billiard ball model'.

4. Realism developed in International Relations as a rejection of idealism in the post-Second World War period.
5. The intellectual roots of realism go back much further. Realism supports its view by reference to a whole series of authors and events going back millennia.
6. Realism is a label given to a particular set of assumptions about international relations which emphasise the importance of states, motivated by national interest and driven by power.
7. Realism does not make a claim to explain every aspect of international relations. It aims to capture the essence of one specific aspect of the world – i.e. power politics.
8. Realism claims to describe a world it is not possible to change and gives us a guide on how to survive in that world.
9. By extension, realism claims to be based on certain essential 'truths' about the human condition.
10. Realists make clear distinctions between the 'domestic' and the 'international' realms.
11. Neo-realism also places central emphasis on anarchy in international relations, but claims to be more scientific in its approach than classical realism.

We need a good war!

Criticisms

While realism was not initially the dominant perspective in International Relations, historically, it has been the dominant tradition in the discipline and perhaps it is for this reason that it has been subjected to so much criticism. Liberalism and structuralism can both be used to develop a critique of realism. In more recent years realism has been subjected to complicated critiques from Critical Theorists, postmodernists, feminists, social constructivists and Green theorists amongst others. These are covered in chapters 4–8 of this book and this chapter on realism might be usefully re-read once an appreciation of the insights of these 'critical' theories has been fully understood and assimilated. Some of the most devastating criticisms of realism and neo-realism concern its epistemological and ontological underpinnings. This is the difficult language of theory and it is, therefore, appropriate to visit this debate in the concluding chapter of the book. At this stage, however, we can consider some of the possible shortcomings or weaknesses of this approach.

1. The fact that realism is simple and understandable is presented as a strength of the perspective. However, an opposing argument would suggest that realism is too simplistic, reducing the complex reality of international relations to a few general laws which are said to be applicable over time and space and which therefore omit much of interest and importance from our analyses.
2. Realism, in emphasising the principle of power politics and the enduring features of the international system, fails to allow for the possibility of real change. Realists accept that great powers rise and fall, and wars come and go, but insist that the basic rules of the game cannot be changed. In failing to embrace the idea of substantive changes, realism is inherently conservative and anti-innovative, meaning that it is highly attractive to, and politically malleable by, those who would have things continue as they are. Whether intentionally or not, realism may also serve to justify injustice on the grounds that nothing can be done to change things.
3. By considering states to be the only important type of actor in international relations and by only viewing the agency of non-state actors such as MNCs as part of state agency, realists have been criticised for not being able to fully account for a range of issues and processes in international relations.
4. While realism has a cyclical view of history (a repetition of patterns of behaviour) it has failed

Falklands War

to successfully make any specific predictions. Most startlingly, realists failed to predict the end of the Cold War; given its pretensions to be, if not scientific, then at least useful, this is a very serious weakness.

5. Realism does not help us explain which decisions will be made by states' representatives, but only why they will be made. Thus statespeople will make decisions rationally and on the basis of national interest. However, how do we know if it is the national interest of State A to attack State B? Perhaps it would serve the national interest better to delay an attack or to seek an alliance against State C. Is national interest a self-evident thing? After the event, when State A has attacked State B, the realist could say this was based on a rational calculation of the national interest, but the realist offers no way of deciding which option is actually in the national interest and simply tells us that this is the motivation.

6. If we accept the possibility that the assumptions of realism are relevant only in a particular context, there is possibly great danger in treating them as if they were universal truths: that is, applicable everywhere and at all times. Far from providing universal truths, realism may simply have seemed the most appropriate way of viewing a short historical phase; the idea of universal truth may have held back scholarship which would have been better directed at freeing us from realist despair.

7. In emphasising the centrality of the state and the national interest, realism encourages people to view the world from a very narrow, ethnocentric perspective.

8. The simplistic view of human nature as being inherently selfish and unchanging has been criticised, in particular by more progressive approaches such as Green Thought and liberalism. Here it is claimed that the nature of the society one lives in can change over time and can thus change human nature or at least allow humans to be less selfish.

9. Realism ignores or significantly downplays the degree to which states might have collective or mutual interests, and so underestimates the scope for cooperation and purposive change in international relations.

10. We should ask if foreign policy really is conducted rationally and indeed what is implied in the idea of rationality. Rationality seems unlikely to be the same for the leaders of states with strong ideological or religious bases as it is for leaders of liberal democracies. Furthermore, even within, for instance, liberal democracies, can we be sure that in the hurly-burly world of foreign policy, decisions will always be made rationally? The decision maker is likely to be bombarded with information, denied sleep and asked to make several choices at once; it seems plausible at least that rationality will be compromised, affected by mood, modified by spur-of-the-moment decisions and so on.

11. The antecedents of modern realism have perhaps been selectively read or interpreted in a biased fashion. As people are fond of saying in relation to statistics, if you select your evidence carefully enough it is possible to prove almost anything. We can simply note at this stage a certain selectivity in the historical memory of realism.

While, in its simplified form, realism can present an easy target for criticism, realism's detractors, bent on exposing its shortcomings, have often found it a formidable task. Indeed after some 15 years (or more) of fending off criticisms on all fronts, realists might argue that the post-9/11 world is one in which realist propositions are clearly vindicated by current practice. For example, the euphoric atmosphere of the post-Cold War period might have opened up a space within International Relations to imagine other possibilities, including the pursuit of human security founded in respect for human rights. However, the security risk to US citizens, highlighted by the terror attacks on the twin towers, the subsequent 'war on terror' and the unwillingness of the USA to listen sympathetically or seriously to investigate allegations of human rights abuses in relation to prisoners in Guantanamo Bay, can on the face of it be used to vindicate realist propositions.

Figure 2.1   A state-centric image of the world.

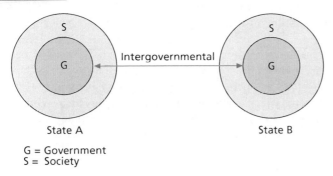

G = Government
S = Society

Source: B. Hocking and M. Smith (1995), *World Politics: An Introduction to International Politics*, 2nd edn, London: Prentice-Hall/Harvester Wheatsheaf, p. 75.

Many realist models of international relations may appear to be oversimplified and therefore useless. However, the realist argument would be that they help us understand what is vitally important about international politics.

Modifications of realism have been proposed by various authors and many differences exist within the broad category of realism. Moreover, realists acknowledge a changing world and are aware of ecological threats, gender issues and so on. However, and crucially, realists believe that their basic assumptions capture the real essence of international relations, and they argue that they are perfectly entitled to privilege some areas and issues in international relations, and, indeed, to marginalise or ignore others. However, it would be difficult to overcome the decades of dominance that realism has had in the discipline and therefore the tendency to regard it almost as a natural starting point for talking about IR, even for those eager to criticise it or offer a more adequate framework for analysis.

Furthermore, while realism may be under attack from all sides in academic circles, it continues to find favour amongst policy makers and statespeople and accordingly is implicit in rationalisations of policy offered by foreign-policy decision makers. We have chosen realism as one of our preliminary chapters for the simple reason that it has indeed provided a backdrop for much discussion in International Relations theory. To an extent this bears out our opening comments about the prevalence of realism, and latterly neo-realism, and the degree to which neo-realism particularly has become the basic point of departure for much 'critical' international theory (see concluding chapter).

Common misunderstandings

1. *It's called Realism because it's realistic.* Some of you may come to regard what International Relations calls 'realism' as being highly *un*realistic. Clearly the adherents of realism regard it as a sensible explanation of the dynamics of the world in which we live, and the name represents almost an unfair advantage in terms of students' initial reaction to it. However, 'realism' should be regarded as simply a name for a particular way of thinking about the world; a label which is understood to imply certain basic assumptions. It is for you to decide if realism is realistic or not.
2. *Realists ignore so much.* Once you understand the basic assumptions of realism and what it regards as important in international relations, you may decide that it fails to address some crucial issues. Environmental degradation, torture, rape and many other issues are ignored by

realists in favour of concentrating on states, state interest and military power. Realists are not ignorant in this sense; they do not deny the existence of other actors, interests and issues. However, they suggest that IR should be about the really crucial aspects of international interactions and thus deliberately limit the scope of their analysis in an attempt to better understand what is vital.

3. *Realists are nasty people.* From the above it might follow that realists are necessarily heartless people who do not care about starvation, repression and rainforests as long as the international system persists and wars are understood and perhaps limited or controlled as much as is possible. The reputation enjoyed by Niccolo Machiavelli helps to perpetuate this idea. While we are sure that nasty realists exist, this is not necessarily the case. Some realists are simply pessimistic about human nature or the international states system to the extent, for them, that any other view is utopian nonsense. In effect they argue that what we would like and what we get may be very different.

4. *Structural realism is the same as structuralism.* No. Structural realism is a name sometimes given to Waltzian neo-realism and bears little relation to the 'structuralism' mentioned in the introduction and expanded upon in the next chapter, except in so far as they do both concentrate on the idea of 'structure' as being crucial in explaining international relations. For structural realists it is the structure of the inter-state system which interests them and which constrains state behaviour, forcing states to act in particular ways.

5. *Anarchy means chaos.* This is an understandable way of thinking. However, anarchy actually means absence of government, a situation which characterises international relations where there is no world government. Thus, states exist in a state of anarchy. Given the existence of international law, order is not entirely absent; this is one important reason why some authors associated with the English School talk of an 'anarchical society'.

> **Structural realism**, with its emphasis on the anarchical structure of international relations should not be confused with structuralism which we discuss in detail in chapter 3.

Further reading

Bull, H. (2002), *The Anarchical Society: A Study of Order in World Politics*, Chichester: Columbia University Press, 3rd edition (largely seen as one of the core neo-realist texts along with Waltz (below) and originally published in 1977, it is often claimed that this is the founding text of the English School of IR theory).

Carr, E.H. (1946), *The Twenty Years' Crisis 1919–1939: An Introduction to the Study of International Relations*, London: Macmillan (along with Morgenthau – below – this is sometimes cited as an influential text within the classical realist tradition, although Carr has also been read as, among other things, a member of the English School, a Critical Theorist and even a proto-Critical Realist (see chapter 7)).

Gilpin, R. (1987), *Political Economy of International Relations*, Princeton, NJ: Princeton University Press (sets out the neorealist approach to International Political Economy – note both the similarities and differences between how Waltz and Gilpin conceptualise 'hegemony').

Keohane, R. (1986), *Neorealism and its Critics*, New York: Columbia University Press (a collection of papers that in various ways critique the assumptions of neo-realism).

Morgenthau, H. (1978), *Politics Among Nations: The Struggle for Power and Peace*, New York: Knopf (a highly influential text not only within the academic discipline of IR, but among policy makers in the USA in the post-Second World War period).

Waltz, K. (1979), *Theory of International Politics*, Reading, MA: Addison-Wesley (possibly *the* major work on neo-realism in IR).

3 Structuralism

Introduction

Although **structuralism** has waned in popularity in recent years, it has been important in the history of International Relations theory, and continues to have relevance today for a number of reasons. First, structuralist calls for justice continue to strike a chord with many people, particularly in the developing world. Structuralism can be seen as a perspective on the world which prioritises the plight of the poor, the marginalised and the oppressed. Structuralists argue that global economic relations are structured so as to benefit certain social classes, and that the resulting 'world-system' is fundamentally unjust.

> It is important to distinguish the **structuralism** discussed here from the 'top-down' structural realism of Waltz – see previous chapter. For structuralists the fundamental units of analysis are not states, but social *classes* and the international system of production and exchange.

Second, structuralism provides an important critique of realism and liberalism. Superficially structuralism resembles realism because both emphasise conflict as a central process in international relations. Moreover, neo-realism and structuralism share the view that conflict is structural because of the framework in which international relations take place. Structuralism also shares common ground with liberal pluralist approaches in emphasising the profoundly interconnected nature of international economic relations and the importance of non-state actors. However, structuralism stresses the conflictual nature of the global economy and structural relations of domination and dependence, rather than the anarchy of the state system, or complex interdependence.

Finally, structuralism highlights the connection between politics and economics. Structuralists stress the importance of the overall structure of relations within which political and economic interactions take place and the processes and mechanisms which support this same structure. That is to say, the individual parts of the world-system – states, MNCs, transnational élites and so on – must be understood in relation to their place in the overall structure of global capitalism. Structuralists believe that states and international institutions play a role in 'managing' the global capitalist order. However, they regard classes as the *key* actors in the global capitalist order. From a structuralist perspective, 'international relations' are conditioned by the nature of global capitalism/economic relations. It makes more sense, therefore, to analyse international relations by reference to the big picture than by examining each and every individual actor, action and event. In this chapter we are using the term 'structuralism' to refer to the idea that individual parts can only be understood in relation to an overall system or to the structure of ordered relationships in international relations.

Structuralism goes by a number of names. It is heavily influenced by Marxist thought and is, therefore, sometimes referred to as structural Marxism, scientific Marxism or neo-Marxism. In the

'Origins' section, below, we will concentrate on the central influence of Marx in structuralist thought, particularly the body of work Marx wrote later in his life, sometimes called 'the economics', 'economic determinism' or 'scientific Marxism'. This work contrasts with the earlier (humanist) writings of Marx which have, in part, provided the inspiration for Critical Theory (see chapter 4).

Structuralism is often referred to as dependency theory, world-systems theory, the core–periphery model and radicalism – these are all elements of structuralism, but they should not be misunderstood as representing the totality of structuralist thought. Structuralism has its own 'language' (often Marxist-influenced) which is not easy to penetrate, and which can be off-putting. Making sense of the subtle differences between these terms can often get in the way of a general understanding of structuralism as a perspective with particular insights.

As with other theoretical approaches, we offer a simplified account of what is a diverse body of work, without overly 'jargonising' the text. We simplify by outlining the guiding ideas and assumptions which are shared by different structuralist writers. We explain how structuralism provides a persuasive analysis of various themes.

Origins

The major, though not only, influence in structuralism is Karl Marx (and to an extent his often co-author, Friedrich Engels). However, Marx's guiding ideas have been developed over the years by many other notable scholars. We only include here a limited number of structuralist scholars and influential works to give a general outline. For this reason, we concentrate particularly on dependency theory and world-systems theory. Although we make reference to other influential neo-Marxist works where appropriate, these have been chosen because they constitute good examples of structuralist thought in ways which are relevant to international relations.

Marx lived a somewhat tragic life dedicated mostly to his writing, philosophy and activism. It has, furthermore, been a tragic death too, in that much of what has been carried out in the name of Marxism, and earned him such opprobrium in certain quarters, would certainly not have met with his approval. Marx was a prolific writer who produced a huge volume of work over his relatively short life. Much of Marx's early work is concerned with the historical and changing nature of material social and economic relations, human nature or subjectivity, and problems of alienation (see chapter 4). Structuralism owes more to the later works of Marx, produced after 1857, in close collaboration with Friedrich Engels.

By this stage in his life Marx was paying much closer attention to the nature of economic relationships in capitalist societies, rather than to specifically 'human' problems. Marx argued that the organisation of the economy and economic relationships – what he labelled the 'mode of production' – formed the material base of society. To give a contemporary example of what is meant by the mode of production, today the West lives in an age when the economy is still largely based on the mass-production of manufactured goods and, increasingly, services. Capitalism is built upon the principles of private ownership of property and the pursuit of profit. Most people go to work every weekday in shops, factories or offices, producing goods and services for the 'boss' (be it a single entrepreneur or huge multinational), which are subsequently sold for a profit in the 'market place'. People do not own the goods and services which they produce but instead are paid a wage for their labour. Moreover, the contemporary economy is characterised by a highly complex division of labour so that the production of a single commodity, like a car perhaps, takes place in a number of factories, perhaps in several different countries and involves very many different people in complex relationships, at different stages of the production process. Collectively, the ways in which goods and services are produced (the division of labour, factory production and so on) and the conditions under which they are produced (wage labour) constitute the 'economic base' or 'mode of production'.

In a series of influential essays, Marx developed a 'labour theory of value', which suggests that the 'exchange value' of any good or service (what in capitalist economies is called the 'price') is really made up of human labour. Marx argued that capitalists paid workers considerably less than the true value of what they produced. In Marx's time employers paid wages which would, perhaps, cover bare subsistence. Marx called the difference between what workers actually produced and what they were paid, surplus value. What we commonly call 'profit' is the surplus value extracted from labour and taken – or in the correct terminology 'expropriated' – by capitalists. Marx argued that capitalism was driven by the accumulation of surplus value.

The accumulation of surplus value could be achieved in one of three ways: capitalists could search out new markets for the products of labour; they could constantly drive down wages in order to extract more surplus value from their workers; or they could replace labour with new technologies (machines). Marx believed that to some extent these strategies were pursued simultaneously and that sooner or later capitalism would collapse as workers were rendered too poor to provide a market for the goods produced, and as new markets were exhausted. Capitalism was then an exploitative system, riddled with tensions, conflicts and inherent contradictions which would ultimately cause it to collapse.

LITERATURE BOX

The Ragged Trousered Philanthropists

Marx's ideas have been influential in politics, sociology, history, economics and philosophy. However, Marx's ideas have also inspired great works of fiction. Robert Tressell's novel is a moving and informative defence of socialist values with a heartfelt message. The novel is centred on a group of painters who are set the task of renovating a house, owned by a wealthy family. As the novel unfolds, a picture emerges of daily toil, in poor working conditions, for pittance wages, and lives characterised by hardship and job-insecurity, by ill-health and fear. The novel charts the ways in which material conditions of life gradually foster a consciousness of social class and the nature of exploitation. Many of Marx's ideas are explicitly discussed, explained or refuted by the central characters in the book.

Of course, human relationships are not just constituted by economic relationships of the kind described above. We interact with other people on a day-to-day basis in the home, in a university, and in many other contexts such as a mosque or church perhaps. Our lives and our relationships with others are profoundly affected by government policies and we have to obey the law. We also 'engage' with others indirectly when we read about events happening away from our locality, or watch programmes on television. Marx believed that the economic 'base' supports a range of other political and social institutions, such as the state, the law courts, the church, the family, the education system, and what we now call the 'mass media'. Contemporary structuralists sometimes refer to these institutions as the 'superstructure' of society. The superstructure is intimately connected with, but conceptually distinct from, the economic base. Marx devoted a great deal of time to trying to elucidate the relationship between the economic 'base' and the political, social and legal 'superstructure'. He believed that ultimately economic forces drove (determined) social and political change, and much of his work was concerned with explaining how and why such change occurred. The relationship between base and superstructure has been much debated within Marxism.

By combining some of Marx's ideas on the historical and changing nature of human societies – known as 'historical materialism' – with Marxist economic analysis, it is possible to construct a coherent analysis of the overall structure of capitalist societies which can then be used to inform our understanding of the individual 'parts'. To simplify, Marx claimed that human societies were made up of various institutions and forms of social organisation which fulfilled a particular function or role in terms of the overall social system. He believed that, as societies changed over time, so too did forms of social organisation, practices and institutions.

Marx believed that the dynamic force propelling change of this kind was economic: that is, the dynamic of change was rooted in the particular 'modes of production' of society. Marx also believed that productive forces developed over time as humanity developed more knowledge of/mastery over, nature. As modes of production advanced and changed, the superstructure of society also changed. So, at different periods in history we find different modes of production – agricultural, industrial and so on – and a corresponding system of legal and political forms of organisation and social relationships. Marx argued that social relations could be characterised in different ways – feudal, bourgeois and so forth.

Marx was not alone in seeing a close 'fit' or correspondence between the economy, social relationships and political institutions. At roughly the same period of history, 'functionalist' thinkers like Durkheim were arguing that the social, political and economic spheres of life were intimately connected. However, whereas functionalists likened society to something like a natural organism, Marx regarded societies as riddled with internal tensions and conflicts. He argued that all forms of social and economic organisation, to date, were based on forms of oppression and exploitation. Moreover, all systems contained inherent contradictions, based on their exploitative nature, which eventually

| **Figure 3.1** | Robert Tressell's novel, *The Ragged Trousered Philanthropists*, encapsulated the idea that people such as these were giving their labour so that others could be rich. Tressell's novel encourages people to look forward to a glorious socialist future. |

Source: Michael Charity/Rex Features.

brought about their downfall. Marx believed that this process of historical change was usually violent. During periods of transition emerging classes struggled for ascendancy over the old ruling order and established their own dominance over the rest of society.

From a Marxist perspective the French Revolution, and the subsequent period of social turmoil/political upheaval, were illustrative of a process by which an emerging social class (the bourgeoisie) rose up and displaced the established ruling class (the *ancien régime* or aristocracy). Marxists continue to view classes in terms of their relationship to society's mode of production. So, contemporary capitalism is characterised by a ruling class (bourgeoisie), which owns/controls the means of production, and the working class (proletariat), who must sell their labour to survive.

Before considering how Marx, and Engels, provided a theoretical framework which has been used to develop a structuralist analysis of international relations we need to draw out the ways in which Marx's ideas about the relationship between economics, politics and society are later used to develop an elaborate structural analysis of capitalism (see the Author Box on Louis Althusser).

AUTHOR BOX

Louis Althusser

The French philosopher Louis Althusser is a good example of a structuralist thinker. Althusser argued that capitalism was a system – a set of ordered economic, political, social and legal relationships – reinforced by a range of institutions, like the family, church and education system. The parts of the system can only be understood in relation to the function they fulfil in the system as a whole – thus, institutions and their practices have to be understood in terms of their place in the overall system of ordered relationships. The structure of the capitalist system determines the nature/purpose of the various parts.

Marxism is often dismissed as 'ideological', but structuralists make their claims on the basis of what they regard as 'scientific' analysis. Though Marx was unable to allow for many factors (and hence was 'wrong' in some of his arguments), he was actually trying to suggest that what was happening was based on certain observable, inevitable processes. History was 'pre-determined' in the sense that capitalists could not prevent their own demise and workers were destined to inherit the world and build a better and brighter future.

REFLECTION BOX

Human beings frequently think of themselves as living in history. That is, people tend to believe that history is going somewhere and so their lives are likely to be better than their forefathers. Moreover, both religious belief systems and modern secular ideologies tend to impute a final purpose to life – this is called 'teleology'. Marxism *is* radically different from liberalism, but have you noticed how both share a view of history *as* progress?

So far we have discussed Marx's ideas about the nature of capitalism as a social, economic and political system, and hinted at ways in which Marx's work subsequently influenced structuralist writers. We now turn to the ways in which Marx (and later structuralist writers) developed concepts and theories which can be used to inform the study of international relations.

Marx was interested in the dynamism of capitalism and the ways it was radically transforming the economic, social and political landscape across Europe. He also believed that, while the crisis of capitalism would occur in a relatively advanced industrial economy (like Britain or Germany), he was aware that the ramifications would be felt in other countries across the European continent. Marx was also a committed member of the Communist International, an organisation dedicated to the task of raising awareness of transnational working-class interests, uniting the working class across Europe and stressing the need for solidarity with the poor and oppressed across the world. However, Marx's ideas contain important omissions if one attempts to apply them to the contemporary world. Marx did not develop a sustained analysis of the state system and did not aim to. What is more important is that his ideas have been utilised by others with a more internationalist orientation.

The work of Lenin is an important stepping stone between Marx's analysis of industrialised capitalist countries in Northern Europe and an analysis of international capitalist expansion and inter-state conflict. Lenin's ideas also draw from the English economist/historian Hobson. We suggested above that Marx believed capitalism would eventually collapse as workers became more impoverished and new markets became exhausted. Hobson, and later Lenin, did not necessarily disagree with Marx's basic thesis; however, they believed that Marx seriously underestimated the ability of the capitalist system to survive in the face of periodic crises. The nature of capitalism, it was argued, was such that it needed to expand in order to find new markets and secure new sources of raw materials and labour.

At the same time, industrialisation furnished the élites of developed European states with the means to undertake campaigns of colonial expansion across the globe. Hobson believed that these campaigns were designed to ensure that rich élites in European states had captive markets and thus were a form of exploitation. Lenin took this basic idea of expansionism and, using guiding ideas on the nature of capitalism provided by Marx and Engels, developed a more sustained analysis of imperialism as 'the highest stage of capitalism'.

CONCEPT BOX

Imperialism and colonialism

Imperialism means the extension of power through conquest. It refers to the extension of a state's hegemonic power/influence beyond its own borders, so much so that it amounts to an empire – the extension of a state's sovereignty over other countries. Colonialism refers to a situation where a group of people settle in a foreign country, establishing some form of domination over the indigenous population and maintaining close links with their 'mother' country. Since successful imperial domination frequently depends upon the loyalty of particular groups in subordinated countries, in practice, imperialism and colonialism might be closely linked.

One of the most effective examples of both colonialism and imperialism is the French invasion, occupation, settlement and annexation of Algeria which began in 1830. Initially the French invaded the Mediterranean coast of the area of the Ottoman Empire which would later become the state of Algeria, in order to expand access to resources and thus increase France's power base. This mission subsequently developed into a policy of settlement and colonisation during the nineteenth century. By 1848 France had annexed Algeria and declared that it was in fact an inseparable part of the French homeland. These actions were resisted to a certain extent by the original inhabitants of Algeria following the initial French invasion, but these efforts were largely ineffective until the Algerian movement for independence gathered pace in the mid-twentieth century. It is important to note that there was a level of integration between French and Algerian culture and nationalism. Usually this took the form of Algerian acceptance of French cultural and political imports (a large number of Algerian soldiers fought for France in World War Two).

Eventually, the Algerian drive for self-determination evolved into a complete military resistance to French domination. The Algerian war of independence began in 1954 and ended in

1962 with Algeria gaining independence from France. While it was a successful decolonisation war, it was also an extremely violent, costly and devastating war (which was characterised by guerrilla warfare, *terrorism*, civilian deaths and large financial costs) demonstrating the importance of national interests and the extent that people would go to in order to achieve them. *The Battle of Algiers* is a film released in 1966 which depicts the war and the processes which led to it.

FILM BOX

Indigènes / Days of Glory

Directed by French-Algerian Rachid Bouchareb this 2006 award-winning film portrays the story of a group of Algerian soldiers who volunteer to join World War Two as part of the Free French Forces. Algeria was conquered and annexed by France in the nineteenth century but Algerians were not given French citizenship. Nevertheless, approximately 200,000 African soldiers fought for France, a large proportion of whom came from Algeria. *Indigènes* tells the story of some of these soldiers as they train and are deployed in the African and then European theatres of war. Running parallel to the stories of combat are personal stories about four Algerian soldiers in particular. Each has his own motivation in joining the army, ranging from escaping poverty in rural Algeria to fighting for equal rights and recognition for Algerians. Ultimately these four soldiers and the other African forces fighting for France are confronted with hardship, discrimination and abandonment. It is interesting to note that large numbers of African soldiers died on behalf of France in World War Two, but neither the fallen nor their countrymen were rewarded with the social, political or economic rights which they had expected for their sacrifices and loyalty to France.

Some have claimed that *Indigènes*, therefore, while telling a war story also represents a critique of European (or largely French) imperialism and colonialism and the exploitation of the colonised subjects that accompanied them. By highlighting these historical events and processes the film demonstrates some of the roots of continuing resentment and tension between European- and Algerian-French citizens.

Imperialism was said to be the highest stage in capitalist development because it would bring about the total exhaustion of new markets in accordance with Marx's predictions. However, Lenin believed that long before that occurred, capitalism would collapse because the search for captive markets and sources of raw materials was already generating conflicts between imperialist powers. Lenin believed that the First World War was the result of such tension and that, along with the working class of industrialised countries, subjugated peoples across the world would eventually rise up and throw off the yoke of imperialist domination, as the world descended into vicious war.

Lenin's ideas about the end of capitalism were popular among intellectuals in the inter-war years. However, with the so-called 'golden years' of liberalism (that is, the economic boom post-Second World War) such ideas quickly became unfashionable, in the West at least, and so structuralist-type explanations did not play a significant role in the early development of International Relations. However, that changed by the 1960s and 1970s when Marxist-derived ideas were picked up by the International Relations community.

So, we now turn our attention to two important theories which *have* been influential in developing a structuralist perspective in the contemporary discipline. In the 1960s and 1970s dependency theory and world-systems theory were becoming influential in areas of the social sciences like Sociology just at the time when International Relations scholars were becoming more keenly interested in the relationship between international economics and international politics. This was, more generally, a time of economic uncertainty and instability. By the early 1970s the international financial community began to entertain doubts about the monetary system underpinned by the US dollar. Oil prices increased drastically and the world economy was subsequently thrown into a deep recession.

At the United Nations General Assembly (UNGA) of 1974, the poorer countries of the world stood together to demand a new (meaning fair) international economic order (NIEO). During the same period, the relaxation of tension in relations between the USA and USSR allowed academic attention to switch to more economics-based concerns. We might say that from Marx through Lenin, through to the emergence of the dependency theory and world-systems theory, combined with the waxing and waning of international affairs, structuralism gradually emerged as a distinctive perspective or paradigm within International Relations.

Dependency theory came to prominence in the 1960s. It developed as a critique of liberal modernisation theory (see the Concept Box below). During the 1950s and 1960s developing countries threw off the yoke of colonialism/imperialism; they demanded and achieved independence. However, this was happening in the context of the Cold War (see chapter 2); Western countries were keen to ensure that former colonial (or Third World) states did not fall into the hands of communist regimes, and encouraged newly independent states to develop capitalist economies. Walt Rostow's influential text on economic growth/modernisation was subtitled 'a non-communist manifesto'. Developing countries were encouraged to allow free enterprise to flourish and to engage in free trade with the rest of the world to encourage competition, economic dynamism and growth.

CONCEPT BOX

Modernisation

The concept of 'modernisation' denotes a process characterised by interconnected economic, technological, industrial, social, cultural, and political change. Modern, 'advanced' societies as opposed to traditional, 'backward' societies, are organised on the basis of secular, individualistic values. In modern societies people are supposedly judged, rewarded and afforded a particular role and status in society according to individual aptitude, achievement or merit, rather than on the basis of family connections, gender or age. Power in modern societies is seen to be exercised through administrative machinery in accordance with abstract rules. Along with the secular institutions like the modern state and legal institutions, bureaucratic procedures and processes are supposed to ensure that people are treated impartially.

Modernisation is typically associated with capitalist development and industrialisation, technological innovation, consumerism, the market economy and increases in population. Modernisation is also associated with improved levels of education, an expanding role for the state, the emergence of political pluralism, respect for civil liberties and rights and democratic, as opposed to authoritarian, forms of government.

Modernisation theory has been refuted both on the grounds that its empirical and theoretical claims are flawed and on the grounds that it is, at best, patronising and, at worst, a powerful justification for a form of neo-imperialism. First, the major criticism of modernisation theory is that it has not worked, even in societies which have embraced its values and prescriptions. Second, in suggesting that 'they' can become like 'us', i.e. the poor can become like the rich, at a stroke it dismisses as a mere 'waiting post' the culture, traditions and histories of many 'less developed countries' and communities.

The *Dependencia* School emerged from the efforts of Latin American intellectuals to account for their societies' demonstrable inability to 'catch up' with the rich countries of North America and Western Europe, even though they had largely followed the advice of the West and endeavoured to 'modernise' their societies and move to free-market economies. Dependency theory attacked modernisation theory, because it was severely misleading in terms of its predictions about the development prospects of the Third World. Indeed, with the notable exception of parts of East Asia, by the mid-1960s much of the developing world found that its relative economic performance was extremely disappointing.

The economic and political climate of the late 1960s and early 1970s was such that developing countries in particular were receptive to critiques of Western-led development models. A key idea of modernisation theorists was that all states would pass through stages of development and that sooner or later all would become advanced, high-consumption countries. However, modernisation theory rejected/ignored the possibility that deep *structural* factors might prevent economic progress and, more important, that the nature of the international system itself might be an obstacle to development. Accordingly, dependency theory developed a critique of modernisation theory which emphasised the structural constraints to development in Latin America.

Key writers in the *Dependencia* School, including Andre Gunder Frank, Raul Prebisch, Henrique Fernando Cardoso and Enzo Faletto, undertook a detailed historical analysis of the pattern of growth and development in Latin America and claimed to find that Latin America actually achieved its most impressive levels of growth and development at times when there was a slow-down in world trade and trading links with developed countries were disrupted. Taking this empirical observation as a starting point, dependency theorists suggested this was because the basic structure of the global economy was such that it worked to further the interests of the already rich, developed economies of the West (or North) and to progressively impoverish already poor countries (the South or Third World). The basic structure of the world economy, the trading regimes that existed, the nature of the markets for basic commodities and so on fundamentally determined the development trajectory of individual countries. Therefore, even as large parts of the world emerged from imperialism and colonialism, the West continued to dominate the Third World – hence the terms neo-imperialism and neo-colonialism. Dependency theory can be considered a variant of structuralist thought because it suggests that we can only understand, in this example, the Latin American part of the world economy in terms of its relation to the world economic system as a whole.

AUTHOR BOX

Henrique Cardoso

As a young academic Cardoso was an opponent of Brazil's military dictators. Accordingly, he lived in exile from 1964 to 1968 and indeed was arrested on his return in 1969. He became a prominent and radical sociologist, best known for the classic *Dependency and Development in Latin America* (with Enzo Faletto) as well as numerous other works in sociology and political economy. His radicalism somewhat subsided as he won two terms as Brazilian President from 1994 to 2002, beating off the Workers' Party candidate and subsequently applying orthodox neo-liberal fiscal policies to the Brazilian economy.

Dependency theory can also be considered a form of economic determinism, in so far as *Dependencia* scholars frequently suggested that the political institutions and social relations which characterised developing countries were a reflection of the economic 'base' – dominated by élites who actually benefited from this exploitative economic system. Liberal economic theory suggests that successful modernisation depends to some extent upon the growth of an indigenous entrepreneurial class. Accordingly, development strategies frequently targeted resources at a 'modernising élite', believing that as countries underwent industrialisation and economic growth, wealth would 'trickle down' from this élite to the masses. They also believed that this élite would imbue liberal social and political values and these would gradually spread from the 'advanced' middle classes to the rest of society. Dependency theorists contended, to the contrary that, while élites did indeed benefit from their particular position in the system, the promised 'trickle down' did not materialise and was unlikely to do so. In fact, as a country ostensibly 'advanced', the masses became progressively more impoverished.

While dependency theory owes much to structuralist analysis, it also offers a critique of the Marxist notion that certain classes have common interests regardless of their nationality. Dependency theorists recognise that transnational élites share some common interests, but they also argue that to some extent the workers in developed countries, while relatively impoverished and exploited, have actually benefited to some degree from the exploitation of the developing world. Earlier theorists of imperialism had recognised that the working classes had rallied to nationalist causes (particularly in war) and were, in some cases, enthusiastic supporters of empire. Taking this further, dependency theorists have shown how the bourgeoisie in the rich countries can exploit the poorer countries and use the profits to dampen the demands of its own proletariat, by providing limited welfare for instance. In this way, dependency theorists have suggested, there might well be obstacles to international worker solidarity. They have questioned Marx's notion of a simple divergence of interests between the proletariat (all workers) and the bourgeoisie (all owners).

Finally, no discussion of the origins of structuralism would be complete without some reference to the work of Immanuel Wallerstein. Wallerstein is particularly known for his 'world-systems theory' (WST). As the name suggests, the idea of this theory is that elements of the world-system cannot be understood in isolation. The logic of the WST argument is fairly simple to outline. At one time we could conceive of all societies as mini-systems – self-contained economic, political and social units with a single culture isolated from one another. These societies were characterised by a simple division of labour and all members had a specific, clearly defined role – hunter, farmer, carer and so forth. Today, there are very few examples of these kinds of societies left in the world. Over time they have been swallowed up by larger systems of social, economic and political organisation.

A world-system is the largest and most complex of all and comes in two types – world-empire and world-economy. According to Wallerstein, prior to the birth and expansion of capitalism, there were examples of world-empires based on the conquest of, and subordination of, peoples across the world. Clearly, world-empires have been based on both economic exploitation and political domination. Examples of such world-empires are all the so-called 'great civilisations' of pre-modern times, such as China, Egypt and Rome. However, in about 1500 a novel type of world-economy emerged in Europe and gradually expanded across the globe (though you should be aware that not all Marxists/structuralists date the emergence of capitalism from 1500). New transportation technology allowed far-flung markets to be obtained and maintained especially when combined with Western military technology to dictate and enforce favourable terms of trade. As this 'capitalism' spread throughout the globe, there developed, on the one hand, a 'core', composed of well-developed towns, flourishing manufacturing, technologically progressive agriculture, skilled and relatively well-paid labour, and high investment; and, on the other hand, a 'periphery', from which raw materials necessary for expansion and certain key primary goods were extracted. In such a system, it was necessary to coerce labour in order to keep down the costs of production. In such circumstances, the periphery stagnated, its towns withered, and those with money, technology and skills moved to the core.

At first, the differences between the core and the periphery were small, but gradually the gap widened as, more and more, the core countries concentrated on the production of manufactured goods and the periphery produced only primary products and basic commodities.

Cost of imported primary products relative to exported manufactured goods for developed countries.

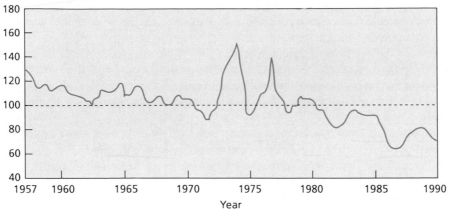

Original source: International Monetary Fund (1983 and 1991), *World Economic Outlook*, Washington, DC: IMF.

Taken from: B. Russett and H. Starr (1996), *World Politics, The Menu for Choice*, 2nd edn, New York: W.H. Freeman, p. 362.

This graph shows how, over time, the price of imports of non-oil primary products from the 'Third World' dropped relative to the price of the manufactures they exported, for developed countries from 1957 to 1990.

Accordingly, uneven development across the world, and the existence of a 'first' and 'third' world is not a consequence of historical lag or a technical hitch to sort out, but actually a function (consequence) of the capitalist world-system. Unlike the core–periphery model characteristic of dependency theory, WST also posits the existence of a semi-periphery – intermediary societies which play an important role in the functioning of the world-system as a whole (see below). When applied to international relations, what this effectively boils down to is an argument that lower levels (states, communities, individuals) matter, but that the highest level (the world-system) constrains behaviour in all sorts of ways (see the Concept Box on the structure–agency debate on p. 109 and revisited in chapter 7). Therefore, it makes no sense to start from the premise that the state is the basic unit of analysis in IR, or posit that states are autonomous 'actors'. It also alerts us to the degree to which social institutions are constantly changing and adapting over time and in the context of a dynamic world-system.

Assumptions

1. 'Human nature' is not fixed and essential. The human subject is social and historical. However, human nature is conditioned by prevailing forms of social, economic and political organisation, and as such, people are products of their society.
2. Individuals can be grouped into identifiable collectivities or classes which might be said to have 'concrete' interests.
3. While recognising the historical and changing nature of human societies, structuralism nevertheless claims to be 'scientific' and 'objective', in so far as it claims to have identified certain 'facts' about the world, and objective laws which determine the course of history.

4. 'Structuralism as science' is clearly distinguished from belief systems or ideology, despite the deep moral convictions of many who have used it as an explanatory theory. In Marxist thought 'ideology' is about sets of ideas and values which reflect specific class interests and which help to consolidate a particular economic order.

5. The nature of international relations is profoundly shaped by the structure of the capitalist world economy, or capitalist world-system.

6. Structuralists make no clear distinction between the national (inside) and the international (outside). From this perspective the state-system is determined by the global capitalist system, or they emerged together and are thus mutually constitutive.

7. Capitalism is a fundamentally unjust social and economic order which generates conflict and disharmony.

8. Capitalism is characterised by internal contradictions and is subject to periodic crises.

9. International politics is shaped by, or even determined by, economic factors.

10. The main 'actors' are states, multinational corporations, intergovernmental organisations, non-governmental organisations and transnational social classes.

11. The state reflects the interests of dominant classes rather than the existence of a genuine 'national interest'.

REFLECTION BOX

Does structuralism deny the possibility of political action or belittle the efforts of heroic struggles throughout the Third World?

Themes

The State and power

The state is a central concept in structuralist theories, but is viewed in a different way from realist or liberal approaches. Structuralists differ over the importance of states in international relations, with some arguing that international political and economic analysis would be better focused on social classes and the nature of transnational alliances among élites. However, even those who prefer such a class-based analysis recognise the actual political division of the world into states, and the role that these states play in helping to maintain class-based inequalities.

In a superficial way, structuralists resemble realists in recognising the importance of the state in IR. However, rather than seeing the state as a sovereign power representing the interests of the 'nation' in international relations, structuralists hold that the state in some sense reflects the interests of dominant social classes. There is, however, disagreement among structuralist thinkers as to whether the state is dominated by élite social classes, or whether it exercises a degree of autonomy.

In classical Marxism and early structuralist theory, the state was seen as a coercive, repressive apparatus supporting an exploitative social and economic order and reflecting the interests of dominant classes. Marx famously described the state as the committee of the bourgeoisie. So-called instrumentalist views are similar to classical Marxism in that they regard the state as a direct instrument of class rule. This school of thought suggests that state policies and actions are designed to consolidate and reinforce the position of the dominant class. In capitalist societies the political and legal systems support the ownership of private property, including the private ownership of the means of production. Since capitalism generates conflict, an elaborate system must be in place to manage

Who are the elites the person speak

Figure 3.3   Increasing 'Third World' debt burden (as a percentage of GDP).

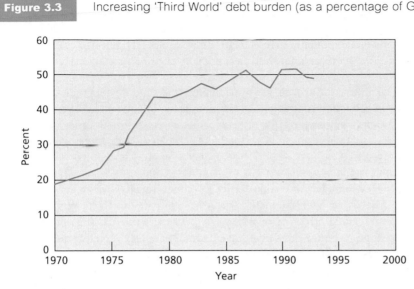

Original source: L. Brown *et al.* (1994), *Vital Signs*, New York: Norton, p. 75 (using World Bank and IMF data).

Taken from: B. Russett and H. Starr (1996), *World Politics: The Menu for Choice*, 2nd edn, New York: W.H. Freeman, p. 366.

or suppress social conflict. These élite classes exercise power for their own ends, and to the detriment of the vast majority of poorer, less privileged people. Structuralists point to the way in which the institutions of the state – the law courts, the police, the military, the economic system – work to protect the interests of the already powerful. As we saw earlier, Althusser saw the law courts, police force and armed forces as integral parts of a repressive, as opposed to ideological, state apparatus. The state quite literally represented the interests of the ruling class. If the ideological state apparatus failed then the repressive forces under the control of the state would be utilised to quell discontent.

FILM/LITERATURE BOX

El Salvador – *Romero* and *Turning the Tide*

International relations are replete with examples of state repression – what has sometimes been called 'state terrorism'. To simplify a complex history, El Salvador was a close ally of the USA in the Cold War (see chapter 2). However, anti-communist and pro-market/pro-US policies in that country created a highly unequal society with a majority of the population living in poverty resulting from a lack of access to resources and money. By the 1970s and 1980s pro-US right-wing governments were only kept in power by extensive repression of left-wing politics, trade union activity and peasant activism; the military, as it had long done, played a vital role in this repression, sometimes covertly but often openly. Elections were rigged, authorities corrupt and people cowed by fear. The state was, in fact, at the service of an élite few known as 'the fourteen families'. This story is partially told in films like *Salvador* or *Romero*, although research into the area – for instance in Noam Chomsky's *Turning the Tide* – will reveal a much more complex situation.

More recent versions of structuralism hold that the state can have a degree of autonomy from the dominant class. The state certainly is not seen as a 'neutral arbiter', but is considered to be relatively independent of specific interests. States clearly do make choices when formulating policies. Moreover, these same choices are sometimes bound to affect some sections of capital adversely. States might even struggle for more autonomy from dominant classes, in response to democratic pressures, perhaps.

However, even if we accept that it has a degree of autonomy, the state is, nonetheless, compelled to deal with the political and economic contradictions inherent in capitalism and is never able to completely escape the constraints imposed by the global capitalist system. In order to formulate autonomous policies the state requires resources, including financial resources which it raises through taxation. Arguably, then, the state relies largely on the capitalist class to bring about an acceptable level of economic activity, which it needs to maintain support.

Of course, states can borrow money from banks, or try to attract inward investment from foreign enterprises or investors. This is, in fact, frequently the case with many Third World countries. However, reliance on foreign capital brings its own dangers, because while the state might increase its autonomy vis-à-vis the dominant class in its own state, it simultaneously increases its dependency on foreign capital. Foreign resources typically come from foreign direct investment, supplied by big multinational corporations, in which case the investor maintains control. The state can, of course, take out loans from private banks or, in certain circumstances, apply for assistance from the International Monetary Fund, or the World Bank. Loans from private banks do not restrict the state's autonomy, although the bank will need to be assured that the money is going to be wisely spent. That said, if the loan proves difficult to service, states can find themselves pushed into a situation of dependency and their choices are then severely curtailed, or the sources of further credit might quickly dry up. Either way, it is clear that, even if we agree that the state has a degree of autonomy from dominant classes within its territory, it is still constrained by global economic realities. This means, of course, that government policy, whatever its ideological basis, is profoundly shaped either by pressures from its own élites, or by systemic pressures, as Henrique Cardoso evidently discovered (see Author Box above). For example, the government of Jordan continually posts annual budgetary deficits of between $1 and $2.5 billion and needs to source capital resources from foreign grants, FDI and private loans. In order to do this, the Jordanian government often has to shape its foreign and domestic policies according to the wishes of the source of the capital.

WORLD EXAMPLE BOX

The debt crisis

To look at the debt crisis is to see how developing countries are severely constrained by world market forces, dominant sections of capital *and* international institutions. In 1973 the oil-producing/exporting countries of OPEC used their collective economic muscle to raise the price of a barrel of oil drastically on the world market. Since many Western (and indeed developing countries) were dependent upon imported oil for their energy needs, they had no alternative but to pay up. Consequently, many OPEC states found themselves suddenly enriched with a glut of so-called 'petrodollars'. These funds were quickly reinvested in Western banks as the receiving countries could not put them all to productive use. At the time interest rates around the world were low and inflation rates were relatively high. For this reason, many developing countries were encouraged to borrow heavily – under the conditions that existed at the time, they were, in effect, getting interest-free loans. Developing countries hoped that these loans would provide a much-needed injection of investment in their economies and so fuel economic development. At the same time Western banks had a large glut of petrodollars and were looking for investment opportunities at a time when Western countries were reluctant to borrow.

However, within a short period of time global economic conditions had changed dramatically. In the first place, countries which imported oil took measures to protect their own economies and began to look for ways to restrict imports, often developing substitutes for commodities which had previously been imported. Consequently, the world market price of many basic commodities fell. The increase in oil prices also resulted in inflationary pressures in Western economies, and, consequently, interest rates increased rapidly. Many developing countries now found themselves in an extremely difficult position; they had large debts, were facing an increasing tide of protectionism in Western economies, were experiencing deteriorating terms of trade for the basic commodities which they sold on the world market, *and* had to pay the new higher price for oil as well as high rates of interest on their loans. In such circumstances, the level of debt escalated and many countries found that they were unable to repay even the interest on their debt (see Figure 3.3, p. 87).

In 1982 Mexico announced a moratorium on its debt and the financial world was plunged into a crisis. The inability of developing countries to service existing debt sent shock waves through the global financial institutions. In such circumstances private banks were reluctant to offer fresh loans and developing countries were compelled to turn to the only real alternative sources of finance, the International Monetary Fund (**IMF**) and World Bank. These institutions did indeed provide developing countries with fresh sources of credit but, in return, imposed harsh conditions. Developing countries had little alternative but to accept tough 'structural adjustment' packages which included, among other things, devaluation of local currencies, adoption of export-led growth strategies, and cuts in welfare provision. The debt crisis and the expanded role that the IMF has assumed in economic policy making in individual states, clearly indicates how state autonomy is severely constrained.

The **IMF** was established in 1944 as one of a number of international institutions which were charged with long-term governance of the international system. The IMF was created to offer financial support to states which face short-term capital shortages and budgetary deficits. A secondary role was to maintain stability in financial markets by ensuring financial resources are allocated where demand exceeds standard supply. However, the IMF has been criticised for placing primacy on market stability instead of development/quality of life issues.

With respect to the overarching global economy as a constraining/determining factor in state behaviour, structuralists (e.g. Wallerstein) make a distinction between 'core' and 'peripheral' states, arguing that in the core the state is relatively strong but functions to advance the interests of the bourgeoisie by preventing other states from erecting political barriers to the profitability of their activities. Core states, then, shape the world market in ways that advance the interests of some entrepreneurs against those of other groups. Core states cooperate to extend and deepen the capitalist world-system. The most powerful states, for example, the USA, Japan and Germany, work together (and through their influence in international financial organisations like the OECD, the World Bank or IMF) to ensure the survival of an international capitalist economy, which benefits élite classes across the globe.

It follows from this that, while structuralists believe that states are of central importance, the study of international relations must also extend to a range of other 'actors' like the World Bank, International Monetary Fund, and multinational corporations. Core states also seek to reinforce the advantages of their producers and to legitimise their role in the world-system by imposing their cultural dominance on the world.

Table 3.1 The concentration of wealth in a few countries.

Country/Area	No. of countries	Share of world GDP %
United States		27.1
Japan		15.3
Germany		6.6
France		5.2
Italy		4.6
UK		4.4
Canada		2.7
Other industrial countries	16	10.5
Industrial countries	23	76.4
Developing countries	138	23.8
WORLD	161	100.0

Original source: IMF (1991).

Taken from: C. Mulhearn (1996), 'Change and development in global economy', in C. Bretherton and G. Ponton (eds), *Global Politics: An Introduction*, Oxford: Blackwell, p. 160.

Although structuralists do not emphasise states but rather social classes, state-based inequality is not an unimportant and unrelated feature of international relations for them. This table shows the dominance of share of GDP by the industrial countries, especially the largest five or six.

In developing an analysis of the interconnections between states, the state system and global capitalism, structuralists have also elucidated the key concept of power. Power to structuralists is not about relational 'trials of strength' (i.e. who wins the war) but something much more subtle. Power is embedded in social relations; that is, it is a part of the structure. Power thus involves the inequalities of capitalist class relations and core–periphery relations. It also involves less tangible ideas such as persuasion or influence and may be 'invisible'. One person or group may have power over others not just through threats and coercion but via ideology and manipulation. In this way, power relations may come to be seen as such a 'natural' order of things that no one is consciously aware that power is, in fact, being exercised.

ANALOGY BOX

The happy slave

The operation of the global capitalist economy might not always appear conflictual, oppressive or exploitative, because these relationships are often not overt or obvious. The factory worker may be happy with life. Although the notion of the 'happy slave' does not originate from Marxist/structuralist thought, it is nevertheless useful in illustrating how power relations can be subtly disguised.

It is possible to imagine a society where slavery is the norm. As it is the norm, people do not question that slavery is part of the 'natural' order of things. Within this society a particular slave owner may provide their slaves with healthcare, education, food, excellent accommodation and working hours. The slave, in turn, may be very happy with his/her lot. Though as outside observers we can see a power relationship, perhaps neither the owner nor the slave perceive their relationship as one of power but rather as one of benevolence and mutual respect within the context of an entirely natural state of affairs. To extend the analogy, perhaps power is a facet of all sorts of social relations from the factory owner and worker to the husband and wife (see also chapter 6).

Institutions and world order

It might be argued that Marxism has made no real contribution to IR theory, because it has everything to say about economics and nothing to say about international politics. Marxists reject this idea because they regard economics as an autonomous sphere of human activity linked to socio-political factors. The economic substructure involves the mode of production and the social relations of production, and the superstructure involves the exertion of (political) power by one class over another. Structuralists follow Marx in insisting that politics and economics are intimately connected. Unsurprisingly, then, structuralism has made a contribution to our understanding of world order and institutions. In this section we concentrate on how world order is conceptualised in dependency theory and world-systems theory and then comment briefly on the role of institutions.

Figure 3.4　With exceptions in terms of gender and traditional dress, the élites and leaders of most countries look strikingly similar, adding some credence to Structuralism's class-based analysis.

Source: Action Press/Rex Features.

As suggested earlier, structuralists conceive of world order as a capitalist system of interconnected sets of social, economic and political relations which collectively constitute a structure. From a structuralist perspective modern capitalism has now expanded to become a global system; local, national and regional economies now form part of a much larger interconnected economic system and are conditioned by that system. Similarly, the conditions of life for individuals, social groups and even states, are determined by their place in the overall, global capitalist system.

In essence, structuralists see this global capitalist system as being structured along both a vertical and horizontal axis. Relations between states are structured hierarchically between those who are wealthy and powerful – the core – and those who are poor and without much influence – the periphery. There is also a horizontal structure of class relationships, namely the relationship which exists between élites in both core and periphery countries. Élites in both the rich 'North' and poor 'South' share fundamental interests in supporting this system because they actually benefit from the exploitation of other social groups.

AUTHOR BOX

Immanuel Wallerstein (The modern world-system)

According to Wallerstein, the concept of a world-economy assumes that there exists an economy wherever there is an ongoing extensive and relatively complete social division of labour with an integrated set of production processes which relate to each other through a market. Wallerstein (though others disagree) believes that a capitalist world-economy has been in existence in at least part of the globe since the sixteenth century. We have now reached the stage of capitalist development and expansion where the entire globe is operating within the frame of a singular social division of labour. It is meaningful, therefore, to speak of a capitalist world-economy.

The major social institutions of the capitalist world-economy are states, social classes, 'peoples' and households. Wallerstein believes that all of these institutions and social relationships are profoundly shaped (or even created) by the ongoing workings of the world-economy. Therefore, we can speak of a 'world-system'. The main underlying dynamic of the capitalist world-economy is the relationship between capital/labour and the extraction of the surplus created by direct producers (labour), or by others (capitalists) either at the actual site of production or, later, when goods are exchanged in the market place. The principle of private property, upheld by the law and enforced by the state, means that appropriators control the capital and that their rights to the surplus are legally guaranteed. Increasingly these 'appropriators' are not individuals but collective entities like multinational corporations.

Whereas orthodox Marxist analysis emphasises processes of unequal exchange between capital and labour, Wallerstein introduces the notion of a 'core' and a 'periphery' in the world-economy and calls the exchange of products containing unequal amounts of social labour a 'core–periphery relationship'. Wallerstein argues that the structure of the world-economy permits an unequal exchange of goods and services in such a way that much of the surplus value extracted in the peripheral zones of the world-economy is transferred to the core zones. However, unlike dependency theorists, Wallerstein posits the existence of a 'semi-periphery' in the world-economy or world-system. He argues that some states are neither in the core or periphery of the world-economy. Instead they can be thought of as semi-peripheral states. These states are engaged in production activities, some of which are 'core-like' and some 'periphery-like'. An example of these states might be the newly industrialising countries (NICs) in Asia, such as South Korea. So, the structure of the world-economy consists of a tripartite division between the core, periphery and semi-periphery. States and social groups can move, slowly, from one category to another but they remain within the overall determining structure of the world-economy.

[handwritten: how is this defined?]

> **REFLECTION BOX**
>
> Does Wallerstein's claim that a capitalist world economy has existed since the sixteenth century have any impact on arguments which claim that globalisation is a distinctly contemporary phenomenon?

[handwritten margin notes throughout: still true China Mex Brazil; environ laws? race to the bottom]

Dependency theorists argue that the economies of Asia, Africa and Latin America are on the periphery of the global economy and that they are dependent on the capitalist countries of Western Europe and North America at the centre/core of the system. The trade relations and capital flows between the core and periphery of the global economy are asymmetrical, shifting the economic surplus to the core and undermining the resource base of the periphery. Broadly speaking, countries in the periphery produce primary products like raw materials – cotton or coffee – not manufactured goods like motor vehicles or electronic goods. This degree of 'specialisation' or division of labour perpetuates inequalities. Surplus flows out of the periphery to the core, in the interests of international capital. Peripheral countries (the South or Third World) are not 'catching up' with the core because of their dependence on, and exploitation by, the core (West or North) of the international capitalist economy. Economic growth and development in the periphery is sluggish owing to a lack of technology and investment, which again is a consequence of their dependence on the core.

According to world-systems theorists, capitalism is driven by the imperatives of accumulation – each 'entrepreneur', whether an individual or a big corporation, seeks to maximise their profit. For this reason there is an inherent tendency for the absolute volume of production in the world-economy to expand over time, as more is produced to be sold on local, national or world markets. However, profit can only be made if there is effective demand for the goods and services produced and this is a problem when wages are being driven down. According to Wallerstein, the dynamics of the world-economy ensure that the level of world supply expands at a steady rate, while world demand remains relatively fixed for intermediate periods. This results in reoccurring blockages in the process of accumulation, which in turn generates periods of economic recession and stagnation.

In response to such pressures, capitalists will 'restructure' the network of production processes and underlying social relations in an attempt to overcome obstacles to capital accumulation. Such 'restructuring' might involve attempts to cut the cost of production in core countries by replacing labour with machinery. Alternatively, capitalist enterprises might relocate in the periphery where wages are much lower. Periods of restructuring have a profound effect on class relations both within and between states in the world-system.

Starting from the central premise that economics and politics are intimately connected allows structuralists to make various points about the nature and role of states and institutions in international relations in 'managing' world order (global capitalist relations). Structuralists argue that capitalism is maintained and perpetuated by a range of institutions and practices and by dominant ideologies or belief systems which legitimise the current world order. The fundamental economic inequality which exists between core and periphery determines the nature of the state – put simply, core states are powerful and peripheral states are weak. States in the periphery have little autonomy in relation to the global economy in which they are embedded, because ruling classes in peripheral countries are tied by economic interest to international capital and play a managerial or intermediary role within their own countries for international capital by using control of state power to protect the interests of multinational capital. Structuralists believe that major institutions like the UN, the World Bank and IMF and trading blocs like NAFTA are dominated by élite groups and/or hegemonic states. Thus, we cannot take statements of the World Bank and IMF about their role in poverty alleviation at face value; these organisations have a role in the capitalist structure which helps to maintain current injustices.

How would Wallerstein explain the large differences in economic wealth and quality of life which exists between the rich, industrialised, developed North (the core) and the poor, under-developed South (the periphery)?

Inequality and justice

Whether one adopts a dependency theory or a world-systems approach, it is clear that structuralists see inequality as a fundamental and enduring feature of international relations, because the international system is divided between the 'haves' and the 'have nots'. The 'haves' are (or live mostly in) the rich countries, predominantly in the northern hemisphere. Structuralists argue that these countries, or their capitalist élites (along with smaller local third world élites), constitute a strong centre or core in the world economic and political order, or world-system. The 'have-nots' are the poorer countries of the South or the downtrodden classes; they are the weak and powerless and make up what is known as the periphery.

By focusing on structures of the international system and world economy, world systems theory puts the experience, and plight, of Third World states in an entirely different light from the optimism generated by liberal modernisation theory. For example, the end of colonialism (where Third World countries were ruled as colonies of other states such as Britain) cannot be seen as signalling the end of exploitation of these states by rich, industrialised nations; the 'end' of colonialism simply changes the nature of colonialism from a direct type, based on military occupation, to an indirect type based on economic structures (that is neo-colonialism).

According to this view, Third World interaction with the financial and commercial power centres of the rich states of the first world is undertaken on unequal terms, since the rich countries have used their previously existing position of economic dominance in order to structure the international economy to serve their interests and maintain their dominance. Third World states which have tried to 'opt out' of the system have not fared well economically and so, however unfair the existing situation, most Third World states are dependent upon (and trapped by) it. This 'dependency' has left most Third World states unable to define effectively their own development goals, or to advance the welfare concerns of their populations, because their economies are set up and organised to serve the interests of the industrialised states.

The case of Cuba

Cuba was once a country which sold its sugar to the USA. It was also characterised by oppression and poverty, while being a preferred holiday destination of the USA's rich and famous. The revolution of 1959 sought to end such injustice. However, the USA quickly defined the revolution as communist and refused to trade with Cuba. In the context of the Cold War (see the Film Box on p. 63), Cuba was fortunate in that the Soviet Union saw it as an important ally (given its geographical proximity to its ideological enemy) and stepped in to exchange Cuban sugar for oil, and at preferential rates. Even so, shunned by the international financial institutions such as the IMF, Cuba faced big economic problems. These problems were severely exacerbated by the end of the Cold War and of subsidised Soviet oil, and the loss of its market for sugar. Cuba is relatively isolated from the normal workings of the world economy. Although distributed in a relatively equal fashion, most goods are rationed in Cuba today, and Cuba is struggling to survive in its present form. The case of Cuba suggests that in some senses dependency is a 'lose–lose' situation; states can suffer the injustice of dependent status *or* fare even worse in attempting to set up an alternative. It might be suggested that the only thing worse than being exploited by global economic forces is *not* being exploited by them.

Structuralist-inspired critiques of this kind raise normative questions about how this exploitation can be ended and what would constitute a just international economic and political order. The relationship between the rich North and poor South (core and periphery) is said to be unequal and exploitative. Despite differences between varieties, fundamental to a structuralist argument is the idea that the rich are rich *at the expense of* the poor; put another way, some people are able to enjoy life because of others' misery; this is not just a matter of chance. The global economy is structured by class interests to the benefit of some and the detriment of others.

REFLECTION BOX

Structuralists dismiss the liberal pluralist notion of *inter*dependence, arguing that this implies a balance and fairness which does not exist. To what extent do you think that the complex interactions of international relations are characterised by mutually profitable exchange *or* unfair exploitative relations?

Dependence describes a type of relationship between rich and poor which ensures that money and resources are increasingly concentrated with the former because of the way the world economy is structured. For instance, poorer countries might export raw materials such as, for example, bauxite, and foodstuffs like coffee and bananas, whereas richer countries export manufactured goods, such as cars, fridges and so on. Statistical evidence supports the contention that over the long term the prices of raw materials and food – primary products – tend to decline relative to the price of manufactured goods.

This puts poorer countries at a fundamental, structural disadvantage. Furthermore, richer countries are able to perpetuate this situation because, despite the rhetoric of free trade, richer countries are able to control prices by trade restrictions. The EU, for instance, strictly controls the importation of bananas. Furthermore, technical innovation keeps pushing the development of better products, which have even higher levels of 'value-added'. Of course, some people, plantation owners in Guatemala for instance, are very rich despite the overall poverty which may exist in their country; this ensures that the system is kept going, since there is a commonality of interest between the rich of the core and the rich of periphery.

World-systems theory aims to explain the historical rise of the rich countries (referred to as either the North or the West), as well as the continued poverty of the non-Western (Southern or Third World) societies.

CONCEPT BOX

The Third World

The 'Third World' is a term that began to evolve from the times of the French Revolution. Although the term now obscures as much as it illuminates, in the time of the Cold War the world might be divided into First (Western, capitalist, developed) World, Second (Eastern,

> Communist, industrial) World and Third (Southern, poor, agricultural) World. Nowadays it is recognised that there is a lot which is different about various parts of the developing world and many parts of the developed world which nonetheless exhibit many of the symptoms of poverty of the Third World. Though the term thus has some problems, it is nonetheless useful as a way of talking about the marginalised, excluded and poorer areas of the world. Politically, terms like 'majority world' are more acceptable, but we continue to use the term 'Third World' here because it gives a very real sense of the marginalisation which is key to structuralist thought.

World-systems theory, like structuralism in general, demands a fair redistribution of the world's economic wealth. In order that this should be achieved, world-systems theory provides support for a new international economic order, often abbreviated in written form to the unpronounceable acronym NIEO. Demands for a NIEO involve fair prices for products produced by the Third World and a restructuring of world trade in general. A NIEO can be contrasted with the actual economic order which is a Liberal International Economic Order, or LIEO. Given that this version of structuralist doctrine emphasises the systematic nature of exploitation, and given the stress on conflicting interests, we can safely assume that the rich are not likely to give up their wealth and privilege without a struggle. Therefore, the challenge for the poor is to break free from the structures which constrain them. How to do this, in theory or in practice, is a different matter.

Identity and community

Recognition of the significance of gender and racial discrimination was fairly central to the 'post-Marxist' turn which occurred in the late 1960s and early 1970s in social theory (see chapters 4–6). However, generally speaking neither early Marxist nor later structuralist writers paid much attention to aspects of identity and community that did not easily fit within the broad framework of a global capitalist order and notions of class struggle. Despite the importance of nationalism, as both an ideology and political force in nineteenth-century Europe, Marx devoted most of his time and energies to exploring the theme of class consciousness, class interests and class struggle.

Given the national and ethnic diversity which existed in the Soviet Union, it is somewhat surprising, perhaps, to find that none of the leading Bolshevik revolutionaries, including Lenin and Trotsky, gave sustained attention to the ideology of nationalism. Moreover, the intellectual and political climate of the USSR during the first half of this century was such that there were no serious challenges to Stalin's rather simplistic view of the world 'community' as being fundamentally divided into two opposing blocs or 'camps'. Throughout the nineteenth and early twentieth centuries Marxists tended to regard nationalism, or indeed any other form of identification – religious, cultural, ethnic and so on – as a manifestation of 'false consciousness'; in effect a distraction from the real class-based structures of politics. This view continues to find echoes in some contemporary Marxist work.

That said, in the 1960s there emerged many national liberation movements in parts of Africa and Latin America which were left-leaning, or pro-Marxist-Leninist and, for this reason, it became necessary to develop an account of nationalist struggle which was neither dismissive (as in the notion of false consciousness) nor incompatible with the basic assumptions of structuralism. Thus, in Wallerstein's account of the modern world-system, we find some attention being given to nationalism as a powerful source of political identification.

Wallerstein argues that the increasing definition of state structures has led to the shaping, reshaping, creation and destruction, and revival of the idea of 'peoples'. He believes that these 'peoples' come to see themselves (and are seen by others) as controlling state structures. Through this identification of 'peoples' with the state, 'nations' are created. On the other hand, within the boundaries of the 'nation-state' there are significant groups who are not identified as having rights to control state structures or exercise political power directly. These people come to be seen by 'nationals' as 'minorities'. However, it is important to realise that Wallerstein does not regard national identity as rooted in some real shared ethnic heritage or history. Nations are 'solidarity groupings' whose boundaries are constantly constructed, defined and redefined, and nationalism is a device which is used to strengthen and consolidate the power of the state.

World systems theory incorporates an analysis of those forces which work against the system as well as dominant, class-based, structures. Thus, it is possible to identify a number of oppositional or 'anti-systemic' forces at work in world politics. Nationalism is not all of one kind. Some forms of nationalism certainly work to consolidate capitalism and disguise the exploitative nature of the capitalist world-system. However, some national liberation movements are clearly anti-systemic. Various groups have an interest in supporting and opposing particular definitions of the 'nation-state' and so, according to Wallerstein, 'nationalism' must be seen as both a mechanism of imperialism/integration *and* of resistance/liberation.

Clearly, here we have an analysis of nationalism which is influenced by the underlying theory of class politics. Indeed, Wallerstein goes on to say that anti-systemic movements are organised in two main forms around two main themes: social movements around class and the national movement around 'nations' or peoples. Anti-systemic (or revolutionary) movements first emerged in organised form in the nineteenth century to promote human equality and so were, by definition, incompatible with the functioning of the capitalist world economy. It was the political structure of the capitalist world economy – a series of sovereign states – which compelled movements to seek the transformation of the world-system via the achievement of political power within separate states. However, because the capitalist world-system is based fundamentally on class division and exploitation, which is transnational or global in nature, the organisation of anti-systemic movements at the state level necessarily has contradictory effects. Nationalism counterposes the logical and ideological necessity of worldwide struggle against the immediate political need of achieving power within one state. Whatever the tactic of a given social movement, it achieves power in a state structure and is then constrained by the logic of the inter-state system.

Structuralists have also endeavoured to give some account of racism and sexism in the world-system. According to Wallerstein racism is a belief system which functions to justify the inclusion of certain groups in the workforce and the political system at a level of reward and status sharply inferior to that of some larger group. Sexism has the same objective, although it is reached via a different path. By restricting women to certain modes of producing income and by defining such modes as 'non-work' (through the concept of the 'housewife') sexism works to reduce wage levels in large sectors of the world economy. According to Maria Mies, in the contemporary global economy the coercion of women as 'housewives' remains essential for a system which allowed male workers to be free citizens.

However, while structuralists have attempted to give some account of identity, forms of solidarity and types of community (such as nation-states and anti-systemic movements), it is fair to say that this analysis has been profoundly coloured by their basic beliefs about the primacy of social class and class struggle. Indeed, overall structuralists have tended to emphasise class as the coming together of identity and interests.

Conflict and violence

For structuralists, conflict is intimately connected with the forces of global capitalism. Global economic relations are highly conflictual, because of the tendencies inherent in capitalism – it is built upon and perpetuates divisions between social classes and between core states and periphery states. Conflicts between social groups, and indeed states, are generated by the nature of the system itself. Conflict is not then primarily rooted in the nature of the inter-state system, as realists hold, but arises out of the exploitative nature of capitalism. For this reason, attempts to mediate or resolve conflict by well-meaning individuals or groups are unlikely to be effective.

In the sense of direct physical violence, like war, the link between capitalism and conflict can be seen in terms of imperialism and the violent subjugation of those peoples who opposed it. It has also been claimed, by Lenin for example, that capitalist competition leads to inter-state war, though the evidence here is not clear and might even be contradictory. What is evident is that some conflicts appear to have at least partly capitalist economic motivations. For example, Indonesia's invasion of East Timor was followed by a treaty with Australia on oil exploitation off the Timorese coast. Many observers argue that the US/UN military operation in the Gulf in 1991 was not motivated by liberating Kuwait from Iraqi occupation and upholding international law. Instead they argue that the invasion was motivated by economic interests and the need to secure access to natural resources (oil). Furthermore, the 2003 US-led invasion of Iraq can be seen to have less to do with liberating the Iraqi people from a dictator than making profit from Iraq's resources, the reconstruction effort and the military activity itself.

CONCEPT BOX

Realist and structuralist perspectives on conflict and political struggle

At this juncture it might be helpful to compare and contrast structuralist and realist views on the nature of the inter-state system and forms of conflict and political struggle. You will recall that realists regard states as the primary actors in international relations. Moreover, states are autonomous actors – they are able to formulate foreign-policy goals and take effective action to realise these ends ('the national interest'). Conflicts arise because states frequently have competing interests, are prepared to use force if necessary to realise their objectives and because, in an anarchic system, there is nothing to prevent it. Moreover, realists recognise that political struggle is not limited to conflicts between states. After all, from a realist perspective, conflict is endemic to the human condition. However, realists tend to concentrate on conflict between, rather than within, states.

The structuralist view of conflict and violence among states is different. Structuralists regard the inter-state system as reflecting the interests of élite groups (international capital), and functioning to manage conflicts that arise from the contradictions inherent in capitalism. Political struggles take a number of forms, but they can be reduced to two kinds. The first kind is conflict and struggle among different sectors of capital – which may take the form of inter-state conflict (war) when nationally based capitalist classes attempt to increase their share of the global product, or their access to resources. The second kind is conflict and struggle among opposed social classes – capital and labour. The first kind of struggle is a squabble (albeit often a brutal and bloody one) over the share of global wealth and resources, which leaves the capitalist system intact. The second kind, however, is a much more fundamental conflict between those who defend the capitalist system and those who want to change it.

Another way of looking at violence is as something indirect or structural. Johan Galtung is particularly known for his work on structural violence, which has made an important contribution to Peace Studies. One can suffer great harm, both physical and psychological, if deprived of social and economic security. To this view 'violence' pervades the structures of society, which oppress the working class and other marginalised groups. The economic structure of capitalism works to damage subordinated groups in many and varied ways; they get less education, poorer healthcare and so on, leading to shorter life-expectancies. Feminists have gone beyond the class-based analysis of Galtung's original work to suggest that structures in society also tend to impact negatively on the lives of women (see chapter 6).

Peace and security

As indicated above, the concept of structural violence has been particularly influential in Peace Studies. More generally, structuralist analysis suggests that current patterns of economic organisation generate tensions and contradictions which often result in direct conflict. The possibility of violence and war mean inherent insecurity for large sectors of the world's population. Peace and security, therefore, lie in moving to a socioeconomic system which is not exploitative and so lacks the motivations for war.

Summary

1. Structuralism is a broad perspective drawing upon a Marxist legacy, but also influenced by ideas not directly Marxist in origin.
2. Probably the best known variants of structuralism are dependency theory (the *Dependencia* School) and world-systems theory.
3. From a structuralist perspective, the contemporary world order is constituted by a global capitalist system and a corresponding inter-state system.
4. A fundamental feature of this order is inequality. Capitalism is based on the exploitation of the poor by the rich. In pursuing their (class) interests, the rich (people and states) are able to maintain their position by their exploitation of the poor. This is caused by a fundamentally unjust system, based on structures and characterised by inequality.
5. In line with Marx many structuralists therefore see classes as the dominant actors in IR, despite the importance of the state.
6. Structuralists have not neglected the role of the state-system. Structuralists have developed an analysis of the state as either an instrument used to perpetuate the rule of dominant classes, a conduit for class oppression or, alternatively, as a relatively autonomous entity which, nevertheless, plays an important role in facilitating capitalist expansion and supporting an unjust order.
7. While the world is divided up into rich and poor countries, an accurate appraisal of IR needs to look at how classes promote their interests and how they use the state to help them.
8. Structuralism looks carefully at the role of institutional actors such as the World Bank and IMF and how these help legitimise and maintain existing structures.
9. Structuralism claims that processes of capital accumulation, the extraction of surplus value and exploitation can be measured objectively. We can understand processes of contradiction, crisis and change by reference to these same economic 'laws'. Therefore, structuralism can be viewed as a 'scientific' or 'positivist' approach within IR (see concluding chapter).

10. Despite many insights, structuralism has tended to be marginalised in the study of IR, especially in the US version of the discipline.

Nick Davies' *Dark Heart*

Structuralist writers emphasise both inequality and the structural reasons for this as at the global scale. More recently, it has become more and more clear that the victims of this structure are a global phenomenon and Monty Python's classic sketch 'Constitutional Peasant' from the film *Holy Grail* contains the line that sums it up: 'violence inherent in the system'. Nick Davies' book *Dark Heart* published in 1996 gets to the nub of this issue.

Davies' fantastic piece of investigative journalism begins, and can be read on one level, as a story of terrible human misfortune (in places like Nottingham, Leeds and London in the UK), as he documents the lives of poverty experienced by what he characterises as a 'hidden country' that many people have little contact with, except perhaps when they are asked for money or have their cars stolen. However, on another level Davies is describing what happened to ordinary people when Margaret Thatcher famously declared that there was no such thing as 'society' and implemented policies which cut back on social spending and effectively cast adrift from prosperity a whole raft of the country's most unfortunate citizens to face the vagaries of market capitalism.

Davies is referring to the relentless rise of neo-liberalism. Mrs Thatcher also famously declared 'there is no alternative'. Despite her apparently callous and uncaring nature – exemplified by her support for Chilean dictator General Pinochet – the case for her defence might point out that Britain would have been like King Cnut if it had attempted to hold back the neo-liberal tide. Wherever we lay the blame, the very real and negative consequences of neo-liberal Thatcherism, documented painfully by Davies, might easily be characterised as systemic violence.

Criticisms

Perhaps the biggest criticism of structuralism concerns its level of determinism. This means that the theory suggests that the position of actors within the structure determines the way they behave. States are said to have little autonomy in the way they conduct themselves in terms of winning or losing within the international economy. However, the whole point of the analysis is to suggest that poorer states have very little opportunity to improve their position. This seems to dismiss as meaningless even noble and heroic struggles to overcome such constraints.

This point gives rise to complaints that structuralism is able to outline the evils of international capitalism but has no scheme which will change it. In other words, it is merely a problem highlighting approach as opposed to a problem-solving one. The despair of such a position (which rejects the purely Marxist determinism of inevitable revolution) may be regrettable or frustrating but is again part of the idea that the rich countries have things effectively 'stitched up'. Some structuralists, most notably Wallerstein, have sought to fight their way out of this corner but then find themselves trapped in another (teleology – see below).

A further criticism of structuralism is that it is reductionist: that is, it reduces all phenomena – war, economic crisis, inequality, aspects of identity and so forth – to the dynamic of capitalism and to social class and class struggle. What this means in practice is that structuralists have failed to ask a whole range of questions about gender, ethnicity and identities of other sorts. They have reduced a highly complex situation to one which is wholly explained by class, when, in fact, patterns of oppression are multi-faceted and overlapping ones, where even class loyalties are not always easy to ascribe in a way which helps predict behaviour and attitudes. A related criticism concerns the way that interests are understood. Is it really possible that interests are so fundamentally determined by social class? Or that interests are really this fixed? (See chapter 6)

In adopting the Marxist heritage, which emphasises the oppression of the working class, structuralism (though it may have no road map to get there) implicitly suggests an end point to history. The end point is socialism, at which point the good life will be enjoyed by everyone. Quite apart from the fact that much of what Marx predicted as inevitable has not happened, this teleological position can be criticised because the explanation of what *is* happening (the dynamic of history and social change) is coloured by the assumption that a socialist society will eventually emerge – that is to say, the posited end point colours the explanation of past and present events. Moreover, not only does the above suggest that the 'end point' influences the theory, but it also reduces different cultures to mere temporary stages or impediments, rather than allowing them intrinsic value.

Overall, however, we might conclude by saying that more thoughtful critics of Marx have recognised the structuralist contribution, as well as noting its weaknesses.

Common misunderstandings

1. *If classes are the predominant actors then states are unimportant.* No, just as realists do not deny the existence of MNCs, NGOs and so forth, structuralists are not oblivious to a world divided into states. Indeed, structuralists have attempted to theorise the nature and function of states and other 'actors' in terms of the way they promote certain class interests.

2. *Structuralists have a plan to end injustice.* Not necessarily. In fact, a major criticism of some structuralist theories is that, while they are very good at telling us what is wrong with the world and how this situation came about, they are not very good at telling us what remedial action to take and how the situation is likely to improve.

3. *Structuralism is Marxism.* Not so. Although Marx's influence is clear in much structuralist writing, you cannot use structuralism and Marxism as if they were entirely synonymous. It is more accurate to say that structuralism is inspired by, or indebted to, Marxism in terms of the way it approaches international relations.

4. *Structuralism is unified.* Only in the sense of a concern for the poverty and underdevelopment of the third world. There is, in fact, enormous variety within structuralist literature. Some structural approaches tend to relate to a particular epoch and have been developed for a particular reason (for example, dependency theory) whereas others, like the work of Wallerstein, are developing in some new and interesting directions, to take account of factors such as the possibility of counter-hegemonic resistance and environmental issues.

5. *Structuralism is Marxism's biggest contribution to IR.* The work of Karl Marx and Friedrich Engels inspired a school of thought which came to be known as Marxism. While Structuralism does emerge as a result of Marxian analysis, so do other perspectives which offer critical interpretations or views on international relations. See chapters 4 and 5.

Further reading

Arrighi, G. and Sliver, B.J. (2001), 'Capitalism and World (Dis)Order', *Review of International Studies*, Vol. 27, Special Issue, pp. 257–79 (despite its waning popularity, a more recent example of Marxist-inspired writing).

Baran, P. (1957), *The Political Economy of Growth*, New York: Monthly Review Press (an early example of structuralist work).

Cardoso, F. and Faletto, E. (1979), *Dependency and Development in Latin America*, Berkeley, CA: University of California Press (the Latin American experience; home of the idea of the *Dependencia* School).

Galtung, J. (1971), 'A Structural Theory of Imperialism', *The Journal of Peace Research*, Vol. 8, No. 1, pp. 81–117 (structuralism heavily influenced – at least for a while – emerging ideas of 'positive peace' in Scandinavian Peace Studies).

Harvey, D. (2003), *The New Imperialism*, Oxford: Oxford University Press (a contemporary application of structuralist insights in international contexts).

Rodney, W. (1972), *How Europe Underdeveloped Africa*, London: Bogle l'Ouverture (dependency theories are not merely applicable in the context of Latin America).

Wallerstein, I. (1974, 1980, 1989), *The Modern World-System* (Vols 1 to 3), San Diego, CA: Academy Press (perhaps the most famous structuralist writer, whose detailed ideas are still being developed today).

4 Critical Theory

Introduction

Critical theory has become influential in international relations since the mid-1980s, when, even before the end of the Cold War, Marxism fell out of favour because of its structuralist and economic biases. As a result, the debate turned to a number of new approaches that had been developed in other disciplines of the Humanities and Social Sciences, including feminism and postmodernism. For reasons that we will discuss in the following chapters, these can be labelled 'critical' as well, though in this chapter the term 'Critical Theory' (with a capital 'c' and 't') refers specifically to a school of thought that has its intellectual roots in Marxism, but addresses some of Marxism's perceived short-comings and so is sometimes also referred to as 'post-Marxist'. Since Critical Theory and structuralism are both influenced by Marxist thought, you will find some similarities between, for example, critical conceptions of world order and institutions on the one hand and structuralist accounts as outlined in chapter 3 on the other. However, Critical Theory differs in important respects from structuralism and, hence, warrants separate treatment.

As with all 'critical' perspectives, a first encounter with Critical Theory can be daunting, because it requires us to be reflective about our everyday practices and the relationship between our 'theories' and the way that we act. This emphasis upon critical reflection in turn serves to highlight the import-ance of the ideational realm in IR: the role of ideas, culture, communication and inter-subjective negotiation and dialogue. This notion that there is an intimate connection between theories or ideas and actual social practices is difficult to grasp, so to illustrate this point, we will briefly revisit our discussion of economic liberalism.

Liberals regard the individual as separate from, and existing prior to, society. In liberal thought society is viewed as the product of relationships between individuals which are based on various sorts of voluntary contracts such as the marriage contract, the contract between workers and employers and the contract between buyers and sellers in the market place. The economy is thus the product of trans-actions between individuals made on the basis of choice. Freed from the dictates of traditional duties and obligations, individuals are free to compete in an open and competitive system. In this competi-tion some succeed and others fail, but the outcome is decided by individual skill, aptitude and hard work, and so it is a fair system. It follows from this that the state should, as far as possible, refrain from interfering in society or in economic activity.

What interested Marx was how and why this powerful ideology was taking hold at a time when capitalism was, in fact, creating a grossly unequal society. The emerging new middle class did, indeed, enjoy more freedom, but an increasingly large group of workers were living in poverty and had to sell their labour on a daily basis in order to survive. There seemed to be a contradiction between dominant ideas about the nature of the social and economic system and the actual, or material, conditions of people's lives. From the point of view of the emerging bourgeois class, liberalism did, indeed, seem to describe the reality of their lives. However, if the impoverished working class, or proletariat, were asked to describe the conditions of *their* everyday lives, they would be more likely to use terms like, 'oppressive', or 'exploitative' and see themselves as having few choices and little opportunity to exercise any control. Thus, liberal ideology legitimised economic and social relationships and practices that were inherently exploitative.

HISTORICAL BOX

The condition of child labour in Victorian England

Marx wrote much of his best work while living in Victorian England. At this time, it was not uncommon to find children, many as young as five or six years old, working for up to 19 hours a day and, in consequence, suffering bad health. The following abstract of the evidence of one Samuel Coulson, to the Committee on Factory Children's Labour in 1832, illustrates graphically the harsh conditions of life for thousands of children.

At what time in the morning did those girls go to work? In the brisk time, for about six weeks, they had gone at three o'clock in the morning and ended at ten, or nearly half past ten at night.

What intervals were allowed for rest or refreshment during those nineteen hours of work? Breakfast a quarter of an hour, and dinner half an hour and drinking a quarter of an hour.

Was any of this time taken up in cleaning machinery? They generally had to do what they called 'dry down', sometimes this took the whole of breakfast or drinking and they got their dinner or breakfast as they could.

Had you great difficulty in awakening your children in this excessive labour? Yes, in the early time we had to take them up asleep and shake them, before we could get them off to their work.

Had any of them any accident in consequence of this labour? My eldest daughter caught her forefinger nail and screwed it off below the knuckle, and she was five weeks in Leeds infirmary.

Were her wages paid during that time? As soon as the accident happened, the wages were totally stopped.

(Abstract taken from *The Report of the Committee on Factory Labour in 1832*, reproduced in H. Allsopp, *The Change to Modern England*)

There were then at least two contrasting views of the nature of 'reality', which gave rise to different judgments about the just or unjust nature of the current social and economic order. It followed from this that liberalism did not describe a 'truth' about human nature and society, it merely reflected the point of view of the dominant class. However, liberalism had established itself as a dominant understanding or explanation about the world – a kind of 'common sense' – which in itself was an important factor in consolidating support for the capitalist system.

Clearly, if a central concern with inequality and exploitation also informs structuralist thought, how is Critical Theory different from 'orthodox' or structuralist variants of Marxist thought such as neo-Marxism and dependency theory? First, while structuralists concentrate on the actual structure and the 'mechanics' of the capitalist system – the processes by which unequal relations between social classes, and indeed, countries are reproduced – Critical Theorists (particularly those inspired by the work of Antonio Gramsci) emphasise much more the importance of culture and ideology in perpetuating certain sorts of social relationships, or conversely, challenging them.

Second, orthodox Marxist thought holds that society can be understood scientifically. This is because the actual processes of exploitation and expropriation in capitalism can be clearly observed and the major inequalities in the distribution of wealth and income which emerge in consequence measured objectively. Moreover, changes in the economic organisation of society are deemed to impel or determine changes in the organisation of societies. For this reason it is possible to understand the dynamic that drives historical change and to make predictions about what future social and economic order will emerge out of the ashes of the old one. From this perspective, some versions of 'the truth' are better than others, because they are better able to grasp the exploitative nature of capitalism and the forces at work that will eventually lead to its collapse. In contrast, Critical Theorists hold that *all* knowledge is ideological – intimately connected with social practice and the pursuit of

Figure 4.1   Aid given by richer countries as a percentage of GDP.

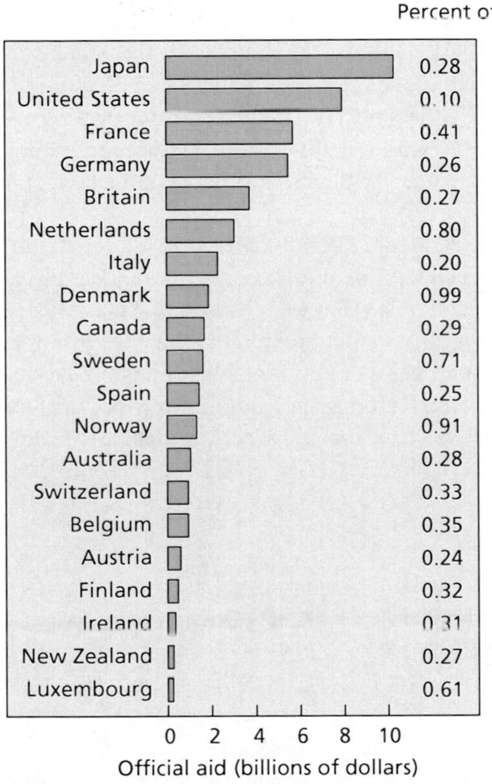

Percent of GDP

Country	Percent of GDP
Japan	0.28
United States	0.10
France	0.41
Germany	0.26
Britain	0.27
Netherlands	0.80
Italy	0.20
Denmark	0.99
Canada	0.29
Sweden	0.71
Spain	0.25
Norway	0.91
Australia	0.28
Switzerland	0.33
Belgium	0.35
Austria	0.24
Finland	0.32
Ireland	0.31
New Zealand	0.27
Luxembourg	0.61

0   2   4   6   8   10
Official aid (billions of dollars)

Original source: *The Economist*, 3 and 26 July 1999.

Taken from: C.W. Kegley and E.R. Wittkopf (1999), *World Politics: Trend and Transformation*, 7th edn, New York: St Martins, p. 163.

Reflection – in trying to address the inequalities that Table 4.1 (overleaf) demonstrates (and the consequences thereof) rich countries give away money in the form of overseas aid. The UN agrees that the level to aim for should be 0.7% of GDP. Although the second most generous in absolute terms, the USA gives only 0.1% of its GDP. However, it does of course spend many times this on overseas adventures in support of the current global order.

interests. We can only evaluate theories according to how far they capture the mood of the times and the configuration of forces at work in any given society and historical period, and whether they support or challenge the status quo. However, and in contrast to postmodernists, Critical Theorists still cling to the idea of emancipation, as we will further elaborate below, and that some ways of organising economic, social and political life will be better than others. There is therefore still a belief in Critical Theory that theory is supposed to provide alternatives, rather than merely problematising the present.

Third, Critical Theorists argue that our theories about the world and the practices which they support and perpetuate are so intimately connected that it is meaningless to see theory and practice as distinctive realms of human activity. We employ our critical capacities to make sense of our world; on the basis of this 'knowledge' we act, and our actions then have the effect of confirming the 'correctness' of our theory. To borrow an expression from contemporary parlance, we might say we can 'make it happen' (recall Barack Obama's rallying slogan 'Yes, We can!'), providing we have a realistic sense of what is possible in any given circumstance or period of time. At the same time, our action changes existing 'reality' and has an impact on what we and others come to think of as 'possible'. Contemporary Critical Theorists believe that social theory – and in this view IR is a kind of social theory – is concerned with understanding the activity of the thinking person, and moments of reflection and self-understanding. The express purpose of Critical Theory is to further the self-understanding of groups committed to transforming society. Critical Theorists have, therefore, reminded scholars that understanding and explaining the international/global domain does not simply involve identifying the structures and processes which will be the object of study, but also reflecting critically upon what can be said to constitute knowledge of the world, and what our knowledge is for. As we will elaborate below, Critical Theory is centrally concerned with possibilities of human emancipation from oppressive forms of social relationships.

Fourth, Critical Theorists do not hold such a rigid or deterministic view of the relationship between the economic and social system, or the dynamic of historical change. It may be the case that there is a close fit between economic organisation (capitalism), social relations (the class system) and the kind of political organisation (states) that exists. It is undoubtedly also the case that the broad structure of the economy and the existing class system places important constraints on the degree of change which can be generated by oppositional social groups and through the political process. However, Critical Theorists view society and the state as having a certain degree of autonomy, reflecting the complex configuration of forces at work in society. Critical Theorists argue that, while

Table 4.1 Global income distribution, 1960–90

Year	Percentage of global income going to richest 20 per cent	Percentage of global income going to poorest 20 per cent	Ratio of richest to poorest
1960	70.2	2.3	30 : 1
1970	73.9	2.3	32 : 1
1980	76.3	1.7	45 : 1
1990	82.8	1.3	64 : 1

Original source: L.R. Brown and H. Kane (1995), *Full House: Reassessing the Earth's Population Carrying Capacity*, London: Earthscan.

Taken from: C. Thomas (1997), 'Poverty, development and hunger', in J. Baylis and S. Smith (eds), *The Globalization of World Politics*, 1st edn, Oxford: Oxford University Press, p. 456.

Like structuralists, Critical Theorists are interested in inequality. This table shows clearly that this is a worsening position.

capitalism is an exploitative and oppressive system, it does generate certain opportunities for social change that oppositional groups can use to their advantage. So, for example, while critical of the liberal ideology of so-called individual freedom and choice, Critical Theorists nevertheless see some value in working for change through the democratic process and certainly in democratic values and practices more broadly defined.

Fifth, some Critical Theorists recognise that class is not the only form of domination or oppression in capitalist societies. As we will see in chapter 6, some feminists argue that in the eighteenth century, when liberals were celebrating the birth of a new world of freedom, equality and opportunity, women were not allowed to vote and many women were not allowed to own property; they were, in other words, wholly dependent upon men. Moreover, theorists like John Locke explicitly excluded women and men who did not own property from his vision of a polity comprised of free citizens. If we observe societies across the world today, we find that it is not just social class that is a major indicator of social inequality, but also nationality, ethnic origin, race and gender. For this reason, many contemporary Critical Theorists concentrate on a number of different kinds of social inequality and exclusion. These scholars are sometimes referred to as 'post-Marxists'.

To simplify the discussion of Critical Theory somewhat, here is a summary of the main features of a critical perspective:

1. The world should be understood primarily in terms of the major economic and social forces generated by capitalism, which are now international or global in scope.
2. States and institutions should be understood primarily in terms of the functions they perform in supporting global capitalism.
3. While a 'real' world exists, our understanding of the world is always mediated though ideas, concepts and theories which are a product of critical thought and reflection.
4. All knowledge is ideological – it is a reflection of the values, ideas and, crucially, interests of particular social groups.
5. Culture and ideology are, in themselves, an important and powerful force working to support or challenge the existing economic and social order.
6. International relations (or politics) constitutes a struggle between a variety of social groups and movements – or social forces – some of whom have an interest in supporting the status quo, while others struggle to change it.
7. Through political action human beings can challenge existing structures and achieve emancipatory forms of human existence.
8. Theory should be directed towards uncovering impediments to change and identifying the emancipatory potential of certain social groups and forces. Knowledge should be directed towards the project of human emancipation.

Origins

Critical Theory draws upon the early Marx and other social theorists like Max Weber. For this reason, Critical Theory is sometimes called 'open' Marxism or 'Marxist humanism'. Contemporary Critical Theory also owes much to the work of a number of writers in the Frankfurt School tradition and some – like Gramsci – outside this tradition. While potentially we could include a great many writers and thinkers in this section on origins, arguably the Italian communist Antonio Gramsci and the German social theorist Jürgen Habermas have had most impact on the development of Critical Theory in IR.

As we saw in the previous chapter, the later work of Marx was centrally concerned with economic relations and the relationship between the economic 'base' and social and political 'superstructure' of capitalist societies. This has been very important in the development of structuralism. There are, of course, continuities in Marxist thought. Throughout his life, Marx dedicated his energies to developing an analysis and a critique of capitalism. However, the young or 'early' Marx was particularly interested in how capitalist society affected the human person or subject, and particularly with problems of human alienation.

Marx believed that people were, by nature, social beings and so needed to live in social groups. Human beings were also creative beings, in the sense that human beings made and used tools which, in turn, helped them to create various artefacts. In a very real sense, human beings created their own social world. Yet, in capitalist societies human beings seemed to experience a sense of disaffection and remoteness from society because of how it, and its methods of production, were organised. Marx's theory of human alienation thus suggested that disaffection and a sense of remoteness lay in the particular form of social organisation which existed under capitalism. It also implied that a major purpose of theory was to understand how human beings could overcome such conditions and, in so doing, achieve emancipation.

REFLECTION BOX

It has been argued by some people who have, for one reason or another, come to live in Western society that some people in Western society appear to drink, not so much because they have the money to do so, or because they enjoy it, but because they actually *need* to escape. You might put such observations in the context of Marx's ideas on alienation and disaffection and/or contrast them with ideas of the alienating effects of modern industrial society highlighted by some green perspectives in chapter 8.

In capitalist society, the products of human labour – commodities – were no longer produced to satisfy human needs, but in order to be sold on the market at a profit. The profit was kept by the factory owner, who accumulated wealth in this way. Human labour was no longer viewed as something physically and socially necessary for the survival and welfare of the community, but rather as an 'input' into the production process. Under capitalism some people – principally workers – no longer owned the means of production, or even the products of their own labour. Labour rather became a commodity that could be used in a one-sided contract by capitalists, who owned the means of production, paid wages and so claimed ownership of what was produced.

For this reason, society was not experienced as beneficial and necessary to human beings, but as hierarchical and oppressive. The class system was deeply exploitative, allowing some people to benefit by capitalising on others. Marx argued that not only did capitalists own the means of production, but they were also able to rule through the force of ideas or ideology. Marx believed that this was the reason why society and human life were so awful for the vast majority. Human beings had lost their sense of themselves as inherently cooperative beings and experienced a sense of estrangement from others and ultimately from themselves.

Marx was not content merely to criticise capitalism but wanted to see this miserable state of affairs brought to an end. The central insight of Critical Theory can, perhaps, be summed up in Karl Marx's famous remark that while 'philosophers have understood the world, the point is to change it'. In simple terms, according to Marx, in all human societies throughout history there have been rich, powerful people and poor people, who have little control over their lives. Furthermore, in all societies throughout history there have been dominant or ruling ideas or ideologies which have been used to justify this state of affairs. According to Marx, philosophers pondered the purpose of life, but too often they have regarded themselves as detached from the preoccupations of everyday existence.

Marx, however, believed that it was impossible for intellectuals to be detached or impartial. Philosophies and theories about the world were not based on 'eternal truths', but were reflections of the historical and social conditions prevailing at the time. Intellectuals were involved in the activity of producing knowledge or 'truths' about the world which worked either to support social relationships of dominance or to challenge those of subordination. This included social institutions and practices which created and perpetuated inequalities. In this sense, then, knowledge is inherently social and political. Marx expressed moral outrage at the terrible conditions under which many men, women and children were condemned to live (see the Historical Box above). Marx believed that intellectuals should nail their colours to the mast, so to speak, by taking a position on issues of poverty and inequality and by reflecting on how they could help to bring about positive social change.

Human nature was not, Marx argued, immutable (unchangeable). People's characters or personalities – their subjectivity – were created through active engagement in social relationships. Similarly, forms of economic, social and political institutions were the product of such social interaction, established at different periods in history to fulfil certain needs or functions. What we commonly call social 'structures', such as the class system, or institutions like the family, also emerged in particular historical epochs and changed over time. It was, therefore, possible for humankind to be emancipated from repressive social relationships and forms of exploitation. In the early work of Marx, this notion of emancipation was tied to the recovery of one's sense of self, control over one's own life and in enjoying harmonious, fulfilling relationships with others.

CONCEPT BOX

How do things change? The agent–structure debate

The so-called agent–structure debate has been important and contentious in social science (see also the chapter on Social Constructivism). It is not as complicated as it sometimes sounds. In chapter 2 we considered briefly how Waltz's *Theory of International Politics* had addressed the inadequacies of realism in relation to questions of structure and agency and had tried to develop a model of both the dominant structure (the international system, the distribution of capabilities and so on, and problems of anarchy) and the main agents ('units' or states) in international relations.

Critical Theorists have rather different views on the relationship between structure and agency. They recognise that opportunities for human intervention or agency are *constrained* by historical circumstance (the dominant structures and practices of the contemporary capitalist world order), but are more optimistic about the possibilities of achieving change through political action. In this model states are not privileged as the only significant actors in IR; social movements and NGOs can also serve as radical social forces that generate change. Critical Theorists argue that those committed to the cause of human emancipation can point the way forward by analysing the nature of social repression – the kinds of structures that exist – and suggesting ways in which social, economic and political systems might be changed. Rather than offering a 'blueprint' for a perfect or Utopian society, however, Critical Theorists pay attention to the prospects for change which are emerging in the existing order. Societies are always to some extent undergoing forms of change and transition. If these tendencies are correctly understood, it is possible to intervene and influence, to some extent, the direction of change. Human beings could, then, become conscious agents of social change.

In the twentieth century the Frankfurt School continued to develop Marx's analysis of capitalism as a social and economic system. Frankfurt School scholars combined Marx's interest in capitalism with processes of rationalisation characteristic of the modern world. (In this respect, Frankfurt School scholars also owed a significant debt to the social theorist Max Weber). The term 'modern' in this usage refers to interrelated historical developments such as the secularisation of political authority in the form of the state, and the development of industrial capitalism. As Marx had observed, modern societies were characterised by a complex division of labour and a high degree of social differentiation. People also increasingly saw themselves as individuals rather than, say, members of a particular family, community or religious group. Modernity not only changed the way in which people lived, but also the way in which people thought about themselves and their lives. The modern world was one in which people believed in progress – history was moving forward and they were 'going' somewhere.

It is not surprising to find that this period of history also produced a prodigious legacy of social and political thought, much of which was universalist, secular and anti-authoritarian, seeing the major sources of social evils in prejudice and intolerance. Enlightenment thinkers concentrated on the possibilities inherent in throwing off the dictates of custom and tradition and organising society in a more rational way, in the interests of human progress and emancipation. In this respect, then, Marxism is very much a modern discourse. Indeed, Frankfurt School thinkers recognised that modernity and the Enlightenment represented a major step forward in the development of the human race, because for the first time people were able to imagine the possibility of change and progress and so, potentially, gain some control over their destinies. However, Frankfurt scholars also saw a 'dark side'

Figure 4.2   'The dark side of modernity': Stalin's series of 'Gulags' (brutal prison labour camps), extensively reported on by Alexander Solzhenitsyn, reveal left-wing alternatives to not always be as progressive as their adherents would suggest.

Source: Sipa/Rex Features.

of modernity. Drawing upon Weber's work, the Frankfurt School developed an analysis of how the growth of large-scale economic and commercial enterprises, combined with the increasing reliance upon and deference towards scientific knowledge and technical expertise, was creating a situation in which a sort of instrumental 'means–ends' rationality dominated more and more areas of life.

In classical political thought, politics as an activity was seen to be directed towards realising the conditions in which it was possible to live the good life (meaning in this context, a life guided by principles of morality and justice, rather than in the material sense of a 'good standard of living'). However, in most modern societies politics had been reduced to managerialism and finding technical solutions to a range of human problems, rather than examining the root causes of those same problems. Similarly, human knowledge was not seen as something that should be used to advance the position of human beings generally, but as an instrument of control. In their everyday working lives, busy people were preoccupied with the task in hand, and spent little time reflecting on the ultimate purpose of life, or path to human happiness and satisfaction. In society at large, capitalism manufactured a desire for consumer goods, which meant that people were encouraged to buy into consumerism and seek fulfilment through the ownership of *things*. In such circumstances, the capacity of people to think critically and reflectively was gradually being lost.

As noted above, Marx believed that eventually capitalism would reach a major crisis and collapse. He also believed that the social conditions were emerging which would enable workers to develop a consciousness of their exploitation and through the process of revolution take control of their destiny. However, Frankfurt scholars began writing in the light of one major crisis of capitalism – the worldwide depression of the 1930s. In the 1930s, in some countries, rather than rallying to the socialist cause, the working class had lent their support to right-wing populist, even fascist, movements. In addition, even where socialism *had* triumphed – in the Soviet Union, for example – it had proved to be a travesty of what Marx had envisaged. Rather than realising the conditions for the emancipation of working people, Stalinism was characterised by widespread repression and tyranny.

FILM BOX

German Expressionist cinema in the Weimar Republic

It is interesting to note that during roughly the same period that Frankfurt School scholars were debating the promise and problems of modernity against the backdrop of rising fascist sentiment in German society, many of the same themes and preoccupations were played out through the medium of German Expressionist cinema.

The rise of cinema as a cultural artefact was intimately connected with the emergence of (modern) urban living, the growth of the city, and mass society. Early cinema (and indeed much contemporary cinema) sought to represent the collective experiences and situations of modernity such as mass transport, traffic, street lighting, the crowd – all engendered by capitalism and industrialisation. Cinema was also dependent upon the financial and commercial structures of capitalism if it was to evolve into an institutional form, enabling the production of film as a mass-entertainment *product*.

The representation of the city and the kinetic, fragmentary experiences and visual excitement of city life often served to eulogise the modernist ideal of the city as a Utopia. Such imagining took a more material guise in the architecture of Le Corbusier and his contemporaries, in their conception of an ideal planned city. One such film was *Berlin, Symphony of a Great City*, a studiously modernist work. Yet, at the time it was released the values and mores which it both represented and championed were viewed by some sections of German society as degenerate. During the 1920s this position was also explicitly tied to a critique directed against the democratic government of the republic and its 'soulless' culture, nowhere more materially manifest than in decadent Berlin.

Indeed, many films of this period were characterised to some degree by a looking back to Germany's Romantic literary and musical traditions such as in Murnau's *Faust* (1926). These narratives praised folkish and traditional values of countryside over the city, and, in some cases, were in direct opposition to the new urban ways of life celebrated in *Berlin, Symphony of a Great City*. The darker inflections of modernity also found expression in films like Fritz Lang's bleak dystopian vision of *Metropolis* (1929). The dominant critical appraisal of German Expressionist cinema emphasises the reaction of Germans to the First World War and the ominous slide of Weimar Germany into Fascism. Siegfried Kracauer saw the looking back towards Romantic traditions in films such as *Faust, The Golem* and *Nosferatu* as being symptomatic of the 'retreat into the shell' (Siegfried Kracauer, *From Caligari to Hitler*, 1947) of the German psyche in the inter-war period. See Denzin, *The Cinematic City*.

Frankfurt School thinkers were forced to confront these unpleasant realities and to try to explain why working people had failed to revolt against capitalism. In trying to explain the continuation of capitalism despite crisis, Frankfurt School thinkers turned to the crucial role played by the education system and the mass media in consolidating support for capitalism, as well as organisations like the police that were used to forcibly put down strikes or other open displays of revolt against authority and private property. In this way, Critical Theorists came to understand that, while the economic organisation of society was important, other social institutions played a vital role in supporting capitalism. Through the education system and the mass media, for example, people were indoctrinated into accepting 'received truths' about the world which prevented them from understanding the true nature of the exploitation they suffered.

Frankfurt scholars also noted that changes associated with developments of the capitalist economy in the twentieth century had brought about schisms among workers – for example, a gulf between the regularly employed, casual labour and the unemployed. The introduction of labour-saving technologies produced mass unemployment in the 1930s, and the lives of the employed were better than those of the unemployed. The unemployed had very little to lose and so were more likely to take risks. However, these groups lacked organisation and consciousness. Class consciousness also diminished as tasks and knowledge became more and more fragmented, because people began to see themselves more in terms of their specialist role or job, rather than as simply 'workers'. Disillusioned with the lack of revolutionary potential in the working class, many Frankfurt School thinkers began to look for other sources of resistance and other possible agents of wide-scale social change. For example, in the post-Second World War period there was an explosion of nationalist discontent across areas of the world previously subjected to colonial rule. Later in the 1960s and 1970s, in the wake of a new wave of political radicalism sweeping across the Western world, a number of social movements emerged which organised themselves around everything from ecological issues, racism, human rights violations, civil liberties, sexuality and gender discrimination. Contemporary Critical Theorists similarly look beyond the industrial working class to the 'counter-hegemonic forces' which frequently take the form of 'new' or 'critical' social movements, engage in struggles to resist global capitalism and are, as such, potential agents of social change.

Gramsci's work on **hegemony** has also been very important in critical International Relations theory, particularly in relation to the study of world order and institutions. Gramsci highlighted the central importance of ideology in maintaining class rule and in bringing about social change. Gramsci argued that ruling groups were able to legitimise their rule by persuading people that it was just and fair. He insisted that, in order to bring about change, it was necessary to not only win the battle 'on the ground', but also in the realm of ideas. Counter-hegemony involved, therefore, not only social and political struggle against capitalism, but also the development of an alternative set of values, and, crucially, an alternative set of concepts in order to think about and describe the current social 'reality' and possible alternatives.

> Note the different uses of **'hegemony'** in Critical Theory and in neo-realist theories of 'hegemonic stability'. Neo-realists focus on dominant states whose hegemony is largely based on their military might, while for Gramscians, hegemony is the project of social forces that are able to set the parameters of public debate, mostly through other means than violent coercion.

As we have seen from our brief discussion above, increasingly critical thinkers have become, if not disillusioned, then certainly more circumspect, about the possibility of working-class revolution. Moreover, Critical Theorists have become much more sensitive to the multiple oppressions inherent in capitalism. From a critical perspective, capitalism is transforming the world radically, but in the process it is generating major forms of inequality based on class, race and gender. Capitalist enterprises are devouring more and more of the world's precious resources in order to promote mindless consumerism in the name of 'freedom of choice'. Moreover, the search for markets is destroying traditional societies and the way of life of many of the world's peoples.

However, while this more nuanced analysis of the global impact of capitalism might have more explanatory power, once the analysis of capitalism moves away from a central concern with class, what happens to the project of human emancipation? How can Critical Theorists develop a conception of a fair and just society, if it is no longer a question of getting rid of inequalities rooted in social class? Who will be the agents of radical change? Moreover, what does it mean to be 'emancipated'? Jürgen Habermas has become an influential figure in critical thought because he seems to have an answer to these questions. While Habermas has not devoted much attention to international politics in his own work, IR scholars have drawn upon key concepts and ideas in his work in the service of developing a critical international relations theory and in opening up a new research agenda within IR (see the Concept Box below).

A key concern of Critical Theory has been how to develop institutions and forums in international politics that facilitate negotiation. In this way conflicts are settled by consensus rather than power, although Critical Theorists differ from, say, neo-liberals as to how this might be achieved. We might argue that the 'fourth debate' or the 'next stage' in the development of IR (discussed at greater length in chapter 7 and in the conclusion to this book) was, in part, inspired by a desire to escape from realist/neo-realist despair and to challenge the idea that international politics would always be dominated by the pursuit of power and the instrumental and/or strategic interests of states.

Habermas was critical of positivist approaches to the social sciences because he believed that the knowledge they generated was essentially knowledge generated in the service of social control. Critical Theorists believe that knowledge about the social world is sought in the interests of furthering human emancipation, or at least it should be. Following a typology first developed by Frankfurt School scholars, Richard Ashley (who would later come to be identified with postmodernism/post-structuralism in IR – see the following chapter) argued that there were different kinds of knowledge: knowledge that served a technical interest in understanding and extending control over nature and society; knowledge that arose from a practical interest in understanding how to maintain social order among communities; and knowledge born of the emancipatory interest human beings held in identifying and eradicating unnecessary social confinements and constraints. Andrew Linklater (discussed at greater length in the Author Box on p. 122) has been one influential IR theorist who has drawn upon Habermas to suggest new institutional arrangements that facilitate open dialogue and allow the conduct of international relations to become more consensual and less coercive.

In one crucial respect Habermas's work represented a major departure from Marxist analysis. Habermas argued that, hitherto, Marxist analysis had failed to pay adequate attention to the central importance of communication in shaping consciousness and developing understanding of one's self and one's relationship to others. Marx was correct in stressing the inherently social nature of human beings. However, Marx limited himself to analysing the particular kinds of social organisation that existed. The sociability of human beings is, of course, also expressed through language. Habermas argued that the role of language and communication had been neglected in critical thought. According to Habermas, communication – the use of language and the manipulation of symbols – allows a sort of collective learning process to take place. Through language and communication, human beings construct **intersubjective** knowledge about the world.

> **Intersubjective:** intersubjective meaning is that established (or constructed) through the interaction of 'subjects'. The idea implies that 'meaning' is established through interaction or dialogue between conscious subjects.

This emphasis on the importance of communication and human understanding led Habermas to advocate a process of open dialogue and democracy in the interests of furthering human emancipation. Habermas was a very modern thinker in the sense that he valued the modern achievement of being able to criticise, challenge and question authority and existing duties and obligations. Habermas believed, however, that such criticism was only a prelude to developing a better understanding of what it meant to live in a moral society in which people were treated justly. He argued that the formation of self-understanding, self-identity and moral judgements concerning justice were intimately linked; we become aware of our own self and our own needs and desires by entering into dialogue with others and becoming aware of the needs, interests and desires of others. Habermas also moved away from orthodox Marxist thinking by arguing that social movements promoting feminism or green issues or indigenous peoples also resisted the extension of 'technical' or 'means–ends' rationality into all spheres of social life, promoted alternative values, and so could contribute to an emancipatory politics. However, this emancipatory politics was no longer rooted in the notion of labour free from alienation. Emancipation was about extending the realm of moral understanding and justice in human life. Habermas was committed to the democratic process because it fostered dialogue and this was necessary in order to further develop our moral codes and thinking about justice.

The problem is, of course, that a process of genuinely open dialogue is difficult to achieve in a divided society where people have different – even opposing – interests. Habermas recognised this problem, but insisted that it was, nevertheless, an ideal to be striven for. For this reason, much of his early work was concerned with the condition under which it was possible to create an 'ideal speech situation'. In an ideal speech situation, all people would be able to participate in open dialogue, black or white, rich or poor, Christian or Muslim, male or female. In such a situation, people might be encouraged to consider the perspective of the 'other', rather than just their own selfish interest.

CONCEPT BOX

Critical Theory as the 'next stage' in IR theory

In the first instance, IR scholars drew upon Critical Theory to develop a critique of the dominance of positivism in IR. We will return to this critique in our concluding chapter. However, beyond this initial project of critiquing the 'mainstream' or 'orthodoxy' in IR, a number of scholars pointed to ways that Critical Theory – and the ideas of Gramsci and Habermas particularly – could advance substantive research and theoretical understanding in IR. For example, Robert Cox, an influential figure within International Political Economy (see the Author Box on p. 120), not only used key ideas from Critical Theory to criticise the dominance of 'problem solving' approaches to IR, but also drew upon Gramsci and others to map out a critical conception of 'world order' as a radical alternative to the neo-realist conception of the state system and international anarchy.

Scholars such as Andrew Linklater and Mark Hoffman, saw great promise in Habermas's concepts of discursive ethics and communicative action in opening up new theoretical departures in IR theory that would help us escape from the realist/neo-realist 'tradition of despair'. For example, Habermas' concepts of communicative action and discourse pointed to possibilities of dialogue across international (and indeed other) boundaries as a first stage in understanding the conditions under which global justice was possible. During the 1980s scholars who embraced Critical Theory engaged in a debate with their detractors in the pages of a number of influential IR journals (particularly *Millennium* – see Further Reading). What emerged from such debates was a recognition that dialogue, intersubjective negotiation and respect for the 'other' was every bit as much the 'stuff' of international relations as war and oppressive practices like imperialism.

However, these debates also revealed uneasiness in some quarters about the universal aspirations of Critical Theory. Post-structuralists rejected the idea that 'common understanding' could be secured through dialogue because cultural (and other) differences meant that often people talked at cross-purposes – there was not and could not be a 'universal' point of view. Moreover, rather than seek 'common understanding' or aim at achieving an intersubjectively negotiated 'universalism', we *should* embrace the pluralism and diversity of humanity.

On a more practical level, it was argued that the 'ideal speech situation' which must in theory be secured before dialogue could ensue, was impossible to achieve in reality. For example, feminists argued that 'communication across boundaries' often marginalised women's voices. Furthermore, it was doubtful whether communicative rationality could overcome the problems of the pursuit of interests and power in international relations. The problem of power in IR in turn highlighted the dominance of Western states and a particular type of Western rationality in international public spheres, undermining the notion that participants in dialogue had equal access and influence.

Assumptions

From the above we can suggest the following assumptions common to varieties of Critical Theory:

1. 'Human nature' is not fixed or essential, but shaped by the social conditions that exist at any period in time.
2. These conditions, and therefore world politics, are themselves shaped by historical struggles between different social forces.
3. Individual people (subjects) can be grouped into identifiable collectivities which might in turn be said to have concrete interests.
4. Despite differences – for example, race, ethnicity, gender, class – all human beings share an interest in achieving emancipation. Critical Theory is, thus, universalist in character.
5. There are different types of knowledge. Traditional, positivist science is interested in 'problem-solving' knowledge. Critical Theory is interested in knowledge that will lead to emancipation.
6. Core to emancipation is the achievement of dialogue in which those communicating take each other seriously and do not try to impose their argument on the back of their more powerful status.

Themes

Thus far we have been concerned to differentiate between Critical Theory in IR in the Gramscian tradition and Critical Theory that draws upon ideas from the work of Jürgen Habermas. We now turn to how Gramscian and Habermasian ideas have been used to help us make sense of some of our core themes in IR.

The state and power

You will recall from chapter 2 that realism takes the nature of the state and the state system as a basic starting point for theorising international relations. In so far as realists are interested in economics, it is only as it affects state behaviour, or constitutes an issue in international politics. From a critical perspective, it makes no sense to treat the state as the basic unit of analysis in international relations, nor does it make sense to separate economics from politics in this way. In the first place, the state is only one form of political organisation to exist among human beings. From a critical perspective, understanding the historical nature of the state and the state system is crucial, but this historical understanding is lost if we adopt a 'state as actor' approach to international relations.

We suggested above that Critical Theory is oriented towards the project of human emancipation. It follows from this that, when Critical Theorists engage in the process of thinking about the forms of political, social and economic organisation that exist in the world, they are explicitly seeking to answer the question: how far do existing arrangements constrain or facilitate the project of human emancipation? In relation to the current 'world order', key questions for Critical Theorists are: What is the state? Why did the state become the dominant form of political organisation globally? What kind of world order might there be in the future? What tendencies can we see in the existing order that point the way to future changes?

Before the world was constituted as a system or society of nation-states, there existed many different forms of political organisation across the world. We have become accustomed to thinking about the state and the state system as a European invention, but something akin to what we would now recognise as a system of states emerged in Northern Africa between AD 900 and 1500, closely linked to the expansion of trans-Saharan trade. During roughly the same period, much of the world was divided into large empires, e.g. the Mongol Empire (1206–1405), or the Ottoman Empire (1301–1520). In much of what we now call Western Europe, there existed a system of Feudal Monarchy between 1154 and 1314. What we would now recognise as the modern state system gradually evolved in Northern Europe between 1500 and 1688 and was consolidated by the rise of nationalism in Europe between 1800 and 1914.

At the time that the state system was emerging, European merchants and traders were embarking on a voyage of 'discovery', seeking out new trading opportunities in far-flung corners of the world. This, in turn, saw the emergence of Spanish and Portuguese colonies in Latin America, parts of India and in South East Asia between 1500 and 1600. Between 1600 and 1713 waves of British, French and Dutch expansion occurred, resulting eventually in the colonisation of territories throughout Africa, the Indian sub-continent, South East Asia and the West Indies. Here the trade in luxury goods like spices was central to the expansion of world trade and the emergence of a new form of political organisation around the world. The Industrial Revolution only intensified the search for new markets, and generated new forms of political control, as Europe came to dominate much of the globe during the eighteenth and nineteenth centuries. Many former colonies did not achieve formal independence until after the Second World War.

HISTORICAL/WORLD EXAMPLE BOX

The trade in spices

In northern Europe before the invention of winter feed for cattle in the late seventeenth century, many beasts were slaughtered every autumn and the meat was preserved for winter eating, hence the high demand for spices both as a preservative and condiment. Pepper grew in many parts of southern Asia, while cinnamon was found in Ceylon (Sri Lanka) and nutmeg in the Banda Islands. In the sixteenth century trade in these goods had been organised and shared out among Malay, Indian, Persian, Arab and Portuguese merchants. In the seventeenth century, by a combination of diplomacy and force, the Dutch East India Company seized control of the source of many valuable spices and established a virtual monopoly on their trade into Europe. The Dutch East India Company is an early example of a transnational enterprise. (Information from Barraclough, G. (ed.) (1978), *The Times Atlas of World History*, London: Times Books.)

We will not labour the historical development of the different kinds of 'world order' here; suffice to say that the state appears to be a particular kind of political organisation, which emerged at a time of early capitalism in Europe and has gradually been adopted all over the world. Regardless of precisely how this relationship is conceived, the close connection between the emergence of the state system and capitalism is central to critical approaches to International Relations. The state system has developed in conjunction with, or alongside, a capitalist world economy and an over-arching culture of modernity. For this reason, from a critical perspective it makes no sense to view economics and politics as distinct realms of human activity – political and economic forms of organisation are intimately connected. Moreover, a critical conception of world order does not begin and end with different types of political organisation. World order also includes economic forms – patterns of trade and commerce and emergent markets – and the particular configuration of social forces – merchants, traders, industrialists and workers – who are all, in some way or other, drawn into this global system.

The state clearly performs a number of roles which are vital for a capitalist economy, including the provision of a system of law to regulate contracts between individuals and companies, and a police force to ensure that society remains orderly. Orthodox Marxists hold that the state mediates conflict resulting from class struggle. In this way, the state legitimises and ensures continuing class rule. The state also maintains conditions conducive to economic growth ('capital accumulation' in Marxist jargon). While there are some similarities, there are important differences between Critical Theory and orthodox Marxist views of the nature and role of the state.

First, Critical Theorists pay much closer attention to the role of ideology in maintaining the rule of dominant groups. The concept of hegemony expresses the idea that dominant groups establish and legitimise their rule through the realm of culture and ideas. Hegemony is seen to rest on a broad measure of consent; nevertheless, it functions according to basic principles that ensure the continuing supremacy of leading social classes, within the state. The stronger the ruling group, the less need it has to use force. Hegemony is the outcome of class struggle and serves to legitimise capitalist rule. Gramscians use the term 'hegemonic project' to refer to the way in which classes present their particular interests as the interests of all people – that is, universal interests. In this way, particular classes are able to maintain their power.

Second, hegemony is used in Critical Theory to describe the dominance of certain major states in the world. Critical Theorists argue that, while we now live in a state system in which all members are formally equal, different states perform different functions to facilitate the opening-up of global markets and the operations of capitalist enterprises, and have different power and influence. So, for example, in the current world order the USA is the major, hegemonic state which works to ensure that the world is 'made safe for capitalism'.

Third, Critical Theorists argue that the state does not reflect the interests of dominant social classes in a straightforward way. It certainly plays an important role in supporting an oppressive social order. Gramsci argued that hegemony was exercised by a class via the agency of a party or through the state. Clearly, the historical emergence and evolution of the state and the state system has worked to ensure that capitalist economic and social relations are fairly securely embedded across the world. However, as noted earlier, contemporary Critical Theorists regard the state as relatively autonomous. This means that the state reflects both the interests of capital, and also pressures from counter-hegemonic groups.

The degree to which counter-hegemonic groups achieve influence varies over time (see the earlier discussion of structure and agency). In the current period, the globalisation of capital has undermined the autonomy of the state and its ability to meet the demands of its citizens for welfare and economic and social security. The so-called 'rolling back of state', which has been a phenomenon across the industrialised world during global restructuring, must be seen as a means of insulating economic policy from popular pressures, specifically the demands of poor groups. At the same time, trade unions have been weakened and the position of capital in the production process significantly strengthened. Thus, in the contemporary world order capitalism is fairly securely embedded. Moreover, neo-liberalism serves as a powerful ideology in furthering the hegemonic project of dominant states and social forces. However, we can also identify 'counter-hegemonic' tendencies and social forces that struggle to achieve new ways of living. For example, the Green movement or radical forms of feminism both seek to reconstitute human societies and human relationships on the basis of radically different social and political values.

WORLD EXAMPLE BOX

States and Markets: the de-regulation and re-regulation of finance

Historically, control over interest rates has allowed governments to exercise some influence over other major economic indicators such as the rate of inflation. For this reason it has been considered a vital tool of economic policy for any government seeking to manipulate the economy to achieve certain goals like full employment and the redistribution of wealth through taxation or the provision of welfare goods (characteristic of the post-war Keynesian consensus period).

One of the first acts of the British Labour Government on assuming power in the summer of 1997 was to hand over the control of interest rates to the Bank of England. In doing so, then Chancellor (now Prime Minister) Gordon Brown was in effect admitting that government control over the economy was impossible in an age of globalisation, and that henceforth social democratic parties, like the British Labour Party, would have to work with the forces of global capitalism, rather than against them. From a critical perspective actions like these represented a fundamental shift in the balance of global social forces in favour of capital and against labour.

Interestingly, if we fast forward to 2008–9, it becomes apparent that financial re-regulation of markets is now very much back on the international political agenda. In the absence of regulation, competition in financial markets has led to irresponsible loose lending and increasingly risky forms of investment, leading to a massive failure in public confidence (which is vital to the smooth functioning of contemporary capitalism) and a near collapse of global financial markets. In this context, there have been growing demands that states once again assert a degree of control over markets. It is doubtful, however, that this trend really represents the reassertion of labour power, since the ensuing recession has led to the loss of hundreds of thousands of jobs across the world and, moreover, many ordinary tax payers will ultimately foot the bill for the bank bail-out regardless of whether or not they benefited from the initial financial 'boom'. It seems that we are now living in an age where the state's role in the economy has been reduced to that of intervention in the interests of 'crisis management'.

Figure 4.3 Never a frown with Gordon Brown? The decision by the incoming Labour Government in Britain in 1997 to hand over control of interest rates to the Bank of England showed the increasing limitations on states to act as they wished in the face of global financial pressures.

Source: Alistair MacDonald/Rex Features.

It follows from this discussion of the state system and world order, that power cannot be understood solely in terms of the military and/or economic might of the state. Clearly, power is exercised directly by states in some situations. In 'making the world safe for capitalism', the USA has intervened in conflicts all over the world in order to try to influence the outcome in ways which favour global capitalism. However, power is also exercised through a range of other social institutions, and works to support a particular kind of social order. The state supports a capitalist order. In so doing, the state supports particular kinds of power relations that exist among social groups: for example, the power of business and commerce over workers, the power of multinational corporations over local communities dependent upon the employment it generates and the power of currency speculators, investors and traders in basic commodities to shape the global economy and influence the distribution of wealth throughout the world. Social and economic power is also exercised insidiously through the spread of certain ideas and beliefs in society that work to legitimise the existing order.

Institutions and world order

Robert Cox (States, Social Forces and World Order)

In 1986 Robert Cox outlined what has become an extremely influential conception of 'states, social forces and world order'. Cox suggested that advances in communications and the globalisation of finance have brought about a radical change in the way production is organised across the globe. In the nineteenth and early twentieth centuries the production of goods and services was confined to particular countries, and products were then traded between countries. However, today the production process is spread across countries. For example, the production of different car components might be spread across a number of countries, and the assembly of these various components to make a car might take place in another part of the world. This method of production has brought with it a new model of social relations based on a core–periphery structure of production, with a relatively small core of relatively permanent employees in the North, handling finance, research and development and technological organisation, and a periphery consisting of the dependent components of the production process. This has allowed capital to take advantage of a more precariously employed labour force segmented by ethnicity, gender, nationality or religion.

To some extent these groups have displaced class as the focus of social struggle, but like the 'old' working class they derive their force from the resentment they feel at the exploitation which they suffer. Disaffected groups must organise transnationally if they are to be an effective oppositional force. However, increasingly, as the economy globalises, major economic classes become organised globally in response, in order to achieve hegemonic domination, while disadvantaged groups are fragmented along the lines of nationality, ethnicity, class and gender. In response, trade unions and other groups have attempted to organise globally in order to strengthen workers' rights, but their efforts have been thwarted by the logic of competition. For example, the International Labour Organisation (ILO) has endeavoured to develop global standards in relations to workers' rights and conditions of employment throughout the world, but have – ironically – often faced opposition from developing countries who fear that their 'competitive edge' (effectively a cheap and flexible labour force) will be eroded.

Unsurprisingly, Critical Theory has made a major contribution to our understanding of world order and institutions. We have already seen how a critical conception of the state leads to a particular view of the nature of world order. At this point, it is helpful to develop this notion of world order a little further and to attempt to explain how it helps us to understand the role of international institutions such as the International Monetary Fund and the World Bank. As we saw above, in the post-Second World War period the state has become 'internationalised' in the sense that it has become the dominant form of political organisation across the world. The state has become internationalised in a second sense; its traditional regulatory functions are now performed by different states and organisations. If we think about the state in terms of what it does, the control and regulation of capitalism, rather than as an entity or 'actor', we see that these functions are now dispersed among different states in the world and among a range of international institutions and regimes.

The Gramscian notion of transnational class alliances and hegemonic domination has been successfully applied to the conception of world order. Critical Theorists adapted this idea to suggest that the dominant state in the world creates order on the basis of ideology. For example, the Bretton Woods System (BWS), which was discussed at greater length in chapters 1 and 2, would not have been possible without the support of a hegemonic state – the USA. The USA played a number of crucial roles in establishing the BWS and making it work effectively. Perhaps most important, the USA provided vital ideological support for the new world order, arguing that free trade and monetary stability would allow freedom and democracy to flourish throughout the world.

As is apparent in our earlier discussion, world orders do change and alternative political, economic and social arrangements can and do emerge. Critical Theorists are concerned with the nature of such change and the ways in which social forces and social structures enter periods of transition. The existing order is not 'fixed', because social structures comprise institutions and the prevailing socioeconomic form of organisation and ideas.

Although social action is constrained by structures, these can be transformed by collective action involving leading or subordinate groups in society. Stephen Gill and David Law argue that there are new sources of conflict and cleavages that are working their way slowly but surely into the foundations of world politics. Counter-hegemonic forces are challenging prevailing institutional and political arrangements. Gill also argues that there is an urgent need for a counter-hegemony based on an alternative set of values, concepts and concerns, coming perhaps from organisations like Amnesty International, Oxfam and Greenpeace. These movements exist within states, but they have grown up in different parts of the world and are transnational in essence. Intellectuals also have a role to play in generating change by developing a 'counter-hegemonic' set of concepts and concerns to deal with the problems of militarism and economic and social inequalities.

Identity and community

So far, in our discussion of themes, we have concentrated on Gramscian Critical Theory. At this juncture, it is appropriate to consider the ways in which Habermasian ideas have been influential in International Relations. In our discussion of the state above, we tended to concentrate on the roles and functions which it fulfilled for capitalism, but suggested that to some degree the state also reflects the struggle for political influence among oppositional groups. Critical Theorists such as Andrew Linklater are interested particularly in how far the state and the state system open up or close off possibilities for human emancipation.

Enlightenment thinkers believed that the modern state created the conditions in which it was possible to live under the rule of law and according to principles of justice. Furthermore, people, or at least some people, enjoyed the status of active citizens, playing a role in deciding the politics of their country in the public sphere where issues of law, justice and morality were debated openly, rather than of subjects who simply obeyed the monarch. In so far as 'emancipation' was closely connected with a sense of autonomy and control over one's life, this was a major step forward for human beings.

The rise of nationalism as a powerful ideology in the eighteenth and nineteenth centuries strengthened the claims of the state to be the sole legitimate representative of citizens, in the first place by extending citizenship rights and, secondly, by inculcating a feeling of emotional attachment to the nation-state. As we saw in chapter 2, realists continue to regard the state as the dominant form of community and the only significant expression of political identity in the world. In the twentieth century nationalist sentiment worked to challenge the authority and legitimacy of existing state boundaries. However, radical and secessionist national movements, acting under the banner of the rights of people to self-determination, only strengthened the attachment between the individual and the 'national homeland' and thus consolidated, rather than weakened, the state system.

In some respects, the expansion of the state system can be viewed as a positive development, because it extends the principles of self-determination and citizenship to more and more of the world's peoples. However, at the same time, the nation-state embodies something of a moral contradiction, because it is at once both an inclusionary and exclusionary form of political community. The nation-state is inclusionary, because it is founded on the idea that all citizens are equal. There are certain rights which flow from citizenship and these should be enjoyed by every member of the community. All citizens are, therefore, of equal moral worth. However, the nation-state is by its very nature exclusionary. It discriminates against 'foreigners' on the grounds that they are different. The differences between 'insiders' and 'outsiders' are held to be morally relevant. The bounded community of the nation-state excludes people whose 'difference' is deemed to threaten the state's distinctive identity. International law sets out just what obligations states owe to non-citizens temporarily residing within the boundaries of the state, who, among other things, must be protected from harm; in certain cases states might extend temporary rights of asylum to foreigners who fear persecution in their homeland. Nevertheless, while, say, the British state has a certain obligation to 'foreigners', these are clearly not the same as or equal to the obligations owed to 'nationals'. Moreover, the boundaries of the communities are constantly being policed to ensure against 'invasion' from outsiders, so much so that we regard 'foreigners' as a threat to the extent that we can even debate the morality of the use of nuclear weapons to deter outsiders from encroaching on our 'space'. The emancipatory project at the heart of Critical Theory necessarily raises questions about the limits of political community, how boundaries between self and other are constructed and the moral implications of this.

Critical Theorists are interested in how the boundaries of community change over time. So, historically, certain groups, for example, women and working-class men, have been denied citizenship on the grounds that they are 'different' – less rational and not up to the demands of active citizenship. Women, for example, were held to be in need of strong moral guidance from their menfolk. Of course, working-class men and women have made great strides in overcoming such prejudices and now enjoy rights of citizenship in most states around the world although, as we will see in chapter 6, significant forms of discrimination still exist.

Since the UN was established in 1945, there has been a gradual development of human-rights law which recognises the equal moral worth of every human being. The widespread commitment to respect human rights seems to suggest that there exists amongst humankind a moral conviction that all individuals belong not only to sovereign-states, but to a more inclusive community of humankind even if, in practice, this has been denied to some groups. Arguably, we might now be witnessing the eclipse of the sovereign state system in favour of more cosmopolitan forms of identity and community. As is evident from our earlier discussion of world order and the increasingly globalised nature of social relations, expressions of loyalty and solidarity can be both sub-state and transnational. Social movements give expression to, or reflect, the plural forms of identity, loyalty and solidarity. These groups express commitment to various 'communities' and, increasingly, these are transnational in nature.

AUTHOR BOX

Andrew Linklater and the transformation of political community

New forms of political identification and expressions of transnational 'community' have prompted Critical Theorists to pose questions about the extent to which human beings owe obligations to the people of the world rather than simply fellow-citizens. Andrew Linklater argues that Critical Theorists remain committed to the creation of 'the good society', which is not limited to the nation-state. His point of departure is the need for a return to the classical understanding of politics as orientated towards the emancipation of people. The first stage in this project is to understand the way people learn how to exclude those deemed to be 'different' from the moral community. This necessarily involves moving beyond a conventional Marxist concern with social class to consider how people of different races, ethnic backgrounds and gender have been, or continue to be, discriminated against.

As well as understanding the dynamics of social exclusion, however, it is also important to recognise that these practices are challenged by groups involved in both national and transnational political action. Moreover, there are many arenas where people think about and debate moral and political issues. Drawing upon Habermasian ideas about the importance of communication and dialogue in achieving an emancipatory politics, Linklater highlights the multiple 'public spheres' in which these kinds of debates take place. He claims that political communities are already being transformed by, for example, struggles over equality, rights, claims to resources and notions of obligations to others, and how they might change more radically in the future.

Inequality and justice

While there are variations and nuances within different strands of Critical Theory, all Critical Theorists share a fundamental commitment to human equality. In contemporary Critical Theory other forms of inequality and discrimination, such as sexism and racism, and the denial of human rights to some groups, are also recognised as highly significant. However, once the multiple sources of oppression are recognised, it raises the question of how can a more equal and just world be realised.

Critical Theorists are sceptical of liberal schemes because these grant formal equality to people, while also sanctioning a social and economic order that generates great inequalities in wealth and power. However, they also recognise that, while experiments in state socialism have been partially successful in creating a more equal society, this has often been at the cost of widespread oppression and tyranny. The great challenge for Critical Theorists is to realise an emancipatory politics which is socially inclusive and democratic. In a world divided along lines of nationality, ethnicity, religion, culture, class, sexuality and gender, how can such a project be realised? There have been a number of responses to this question. One response has been to draw upon Habermas' notion of dialogic politics. Dialogic politics appears to meet the needs of a world in which the nation-state remains significant, but which is no longer the only site in which debates about equality and justice are taking place, and a time when liberal and/or Western visions of equality and justice have been subject to criticism.

It is recognised that it might not always be possible to reach agreement, especially in situations where societies have radically different forms of government and cultural preferences. Dialogue does not necessarily have to reach consensus. The primary function of global communities of discourse, according to Linklater, is to reflect the heterogeneous quality of international society. However, the commitment to dialogue requires efforts to build wider communication channels. The universal communication community may be unobtainable, but it remains the ultimate standard of social criticism to which we should aspire.

Conflict and violence

From this perspective, human conflict is not rooted in the problem of anarchy *per se*, but in the nature of global capitalism. The Gramscian variant of Critical Theory accepts, with some qualifications and modifications, the more orthodox Marxist view that major wars this century have been caused by the search for raw materials and resources and the forcible opening up of large areas of the world to capitalist expansion. On the other hand, many struggles for 'national' liberation have come about in response to forms of colonial or imperialist domination. Capitalism, by its very nature, generates conflict and violence.

A second variant of Critical Theory influenced by Habermas has taken the notion of intersubjectivity, dialogue and negotiation as a starting point for understanding how peaceful change can be promoted. While we are unable to include a detailed discussion of key works in this text, we draw your attention to the potential of applying Habermas' ideas in relation to processes of diplomatic negotiation and conflict resolution.

CONCEPT BOX

Beyond Power Politics

One way to understand Critical Theory is to contrast Critical Theory with Realism. Realists regard the international realm as an area of power politics in which states must necessarily prioritise the aim of achieving security and safeguarding their (national) interests. Realists take the problem of 'anarchy' as a given. They believe that, regardless of how the world came to be organised as a system of nation-states, where there is no sovereign centralised authority, this is the world order that we currently live in. Anarchy confronts individual states and statesmen with certain 'problems' that must be confronted (hence, realism is a 'problem-solving' theory in Cox's term). Notably the 'problem' that the state has enemies and might be subjected to hostile aggression or even military attack at any time. This being the case, states – or statesmen – must necessarily think strategically and act instrumentally. State action is thus *strategic* and *instrumental* and the international realm is dominated by strategic and instrumental behaviour. In contrast, Critical Theorists argue that world order is not immutable, but can be changed for the better. Thus, strategic interest in the control and manipulation of others need not necessarily prevail in IR, because anarchy and power politics are not enduring features of international relations. Critical Theorists argue that theory should be directed towards understanding the possibilities for change and how to exploit possibilities for change, so that a – new – politics of negotiation rooted in recognition of and respect for differences is realised. Critical Theorists are deeply concerned with the ethical dilemmas and responsibilities inherent in the practices of world politics and the theorisation of IR.

Peace and security

As is evident from our brief discussion of the role of the USA since the Second World War, Gramscians are highly critical of realist and liberal notions of peace and security and how they might be achieved. International institutions largely reflect the interests of hegemonic states who act to ensure that world markets remain stable, contracts are honoured and open revolt is suppressed. For Critical Theorists, genuine peace and security will only be achieved when the major contradictions of capitalism which generate economic crisis and instability are overcome, when people are no longer treated as the means (labour) to an end (production for profit) in a thoroughly exploitative and alienating system, and when the earth's resources are no longer squandered recklessly to satisfy the wants, rather than needs, of consumers. Some strands of Critical Theory inform the developing **school of critical security studies** within International Relations.

Critical security studies

The changed political circumstances of the post-Cold War world and new theoretical departures in IR, such as Critical Theory, have encouraged a radical rethinking of the concept of 'security'. As we highlighted in chapter 2, for much of the Cold War period, realist, and later neo-realist, discourse dominated thinking about security. Disenchanted with what had become a realist/neo-realist 'orthodoxy' in IR, a new school of 'critical security studies' emerged in the post-Cold War period which challenged the fundamental assumptions of realisms, and argued for a radical new approach to security.

Krause and Williams have argued that the debate within security studies has arisen out of three related areas. First, the end of the Cold War and the collapse of the Soviet Union (events which realist analysts had failed to predict, and did not appear to be able to explain convincingly) meant that there was an urgent need to think about what security might mean in a post-Cold War world.

Second, and relatedly, the need to make the discipline relevant to the concerns of contemporary international relations. For example, the resurgence of nationalisms and inter-ethnic conflicts across the post-Cold War world put issues of identity firmly back onto the agenda of International Relations, while phenomena like population growth, migration, poverty, global recession, global warming, pollution and the rapid and indiscriminate use of the world's natural resources were increasingly being articulated as 'threats' to the future well-being and security of humanity as a whole.

Third, discontent with the ontological and epistemological assumptions of realism/neo-realism opened up a wide-ranging debate about what security now means, whose security matters and how security can best be promoted or achieved. We will leave debates on ontology and epistemology for the time being, but they are taken up and developed in the concluding chapter. At this stage it is enough to note that critical security studies no longer privileged the state as the *fundamental referent* of security and the 'conflict and war' dominated understanding of security central to realism/neo-realism.

The **school of 'critical' security studies** also embraces social constructivists whose work will be discussed at greater length in chapter 7.

While there are important differences between Critical Theorists and constructivists (collectively making 'critical security studies'), what they have in common is a concern with the processes through which individuals, collectivities and 'threats' get constructed as 'social facts', rather than concentrating on supposed 'objective' threats to the state that are 'out there' in the real world. The security debate has also led to a problematisation of dominant conceptions of identities and boundaries in which traditional approaches to security have been framed. Here the work of post-structuralist scholars has also been influential (see chapter 5, particularly references to David Campbell's work).

Summary

1. Critical Theory became influential in IR from the 1980s onwards.
2. Like structuralism, Critical Theory is influenced by Marxism, though more by the early 'humanistic' Marx, in contrast to structuralism which takes more inspiration from later 'economistic' and 'scientific' Marxism.
3. Critical Theorists see an intimate relationship between theory and practice.
4. Critical Theorists hold that knowledge is ideology, not truth, although some believe that it is possible to negotiate or agree upon propositions.
5. As well as roots in Marx, Critical Theory has also evolved from the ideas of the Frankfurt School (particularly Jürgen Habermas) and Italian Marxist Antonio Gramsci.
6. Critical Theory is very much a 'modern' project, because it aims to further human emancipation. However, Critical Theory acknowledges and seeks to overcome the 'dark side of modernity'.
7. Many Critical Theorists recognise that class-based oppression is not the only form inherent in capitalist societies. Other oppressions include those on the basis of ethnicity, gender, nationality and so on.
8. Contemporary Gramscians see 'counter-hegemonic' forces (struggles to resist global capitalism) in terms of new social movements (women, environment for example) and look beyond the industrial working class for potential agents of social change. Habermas similarly believes that social movements are a radical force in international politics because they ascribe to value systems and advocate ways of living that challenge dominant (capitalist) forms of economic and social organisation.
9. Critical Theory makes us aware of the historically contingent nature of certain features of human life and reminds us, therefore, that international relations are not fixed or immutable.
10. Critical Theory makes claims in the name of all of humankind – it is universalistic. For this reason, it questions forms of exclusion or discrimination which make distinctions between different groups of people. This necessarily raises questions about how we define ourselves, and how we distinguish ourselves from others, leading to consideration of how boundaries between communities are drawn and the consequences of this.

Criticisms

One criticism of Gramscian Critical Theory is that it concentrates too much on the significance of social class and class relationships and, in consequence, is blind to other forms of inequality and exclusion. As we have seen, this criticism is not entirely justified, as many Critical Theorists do recognise the significance of gender inequalities or that people can be discriminated against, excluded or somehow treated differently according to their sexuality, race or ethnic origins. However, it is fair to say that there is a tendency among Gramscians to continue to concentrate on (or privilege) social class in their empirical work.

A related criticism is that Gramscians privilege class in their conception of 'interests'. We might regard ourselves as having concrete interests which derive from our gender or nationality. Moreover, our notion of where our interests lie might also change significantly over time. Even within capital, there might be different interests depending on whether the capitalist is an industrialist or involved in commerce and this undermines to some extent the notion of transnational class alliances.

In relation to Critical Theory inspired by Habermas, critics have argued that the 'dialogic' model is flawed because access (the ability to have one's voice heard) is inevitably restricted by existing inequalities. It is impossible to establish an 'ideal speech situation'. By and large, the poor (those with little education or access to technology) are likely to be seriously under-represented. A related criticism is that the dialogic model of politics fails to take into account the fragility of a moral point of view in a world characterised by massive inequalities: that is to say, the powerful are unlikely to concede their advantage, under critical review, even if 'justice' demands a redistribution of resources and wealth.

Finally, the universalistic aspirations of Critical Theory have been challenged. For example, postmodernists argue that it is impossible to establish what *is* morally right or just, even through the process of intersubjective dialogue, because there is no agreement about these issues across cultures. The most likely result of a (critical) project of this kind would, then, be a profoundly Western, middle-class and gendered conception of a 'good society', masquerading as a 'universal' point of view.

Common misunderstandings

1. *Critical Theorists are so-called because they criticise other perspectives like liberalism or realism.* No. It is certainly the case that critique and criticism is an important aspect of Critical Theory. It is only through critique and criticism that the interested, partial and ideological nature of knowledge claims can be exposed. However, Critical Theorists are also interested in going beyond criticism, and so concentrate mainly on how theory can be used to inform an emancipatory project.

2. *Critical Theory is the same as postmodernism.* No. As you will see in the following chapter, postmodernism and Critical Theory are different in many important respects. However, confusion arises because the term 'critical theory' is sometimes used in a generic sense to describe a number of post-positivist approaches including the Frankfurt School, postmodernism, feminism and even Green thought.

3. *Critical Theorists believe that the collapse of capitalism and worldwide socialism is inevitable.* No. While this view of history is found in much orthodox Marxist thought (see preceding chapter), Critical Theorists argue that economic, social and political change is something which must be struggled for. A much greater emphasis is placed, therefore, on the need for human intervention – agency – and political struggle, in bringing about change.

4. *Critical Theorists argue that there is no 'real world'.* No. In contrast to postmodernists (see following chapter), Critical Theorists emphasise the existence of real material structures and power relations. However, Critical Theorists contend that our understanding of the nature of this reality is always mediated through ideas and concepts, which are in turn related to concrete interests. Therefore, Critical Theory – while not neglecting the material realm – places much greater emphasis on the ideational dimension of international politics.

5. *Critical Theorists hold that social class is the only significant division which exists in human society.* Not quite. Certainly, Critical Theorists are interested in class divisions and social inequalities rooted in social class. Some might even believe that these are indeed of major significance. However, most Critical Theorists now accept that there are many forms of social inequality and many forms of oppression, discrimination and social exclusion.

Further reading

Ashley, R.K. (1981), 'Political Realism and Human Interests', *International Studies Quarterly*, Vol. 25, No. 2, pp. 204–36 (a very early and still influential article on the need to develop a Critical Theory of IR).

Cox, R.W. (1986), 'Social forces, states and world order', *Millennium: Journal of International Studies*, Vol. 10, No. 2, pp. 126–55, reprinted as 'Social forces, states and world orders: Beyond international relations theory' in R. Keohane (ed.), *Neorealism and its Critics*, New York: Columbia University Press, pp. 204–54 (another influential piece within the Critical IR literature, particularly useful in setting out the distinction between problem solving and Critical Theory).

Diez, T. and Steans, J. (2005), 'Habermas and International Relations: A Useful Dialogue?' *Review of International Studies*, 31, 1, January, pp. 127–40.

Gill, S. (2003), *Power and Resistance in the New World Order*, Basingstoke: Palgrave Macmillan (a good example of the treatment of globalization from a Critical Theory perspective, investigating the emergence of new forms of resistance).

Hoffman, M. (1988), 'Conversations on critical international relations theory', *Millennium: Journal of International Studies*, Vol. 17, No. 1, pp. 91–5 (along with Rengger – below – an important article in taking the debate about Critical Theory and IR forward).

Jones, R. W. (2000), *Critical Theory and World Politics*, Boulder, Col: Lynne Rienner Publications Inc.

Linklater, A. (1988), *The Transformation of Political Community*, Oxford: Polity Press (an important work that applies Habermas's Critical Theory to IR).

Linklater, A. (2007), *Critical Theory and World Politics: Sovereignty and Humanity*, London: Palgrave.

Rengger, N.J. (1988), 'Going critical? A response to Hoffman', *Millennium: Journal of International Studies*, Vol. 17, No. 2, pp. 81–9 (a cautious response to Hoffman – above – that alerts us to some of the problems in using Critical Theory in an international/global context, inherent in its universalist claims).

Rengger, N. J. and Thirkell-White, T.B.(2007), *Critical International Relations Theory after Twenty-Five Years*, Cambridge: Cambridge University Press.

Roach, S.C. (2009), *Critical Theories and International Politics*, London: Routledge.

5   Postmodernism

Introduction

Postmodernism has become something of a buzzword in the social sciences and humanities, and one that often provokes very strong reactions: many oppose it, and those labelled 'postmodernists' also tend to reject the label. It is hardly surprising then that the student engaging with postmodern thought for the first time encounters a number of difficulties. First, the very term 'postmodern' creates some confusion. It is sometimes used to connote a cultural change, a difference (although not necessarily a purely temporal one) from modernism. In other contexts it is used synonymously with

Figure 5.1   Postmodernism is about more than wacky building design, and can be used to critique many central ideas and concepts in 'mainstream' International Relations.

Source: Jose Fuste Raga/Corbis.

poststructuralism, which is a particular philosophical approach grounded in a critique of, but also building on, structuralism in linguistics. Second, postmodernism challenges, or subverts, many of the ideas central to International Relations theory. Relatedly, a third difficulty lies in the complexity of the work itself. The student needs a fairly sophisticated understanding of the political institutions, forms of social organisation and social practices associated with modernity, and the philosophical underpinnings of modern social and political thought, in order to fully appreciate postmodern critiques of IR. Finally, there is a question of definition. What *is* postmodernism? Is postmodernism a critical theory, and if so, how is it different from Critical Theory as discussed in chapter 4? Is postmodernism really synonymous with poststructuralism? Do these scholars share a distinctive approach to the study of world politics?

CONCEPT BOX

Postmodernism or poststructuralism?

Often the terms 'postmodern' and 'post-structural' are used interchangeably. At this point it is useful to sketch out in simple terms the differences between them in the interests of clarity. Postmodernism is centrally concerned with the nature and consequences of modernity and develops a thoroughgoing critique of the Enlightenment project. In contrast, poststructuralism is more concerned with the nature, role and function or dysfunction of language – how social meaning is constructed and contested through language. In International Relations, the two terms entered the discipline through their US-American reception in Cultural Studies and other humanities, where their common theme of questioning grand, unified and universalist narratives had been combined. As it happens, scholars working from a 'postmodernist' or 'post-structuralist' perspective tend to not like such labels anyway. For you, as well, it should be more important at this stage to grasp the general critique of power relations, dominant forms of knowledge and social practices which arise from both post-structuralist and postmodernist insights.

A good starting point for understanding the origins of postmodernism is the wave of political radicalism that swept across the Western world in the late 1960s. Just as (post-Marxist) Critical Theory (see chapter 4) was, in part, born of the politics of the New Left, the origins of postmodernism can be seen in the identification with a range of disaffected groups such as student protesters, feminists, environmentalists and gay liberationists. While advocating political radicalism, many on the Left were dissatisfied with the continuing emphasis on the importance of economically determined social class in left-wing political movements. They believed that this emphasis neglected other issues such as racial or gender discrimination. As we will see in the following chapter, during this period feminists were drawing attention to the repressiveness of social relations previously dismissed as 'private'. It was also a time of nationalist struggles against colonial and imperialist domination, with people in many parts of Asia, Latin America and Africa demanding the right to self-determination in the name of 'the people', while minorities in Western countries were documenting the ways in which they suffered forms of discrimination or exclusion from the mainstream of society.

To the New Left, oppositional or radical politics involved often novel forms of resistance to myriad practices of domination and exclusion. As we saw in chapter 4, the experience of widespread persecution and political violence in the Soviet Union had generated scepticism towards the promise of Marxism, even amongst those committed to the cause of human emancipation. In attempting to understand social inequality, Marxists had pointed to the divisiveness and exploitative nature of capitalism, and offered up a vision of a socialist society as a panacea for contemporary ills. Many of the

New Left began to argue that in their attempt to generate the impetus to widespread social change, Marxists had 'universalised' the conditions of human emancipation, at the cost of marginalising and silencing large numbers of groups and people.

AUTHOR BOX

Deconstructing binaries: Jacques Derrida

Jacques Derrida (1930–2004) was a French philosopher who argued that much philosophical thought was metaphysical – that is, it was a belief system which depended ultimately upon an appeal to an ultimate truth, or a solid foundation – for example, the idea of God, or the human subject. In so far as human language is used to convey these ideas, Derrida called this single 'truth' a transcendental signifier – that is, the definitive word which gives meaning to all others. In the final analysis, metaphysical belief systems are based on a fiction, but a whole hierarchy of meaning is then constructed upon this. Derrida pointed out that many philosophers had used the opposition between nature/culture as the basis for their theory. The notions of archaic man living in a 'state of nature' and the desire to establish 'society' are, by now, familiar to you. The structure of the nature/culture dichotomy repeats itself in other binary oppositions: man/woman, national/international. The first term in each of these oppositions constitutes the privileged entity; the second term is always viewed as in some way inferior. Such binary oppositions are used to draw rigid boundaries between what is acceptable and what is not, between self and non-self, truth and falsity, sense and nonsense, reason and madness, central and marginal. It is from Derrida that we get the notion of *deconstruction – a critical method of reading a text to expose the ways in which meaning is constructed.*

HISTORICAL BOX

Enemies of the people

When the Bolsheviks seized power in Russia in 1917, they promised to create an equal society across the territory they controlled, where people were free from want. They also hoped to provide the inspiration and leadership for oppressed peoples across the world. In a few years that vision had degenerated into a nightmare. Under the rule of Stalin the Soviet Union became a land of forced industrialisation and forced collectivisation of agriculture. The latter process saw peasants driven from the land or starved into submission. During the same period religious groups were persecuted for their beliefs and ethnic minorities often treated with suspicion. One of the main pillars of the regime of terror and control created by Stalin was a system of forced labour camps made famous in the work of Alexander Solzhenitzyn. At the height of Stalin's reign of terror, some 8 million people were held in captivity. Often the captives were intellectuals – writers, scientists, artists and teachers. Each and every one had been labelled a 'counter-revolutionary' or 'enemy of the people' for daring to speak out against communism, or in many cases, for much less (for suggesting that there were problems or shortcomings in this particular manifestation of a socialist society or merely because someone had denounced them). Of course, we cannot blame Marx for deeds perpetrated in his name. Nor can we conclude that this particular experiment in collective ownership 'proves' that communism does not work. However, postmodernists claim that the experience of the Soviet Union during Stalin's reign of terror is a powerful illustration of the uses and abuses of power justified in the name of grand, all-encompassing doctrines like Marxism, and of the problems of modernity's belief in the possibilities of centralised control.

Postmodernists are not just suspicious of Marxism, but are wary of all universalising visions which claim to have uncovered the causes, consequences and solutions to human misery and offer a blueprint for a better world. Inevitably, reducing the source of all our ills to a single cause disguises the complex and varied ways in which power operates throughout society and the many different forms of inequality and discrimination that exist. Moreover, such doctrines can potentially provide a powerful justification and legitimisation for a system of rule in which opposition is suppressed in the name of 'progress' or 'emancipation' and which frequently works to perpetuate the position of a self-interested élite.

Finally, given that postmodernists express such incredulity towards 'meta-narratives' like Marxism – that is to say, that postmodernist thinkers have difficulty believing all-encompassing theories or explanations – it would be somewhat surprising to find postmodernists subscribing to a coherent, comprehensive world view or grand vision of international relations. Rather than sketch out a perspective on international relations, therefore, postmodernists prefer to engage in a critique of such projects and concentrate instead on what is different, unique and seemingly defies grandiose forms of theorising, in order to open up space to think 'outside the box' and from different, often marginalised, angles. On the other hand, postmodernist thinkers welcome the proliferation of perspectives and approaches in IR during the past two decades. Far from seeing this as a weakening or undermining of IR as a distinctive 'discipline', postmodern thinkers argue that scepticism and uncertainty combined with a plurality of world views, visions and voices, is an appropriate response to a highly complex world.

It is partly because of this emphasis on a plurality of world views that, having situated postmodernism broadly on the left of the political spectrum, you should be aware that postmodernism has also been described as profoundly conservative because it does not provide a blueprint alternative and is therefore supposed to lead to relativism. This criticism ignores or rejects the critical impetus of deconstruction, but it shows that it is not easy to make sense of postmodernism in terms of simple dichotomies like left/right or radical/conservative. This is yet another difficulty that the student must negotiate.

CONCEPT BOX

The purpose of critique

Through the critical analysis or investigation of a text or writing, it is possible to draw out the hidden assumptions that underpin attempts to understand or explain certain events. The function of critique is to demonstrate how theories that profess to be based upon universal categories or basic 'truths' about the human condition inevitably produce a partial or distorted view.

Taking the example of realism. Realists claim that states, like 'men', are self-interested 'actors'. Moreover, the international realm is like a 'state of nature'. Therefore, states must always look to their own security and act prudentially, which means safeguarding the 'national interest'. In this way, realism makes certain claims about what can be said to exist – what is 'real' or tangible – a system of states, a precarious or stable 'balance of power', genuine threats to security, concrete national interests and so forth. Realists also claim to 'know' something about this world. This knowledge is based on a mixture of age-old 'truths' about the human condition, which philosophers have recorded, historical analysis (the preponderance of wars, perhaps, or shifts in the balance of power) and empirical observation (we can see people and states behaving like this on a daily basis).

However, if we unpack, or deconstruct each of these assumptions, we find that they are all problematical. For example, states are 'real' in the sense that they are constituted by a territory, government, a people and sovereign jurisdiction recognised by international law. However, the state is not 'real' in the sense of being a unified 'actor' with a concrete identity or single purpose. The state is made up of an array of institutions and bodies, and within those institutions there are very many decision makers. Moreover, within that given territory there might well be numerous groups and individuals who have access to power, or, conversely, are without influence. In order to make the notion of the state as a unified, coherent actor 'real', realists resort to claims about the selfish nature of 'man', but this view is surely coloured by how 'human nature' has been understood in certain cultures and perhaps in different periods of time. For example, some feminists argue that the kind of behaviour realists ascribe to the state as 'man writ large' – aggressive, dominating – is commonly associated with male, and not female, 'nature'.

The notion of threats, danger and an international state of nature is constructed by drawing upon powerful images of anarchy, and metaphors which present the natural world as hostile and disorderly. Insecurity arises from a fear of not being in command or able to control our environment, and in which the body politic is, consequently, in constant danger of being overwhelmed, invaded or otherwise violated. This analogy of international relations as a 'state of nature' is based on a distinctly modern view of our relationship to nature (see chapter 8 for a fuller discussion of this point). Some might argue that the individualism inherent in realism – isolated, bounded, autonomous states – constitutes a rather strange understanding of how people (or, indeed, states) form relationships with others and how they behave towards others. Furthermore, we need only recall our earlier discussion of liberal pluralism or structuralism or Critical Theory to realise that the nature of world order is disputed – there are many views of what can be said to 'really' exist. Also, the concept of 'national interest' is difficult to pin down. Liberal pluralists, for example, claim that there are always competing visions of what is in the 'interest' of the people or nation, while structuralists argue that the state reflects the interests of élite classes. We will return to this idea of critique later in the chapter. At this stage, suffice it to say that postmodernist critique aims to show how, in this case, realism offers at best a partial view of international relations. At worst, we could say that the claims that it makes about the world are based on the world view of powerful men in the West at a particular period in history and are both distorting and exclusionary.

This is not to say that postmodernist scholars simply reject everything as bias, perverse or a reflection of the perspective of the powerful. Postmodernists are not necessarily cynics or nihilists. However, postmodernists are different from, say, liberals or Critical Theorists, because they are more willing to admit that ultimately there might not be any solid grounds, or ultimate source of appeal, on which to establish the 'rightness' or 'wrongness' of particular value systems, beliefs, or world views. They certainly do not claim to have an insight into the 'truth' about the human condition, or the inherent virtue or wickedness of a particular action or event. Instead, they see it as the defining nature of politics that there is a choice between various 'truths'. Indeed, one could even argue that the emphasis on what William Connolly once called the 'ethos of pluralization' (in contrast to a mere belief in pluralism) makes postmodern thought deeply ethical, although in a different sense from other critical or normative theories.

We are running ahead of ourselves here, however. We return to postmodern critique of established perspectives or 'stories' of IR and their celebration of value pluralism and diversity later. First, though, while recognising that it is difficult to present this collection of approaches, authors and topics as a coherent theoretical perspective, we endeavour to make good our promise to make the complex accessible, and attempt to identify some of the core themes which recur in the postmodern IR literature, even though those scholars often labelled 'postmodernists' are themselves reluctant to accept pigeon-holing and labelling.

From a postmodernist perspective, the study of world politics (a term preferred to International Relations for reasons which are elaborated on below):

■ investigates the ways in which power operates in the discourses and practices of world politics;
■ maps the many and varied ways that political space is constructed and utilised by individuals and groups;
■ unpacks the complex processes involved in the construction of political identities;
■ celebrates differences and diversity among people and across cultures;
■ encourages a proliferation of approaches and world views, because this has the effect of displacing or undermining 'orthodox' or hegemonic forms of knowledge and power;
■ highlights issues or concerns frequently dismissed as trivial or insignificant in order to give a voice to, or empower, people and groups who have been marginalised in the study of IR.

Origins

The body of work labelled 'postmodern' has made an important contribution to the study of International Relations since the 1980s. However, as already indicated, the intellectual origins of postmodernism go back further. A diverse array of thinkers have influenced/inspired contemporary postmodern scholars. In this chapter we concentrate mainly on the ideas of two – Foucault and Derrida.

CONCEPT BOX

Modernity and the Enlightenment project

The term 'modernity' is used to refer to two related processes. First, to institutional transformations that have origins in the West. Second, to a fundamental transformation of political and social thought which occurred with the emergence of modern science. The Enlightenment refers to a period of European history, from the seventeenth to the nineteenth century, during which tradition and religious doctrine were challenged by the rise of modern science and certain 'enlightened' or progressive views of humankind's capacity for reasoned thought and moral development. Enlightenment thinkers were committed to scientific, logical and rational forms of knowledge. This manifested itself in scepticism towards traditional forms of authority.

Together, these developments gave rise to the 'Enlightenment project' of human progress and emancipation. The development of modern industrial capitalism allowed for more rational organisation of society, while modern science held the promise of a 'science of society', which would lead to the discovery of 'laws' governing the social world. This kind of thinking implicitly challenged the idea that the existing social and political world reflected a unified moral order ordained by God. However, Enlightenment thinkers were convinced that the steady growth of human reason and the gradual elimination of ignorance and suspicion would culminate in the moral and political unification of humankind. This Enlightenment project rested on a belief in the possibility of discovering universal 'truths'.

For this reason, universalistic doctrines, like liberalism or Marxism, hold that there is no justification in drawing boundaries of, say, human rights, or human dignity and respect more narrowly than around the whole human race. Consequently, they protest against needless human suffering wherever and whenever it is manifest. So, Enlightenment thinkers challenged practices of oppression inflicted on people in the name of larger orders or a 'common good' – whether it be family honour, or the glorification of God, or the nation or the leader. This is entirely consistent with the rejection of doctrines like the 'divine right of kings' or a heroic view of great warriors, which clearly places greater importance or value on people who embody special qualities that set them apart from the rest of us. Instead history (social change) is driven by the trajectory of the societies in which we live and possibilities which they allow for producing social change and human progress.

One of the most powerful ideas in Enlightenment thinking is that ordinary, everyday life has intrinsic value. For this reason, Enlightenment thought is sometimes referred to as 'humanism'. You will no doubt recognise these ideas as central to liberalism. The modern person, or subject, is worthy of respect. This gives rise to the liberal notion of the moral autonomy of each individual and the idea that the person possesses certain inalienable rights. It is because people understand rational principles that it is possible to organise society on a rational basis and according to the rule of law. However, structuralism and Critical Theory also emphasise the dignity and moral worth of ordinary human life. In orthodox Marxism, this modern, Enlightenment, view of man as the measure of all things is expressed through a belief in the dignity of work. Indeed, the common working man is no insignificant minion destined to toil, but rather the central actor in a great drama – the unfolding of history and human destiny. As we see in later chapters, strands of feminist and 'green thinking' subscribe to an essentially Enlightenment view of progress and emancipation.

Surely, one might think, modernity and the Enlightenment are built on a vision of hope for the future of the human race, so why do postmodernists subject these ideas to such intense criticism? In part, this criticism of the Enlightenment project is a consequence of the rise of fascism in the 1930s, which plunged Europe into a new 'dark age' characterised by war, destruction and horrifying acts of cruelty and barbarism. The experience of a modern nation seemingly submitting willingly to the iron will of the *Führer* in the interests of the glorification of the Aryan race, wartime atrocities such as those perpetuated at Kerch in the Crimea and the Nazi death camps at Auschwitz and Belzec, seemed to defy the idea of history as progress and cast doubt on the West's claims to be advanced and civilised. In more recent years, the spectre of nuclear war, environmental degradation, and widespread feelings of alienation and hopelessness, which seem to be endemic to advanced capitalist societies, have added further to the criticism of the image of the West as a bastion of progress.

The 'final solution'

The most obvious manifestation of Hitler's fanatical hatred of Jewish people was his determination to exclude them from every area of German society and everyday life. At first, this policy took the form of 'voluntary' emigration or forced expulsion. However, as Nazi forces occupied more and more of mainland Europe, Jews had fewer means of escape from persecution and fewer places to hide. A few weeks after the German occupation of Poland in September 1939, Reinhard Heydrich, the head of the Third Reich central security services, issued an instruction that Jews were to be grouped together 'as a means to the final end'. The 'final end' or 'final solution' was the mass extermination of the Jewish people. Initially, herded together and held captive in ghettos across Europe, the Jews were transported to camps deep within the occupied territories. Here millions of people died as a result of torture, hard labour or starvation, or by asphyxiation through gassing.

You might object that, however terrible, the experience of Nazi fanaticism and the spectre of concentration camps is an aberration in European history and so cannot be taken as evidence of the bankruptcy of the Enlightenment project. Moreover, is not fascism a rejection of everything the Enlightenment holds dear; the intrinsic value of the human person and moral dignity? This would certainly be one interpretation of events. However, from a postmodernist perspective, far from being a deviation, the 'final solution' is a consequence of trends set in motion by modernity – the rational organisation of society, the prevalence of 'means-ends' instrumentalism, the existence of social hierarchies and chains of command, the means to transport people across vast territories, and the factories of death in which people were systematically killed and their remains efficiently disposed of. From this perspective, the Nazis saw the final solution merely as a technical problem, and industry and the rational organisation of society allowed a technical solution.

You will recall that this stark realisation of a 'dark side of modernity' was also central to the 'critical turn' in Marxism in the 1930s, which gave birth to the Frankfurt School. Frankfurt School scholars understood the danger of an all-pervasive technical, means-end rationality. It was necessary, therefore, to return to the vision at the heart of the Enlightenment – human emancipation – and reflect critically on how current conditions facilitated or threatened the realisation of this vision. Critical Theorists believe that it is still possible to salvage an emancipatory project through a reformulation of Marxism. Postmodernists do not think so. They are profoundly sceptical of any attempt to establish universal categories or explanations. Moreover, postmodern thinkers have argued that all attempts to establish the universal conditions for human freedom and emancipation will inevitably be used in practice to subordinate and marginalise those who are deemed 'different'. This is because power/knowledge relations, which we discuss in greater detail below, are always at work in social relationships. To illustrate this point, postmodernists point to the ways in which liberal ideas about rationality, civilisation and progress have also been used historically to divide up and categorise the world's people as 'advanced' or 'backward', 'civilised' or 'barbarian' according to what were actually European (or Western) social, political and cultural values. They pointed out that the Enlightenment period was accompanied by the widespread oppression of many peoples in the cause of spreading the benefits of civilisation.

Figure 5.2   In the aftermath of World War Two, the 'dark side of modernity' became depressingly apparent in the concentration camps found across central and eastern Europe.

Source: Corbis.

Pulp Fiction

Quentin Tarantino's *Pulp Fiction* can be seen as a celebration of postmodernism through its eclectic attitude to combining storylines and symbolic references to other movies. Despite the violence of the movie, there is little, or at least little obvious, social commentary in *Pulp Fiction*. This movie is a collage on several levels. Most obviously, it works as a collage by telling four stories that are only linked by one incident, which is shown last. More intriguingly, perhaps, Tarantino makes references to a whole range of other movies in film history, and sets his story against a soundtrack that again makes reference to the past, in particular the 1950s and 1960s. In this way *Pulp Fiction* refuses the conventions of linear time-lines and authentic representation characteristic of social realist films, but also mixes and matches styles and cultural reference points from different periods, thus challenging the notion that stories (real or imagined) are necessarily coherently embedded in particular times and places.

The implication of the critique of the Enlightenment was that, while the Enlightenment had been presented as a period in which mankind has been liberated from ignorance, the discourse of rationalism characteristic of the 'modern' age has been imbued with bias. Postmodernist thinkers argue that there are varied forms of social organisation and many different kinds of cultural practice. These are not inherently 'good' or 'bad', 'progressive' or 'backward', though they are often adjudged as such by reference to some supposedly superior model – the Western world. Similarly, the model of the rational subject, held to be a universal characteristic of 'man', actually described a particular kind of view of human 'nature', or subjectivity, which was European, bourgeois and masculine – the new élite which emerged from the ashes of feudal society. Any manifestation of human life and being which appeared to contradict or challenge this view has immediately been labelled as alien, ignorant and, more important, threatening.

Postmodernist thinkers have drawn heavily upon the work of the French philosopher Michel Foucault. Foucault's work is extensive, so here we will concentrate on just a few central ideas – Foucault's view of the power/knowledge relationship, his ideas about discourse, and his conception of the human person, or subject. For Foucault, the discourses in which we engage are not controlled by us. Rather, they are powerful in themselves in that they generate a particular knowledge, including core concepts and problem-definitions with which we operate, and which we most of the time accept without questioning. This means that there are no undisputed 'truths' about human 'nature' or human life. Everything that we think we 'know' for sure is tied to our particular discursive contexts. We 'know' because we believe these things to be true. We believe these things to be true because we are taught in schools, or told by scientists, technical 'experts', bureaucrats and policy-making élites. While the most powerful people in society are in a much better position to have their views accepted as 'truth', and are able to dismiss or trivialize alternative views, they do not control discourses. Rather, the meaning of whatever they say makes sense itself, only against the background of a wider discursive context. This illustrates once more that power does not rest with individuals but within discourses.

However, this does not make postmodernists uncritical of hierarchical structures. One 'truth' that they contest is, for instance, the distinction between canons of 'knowledge' taught to us in schools and universities and myths, stories, narratives and the kind of 'common sense' which is passed down in families and local communities. Postmodernist authors see this distinction as a consequence of modernity and the Enlightenment, privileging particular forms of knowledge, as well as particular discursive and societal positions over others.

CONCEPT BOX

Discourse

According to postmodern thinkers, a discourse is not simply an account or a story *about* something or somebody. Discourses are practices that systematically form or create the objects that they speak of. This is a complex idea, so let us try to unpack it further by taking the concrete example of discourses on 'women'. Throughout history, in works of art and pornography, in literature and folklore, in philosophy and science, there has been a great deal written on the subject of 'women'. People called 'women' have been variously represented as virtuous goddesses or treacherous witches, as caring wives/mothers, or scheming whores, as autonomous individuals each possessing free will or naturally subordinate and suited to a subservient role. So what are we to make of these creatures called 'women'? Do we conclude that the cumulative wisdom tells us that women are goddesses? Or witches? Or paradoxical creatures embodying complex personas?

Feminists would caution that these stories about women do not necessarily tell us anything at all about the 'true nature' or 'essence' of woman, because they have usually been written by men. These are not, then, accurate or even partial, pictures of what women *are* (the 'essence' of women). How could men possibly know what women are? However, feminists have not been successful in identifying a female 'essence', as we will see in the following chapter. De Beauvoir argued that woman was what she could be, while others have simply concluded that woman is an enigma, a question. However, just because we cannot identify an essence that is 'woman', it does not follow that discourses on women are of no consequence. Claims about women's 'true nature' have informed laws, social policies, institutions and practices throughout history, from, say, marriage and divorce, to 'proper' education and training, to who can or cannot fly an aeroplane or vote in an election. Discourses inform or create concrete practices, which become part of discourses. Or we might say, discourse is itself a practice. A discourse is not about a 'real' thing, or event, or category of person like 'woman'. Discourse creates the thing it speaks of, because it invests meaning into an empty term like 'woman' and, in so doing, creates a 'real' category of people. The lives of people called 'women' are then profoundly shaped by the concrete practices that flow from this same meaning.

However, while language is important, it would be wrong to simply equate discourse with language. Many scholars have moved to include images, symbols and non-textual practices in their notion of discourse. Undoubtedly, all of these play a role in the construction of meaning. However, at some point pictures or symbols will have to have been rendered meaningful through language in the first instance.

As a consequence of this critique, there is no hierarchical distinction between, for example, a great work of history or science or social science, and a work of fiction. We may believe that Darwin's *Origin of Species* or de Beauvoir's *The Second Sex* have more insight into the human condition than, say, *Buffy the Vampire Slayer*, but to the postmodernist, all of these are important sources of how meaning is generated. In this respect Foucault's ideas about knowledge/power and discourse are similar to the Marxist view of knowledge as ideology – the world view or 'truth' of the powerful which masquerades as 'common sense', except that in the Foucauldian sense, there is no clear truth against which another view can be characterized as 'ideology'.

While postmodernist thinkers thus share some common ground with Critical Theorists in the Marxian tradition, Habermasian Critical Theorists hold that through dialogue aimed at consensus we can arrive at intersubjectively shared understandings that at least minimize the influence of power. Postmodernist thinkers, in contrast, argue that there is always power in such understandings, and that dialogue can never be power-free. Postmodernism therefore is a critical theory (note the small 'c' and 't') in the sense that it problematises and undermines supposedly self-evident truths that carry with them power and domination. However, in contrast to the Critical Theory of, for instance, Robert Cox, it does not accept any secure foundations for alternative truths, including the notion of 'social classes', and therefore also rejects the project of constructing alternative world orders as guidance for political action.

All of this does not mean that postmodernists would deny that there is a reality 'out there'. Of course there are states and there are wars, there is suffering and there is hunger. The point, however, is that we do not have direct access to this reality. Like social constructivists (chapter 7), postmodernists argue that the social reality is discursively constructed; states, for instance, only exist because of particular discourses tied to particular historical developments. However, postmodernists also contend that we can never speak about any reality objectively; reality is not directly accessible to us, and our understanding of it is always mediated and informed by particular discourses. We can never be free of the power/knowledge nexus – it permeates all aspects of our day-to-day life. Knowledge, then, presupposes power relations and we can only ever adopt an attitude of scepticism and critique. From a postmodern position, whenever we are confronted with a 'story' about the world, we must ask: Where does power reside? How is it exercised? To what end? How are particular configurations of power relations implicated in this view?

CONCEPT BOX

Telling stories . . .

Postmodernist thinkers, influenced by Jacques Derrida, claim that in a sense we can think of the social world as being like a book. We use our critical faculties to 'read' and interpret the world, just as we would read a book. The world is like a text, because it has no meaning independent of this interpretation. You might object that a book *does* have a meaning. The meaning of a story or an account is invested in the work by the author. For example, we are the authors of this book. We are endeavouring to convey something of the world of international relations. As readers, you are attempting to discover something about international relations by interpreting the meaning of words, analogies and examples that we have used. But are you learning anything about the world of international relations directly? Are you not learning about our perspectives and interpretations? Is your reading of these perspectives and interpretations not coloured by your own preconceptions (thus investing our words with meanings we may not have intended)? And are our perspectives and your reading of them not based on a wide range of other sources – from the works of philosophers to newspapers, films and magazines?

Postmodern thinkers reject grand theories or meta-narratives, including the idea of God or Rationality or any other authoritative voice. The world has no 'author'. God did not create the world in six days; this is only a story about the world gleaned from the Bible. History is not the history of class struggle; this is an interpretation of history that comes to us through the pages of *The Communist Manifesto*. There is no hidden meaning of life which we can one day hope to discover. Postmodernists often speak of the 'death of the author' to convey the contested nature of knowledge, meaning and interpretation. We can only 'read' and interpret the world, or read and interpret other interpretations.

There are some similarities here with the interpretative or hermeneutic tradition of thought. However, postmodernists do not accept the proposition that there is a single world, which we are all interpreting. In so far as we have *shared* meanings, these must be understood as 'intertextualities', rather than 'truths' arrived at by a shared understanding of events, processes and practices 'out there' in the real world. There are very many different stories or texts, and many different interpretations of dominant texts. Indeed, meaning is derived from the interaction of the reader with the 'text'. Since the social world is made up of such interpretations or discourses, we could say that interpretation constitutes the social world.

According to Foucault, the idea of a rational, autonomous human subject is also a fiction. In his earlier work Foucault presented a view of the human subject as a body, an empty vessel, a product of the power relations to which we are all subjected throughout our lives – in sexual relationships, in the family, in the school, by exposure to media and communications, by conscription into the armed forces perhaps, by the regulation and supervision carried out by the police force and law courts, by the discipline we are subjected to in the workplace and so forth. Unsurprisingly, this view of the human subject has been criticised as anti-humanist and profoundly pessimistic. If we are only ever the product of discipline and punishment, how can we ever escape? Towards the end of his life,

Foucault began to change his views somewhat. Certainly, most contemporary postmodernists do recognise the capacity for resistance and empowerment. If this was not the case, we would not find examples of opposition, or different perspectives and 'stories' about the world. Indeed, postmodernists see inherent value in a multiplicity of approaches and perspectives on world politics, not because collectively they will increase our stock of knowledge and take us closer to the truth, but because they allow us to see the world through different lenses, enable us to hear diverse voices articulating various issues and concerns, and so undermine the truth claims of orthodox or hegemonic world views.

In developing this critique of the Enlightenment, postmodernists also develop a critique of philosophy. In so far as philosophers have sought to understand the truth about the human condition and speculate about the ends of human life, philosophy is rejected on the grounds that there can be no single truth and no one conception of the good life. Derrida was critical of Western philosophy because it is phonocentric – centred on one authoritative voice. It was also logocentric – committed to a belief in some presence, or reality. Derrida argued that this occurred because of the human desire for certainty, the need to posit a central presence – something or someone there at the beginning of time and whose idea or will is being played out throughout history. If Enlightenment thinkers were concerned to challenge the one authoritative voice of God, they were never able to quite give up on the idea of a point of origin and ultimate destination – the human subject, human progress and a better future for the world.

Indeed, postmodernist thinkers criticise this view of history as 'progress'. Human history should not be viewed, as some Enlightenment thinkers have suggested, as a gradual journey, or an unfolding of events, destined to culminate in a more rational world and freedom for the human race. Postmodernist thinkers argue that there is no overall pattern, no end point or destination in history. Foucault was also deeply critical of the idea that human history should be seen in linear terms – as the logical and necessary progression of the human race. He criticised traditional history that interpreted historical events in terms of some grand explanatory system – attempting to track and interpret events in accordance with some preconceived ideas about the overall direction and pattern of history.

Foucault used a method called 'genealogy' to trace the discontinuities and ruptures in history, in order to emphasise the singularity of events, rather than seeking to identify historical trends; in effect, to show that history had become accounts of the powerful. In so doing, Foucault was attempting to show what had been marginalised or neglected in traditional accounts of history. If traditional history focused on the big events, or the heroes and villains, and, say, Marxism focused on history as the history of class struggle, Foucault's genealogy was designed to show what and, crucially, who had been neglected in these accounts and so, effectively, denied a history. Since the legitimacy of the current social and political order is embedded in certain interpretations or stories about the past, it is possible in this way to delegitimise the present social and political order and expose the current configuration of power relations. Foucault was, for instance, fascinated by mental 'illnesses' such as schizophrenia because here was a concrete example of people who manifested 'split' or multiple subjectivities and who were often not able to locate themselves in time or space. It is important to understand Foucault did not regard these people as 'mad', because the notion of 'madness' was another manifestation of intolerance and the desire by the powerful to marginalise, or incarcerate the 'different'.

Postmodern thinkers invoke the notion of 'otherness' to refer to the voice that is silenced, or the experience that is marginalised when the 'truth' is asserted. The concept of the 'other', which is a major theme in the work of Jacques Derrida, is employed to confound the notion that there can be universal truth grounded in a conception of universal reason, that there are universal experiences or universal values. Experiences, values and knowledge claims are always particular. That projection onto a universal scale involves a two-step process. First, it rests on the logocentric practice of creating a dichotomy between, say, one value (attributed to the self) and another, and turning this dichotomy into a hierarchy so that the 'other' becomes inferior and often a threat to the self. The interesting thing about this is that the self only becomes meaningful by being put into such a dichotomy. Without the difference to the 'other', there would be no self. Imagine a world without borders: in such a world, we could not talk about the UK, India, Nigeria or Canada. The second step then is to assume that the self, which exists only because of the inserted difference, is in fact universal in nature. This is how imperialism in its various guises works; it turns particular experiences, cultures and values into universal ones, and at the same time constructs different experiences, cultures and values as 'others' that need to be dominated and transformed because they constitute a threat. Powers that are seemingly non-imperialist, however, perform similar logics, as is evident in the US attempt to 'civilise' and 'democratise' the Middle East, or the notion of the European Union as a 'normative power' that purports to promote universal standards of human rights or environmental change yet in doing so constructs itself as the 'shining light' in the world, and example to follow and a 'force for good'.

Assumptions

1. Human 'nature' is not immutable. The human subject is 'open' and malleable, a product of practices of subordination and resistance.
2. Human values, beliefs and actions vary according to the wider social and cultural context. There are no characteristics or values with universal applicability. The behaviour/actions of people and particular values can only be understood and judged in terms of specific cultural meanings and contexts.
3. We cannot outline any general theory which helps us to 'make sense' of the world, or prescribe a blueprint or scheme for universal human emancipation.
4. Meaning is always the product of discourse, and of power that rests in discourse and that makes us define problems and solutions in particular ways. Such meaning therefore needs to be problematised in order to be able to consider alternatives that were previously marginalised.
5. There are no 'facts' about the world. All we have are interpretations and interpretations of other interpretations of 'reality'.

REFLECTION BOX

When you started your course in International Relations, you probably came with a variety of firmly held beliefs about international politics. Try to make a list of these beliefs – perhaps about what the national interest is, which values should be defended internationally, or what the main threats to security and peace are. Can you trace these beliefs to your particular discursive context? What are the 'others' involved in your perspective of the world? What are possible alternatives that you have simply discounted because of your preconceptions?

Figure 5.3   The world viewed from China.

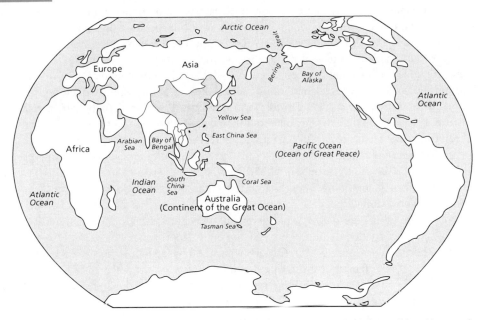

Original source: G. Chieland and J.P. Rageau (1986), *Strategic Atlas: World Geopolitics*, Harmondsworth: Penguin, p. 17.

Taken from: B. Hocking and M. Smith (1995), *World Politics: An Introduction to International Politics*, 2nd edn, London: Prentice-Hall/Harvester Wheatsheaf, p. 38.

Reflection – this map of the world *might* make British or European readers feel uncomfortable, but is it an any less valid interpretation than the one you might be used to?

Themes

If you are now operating in postmodernist mode, perhaps you will have already adopted scepticism towards the study of 'international relations'! Perhaps, you will ask: how are power relations implicated in perspectives and world views? Which views of the world are accepted as valid and which are not? What other possible stories could we tell about the world? You might also desire to unpack or deconstruct the language, symbols and images that are invoked in particular discourses. Or maybe you want to challenge the very notion of 'international relations'. The conception of the nation-state makes certain assumptions about identity and community, of course. It assumes that we identify first and foremost with members of the national group and owe primary allegiance to 'our' state. Perhaps you would now argue for a more open, ambiguous and messier notion of 'world politics' on the grounds that it better captures the nuances and complexities of the world you are striving to 'make sense of'? It is in this context that we can focus on how postmodernism critiques existing perspectives on IR and champions radical new ways of thinking about the general domain of world politics.

The state and power

At first sight the state-centric orientation of much IR theory is not unreasonable. The nation-state has constituted the dominant form of political organisation in Europe since the seventeenth century. In the European context the birth of the state as a form of political organisation was closely associated with the rise of nationalism. Forces of nationalism have played a large part in post-colonial and revolutionary struggles for 'national independence', which have, in turn, encouraged the proliferation of states around the world. Moreover, the defining characteristic of the state is sovereignty – exclusive jurisdiction over a people in a given territory and the right to act on their behalf in relations with others. Is it not reasonable then to start out from the position that the state is the main actor in international relations and acts to secure the 'national interest'?

From a postmodern position we cannot take the state to be our unquestioned starting point for the study of IR for much the same reason as Critical Theorists reject state-centrism – states have emerged during certain historical conditions. In earlier periods, there were many and different 'sites' of power and authority which claimed the allegiances of peoples. Postmodern scholars also argue that mainstream IR theory, in taking the state as a pre-given entity, neglects important questions about why the world has come to be divided up in this way. State-centric approaches fail to ask how sovereignty – centralised authority – has been produced, and what the consequences are of carving up political space in this way. It is to these questions that the discussion now turns.

Postmodernists would not deny the importance of the concept of the state in IR. However, they encourage us to think about the state as 'actor' in a radically different way. Rather than taking the existence of the state as given, postmodern thinkers argue that it actually takes a great deal of time and effort to 'make' a state. Not only must the state constantly patrol and police demarcated boundaries (contested or otherwise), but élites also have to expend considerable effort on retaining the allegiance of the people. The shorthand term for the making of the state is 'statecraft'. In conventional diplomatic history or orthodox accounts of foreign policy, statecraft refers to statesmanship – foresight and skill in the art of government and in conducting relations with foreign powers. While postmodernists would not necessarily contest this definition, they contend that it is mistaken to view diplomacy or foreign policy as the expression or execution of some pre-given national interest. Statecraft is an ongoing, dynamic process, whereby the identity of state is actively created and recreated. Every day, political élites are involved in practices such as the making of speeches, the exercise of diplomacy, and the formulation of foreign policy that constantly serve to mark out the boundaries and identity of the state.

CONCEPT BOX

Discourses of nationhood and national identity

The idea of investing the state with a concrete identity is difficult to grasp, so let us take the example of how the idea of 'Britishness' is acted out on a day-to-day basis. Nationalists frequently claim that the people of a given land – the 'nation' – have existed since time immemorial. A great deal of academic writing on nations and nationalism endeavours to trace back the origins of nations in certain ethnic groups or through a historical lineage stretching back to ancient times; such as Anthony Smith's notion of 'ethnies', for example.

In an influential book Benedict Anderson claimed that nations were not 'real' entities, but 'imagined communities'. That is to say, the idea of nationhood has been constructed through symbols, myths and narratives, which allowed people to imagine that they shared a deep bond based on blood-line and/or a common history, interests and destiny. Anderson claimed that, far from being ancient, nations were, in fact, a relatively recent phenomenon. It was only with the advent of modern transport systems, the imposition of common time zones, the invention of modern print media and the centralisation of authority in the state, that people began to imagine themselves to be a part of one community. State-building projects and modern warfare have both manipulated and perpetuated this notion of 'nationhood'.

If we take the example of the British nation, here we have islands comprised of more than 60 million people. Even if we exclude from our definition of 'Britain' the troubled province of Ulster, where contested ideas of nationhood and sovereignty have led to bitter and bloody conflict, we find that 'Great Britain' is an island of considerable diversity. It is made up of three distinctive countries, England, Scotland and Wales. Many – though certainly not all – Scottish and Welsh people feel themselves to be different from the English and, indeed, may perceive the notion of 'British-ness' to be merely an imposition of some notion of 'English-ness'. This feeling of 'difference', whether it has positive or negative connotations, is undoubtedly part of the reason why Scotland and Wales have demanded a greater degree of self-rule in recent years. However, the decentralisation of power to Scottish and Welsh Assemblies, has, in turn, increased demands for greater autonomy in regions of England like the North East and South West, which have been backed by claims of 'cultural differences'. Of course, we cannot prove in any objective way that these claims have any substance, or that perceived differences are based on 'real' differences. The point is that the idea of nationhood and community is contested. Add to this, the very large numbers of British citizens spread across the various territories and regions, who have parents, grandparents, partners or close relatives who were born in the Indian sub-continent, the Caribbean, Africa, the Baltic States or some other European country, and a picture of a diverse and multicultural society begins to emerge.

It is clearly difficult to sustain the notion of a coherent and unified nation in the context of diversity and complex feelings of identity and allegiance, yet on a day-to-day basis the idea of 'Britishness' is played out, or performed, on the international 'stage'. Politicians debate the implications of European Union for British sovereignty, or the 'problem' of 'bogus' asylum seekers. At the same time, officials and representatives of the British state are involved in diplomatic missions, states-people take part in international conferences, and British forces patrol the seas and airways, and police territorial boundaries – all in the name of 'British interests'. In all of these ways, the idea of a unified nation and a distinctive 'Britishness' is performed.

How then is the state made to appear like an entity and cohesive, purposive actor? Postmodernists argue that the state is made to appear like it has an 'essence' by performative enactments of various domestic and foreign policies. Through the performance of both foreign and domestic policy, by entering into diplomatic relations with other sovereign bodies and, sometimes, through acts of war, the boundaries of the state are constructed, policed and patrolled. State practices are then legitimised through the articulation of national identity, community and interests, which in turn rest on oppositions between self and other. The state is never finished; statecraft is a dynamic ongoing process. Similarly, the state, and how we think about the state, is always undergoing processes of transformation.

You might object that, while closely connected, the concepts of state and nation are distinct. Realists would contend that, notwithstanding the diversity within the citizen body, the concept of 'national interest' is valid because ultimately the state guarantees the security of the citizen body. Some realists prefer not to rely on arguments about nationhood to justify their position and contend that we obey the state because it is prudent to do so – the state protects us; if we betray the state (treason) we can be killed. Moreover, the world is divided up into entities called 'states' and the defining characteristic of a state is sovereignty.

Simulating sovereignty

Postmodern thinkers like Cynthia Weber have referred to the notion of 'writing' the state, or simulating sovereignty. To go back to our earlier metaphor of the world as a text or book, this notion of 'writing' conveys the idea of inscribing modes of representation: that is, meaning is inscribed in a text through the act of writing – the use of words, signifiers, symbols, metaphors and images, which we read, interpret and, at some level, understand. Similarly, concepts, ideas and fictions – the state, or security, or sovereignty – are portrayed or represented to us as having a concrete existence or 'truth'. To write 'the state' is to give the state an 'essence' or, more properly, a presence – a concrete identity or existence. The presence of the state having been established, certain practices are then infused with meaning and thereby legitimised – the policing of boundaries, acts in the name of 'national security', the crime of treason and so on. In Weber's argument, it is the very practice of intervention that reproduces (simulates) the notion of a sovereign state.

Given our earlier discussion of the nature of discourse, however, we would be surprised to find postmodernist thinkers being lulled into a conversation about the so-called 'objective' characteristics of the state, or the ultimate foundation of sovereign authority. The postmodernist perspective on sovereignty shifts the focus from the 'objective' characteristics of sovereignty onto how the discourse of sovereignty has profoundly shaped our thinking about political life. In concentrating on discourses of sovereignty, the aim is not to define sovereignty or pin down the essence of sovereign power. Adopting a genealogical method, it is possible to show how the meaning of sovereignty has changed over different historical time periods and according to the context in which the term has been evoked. This implies that we need to understand how different configurations of power/knowledge have shaped our understanding of sovereignty.

Security and identity

Drawing upon the work of Derrida particularly, many postmodern thinkers have argued that the 'making' of the state necessitates the construction of a hostile 'other'. A discourse of threat or danger is central to the making of identities and the securing of boundaries. Thus, the political cohesion of the USA relies on the construction of hostile 'others', or what is called a practice of 'Othering'. During the Cold War period in US foreign policy, the Soviet Union was constructed as a unified and cohesive actor – a 'red menace' bent on world domination. The Soviet Union covered a large geographical area and embraced a vast array of peoples of different classes, genders, nationalities and cultures, but was presented as an entity with cohesive identity and purpose – or subjectivity.

Adopting a postmodern position on security, foreign policy and diplomacy gives us a much more fluid and dynamic understanding of politics and the power relations that underpin dominant discourses of political space and identity, than that provided by state-centric perspectives. It allows us to see that these practices effectively carve up political space on a global scale and determine what constitutes 'threats'. Not only does this serve to legitimise high levels of expenditure on armaments and political violence in the defence of the nation and its boundaries, but it also disguises internal division and dissent. Far from being politically, socially and culturally cohesive units, 'nation-states' are frequently rent by internal turmoil; legally recognised but lacking domestic legitimacy. However, sovereignty confers on the state ultimate power over the citizen body.

David Campbell, *Writing Security*

David Campbell's book *Writing Security* shows how US foreign policy has relied on so-called 'discourses of danger'. Such discourses have been able to 'create' enemies externally as well as externalising internal dissidence/difference. Campbell calls these discourses 'foreign policy' in that they represent people and things as 'foreign' and thereby construct who and what the 'self' is – in contrast to traditional Foreign Policy, which he considers to be but one facet of this broader notion of foreign policy. As Campbell himself puts it, 'the ability to represent things as alien, subversive, dirty or such has been pivotal to the American experience' (p.2). He argues that this was not just some Cold War necessity but is an ongoing feature of US politics; thus, just as women, blacks, foreigners, radicals, the 'insane' and the sexually deviant were often the targets of anti-communism's discursive practices, so anti-narcotics discourses of danger in the post-Cold War period 'have identified the same groups as of concern' (p.205), and branded them as un-American, or America's 'other' that defines what it means to be 'American'. Apart from social exclusion, the consequence of these practices is that contemporary problems are seen to reside in, and are therefore tackled in, countries other than the USA, while they are deeply enmeshed with US-American domestic life.

David Campbell suggests that the state requires a 'discourse of danger' not only to secure its identity, but also to legitimise state power. Some writers argue that modern statecraft is built upon a set of practices that work to subdue resistance. The consequence of this is that citizenship is equated with ultimate loyalty to the nation-state and the elimination of all that is foreign. Threats to security are seen to be in the external realm and internal dissent is quelled.

We should note, however, that more recent work such as that of Lene Hansen has pointed out that not all representations of the other necessarily construct the other as danger. Indeed, differences between self and other can take a variety of forms, and sometimes those represented as inferior in a binary opposition accept this notion in order to project a new identity that is more like the universal good that they aspire to. Some of the discourses taking place in EU membership candidate countries, particularly in the Central and Eastern European countries after the end of the Cold War and before the EU enlargement rounds in 2004 and 2007, are examples of such 'positive othering'. Yet another variation, shown in the work of Ole Wæver, is the EU discourse to see its own, war-torn past as one of the others, against which the new, peaceful Europe is constructed in what Thomas Diez calls 'temporal' as opposed to a 'geopolitical' form of 'othering'. While such a temporal othering may be normatively preferable because of the self-reflexivity it entails, it is not unproblematic: it, too, is not devoid of power, and it feeds into the already mentioned discourse that tends to neglect the many 'past' characteristics still present in today's Europe.

Identity and community

If, however, the state and national identity is a 'problem', how might we re-articulate or revise conceptions of community and belonging? Postmodern scholars accept that the nation-state is an important expression of political community. However, they point out that it is certainly not the only significant expression of identity or community. That dominant ideas of identity and political community are confined to identification with the nation-state is in no small way a consequence of the way in which the creation of state boundaries in Europe was closely linked with the rise of nationalism as a powerful discourse and political force and war as an all too frequent expression of this. However, if we focus solely, or mainly, on the nation-state, we may well miss other significant expressions of community and identity. State-centric models of international relations marginalise the political significance of social movements, which identify on the basis of class or gender or are organised around specific issues, such as the environment.

Postmodern scholars embrace at least aspects of the idea of globalisation, not because it necessarily captures real material processes or developments, but because it represents a powerful challenge to state-centrism in IR. That said, in true Foucauldian spirit, postmodernists are also sensitive to the power relations that underpin discourses of globalisation – that is to say, globalisation is itself a contested term for a contested process or project. It is important to realise, therefore, that postmodernists see value in any idea or perspective which encourages us to think about the world differently, but are alert to the discursive contexts in which claims about the world are made. Nevertheless, 'globalisation' might be encouraging new forms of identification and expressions of identity and solidarity which cut across state boundaries. Therefore, the concept of globalisation opens up possibilities for revising identity and community.

CONCEPT BOX

Hybridity

The notion of hybridity implies the mixing of different elements of identity to form something new. The concept of hybridity is particularly associated with the ideas of Homi Bhabha. In order to flesh out the concept of hybrid identities, it is helpful to consider further the ways in which globalisation is relevant to the study of identity. Globalisation implies increased travel, the growth of media and communication and a generally 'smaller' world. In a globalised world, therefore, cultural encounters and mixings are likely to become the norm. For example, it is *possible* that somewhere out there is a Bangladeshi woman. She is the daughter of a Bangladeshi man and an American woman, herself the daughter of German Jews who fled the Nazis. This hypothetical woman grew up in Turkey, though she was educated in English. If this person exists, the only people to share her particular mix of identities are likely to be her siblings, who even then will be unique perhaps owing to gender, sexuality and so on. Indeed, one of the authors of this book has a son who has three citizenships by virtue of having parents with two different nationalities and having been born in a third country, and who within the space of his first three years has already lived in two different countries, growing up trilingually. Such hybrid identities may still be the exception, but they are by no means rare in today's world.

It is interesting to speculate on what all this means. Perhaps hybridity, mixing and transmission of ideas mean more than anything else that the stereotype is increasingly hard to 'hold on to'. Are the reinforcement of ideas such as the 'American Way', the remodelling of ideas in say 'Cool Britannia' or attempts to deny or frustrate global trends by, say, 'protecting' the French language from Anglicisation worthwhile projects or discourses of the powerful, whose power is dependent on these discourses? The attempts of politicians to (re)define 'Britishness' and instil a sense of national pride at the beginning of this century, for instance, can be seen as one part of a broader struggle to define identity in a world in which notions of identity are no longer taken for granted.

Postmodernists are interested in social movements because they see them engaging in a politics that challenges the rigid inside/outside boundaries of state-centric analysis. Innovative technologies are being used by a wide variety of social movements to network, campaign and articulate dissent and resistance. All of this political activity is being carried out in a particular 'space' – cyberspace –

which is outside the jurisdiction and control of individual states though, ironically enough, vulnerable to hacking and virusing by individual people. Accordingly, postmodern scholars argue, we need to radically rethink our conceptions of global political space.

R.B.J. Walker, *One World, Many Worlds*

Walker has been an influential figure in the development of postmodern/post-structuralist thought in International Relations. In this work Walker outlined how he saw the significance of new social movements, in relation to questions of identity, solidarity and political action. Their special significance lies in the way they sometimes respond to the challenges they identify. They find new spaces in which to act, thereby challenging the prevailing topography of political life. They discover new ways of acting, thereby challenging the prevailing conceptions of how people ought to behave towards each other. They extend the horizons of what it is possible to know and to be as human beings, thereby challenging the boundaries of received ethical, aesthetic, and philosophical traditions. Critical social movements struggle in particular circumstances, and yet they also recognise that specific struggles require new forms of interaction between peoples, new forms of human community and solidarity that cut across social and territorial categories established under other historical conditions.

Inequality and justice

This concern with novel forms of identification and expressions of community necessarily raises questions of how we conduct our relationships with others. Given the central concern with the power/knowledge nexus and general scepticism towards Enlightenment discourse, we might expect to find postmodern scholars adopting a rather cynical approach towards questions of justice and moral right. No doubt, some postmodern thinkers are sceptics in this respect. However, this is far from true of all postmodernists working in the field of IR. Some postmodern scholars attempt to go beyond critique, and suggest that postmodern insights are helpful in addressing a range of human problems and concerns. Postmodernist thinkers are interested in questions of justice and concrete inequalities. However, postmodernists tend to concentrate more on the moral and ethical implications of a diverse, culturally heterogeneous world. That in turn raises questions of morality and ethics in world politics.

Questions of morality and ethics cannot be understood purely within the boundaries of nation-states. As was suggested above, Enlightenment thinkers saw the human race as engaged in an effort towards universal moral and intellectual self-realisation and as the subject of a universal historical experience. The nation-state was seen by many as a political space in which ethical behaviour was possible. However, as Critical Theorists have pointed out, there is a moral paradox at the heart of the nation-state – excluded 'others' are not regarded as equal to insiders. So, here 'difference' is dealt with through processes of exclusion and unequal treatment.

A second problem with approaching questions of justice or ethics from a state-centric perspective is that, as we will see in chapter 8, the nation-state is ill-equipped to cope with the many problems facing humankind. The state provides no secure boundaries against the threat of global economic crisis, environmental pollution or nuclear attack. Moreover, when this orientation towards the other is coupled with radically different conceptions of political community and political space, it becomes clear that demands for justice can come from above *and* below the state. Ethical issues and dilemmas arise in a range of contexts. Questions of justice and ethics necessarily arise in the practices of the

World Bank, the United Nations, or a multinational corporation, for example, and also from the demands articulated by, for example, minorities, social movements or indigenous peoples.

Postmodernists are, of course, at pains to point out that power is everywhere and power relations can never be completely overcome. However, the response has been to argue that we must, nevertheless, try to conduct our relations with others on an ethical basis. One of the central questions in traditional IR theory is what do 'citizens' owe to others? A postmodern ethics refuses to start out from the assumption that we are above all else citizens of pre-given states. Rather it suggests starting from the question: what do I/we owe to others? So, postmodernism begins from the position of the other. Postmodern thinkers ask: How does recognition of, and respect for, 'the other' make certain claims or pose specific obligations on me?

Recognition of the inadequacy of the state, and calls to rethink our approach to questions of identity and community, necessitate rethinking what it means to have solidarity with others, and in what it now means to behave in an ethical and just way towards others. For this reason many postmodern scholars are interested in discourses on ethics and moral obligation found in, perhaps, writings on human rights. However, it is important to recognise that postmodern thinkers do not start out from the abstract notion of universal reason as a basis for rights claims. Rather they are interested in how we can develop an ethics based on respect for concrete others out of discourses and practices which already have some currency. At the same time, postmodernists want us to rethink the basis for 'rights' claims, or notions of morality and ethics, so that they are sensitive and responsive to differences.

Conflict and violence

From a postmodern perspective, violence is not endemic to international relations because of conditions of 'anarchy' or because states constantly face real threats to their security from hostile foreigners. The construction of the 'outside' as hostile and threatening, legitimises violence in international relations. Furthermore, violence is actually central to the very constitution of the state. The state is, to borrow Max Weber's phrase, that institution which holds a monopoly on the legitimate use of force. The state exercises authority through the political and legal system, but this is backed up by the coercive arms of state power, the military and internal police forces. At the very heart of the state are discourses and practices of violence. This casts considerable doubt on the claim that the state is a 'progressive' form of political organisation.

Institutions and world order

Institutions and world order have not been prominent themes or preoccupations in postmodern IR. However, postmodern IR scholars have engaged in critiques of existing discourses of 'world order' and key concepts like 'governance'. Richard Ashley's critique of governance, sketched below, provides you with a flavour of this work.

CONCEPT BOX

Governance as 'imposition'

In his article on 'Imposing International Purpose' (see Further reading: Critical Theory), Richard Ashley develops a critique of much of the contemporary literature on institutions, regimes and ideas about 'governance' that have much currency within contemporary International Relations. Taking issue with the neo-liberal institutionalists in particular, Ashley starts from the prior distinction that is often drawn between the regularities that structure relations between states and which thus constitute the 'objective reality' or 'objective conditions' of life (for example, the global market) and those rules and norms that are constructed by actors to regulate their relationships and which are intersubjective in nature. Ashley calls into question this distinction, because it presents structures as the objective conditions of life and as such devoid of purpose and independent of specific knowledge practices. Ashley argues that these 'structures' are contingent effects that are imposed in history through practice. Moreover, they are imposed to the exclusion of other ways of structuring collective existence (note the Foucauldian influences here). As such, 'structures' embody a collective intentionality that similarly exclude other ways of structuring collective existence. The existence of structures disciplines resistances and silences competing practices (pp. 251–4).

Ashley's critique of governance as 'imposition' or 'imposed intentional purpose' can be illustrated with an example from current practice. Globalisation is sometimes presented as a 'structure', an objective condition of life which states must negotiate. Multilateral institutions, such as the International Monetary Fund (IMF) and World Bank play a key role in global (economic) governance, devising policies and projects that work with the forces of globalisation. However, it could be argued that globalisation has been facilitated by the 'rules' made by the IMF, the World Trade Organization (WTO), the World Bank and many states around the world. Neo-liberalism – as a dominant knowledge structure and political project – has facilitated the expansion of investment and markets, but it also sets the parameters within which certain policy options (rather than others) are then adjudged 'feasible' or otherwise. Moreover, while ostensibly committed to being more accountable and transparent, opportunities for NGOs to play a role in international economic and social policy-making are, in reality, limited to those NGOs whose goals coincide with the neo-liberal policies and agendas of multilateral economic institutions. Thus, both the norms and mechanisms of 'governance' work to promote a neo-liberal agenda while 'disciplining and silencing' other voices, practices and projects. Much of the current literature on governance represents 'structures' as objective conditions that impose certain limits and conditions on political life. This tends to disguise the ways in which political projects can be furthered through institutions, networks and processes of governance.

Summary

1. Postmodernism is not easy. It challenges many ideas central to International Relations.
2. Postmodernism is not simply about the period of history following modernity, but provides ways of thinking about the consequences of modern thought and practice.
3. Despite some leftist origins, postmodernism has been accused of profound conservatism. Its questioning attitude is just one reason why it is difficult, if not impossible, to categorise politically.

4. Postmodernism inquires into multiple power/knowledge relationships.
5. Postmodernists have been concerned with drawing out hidden assumptions (making visible the invisible) by a process of critique.
6. Postmodernism does not mean a person can have no values or should believe in nothing; rather that they should be tentative about the grounds for the claims they make based upon these.
7. Particularly important authors are Jacques Derrida (1930–2004) and Michel Foucault (1926–84), but postmodernism is much more difficult to pigeonhole than, say, realism.
8. Postmodernism uses various methods including genealogy. This seeks to highlight the singularity of events rather than trends, in order to reveal the idea that all history is written by the powerful.
9. In undermining much of IR, postmodernism might be considered better taught *before* students have the discipline's 'truths' instilled in them. For this reason it appears in this book despite its difficulties.

Criticisms

Some critics have argued that postmodernism has no real 'relevance' to IR. That is to say, postmodernism is not policy-orientated and so cannot be used to inform the conduct of international relations. This can be contested on the grounds that many postmodern ideas – for example, on ethics – *can* inform policy. Moreover, this kind of criticism is based on a rather narrow definition of what constitutes international relations or international politics.

The postmodernist suspicion of meta-narrative and grand theory has led some critics to argue that postmodernism will merely generate endless empirical studies, in which the scholars admit to doing no more than 'interpreting' or 'telling stories' about discrete areas of interest. However, such criticism neglects the importance of critique in postmodernist thought. Moreover, it implicitly assumes that grand theories and metanarratives are useful or insightful.

A further criticism often levelled at postmodernism is that it gives us no way of distinguishing between 'good' and 'bad' forms of knowledge. A related criticism would be that, if we cannot grasp life from a single perspective, and power is everywhere, ultimately this means we cannot judge the validity of different discourses. An extreme example of this, in more senses than one, would be that postmodernism cannot judge the validity or assess the ethical danger of a text like Adolf Hitler's *Mein Kampf*. Again, denying the ultimate foundation or 'truth' of particular world views or values or texts does not necessarily mean that we cannot be opposed to some positions. Indeed, critique and deconstruction can be important political tools in themselves, revealing the partiality and bias of a particular position or doctrine and so undermining its claims to be based on a truth. This criticism of postmodernism is, perhaps, based on a misunderstanding of 'responsibility'. Having no 'universal truth' or 'universal agent' does not mean that postmodernists do not have to take responsibility for their actions. Indeed, as we have seen, postmodernists reject totalitarian truths and celebrate diversity. To that extent, the suppression of diversity, as displayed in fascism, marks a limit to the postmodernist toleration of difference.

Postmodernism has been described as a profoundly conservative position. This criticism arises in part because of the postmodernist rejection of a blueprint for alternative action or emancipation. As we pointed out in our introduction to postmodernism above, it is not easy to categorise postmodernism as either 'right wing' or 'left wing'. It might be that some postmodern thinkers are profoundly conservative. However, it does not necessarily follow that all postmodernists want to preserve the status quo. Indeed, as will be apparent from the above discussion, many postmodernists identify with oppositional groups.

Postmodernism has also been criticised because it attacks Marxism, but has paid little attention to the violence and oppression inherent in capitalism. In their defence postmodernists might point out that, while Marxism has indeed been a target of critique, many postmodernist scholars have also attacked neo-liberalism and contemporary approaches to modernisation because they legitimise dominant economic projects.

Postmodernism has been criticised as profoundly disempowering, because it has no real conception of agency. It is sometimes suggested that postmodernism, even in its 'oppositional' mode, rejects the notion of a subject with a voice, and so undermines the ability of marginalised groups to articulate their experiences. However, some postmodernists' rejection of subjectivity does not mean that there are no subjects, but merely that these are not sovereign and are embedded in a broader discursive context. As we have seen, a lot of postmodern work is, in fact, aimed at creating space for the articulation of marginalised positions by deconstructing dominant discourses. Such work is sympathetic to human-(subject-) centred analysis and seeks to retain, or salvage, something of the humanist tradition characteristic of the Enlightenment.

Finally, if power is everywhere, but we cannot identify structures of power, for example, patriarchy, or capitalism, who or what are we supposed to be resisting? Moreover, if postmodernists are sceptical about the existence of material interests rooted in, say, class or gender, what grounds are there for collective action? Marxists and some feminists have contended that postmodernism uses the language of dissidence, exile and marginalisation, but has nothing to say about how political action can be used to make the world a better place. One postmodernist answer is that emancipatory projects imply a coherent plan; since power relations are always implicated in visions of emancipation, we can only be vigilant and ask: What are the political consequences of emancipation? Who is the other? What kind of subject positions will be privileged and which will be marginalised through emancipation?

Common misunderstandings

1. *Postmodernism is the same as poststructuralism.* No, but as we demonstrate above, there are similarities and we have tended to emphasise these in this chapter.

2. *Postmodernists think that there is no 'real' world.* It would be plainly absurd to deny that there are, for example, real wars and that real people get killed. However, we can never understand the world directly, so we rely upon interpretations of events rather than the actual events themselves for our knowledge of the world. Moreover, in the contemporary age, as often as not, those interpretations come to us through the media and mass communication. In a sense, we usually find ourselves interpreting images and stories that come to us through foreign correspondents and/or television news bulletins which are necessarily selective and, perhaps, biased in their coverage of events/issues. In such circumstances it is perhaps wise to ask what picture of the world is being presented to us? Whose world view is this? What sort of interpretation of 'what happened' and 'why' is being offered to us here? This is not to say that an interpretation can be contrasted with what really happened. All we ever have are interpretations in which the 'reader' infuses any event or process with meaning.

3. *Postmodernists are all relativists.* Not necessarily. Certainly, postmodernists concede that there is no ultimate foundation for knowledge. Therefore, we cannot say categorically that some cultural values and practices are 'bad' and others are 'better' or 'right' (but see below).

4. *Postmodernists are nihilists who have no values.* Not necessarily. We cannot say categorically that some cultural values and practices are 'bad' and others are 'better' or 'right'. However, this position is not inconsistent with preferring one set of values to another, it is simply a matter of on what basis we justify those preferences. We have also seen that postmodernists value diversity and work against totalitarianisms of all sorts.

5. *Postmodern thinkers deny the possibility of human emancipation, therefore, they are unlikely to oppose oppressive practices or systems of rule.* No. Postmodernist thinkers eschew the term 'emancipatory politics', preferring to speak instead of 'interventions' or 'sites of resistance'. The notion of emancipation is too closely tied to the language of old ideologies such as Marxism, which have frequently engaged in repression when they have succeeded in gaining political power. It does not follow from this that postmodernists will be silent or timid in the face of aggression or oppression, as should be apparent from the earlier discussion of Stalinism and the Nazi persecution of Jews and other minorities.

Further reading

Ashley, R. K. (1988), 'Untying the sovereign state: a double reading of the anarchy problematique', *Millennium: Journal of International Studies*, Vol. 17, No. 2, pp. 227–62 (an early, influential re-reading of the problem of anarchy from a post-structuralist perspective).

Bartelson, J. (1995), *A Genealogy of Sovereignty*, Cambridge: Cambridge University Press (re-visiting the sovereignty debate in IR, employing Foucauldian modes of analysis).

Campbell, D. (1998), *Writing Security: United States Foreign Policy and the Politics of Identity* (revised edition), Manchester: Manchester University Press (helpful in terms of elucidating the role played by identity and processes of 'othering' in the making of foreign policy).

Der Derian, J. and Shapiro, M. (eds) (1989), *International/Intertextual Relations: Postmodern Readings of World Politics*, Lexington, MA: Lexington Books (one of the first texts that attempted to use the ideas of Derrida, Foucault and other influential post-structuralists in an IR context).

Edkins, J. (1998), *Poststructuralism & International Relations: Bringing the Political Back in* (Critical Perspectives on World Politics), US: Lynne Rienner Publishers Inc.

Hansen, L. (2006), *Security as Practice: Discourse Analysis and the Bosnian War*, London: Routledge (an impressive work that revises the conception of Othering and offers one of the methodologically most advanced studies coming out of a broadly postmodernist perspective).

Walker, R. B. J. (1993), *Inside/Outside: International Relations as Political Theory*, Cambridge: Cambridge University Press (generally regarded as a seminal work in post-structuralist IR).

6 Feminist perspectives

Introduction

Most definitions of feminism centre on the demand for equality between the sexes or equal rights for women. For this reason, students new to the study of feminism and/in IR often assume that it is about women. As we will see below, feminists do have much to say on the topic of women, on sexual equality and women's rights. However, this is a very narrow understanding of 'feminism' which does not fully reflect the richness and breadth of this body of thought. Equality and equal rights issues have never been the sole focus of feminism. Moreover, the study of gender should not be conflated with 'women'. For example, as the title of Marysia Zalewski and Jane Parpart's book *The 'Man' Question in IR* suggests, feminists are as much interested in masculinities and the construction of masculinities in international relations as women and constructed femininities. The term 'gender' might be used to refer to men and women (as categories); or it might refer to the material and ideological relations that exist between the two sexes – that is, the term is used to describe one dimension of social relationships. Characteristics which are held to be essentially 'male' or 'female' vary in different societies and across cultures and prevailing beliefs about gender vary across time. It is difficult to substantiate the argument that gender differences somehow reflect essential differences. In contemporary feminist scholarship gender is more often employed in relation to ideological or discursive constructions of 'masculinities' and 'femininities.'

Since there are many strands of feminist theory, it should not be surprising to discover that there are diverse strands of feminist scholarship within IR. As with the other perspectives covered in this book, feminism is not a monolithic body of thought. There are also different ways of categorizing feminist work in IR. For example, twenty years ago, feminist IR scholarship tended to be grouped into different strands/approaches: liberal, standpoint and post-structuralist. In more recent years, Ann Tickner (and others) have identified different 'waves' or generations of feminist scholarship. In this chapter the differences between approaches in feminist IR scholarship are not entirely disregarded. The different intellectual roots of feminist thought are flagged in the 'Origins' section and, periodically, differences within feminist approaches and perspectives are highlighted in the sections on 'Assumptions' and 'Themes', when it is useful and appropriate to do so.

However, this chapter is intended as a first introduction to feminist IR and, as with other chapters, the aims here are to simplify as much as possible while supplying the basic vocabulary, introducing the key concepts and ideas and providing examples of how feminist scholars have contributed to the study of IR. Even while acknowledging that feminism is something of a broad church, it is possible to construct a feminist perspective, in a loose sense of the term: as a way of looking at the world which prioritises certain features, issues or processes. Thus, V. Spike Peterson and Ann Sisson Runyan have adopted the notion of looking through 'feminist lenses' or 'gender lenses' in order to uncover aspects of international relations that have been neglected by earlier approaches such as realism, liberalism or structuralism. Many feminists argue that much discourse about international relations, or in IR, is not neutral, but profoundly gendered; it implicitly assumes a masculinist viewpoint. This does not mean that only women are capable of seeing the world through a feminist or gendered lens, because perspectives are politically and not biologically grounded.

CONCEPT BOX

A feminist lens on world politics

As noted above, feminists IR is not exclusively about women. Nevertheless, one of the central aims of what might be characterized as the first wave of feminist literature in the late 1980s and early 1990s was to 'bring in' women in the study of IR. Also, feminist scholars posed questions that got at some deeper epistemological issues in IR (see Reflection Box below). Feminists asked: what might the world of international relations look like if women's concerns were made central rather than marginal? How might the understanding of power be re-visioned if women's experience of forms of domination, or empowerment were the focus of study? What would be seen as vital to the achievement of security, for example, if the things women feared most were prioritised? This was the first stage in developing a critique of dominant conceptions of international politics. One of the first books to bring feminist insights to the study of IR was Cynthia Enloe's *Bananas, Beaches and Bases* which is included in the Further reading section.

With regard to security, feminists developed radical new ways of thinking about the problems involved in achieving security, in the first place, by developing alterative conceptions of political community and security. In this respect feminist works on a politics of 'mutuality' and an ethic of care were brought to bear on security. Ann Tickner's *Gender in International Relations: Feminist Perspectives on Achieving Global Security* emphasised the insights and values of feminist work on human connectedness, dialogue and cooperation over the then dominant realists' concepts of power as dominance and the ever-present threat of violent confrontation in understanding security. Feminists also challenged the idea that the nation-state was the principle referent of security. The degree to which people felt or actually were 'threatened' varied according to the economic, political, social or personal circumstances of the individual or social group. Gender hierarchies and inequalities were shown to constitute an obstacle to the achievement of genuine security. Like liberals, some feminist scholars linked the realisation of a secure world with human rights. In the past three decades, international conventions and instruments have been developed that address the violation of women's human rights, particularly in relation to violence against women, including violence that occurs within the private or domestic sphere. Feminist work on both security and human rights will be covered in greater depth below.

In summary, adopting a feminist perspective in IR might mean any of the following, or indeed a combination of any of the following:

- Employing gender as a central category of analysis in the study of IR;
- Employing gender as a 'variable' in the study of IR (although this is regarded as controversial in some quarters – see box below);
- Incorporating gender as a core social relation in the study of IR. For example, feminism rooted in an historical materialist tradition typically understands gender as a specific form of power relationship between men and women, or a social relationship of inequality between men and women. Gender relations are seen to be embedded in real-material structures and institutions (the

state, the family, for example) which in turn serve to reproduce gender inequality in varied ways through policies or laws or more informal everyday social practices;

■ Focusing on how discourses on all aspects of international relations are gendered discourses. A number of examples are given below, including gendered discourses in the current War on Terror;

■ Drawing attention to the public/private division as central to our understanding of international relations. For example, child-care and violence within the home/family have historically been regarded as 'private' matters, rather than 'public' and so not within the domain of policy making in governments or international institutions. Today, largely thanks to political pressure from feminist groups, both domestic labour/social reproduction and domestic violence are recognized as international issues;

■ Challenging dominant assumptions about what is significant or insignificant, or what is marginal or central, in the study of international relations;

■ Adopting gender lenses to revise or 'revision' the study of IR.

Origins

The openness of theoretical debates in International Relations in the late 1980s created a space for feminist scholarship in a discipline which had, up until that point, largely ignored gender. However, feminist International Relations scholars draw upon a rich and varied tradition of feminist thought, stretching back to at least the eighteenth century.

As noted above, feminism is a diverse body of thought and there are many ways of categorising it. A full exploration of how feminist theory informs feminist IR would require a chapter-length treatment, so the discussion will be limited to only four strands of feminist thought: liberal, Marxist (or historical materialist), standpoint and post-structuralist.

Liberal feminism

Liberal feminism is very much committed to the modernist and Enlightenment view of how the world should be organised. At this point it might be helpful to refer back to the earlier discussions of modernity and the Enlightenment (see chapters 4 and 5). The modern notion that human societies could progress, along with the emphasis on scientific knowledge rather than traditional belief systems, allowed liberals like Mary Wollstonecraft (1759–1797) and Elizabeth Cady Stanton (1815–1902) to argue that the status of women was one measure of the progressive and civilised nature of society. Although not explicitly calling themselves feminists, women like Elizabeth Cady Stanton gave voice to a set of concerns and demands which we would today clearly identify as feminist. For example, she claimed that the position of women was not ordained by God or determined by nature, but shaped by society.

From a liberal perspective, participation in public life was the key to advancing the status of women. Liberals claimed that women, like men, were capable of intellectual development and moral progress. This meant that women, like men, were rational creatures and so had the right to participate in public life – to vote and, more broadly, to contribute to debates about political, social and moral issues – rather than being confined to the private sphere of the home and the family, represented in public life by the male 'head of the household'. In regard to questions of gender and difference, liberal feminists hold that women and men are basically alike and that perceived gender differences are simply the effects of discrimination. Thus, the political project of early liberal feminists was largely limited to securing for women the rights and privileges already enjoyed by men. Since the 1960s liberal feminists (in Western countries particularly) have been more attentive to gender differences. For example, along with lobbying for women's rights at national and international levels, liberal feminists have also argued that our understanding of what constitutes a 'right' or an abuse of human rights should be expanded to include dimensions of life previously neglected. Again, domestic violence is a good example. This is not to say that only women are affected by domestic violence, of course; only that it was an issue that was originally foisted onto the international political and legal agenda as a 'women's issue'.

REFLECTION BOX

Bringing in women: is gender a 'variable'?

Since feminist scholarship began to make inroads into the study of IR in the late 1980s, there has been an ongoing debate both about the status of feminist theory and the possible contribution that gender analyses can make to the study of IR. While feminist IR has largely been accepted within critical IR theory (broadly conceived), feminists have had a harder time finding acceptance among scholars who subscribe to 'mainstream' (neo-realist and neo-liberal) approaches in IR.

Positivists argue that theory and analysis (and the knowledge it generates) is only legitimate if research conforms to the accepted principles and methods of particular scientific disciplines. Post-positivists in contrast argue that what is generally accepted as 'knowledge' in the field is coloured by consensual understandings of what constitutes a distinctive 'discipline' held by a community of scholars. These consensual understandings include agreement on the dominant preoccupations of IR and how our knowledge of this particular domain can best be advanced.

Keohane argues that rationalist and positivist approaches to IR concentrate on establishing causal laws in international relations (for example, as in democratic transition theory) formulating hypotheses that can be tested in the 'real world'. It is important for scientific enquiry that one's procedures (methods of investigation) are known and capable of being replicated by other scholars. From this perspective feminist scholarship can contribute to IR, but only if feminists emulate existing 'scientific' approaches. What this means in practice is that gender analysis can find a space in IR, but only if we regard gender as one of many 'variables' that might be relevant to understanding the causes (or impacts) of war, for example, or the nature and extent of global poverty perhaps. Thus, the study of gender in IR is reduced to the status of gender as one of many 'variables' that might be used to inform our theories on causality or to quantify 'impacts'.

Most feminist scholars regard themselves as post-positivists. Feminists argue that positivist or scientific analysis is problematic because it assumes that gender is a settled or essential feature of men and women respectively (hence the possibility of identifying a gender variable), which as noted above is at odds with most contemporary feminist theory. Even where feminists appear to embrace essentialism, this is often justified not on the grounds of actual biological/sexual differences, but on the grounds of social experiences, or even because it is a useful strategic ploy – in certain circumstances to achieve specific goals. The assumption that gender can be reduced to a variable is problematic, because positivists are unreflective about how, as Cynthia Weber argues, one is never 'outside' gender. This assertion that 'one is never outside gender' is really the key to grasping the insights that feminism brings to the study of IR. While the 'gender as a variable' approach might serve to expand the boundaries of existing IR, positivist scholars are ultimately asking the wrong kind of questions. Feminist IR is rather more ambitious, seeking to escape boundaries of mainstream discourse in IR. There have been a number of debates and exchanges between feminist and mainstream IR scholars. These are included in the Further reading section at the end of this book and are revisited briefly in the concluding chapter.

It has generally been accepted that liberal empiricism is valuable in 'bringing in' women into the study of IR, but feminist IR scholars have tended not to identify with the intellectual position and political project of liberal feminism. This is because liberal feminism has been deemed to be problematic. As previously noted, this strand of feminist thought carries a heavy intellectual and political baggage from the Enlightenment. Many contemporary feminists believe that the commitment to 'progress' is based on the assumption that modern (read Western) societies are more advanced than other kinds of societies. This has resulted in damaging practices and policies in international politics: for example, constructing women in developing countries as somehow 'backward' or 'oppressed' when this is not necessarily the case. Moreover, liberal feminism tends to make universal claims in the name of 'women', whereas contemporary feminist theory (and feminist IR) is much more sensitive to differences among women (and men), and to the inherent difficulties in separating out gender

Figure 6.1 Women's political participation.

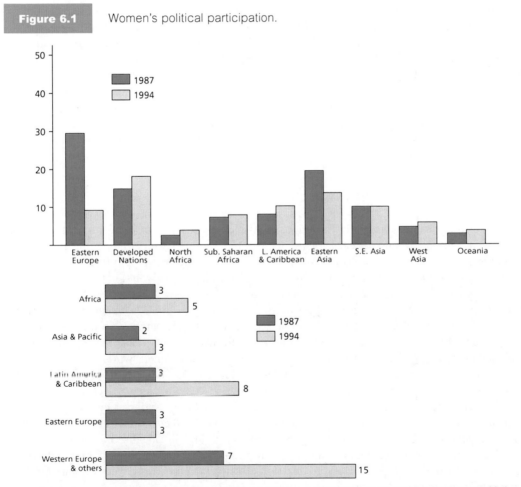

Original source: The *New Internationalist* (April 1995); and the *World Government Directory* (1994).

Taken from: J.J. Pettman (1997), 'Gender issues', in J. Baylis and S. Smith, *The Globalization of World Politics*, 1st edn, Oxford: Oxford University Press, p. 486.
Reflection – these kinds of figures would be of particular interest to liberal feminists. Why do you think a general trend to more women in parliamentary assemblies was sharply reversed in Eastern Europe (and, to a lesser extent, Eastern Asia) from 1987 to 1994?

from other facets of identity, like race or ethnicity, for example. Contemporary feminist theorists pay close attention to the specific and particular factors that shape the lives of women and men in different societies around the world. Whether or not all of these criticisms are justified is a moot point, but there is no space here to go into the core debates integral to feminist theory. Suffice to say, liberal feminism has been very influential in the actual practice of international politics, although paradoxically, not so in the academic study of feminist international relations.

AUTHOR BOX

Mary Wollstonecraft

The English radical thinker and writer Mary Wollstonecraft's feminism was fostered by her own experiences of discrimination. Passionate on the subject of education for girls, Wollstonecraft published a book on the subject *Thoughts on the Education of Daughters* in 1787 and helped to establish a girl's school at Newington Green. However, she is most famous for her 1792 treatise *A Vindication of the Rights of Woman*, in which she used liberal arguments to make the case for equal rights and opportunities for women. The book caused quite a stir at the time, as did Wollstonecraft's unconventional lifestyle. Indeed, to some extent, Wollstonecraft suffered the fate which befalls many women, in that her work was not judged on its merits alone, but rather in the context of her own appearance and behaviour. Wollstonecraft died in childbirth in 1797. The child grew up to achieve her own fame as Mary Wollstonecraft Godwin Shelley, the creator of Frankenstein.

(Information from: L. Tuttle (1986), *Encyclopedia of Feminism*, London: Arrow Books)

Feminist historical materialism

This strand of feminism has its origins in Marxism. At the very time that nineteenth-century liberal feminists were rallying around the cause of women's rights, Marxists were arguing that equal rights would not lead to women's emancipation. While they welcomed the declining influence of religious dogmatism and traditional beliefs, Marxists argued these developments would not necessarily bring the end of women's inequality, because capitalism was simultaneously creating new forms of social subordination and inequality. The gist of the Marxist view of the position of women in society (most fully articulated by Friedrich Engels) was that the emergence of capitalism as a social and economic system brought about a clear distinction between the public world of work and the private realm of the home and the family. This led to particular ideas about what constituted 'work' and 'production', and in this process 'women's work' came to be denigrated and undervalued. The home and the family had come to be viewed as 'private' areas of human life, clearly separate and distinct from the public realm. Here human relations were supposedly based on affection, and particularism. A man's relationship with his wife and family was not then subject to the rather more abstract and universal principles of justice and equality that governed the public world. This idealised view of the family disguised the reality of power relations and inequality that permeated both the public and private realms. The construction of a public/private division effectively served to reduce women, and children to the private property of men.

As the illustration of married life in the 1950s makes clear (see the Literature Box below), the construction of women as people who achieve true fulfilment through the performance of their nurturing, caring and supporting roles prevailed until well into the twentieth century.

Married life

1. Have dinner ready. Plan ahead (even the night before) to have a delicious meal ready on time. This is a way of letting him know that you have been thinking about him and are concerned about his needs. Most men are hungry when they come home and the prospect of a good meal is part of the warm welcome they need.

2. Prepare yourself: take 15 minutes to rest so you will be refreshed when he arrives. Touch up your make-up, put a ribbon in your hair and be fresh looking. He has been with a lot of work weary people. Be a little gay and a little more interesting. His boring day may need a lift.

3. Clear away the clutter. Make one last trip through the house just before he arrives, gathering up school books, toys, papers, etc. Then run a dust cloth over the tables. Your husband will feel he has reached a haven of rest and order and it will give you a lift too.

4. Prepare the children. Take a few minutes to wash the children's hands and faces if they are small, comb their hair and, if necessary, change their clothes. They are little treasures and he would like to see them playing the part.

5. Minimise the noise. At the time of his arrival eliminate all noise of washers, dryers, dishwashers or vacuums. Try to encourage the children to be quiet. Be happy to see him. Greet him with a warm smile and be glad to see him.

6. Don't greet him with problems and complaints. Don't complain if he's late for dinner – count this as minor compared with what he might have gone through that day.

7. Make him comfortable. Have him lean back in a comfortable chair, or suggest he lie down in the bedroom. Have a cool or warm drink ready for him. Arrange his pillow and offer to take off his shoes. Speak in a low, soothing and pleasant voice. Allow him to relax and unwind.

8. Listen to him. You may have a dozen things to tell him but the moment of his arrival is not the time. Let him talk first.

9. Make the evening his. Never complain if he does not take you out to dinner or to other places of entertainment. Instead try to understand his world of strain and pressure, his need to be home and relax.

10. The goal: try to make the home a place of peace and order where your husband can relax.

(Taken from a Home Economics manual, published in 1950)

In the twentieth century Marxist-feminists developed a more sophisticated analysis of the relationship between capitalism, the prevailing sexual division of labour, and gender inequality. A key issue that Marxist feminists highlighted was the contribution that women's unpaid domestic labour made to the capitalist economy. These concerns – women's contribution to the global economy, prevalent ideas about the naturalness of gender roles, and the separation of the public and the private – remain central to contemporary feminist historical materialism. A number of feminist scholars who work in the sub-field of international political economy or in international economic organisations and governance are particularly interested in a set of issues to do with social reproduction, the rolling back of the state and shifting the burden of social care and social welfare from the public to the private. Feminist economics had also been important in the practice of international politics in putting pressure on international institutions to 'make women count' by calculating the value of women's labour and including this value in satellite accounts.

Figure 6.2   The dutiful housewife plays her 'proper' role.

Source: Lambert/Getty Images.

Before moving on, it is important to note that this strand of feminism also emphasises the role of ideology in constructing and reproducing social relations of inequality. Gender differences are constructed as socially relevant and used to justify differential treatment between men and women. From this perspective gender is best understood as both a facet of personal identity (gender is a central facet of identity because individuals are subjected to social pressures to conform to gendered stereotypes) and an aspect of social institutions. Gender differences and gender inequalities are embedded in institutions like the family for instance, but are also reproduced in state policies on reproduction, marriage, welfare and work. In this respect, feminists who work from within the assumptions of historical materialism have something in common with constructivist and post-structuralists in that the ideational realm is afforded importance in understanding international relations. However, the political project of historical materialist feminists is to further the emancipation of women (and other subordinated groups – a point developed further below) and in this respect feminist historical materialism differs from post-structuralist feminism. A good example of an early work in feminist IR that articulated this position is Sandra Whitworth's *Feminist Theory and International Relations* (see Further reading).

Standpoint feminism

Standpoint feminism has its origins in strands of thought that were particularly influential during the so-called 'second wave' of feminism in the 1960s and especially the 1970s. To some extent, standpoint feminism draws upon psychoanalytical feminism (people like Dorothy Dinnerstein and Carol

Gilligan, for example). Today, very few feminists working in IR explicitly self-identify as standpoint feminists, therefore it will be afforded only limited space here, although the insights into questions of epistemology remain valid and relevant to IR.

Standpoint is often criticized as 'essentialist' since it relies on certain ideas about how gender differences give rise to different perspectives. Standpoint theorists argue that women and men occupy radically different 'life worlds'. For example, women's experiences of nurturing and caring shape feminine experience and lead to a distinctive viewpoint. However, most versions of standpoint acknowledge that gender identities are forged through processes of socialisation. Feminist standpoint theorists make strong epistemological and ontological claims about and on behalf of women, arguing that legitimate social knowledge can be constructed from the point of view of women's concrete experiences. In this way, women will move 'from the margin to the centre' as the subjects of knowledge in IR. The above-mentioned book by J. Ann Tickner *Gender in International Relations* is a good example of a work that brought the insights of feminist standpoint into the study of international politics.

REFLECTION BOX

Epistemology concerns the status of the knowledge we generate through theory and research. For example, is it objective fact or subjective interpretation? Epistemology also concerns who can know: who are the 'knowers'.

Post-structuralist feminism

The intellectual influences on poststructuralist feminists working in IR are broadly the same as those on post-structuralist IR scholars as a whole and so need not be reproduced here (see chapter 5). While post-structuralist feminists view gender as discursively constructed and so owe a debt to thinkers such as Michel Foucault, it is pertinent to note that a core concept in poststructuralism – the 'other' – can be found in the work of earlier existentialist feminist thinkers such as Simone de Beauvoir. The work of feminist scholars from other disciplines, such as Judith Butler, has also been central to the development of post-structuralist feminist IR.

As we saw in the previous chapter, poststructuralism can be seen as constituting a radical critique of all meta-narratives of human progress and emancipation. Post-structuralists argue that so-called 'universal' features of human beings or human life are actually particular – that is, based on the Western experience. Rather than advocate projects to achieve women's liberation or emancipation based on the Western model, post-structuralists concentrate on the incremental changes and socially contextualised activities and strategies which women use to improve their position in specific societies. So, for example, a post-structuralist feminist scholar will focus on concrete day-to-day practices, and how these either allow or close off access to resources in any given situation or society, or empower or disempower women and men in various ways.

REFLECTION BOX

Ontology is concerned with the nature of existence. For example, can we talk about 'women' or 'men' as stable categories and/or settled identities?

Post-structuralists eschew strong epistemological and ontological claims made in the name of 'women', arguing that there is no authentic 'women's experience' or 'standpoint' from which to construct an understanding of the social and political world, because women's lives are embedded in specific social and cultural relations. A person's understanding of what it means to be 'masculine' or 'feminine' is constructed through language, symbols and stories that are woven into the fabric of everyday life in different societies. Moreover, post-structuralists argue that gender is discursively constructed. We cannot, then, speak of women as having a fixed ontological essence, nor adopt gender as a stable category of analysis. The meaning of gender depends upon the historical, social, cultural and institutional context in which discourse on gender is conducted. Christine Sylvester's *Feminist international relations: an unfinished journey* and her early work *Feminist Theory and International Relations in a Postmodern Era* are good examples of post-structuralist feminist texts. However, there are number of prominent feminist scholars in IR, including Marysia Zalewski and V. Spike Peterson.

AUTHOR BOX

Judith Butler

Judith Butler is a central figure in contemporary feminist theory. In her influential book *Gender Trouble*, Butler argues that there is no necessary relationship between one's material/biological sex and one's discursively produced gender. One might possess a male body, but not display behaviour generally accepted as masculine. Butler does not deny the existence of the actual or material body, but argues that we can only understand the meaning of the material body through social discourse. It is through discourse that the sexed body (male or female) is invested with social significance.

Butler draws upon Simone De Beauvoir's insight that 'one is not born, but becomes a woman' to demonstrate how gender is not something we are but something we do: gender is a performance. The language we use to describe the body actually constitutes the body. To be a 'man' or 'woman' is thus a performative statement. This notion of 'performance' can be and has been used within other contexts in IR. For example, post-structuralists talk of 'performing the state' or 'performing sovereignty'. Thus, Butler's work has not just been an important influence on feminists working in IR, but in post-structuralist IR generally.

So far, our story of the history of feminist theory and practice has concentrated on feminism in the Western world. However, both the theory and practice of feminism have been shaped by developments in non-Western societies. Historically, Western liberal feminist discourses have been tied up with an inherent faith in progress and development that will eventually help women to achieve genuine equality with men. This Western liberal belief in progress informed modernisation and development projects promoted by UN agencies that were designed to advance the status of women (see below). Postcolonial feminism is deeply sceptical of the idea that progress and freedom for women will come from following the Western model of social and economic development, since their own experiences reveal a history of colonial or imperialist domination. Too often in Western feminist discourse, non-Western women are constructed as 'other'; victims of backward cultural practices and traditions, in contrast to their 'emancipated' Western sisters.

Furthermore, projects to emancipate women assume that we can speak of real 'women' and/or 'women's experiences' without recognising the diversity of women and women's experiences. Gender identities are cross-cut by culture, race, ethnicity, and so on. Moreover, we should not fall into the trap of assuming that culture is always experienced as oppressive, since culture and cultural practices might be celebrated by women in specific societies. This is not to say that postcolonialism is anti-feminist. Postcolonial feminists, like post-structuralists, insist that feminism should be concerned with understanding how women's particular location within a culture or society and the meaning attached to 'femininity' in that context might serve to disempower women or, conversely, allow women access to resources and to enjoy a certain amount of social power. Geeta Chowdhry and Sheila Nair's *Postcolonialism and International Relations*: and Vivienne Jabri and Eleanore O'Gorman *Women, Culture, and International Relations* are examples of such works.

By way of concluding this section on origins, it is helpful to draw out the commonalities and differences in different strands of feminism. While liberal and historical materialist feminisms disagree about how women can best challenge and overcome inequality and subordination, they have tended to hold a fairly optimistic view of the possibilities of human progress. Moreover, it is vital that people become active agents in the process of realising social change. In contrast, post-structuralist feminists argue that no one group possesses a blueprint for universal human emancipation. This is not to say that post-structuralist feminism simply defends the status quo. Power relations are embedded in certain cultural and social practices, so in any given culture, dominant groups will be able to impose definitions and construct meanings and, in so doing, legitimise gender inequalities. It is possible to explore how dominant discourses about gender serve to legitimise particular social practices and how these are, in turn, resisted, but the emphasis is always on the local and the specific context.

Assumptions

1. Feminists do not regard human nature as immutable; liberals believe that human beings are rational beings, but also that human capacities develop through the process of education. Other schools of feminism regard 'human nature' as being differentiated or socially constructed.
2. From a feminist perspective, we cannot make a clear distinction between a 'fact' and a 'value.'
3. There is an intimate connection between knowledge and power and between our 'theories' about the world and our practices – the way we engage with our physical and social surroundings.
4. Post-structuralists apart (post-structuralists reject universal claims), feminist share a commitment to women's emancipation or liberation. Post-structuralists prefer to speak of 'empowerment' and interrogate what this might mean in specific cultural contexts.

Themes

The state and power

As is evident from the above discussion of origins, liberal feminists are interested in improving the status of women around the world, increasing women's participation in public life and gaining access to power. While working within a basically liberal pluralist framework, liberal feminists highlight the absence of women from mainstream analysis. Liberal feminists ask the questions: where are the women in international relations? What is the status of women around the world? How far are women represented or under-represented in international relations? What are the best strategies for overcoming discrimination against women and giving women more control over their own lives and destinies?

'Bringing in' women is a first stage in developing feminist insights into the nature of the state. Looking at the world through a liberal feminist 'lens' allows us to see that the world of international relations is a man's world, in so far as the state's representatives are mainly men-politicians, soldiers, spies and so on. Women have historically been excluded from political power and today remain heavily under-represented in the 'high politics' of statecraft. From a feminist perspective, very few women are involved in the making of foreign or defence policy, so the 'national interest' is always defined by men of statecraft.

As we saw in chapter 1, liberals view the state as a neutral arbiter between competing interests in an open and pluralistic society. Liberal feminists recognise that, historically, the state has not been equal and impartial in its treatment of women. However, for liberal feminists, male domination is largely explained by historical circumstance and accident. Given access to equal opportunities, women can prove that they are the equals of men. In this way, women can gradually overcome deeply rooted social prejudices and prove their abilities in a range of activities including politics. A central question for liberal feminists is: given that the state is now the dominant form of political organisation around the world, to what degree can the state be viewed as a vehicle for women's liberation? For liberals, 'women's liberation' involves, first, gaining the vote, then gaining equal opportunities in education, in social institutions and in the workplace. By enacting pro-woman legislation and outlawing discriminatory practices, the state can help to advance the status of women.

Liberal feminists also argue that male domination of public international life has implications for women's status as citizens. Liberal feminists have thus contributed to a debate on the state and power in international relations, but this has largely been confined to a discussion of the implications of continuing discrimination for the status of women as citizens. Liberal feminists believe that extending rights to women gives them a stake in the political order and 'national community'. Indeed, during the first wave of feminist activism in the nineteenth century, the movement for women's suffrage and citizenship was at the very forefront of feminist campaigns. In more recent years, liberal feminists in the USA have used this argument in their campaign for the right to fight in combat roles in war.

One response to liberal complaints about under-representation and discrimination is to suggest that ultimately the phenomenon of male domination of international life is explained by women's special responsibilities in the 'private sphere' of the home and the family. In order to demonstrate the relevance of gender to international relations and counter this legitimisation of the existing order, we need to unpack the significance of the public/private division in supporting and legitimising male dominance. A second stage in developing a feminist perspective on the state is, then, to make visible the gendered power relationships which permeate all aspects of the state, but which are rendered 'invisible' by powerful ideologies or discourses on the 'naturalness' of the sexual division of labour or the 'socially relevant difference' justification for gender inequality.

HISTORICAL BOX

The Suffragettes

The term 'suffragette' was originally used as a term of abuse against British women who advocated radical action in the cause of women's suffrage (the right to vote). The movement originated in June 1866 when Emily Davis (1830–1921) and Elizabeth Garrett (1836–1917) presented a petition demanding the right to vote, signed by 1499 women, to John Stuart Mill, who agreed to present it to Parliament. The action was not successful. Between 1886 and 1911, a number of Bills came before the British Parliament, but were all defeated. Frustrated by the lack of progress, Emmeline Pankhurst (1858–1928) and her daughters waged a militant campaign to bring the issue to the attention of the wider public, which included chaining themselves to the railings in Downing Street, refusing to pay taxes and even going on hunger strike. One member of the movement, Emily Davison (1872–1913) became a martyr to the cause of women's right to vote when she was killed after throwing herself under the king's horse at the 1913 Derby horse-race. The suffragettes called a temporary halt to their campaign at the outbreak of the First World War in 1914. In Britain, women over the age of 30 were given the vote in 1918. It was another ten years before women achieved equal treatment with men by being given the right to vote at age 21.

(Information from: L. Tuttle (1986), *Encyclopaedia of Feminism*, London: Arrow Books)

In the brief summary above, it was suggested that:

1. gender might be employed as a central category of analysis;
2. gender can be understood as a particular kind of power relationship;
3. the public/private division is central to our understanding of international relations.

How do these propositions inform an historical materialist feminist analysis of the state and power? Feminists working within a historical materialist tradition sometimes employ the concept of the patriarchal state. The state can be seen as patriarchal to the extent that it supports institutions like marriage and a specific form of household and family which both reflect and sustain a male-dominated social order. The state also engages in ideological activity on issues of sex and gender, from birth control to the policing of sexuality and reproductive function and support for heterosexual marriage, to forms of labour legislation and taxation. In complex and varied ways the state is involved in the institutionalisation of gender relations. The state may condone gender-differential terms by sanctioning differential wages. The construction of women as 'dependants' who are identified only in terms of their relationship to men, as wives and mothers, plays a role in limiting rights of citizenship. Obviously, actual laws relating to rights of citizenship vary from state to state, but the point is, all states take an interest in who their citizens choose to marry and the implications of extending citizenship rights to 'outsiders', so these decisions cannot be regarded as entirely a matter of individual choice and inclination.

On the other hand, feminists do not necessarily regard the state as inherently patriarchal. While historically it has been a patriarchal political form that has institutionalised gender inequalities, the state might be viewed as relatively autonomous of specific interests. Feminists organisations and women's groups have successfully lobbied to change government policies and interventions often in ways that bring positive benefits to women. So, the state might be more helpfully viewed not only as a set of power relations and political processes in which patriarchy is maintained, but also as a vehicle through which patriarchy might be contested. From this perspective feminists and pro-women organisations can work through the state to try to achieve positive changes for women. We will return to this critique of the state and citizenship in our discussion of identity and community below.

CONCEPT BOX

The struggle to establish gender-based persecution as grounds for granting asylum

A key idea in feminism is that the private is political. How is this insight relevant to the study of specific issues in international relations?

The widespread acceptance of the idea of universal human rights since the Second World War has meant that a wider range of crimes and forms of persecution have been recognised as grounds for asylum. Persecution is conventionally seen as perpetrated by states against a particular social group defined, perhaps, by ethnic identity or religious belief, or is deemed to have occurred in cases where states have failed to protect such a groups from persecution in specific societies.

Gender-based persecution takes many forms and occurs on a daily basis in countries across the world: for example, forced marriage, forced abortion or sterilisation, or severe punishment for disobeying restrictive religious doctrines or cultural practices. Sometimes such repressive practices are sanctioned by states, but often they are ignored because they are regarded as 'private' or 'cultural' matters and so outside the domain of state intervention. The construction of women as dependants of men, rather than as fully-fledged, independent citizens in their own right is still common today. Consequently, the particular kinds of violence or fear or persecution that women suffer might not be recognised as grounds for asylum. Fundamentally, while feminists continue to argue that the private is political, élites continue to construct violence against women as a 'cultural' phenomenon. Although more than 80 per cent of the world's refugees are women and their children, women face particular difficulties in obtaining refugee and/or asylum status. Their claims have traditionally been ignored or excused through 'cultural relativism'.

There is some evidence that this changing, thanks largely to the efforts of women's organisations and feminist groups around the world who have been actively networking and lobbying to influence the political process, in this case by having women's rights recognised as human rights. After pressure from refugees, asylum-seekers and advocates, the international community has begun to recognise women's claims of persecution based on their gender as a legitimate basis for protection in the form of refugee status. The United Nations High Commissioner for Refugees (UNHCR) issued a set of guidelines for evaluating gender-based asylum claims in 1991 and many countries, including the UK, subsequently followed UNHCR's lead. These developments give some grounds for optimism, marking a significant breakthrough in determining refugee status which could potentially allow many women protection under international law. However, there remains resistance to recognising gender-based violence as grounds for asylum and many countries still refuse to entertain applications of this kind.

This brief account of feminist perspectives on the state challenges the idea that gender relations and the 'private' realm have nothing to do with politics, less still international politics. To borrow Cynthia Enloe's expression, in seeking to 'make feminist sense of international politics', feminists start out from precisely those areas of life usually regarded as 'private'. Moreover, to once again borrow from Enloe, increasingly the 'private is international'.

Identity and community

Some of the most interesting feminist work in IR is being done in the general area of gender, sexuality and sexual identities. This is part of a much broader critical interest in sexualities and identities in contemporary IR which is not exclusively feminist. At this juncture, however, the discussion will concentrate on feminist work on community and identity in IR.

While there has been a tendency in IR to take the existence of states and nations for granted, the boundaries of community are actually carved out through practices: for example, war, foreign policy and diplomacy. One of the most powerful representations of identity is 'national identity' and, for this reason, the notion of 'national interests' has similarly been employed rather uncritically in IR. This is not to say that there is no justification for employing concepts like the 'nation' and 'national interests' as starting points for theorising international relations. Indeed, nationalist ideologies continue to play an important role in world politics, fostering a feeling of distinctive identity and often providing a sense of belonging to 'insiders', while simultaneously serving to exclude 'outsiders.'

Feminists have good reason, therefore, to be interested in the critical interrogation of how nations are constructed and the role of nationalism in state-building projects. Across the world the struggle for popular sovereignty and national independence has stimulated demands for citizenship rights, and women have often benefited from this. Moreover, it is clear that women, like men, frequently have a very strong sense of identification with the nation. However, adopting a feminist perspective on state-building projects around the world reveals that, even while granting women formal rights, nationalism can work to institutionalise male privilege and so impinge upon women's rights as citizens.

WORLD EXAMPLE BOX

The Nicaraguan revolution

The revolution of 19 July 1979 was a profoundly anti-imperialist and nationalist one. At the same time it also sought to address the situation of women in a society profoundly influenced by machismo (macho behaviour) and, accordingly, set up specific women's organisations. The revolution did not succeed (many would argue was not allowed to) certainly not in terms of rectifying profound gender imbalances in Nicaraguan society, but it has stimulated debate about issues such as the double work day and domestic violence which had previously been regarded as in some sense 'normal'.

While the outcome of the Nicaraguan revolution was the outcome of a specific set of economic, cultural and political factors, the experience nevertheless resonates with feminist analysis of many nationalist struggles to realise self-determination or break free from imperialist domination in many other countries. Quite often women, like men, actively participate in the armed struggle, defying conventional feminine stereotypes. Nevertheless, women often find that they are caught in a bind. On the one hand, nationalist struggles offer the promise of not only national, but also women's, emancipation; on the other, the very construction of 'nations' and the necessarily exclusive nature of nationalist identity have profound implications for women whose bodies are controlled in the interests of demarcating identity. The outcome of such struggles is often disappointing from a feminist perspective, although during periods of change spaces might emerge for women to improve their political status and social situation to some extent.

As we saw in the previous chapter, national identities such as Britishness are not homogeneous and stable, but rather constructed. Essential in the process of establishing a sense of identification with the nation and inculcating a nationalist consciousness is the telling of a particular story about the nation and its history. Ideas about gender and women's roles are often a central and powerful part of the 'story' told about the nation, its history and its distinctive identity. The idea of the nation is constructed out of an invented, inward-looking history; a 'cult of origins'. Women are often held to be the guardians of national culture, indigenous religion and traditions. This serves to keep women within boundaries prescribed by male élites.

Women's behaviour is often policed and controlled in the interests of demarcating identities. The incidences of rape in the armed conflicts (that frequently accompany independence struggles) have to be seen as political acts through which the aggressor attacks the honour of other men. Moreover, if women challenge their ascribed duties and roles, they can find themselves accused of betraying the nation, its values, culture and ideals.

So far, our discussion of identity and community has been limited to the nation-state and state-building project. However, feminists are also interested in interrogating other expressions of community and identity. The privileging of nationalist constructions of identity is problematic, because it renders invisible the multiplicity of identities which co-exist within this particular 'political space' and the transnational dimensions of political identification.

For example, during the latter part of the twentieth century, transnational NGO networks have grown rapidly; so too social movements that organise globally. The globalisation of communication technologies has facilitated the growth of transnational networks among NGOs and social movements. Women's groups have taken advantage of the political space opened up by the UN Decade, and more recent UN conferences, as well as networking opportunities to engage in dialogue with women from across the world with diverse backgrounds and cultural experience. Increasingly, women are making use of opportunities provided by communications technologies such as the internet to facilitate transnational networking, to further empower women and to increase the influence which women can have in international politics. There is now an emerging literature on women's use of the internet, which again is included in the further reading section at the end of this book. The use of communications technologies such as the internet was very apparent at the Beijing conference discussed further below. With respect to questions of identity and community, it is interesting to speculate on whether globalisation, the use of communications technologies and the expansion of transnational feminist networks can be taken as evidence of an emerging global feminist identity and sense of 'solidarity' which transcends state boundaries.

WORLD EXAMPLE BOX

Gender, Equality and Cultural Difference

In recent years controversy regarding the status and rights of women from ethnic and religious minority groups in Western countries has become increasingly prominent. In an article first published in 1997, the American feminist Susan Moller Okin argued that, as many Western countries seek to devise new policies that are responsive to cultural differences, the rights of women were being overlooked. The claims of minority cultures or religions often clash with the norm of gender equality as it is formally endorsed by liberal states (even if it is often violated in practice). Multiculturalism might then be 'bad for women', substantially limiting the capacities of women and girls to live with human dignity equal to that of men and boys, and to live as freely chosen lives as they can. For example, many such practices make it virtually impossible for women to choose to live independently of men, to be celibate or lesbian, or have or not to have children.

In response to Okin, Bonnie Honnig has argued that cultures are less univocally patriarchal than Okin suggests and cultural practices are more complicated and ambiguous than that label 'sexist' allows. Moreover, women's groups in varied contexts contest gender relations. There is a danger that feminists who accept Okin's thesis will (unwittingly perhaps) participate in the rise of nationalist xenophobia by projecting a rightly feared backlash onto foreigners who bring their foreign, (supposedly) 'backward' cultural practices with them.

In 2008 the potential conflict between the liberal concept of equality and the concept of cultural difference was much mooted in the United Kingdom when the Archbishop of Canterbury Rowan Williams suggested that the implementation of Sharia Law in some areas of life (notably within the area of family law) was 'unavoidable'. In fact a Muslim Arbitration

Tribunal in Britain had been in existence since 2007 and several regionally based tribunals have been established since then. The use of such tribunals to arbitrate in family disputes has been controversial. For example, some commentators have expressed the view that issues such as domestic violence – which is treated as assault in the secular courts – could be regarded less seriously by these tribunals, thus undermining Muslim women's rights and security.

Some feminists point out that in various ways women and women's bodies have been 'securitised' in discourses on gender, equality and difference, pointing out that what has been missing from these debates are the actual voices and perspectives of actual women from minority communities. This is a pertinent point, not least because once again it highlights the degree to which gender and women's bodies specifically are a site of politics and contestation.

Institutions and world order

Gender is a central factor in understanding world orders, old and new. What does the world order look like when viewed from a feminist perspective? How do the policies of international organisations and institutions like the UN, the World Bank and the International Monetary Fund affect gender relations in countries across the world?

There is a growing feminist literature on gender relations, which is integrated into and informed by an analysis of the changing 'world order'. Of course, in Marxist terms, 'world order' is constituted by global capitalism and the states and institutions which provide a framework in which capitalist economic and social relations are 'managed'. 'Women's work' is frequently unpaid and so not deemed to be part of the activities of states, markets and international institutions which collectively constitute world order. However, not only is the contribution of women's labour highly significant in national terms, but increasingly so in global terms.

Gender is also an observable and significant factor in the current global division of labour. Since the 1970s and 1980s across the world employers have sought to undermine trade unions in order to achieve maximum labour flexibility. Some employers have relocated abroad in order to enjoy the benefits of cheap labour. Frequently this labour force is made up of women. Women are paid less, because women's work is constructed as bringing in a second wage. This has been at a time when the number of female-headed households is actually rising. The impact of neo-liberal development strategies such as structural adjustment is one example of how international institutions both reflect and perpetuate gender inequalities.

CONCEPT BOX

Gender in Governance

The concept of 'governance' embraces not only states, international institutions and regimes, but also non-governmental organisations (NGOs). Governance in the broadest sense of the term embraces a range of state and non-state actors linked together through a variety of networks and institutional arrangements, who collectively engage in decision-making processes, governed by norms and principles, and who are also involved in the implementation, monitoring and compliance of policies at the domestic level (within nation-states). Over the past two decades the number of NGOs has expanded massively, a development facilitated by technological developments. Today, NGOs are an integral part of the process of governance, but the nature and role of NGOs and NGO networks generally is under-theorised and under-researched.

Feminists have contributed substantially to debates about governance and have also produced a wealth of empirical work on gender and/or gender politics in global governance in the United Nations (see below) and also in International Economic Organisations like the World Bank (see Further reading). Since the 1995 Beijing women's conference there has indeed been evidence of a greater commitment to gender equity within the World Bank. For example, the 'Gender Analysis and Policy' thematic group set up in 1995 and the external Gender Consultative Group, comprised of members of the women's movement across the world, is evidence of a greater willingness by the Bank to engage in dialogue about policy, particularly in relation to structural adjustment. Former World Bank President James Wolfensohn pressed for gender equity in the workplace, in private-sector development projects and demanded that gender action plans be incorporated into all of the Banks regional operations. The World Bank also produces an annual report on gender in development. The Bank's poverty-alleviation strategy has promised changes in approach in order to incorporate governance issues, and attention is now focused more closely on participation and improved cooperation with women's NGOs. Feminists have, however, been critical of many such efforts, arguing that marketisation and privatisation programmes promoted by the Bank have often had detrimental effects on poor people and poor women particularly. In such circumstances, bringing in women into governance process only serves to co-opt NGOs, transforming them into compliant neo-liberals who no longer represent civil society constitutencies.

Women are organising to resist the undermining of labour rights, to fight for better working conditions and, in so doing, to draw attention to the particular problems they face as both paid and unpaid workers. Through political struggle women can and do play a role in resisting dominant power relations and bringing about change. Women's struggles typically involve going beyond narrow demands for higher wages and better working conditions. They also highlight the particular problems they face as women who must not only juggle the competing demands of work and family, but also face sexist discrimination. In recent years women have organised internationally to promote women's human rights.

HISTORICAL BOX

Gender mainstreaming at the UN

Since the UN Decade for Women (1976–85) there have been efforts to 'mainstream' gender into the decision-making processes of international institutions. During the UN Decade, a comprehensive survey on the role of Women in Development was produced as a first stage in developing effective strategies to reduce gender inequalities and improve the status of women around the world. Following the Second United Nation's Conference on Women, held in Copenhagen in 1980, an action programme was approved, the main themes of which were later incorporated into the Forward Looking Strategies for the Advancement of Women (FLSAW) adopted at the third UNCW in Nairobi in 1985.

The FLSAW was a significant document for a number of reasons, but one of the main effects of the FLSAW document was to shift the emphasis from the promotion of gender-specific actions or targets within development programmes to a strategy of mainstreaming – incorporating gender concerns into others areas of the UN's work as a matter of course rather than as 'add-ons'. Since the Beijing women's conference in 1995 the promotion of women's human rights has also been mainstreamed in the work of the UN. While there is still resistance on some issues (for example reproductive rights) from countries where religious influence is strong, the majority of the UN member states have agreed on the need to mainstream a gender perspective into their national law-making and policy-making machinery.

Gender mainstreaming has encouraged the growth of linkages between NGOs, individual parts of the UN system, and national and regional policy-making forums. Consequently, selected NGOs now enjoy a role in international and national policy making, although critics argue that their influence is relatively small compared to states. The gradual mainstreaming of gender in other areas of UN work has resulted in the emergence of an 'international women's regime'. In this way, women's groups and feminist organisations are actively working to 'engender' institutions and so shape world order.

Inequality and justice

The incidence of gender inequality in societies across the world is so prevalent and entrenched that it is as close to an established 'fact' as it is ever possible to uncover in social scientific analysis. No society in the world treats its women as well as its men, whether this is measured in terms of the distribution of wealth or income, or the full range of development indices employed by the UN.

Table 6.1   Gender disparity.

	GEM rank	GDI rank	HDI rank
Norway	1	3	5
Sweden	2	1	8
Denmark	3	6	16
Finland	4	5	6
New Zealand	5	9	13
Canada	6	2	1
Germany	7	16	7
Netherlands	8	10	4
USA	9	4	2
Austria	10	12	12
Nigeria	98	78	87
Togo	100	80	89
Pakistan	101	77	84
Mauritania	102	83	95
Comoros	103	76	88
Niger	104	93	104

Original source: United Nations Development Programme (1996), *Human Development Report*, New York: UNDP.

Taken from: J.J. Pettman (1997), 'Gender issues', in J. Baylis and S. Smith (eds), *The Globalization of World Politics*, 1st edn, Oxford: Oxford University Press, p. 490. In the above table, HDI is a Human Development Index based on factors such as life expectancy, education and standard of living. GDI measures the same thing but adjusts in terms of discrepancies between men and women. GEM (Gender Empowerment Index) is about relative empowerment in economic and public spheres and in terms of political representation.

Reflection – why do you think that a country like Denmark is only 16 in terms of HDI, but 6 for GDI and 3 for GEM? In terms of the oppression of women, there is a strong correlation between HDI and GEM, but not always an exact match.

While globalisation has increased employment opportunities for women, women across the world still tend to earn less than men. In a Report on Global Employment Trends for Women 2004 the International Labour Organisation reported that women in the global workforce remain disproportionately in low-paid insecure jobs, despite the increased number of women in the global labour force. In 2003 women accounted for 1.1 billion of the 2.8 billion people in work, an increase of 200 million since 1993, but women were less likely to hold regular paid jobs and more likely to be working in the informal economy, outside legal and regulatory frameworks. Moreover, women earned less than men for the same type of work, even in female-dominated occupations. Women make up 60 per cent of the world's workforce that earns less than a $1 a day.

There are also significant gender hierarchies in the world of paid employment in both public and private sectors. What the statistics do not reveal, however, is the degree to which male authority is still the norm and female authority the exception in the workplace. Diane Elson's work has shown that tax and benefit circuits are also gendered, embedded in assumptions about women's economic dependency on men. In all countries the human-development achievements of women are lower than men, as the table below demonstrates. However, while the statistics paint a depressing picture of the status of the world women's vis-à-vis men, there is evidence that some categories of women, notably young educated women in Western societies, have benefited from globalisation.

Justice has also been a central preoccupation in both feminist theory and feminist practice. From the eighteenth century onwards, feminists in the West have asserted the equal moral worth of women and men and demanded equal rights and justice for women. In so doing, liberal feminists have internationalised the issue and also encouraged an active debate on what should be recognised as a 'human right'.

HISTORICAL BOX

The Convention on the Elimination of Discrimination Against Women

The main developments in women's human rights have been through the work of the Commission on the Status of Women, notably in regard to the development and implementation of the Convention on the Elimination of Discrimination Against Women (CEDAW) and during four United Nations Conferences on Women (UNCW).

The adoption of the CEDAW was one of its major achievements during the UN's Decade for Women (1976–85). CEDAW was the first international treaty dealing with the rights of women in global context. The Convention set out an international standard for what was meant by 'equality' between men and women, covering not only the granting of formal rights, but also promoting equality of access and opportunity.

CEDAW has created a specialist body within the UN system with responsibility for supervising states compliance with its treaty obligations with respect to women's rights and helped to promote women's human rights in other areas of the UN's work. Over time, the Commission has developed linkages with NGOs to strengthen efforts to achieve gender equality. The project of advancing women's human rights has been further strengthen by the forging of networks among women's groups around the world to promote CEDAW.

While there is still resistance to the idea of women's equality and women's human rights among some conservative and religious fundamentalist groups around the world and there is a long way to go before women's human rights are recognised and protected in practice, many

Governments worldwide have now enacted CEDAW and have subsequently revised their domestic legislation to conform to the principles of the CEDAW and with other international and regional human-rights legislation, such as the requirements set out in the Beijing Platform for Action document.

Rights discourse is increasingly being adopted by NGOs in a variety of countries and cultural contexts around the world. Many transnational women's NGOs believe that human rights discourse is politically useful to disempowered groups. Moreover, both the conception and substantive context of human rights has been expanded to incorporate the needs of many groups – including women – previously denied rights.

However, not all feminists favour a rights-based strategy to address gender inequalities and discrimination. Some post-structuralist and postcolonial feminists argue that rights discourse is rooted in a Western tradition, grounded in an abstract, 'universalism' and embedded in Western ideas about 'progress' and emancipation. Furthermore, where rights have been connected to the ownership of property, a traditional source of European law exported through colonialism, the ramifications for women have been enormous, serving sometimes to displace women from land they had previously controlled or from other resources which confer a certain amount of social power on women. These historical examples illustrate, perhaps, the dangers inherent in advocating strategies to address inequality which have been developed in a specific historical context and which may not be appropriate in another.

WORLD EXAMPLE BOX

Negotiating Differences/Negotiating Rights

Feminist theorists and feminist activists tend to adopt an approach to human rights that embraces human rights as a useful political tool for women, but also recognises and respects cultural differences. For example, the transnational network Women Living Under Muslim Laws (WLUML) recognises the multiplicity of women and women's experiences, attempts to build links between local women and non-governmental organisations and provides a platform that allows self-representation and self-expression among different groups of Muslim women in specific national, social and cultural contexts. Nevertheless WLUML explicitly uses the language of human rights in lobbying and advocacy work.

In much of the contemporary academic literature, feminists approach human rights 'from below', attempting to theorise about women's human's rights from practice (as above in the example of WLUML). Rather than relying on unreflective – and gendered/biased – concepts like rationality and universalism, feminists often speak of rights discourse being constructed through intersubjective dialogue (intersubjective universalism) and the content of human rights as 'negotiated' by different groups from varied cultural backgrounds (see Further reading below).

Peace and security

Feminist IR scholars have contributed to debates within security study concerning, for example, who or what should constitute the referent of security in IR, have produced empirical work on security in varied contexts, and have also offered different visions of what security means and how it might be achieved. There is no space here to summarise a substantial body of work and, again, further reading is provided. Briefly, feminists have echoed the arguments of other non-feminist critical thinkers: for example, by engaging in a critique of discourses of state security and discursive constructions of threat which construct a hostile 'other' in the project of legitimising state power. Discourses on the state, security and threats contain a deeply gendered subtext in which the citizen role is in all cases identified with men and the masculine.

The degree to which people feel, or actually are, 'threatened' varies according to their economic, political, social or personal circumstances. As we argued in the introductory section of this chapter, in the contemporary world the security and well-being of human beings is affected by a whole range of factors: the stability of the global economy, poverty and malnutrition, global warming and climate change, ethnic conflict, political oppression, human-rights abuse, and persecution on the basis of religion, ethnicity or gender. Gender hierarchies and inequalities in power constitute a major source of domination and obstacles to the achievement of genuine security.

Liberals feminists argue that we cannot achieve global security unless we recognise and respect the human rights of all people. However, many feminists would support the position that the attempts to build global security upon the basis of a bourgeois human-rights tradition are fundamentally flawed. Indeed, many would argue that non-Western traditions which see the individual as part of the social whole and emphasise human dignity and development are more fruitful starting points for developing alternative conceptions of security. Others have noted affinities between feminist revisions and 'people-centred' approaches to security which simultaneously argue for the equal importance of all people and their security needs, and stress the importance of the collectivities in which people are embedded.

WORLD EXAMPLE BOX

Gender and Food Security

The United Nations Food and Agriculture department recognises that women are crucial to achieving food security in countries around the world. In a report prepared in preparation for the 1995 UN women's conference, the FAO noted that women produce more than 50 per cent of the food grown worldwide. The report also noted that women were active in both cash and subsistence agricultural economies and that much of their work in producing food for the household and community consumption, important as it was for food security, was not counted in the statistics.

Since women play crucial roles in achieving food security, efforts to reduce food insecurity worldwide have to take into consideration the factors and constraints affecting women's ability to carry out these roles and make these contributions, with a view to removing the constraints and enhancing women's capacities. Thus the 'gender blindness' and 'invisibility' of women's roles in and contributions to food security in policy documents had to be addressed. Much of women's work remained invisible, because it was not included in surveys and censuses which still often count as work only that which is remunerated, or ask what is the principal work of a person. Unaware of these differences, policy makers and planners proceed as if they did not exist, as if the situation and needs of farmers were the same, whether they are men or women. Thus, policy making, planning and extension services are built on a partial view of reality and are consequently less effective. See: http://www.fao.org/gender/.

No discussion of feminist contributions to IR would be complete without some discussion of feminist approaches and contributions to peace. Historically, and in many different cultures, there has been a long association between women and peace. For example, the women's suffragette movement in Britain argued that women's maternal urges made them different from men, but that women's peacefulness was evidence of moral superiority rather than inferiority. (Women peace activists sometimes claim a 'natural' peacefulness on the part of women, while some eco-feminists extend the argument to include non-violence towards the planet.) Others, while rejecting biological or essentialist accounts of apparent gender differences, have noted the close association with peace and the 'feminine', and have argued that the experience of maternity on the part of the vast majority of women gives women a special relationship to peace.

Feminist discourse on peace emphasises human connectedness, dialogue and cooperation over dominance and violent confrontation. By assuming a more prominent place in the political arena, feminist peace activists are changing the terms in which public discourse on peace and security is conducted. The need to promote women to positions of influence in international politics in the cause of peace has been echoed by 'moral feminists'. In the 1980s and 1990s moral feminists argued for the inclusion of women in government élites, because the inclusion of women would change the foreign policy of states. Interestingly, Francis Fukuyama argued in an article published in 1998 (see the Further reading section at the end of the book) that the incorporation of women into foreign policies was actually having the effect of feminising and pacifying foreign policy to some degree. However, he concluded that this was a potentially dangerous development, given that these Western liberal feminised states still had to negotiate the power politics that continued to characterise other parts of the world! (See also Tickner's response (1999) in the same section.)

HISTORICAL BOX

The Women's International League for Peace and Freedom

There is a long history of women mobilising in the cause of peace. In 1915 the first Women's International Peace Congress attracted 1200 women delegates. This led, in turn, to the formation of the Women's International League for Peace and Freedom (WILPF). Women's special capacities and capabilities as mothers figured heavily in how the WILPF presented its cause. Many of the women involved in the WILPF appealed to religious ideas or maternalist arguments that stressed women's roles as life-givers and nurturers who had a duty to save their sons from senseless slaughter. This appeal to motherhood made strategic sense in that women's presence within organisations like the League of Nations was welcomed, even in the socially conservative era of the inter-war period, since women's 'innate' caring nature meant that they could contribute to the cause of peace. Women activists within the WILPF also appealed to the perceived link between democracy, suffrage and a more peaceful world order. Having gained a foothold in the League, women activists used that space to promote not just development and peace, but also to advance the principles of equality and women's rights.

Today, the linkage between peace and women's human rights is being made in gender mainstreaming strategies in areas of the UN's work that deal with peace-keeping, humanitarian intervention and disarmament. For example, the United Nations Security Council Resolution 1325 has led to concrete measures to eliminate violence against women in conflict and post-conflict societies, including a detailed review of the impact of armed conflict on women and girls. The Special Committee on Peacekeeping Operations has also taken on board the requirement to mainstream gender issues into peacekeeping operations. Since Beijing, the importance of incorporating the gender perspective in situations of humanitarian emergency has also been recognised. This is an important development which might eventually do much to address the problems of women and children who account for the higher percentage of refugees (in some camps up to 90 per cent).

However, the actual effectiveness of such mainstreaming strategies and the continuing gap between the rhetoric and reality of gender mainstreaming continues to attract criticism from feminist commentators. Nevertheless, these measures are significant in so far as they give increasing credence to the feminist argument that gender is central to our understanding of peace and security at all levels. Furthermore, these kinds of activities illustrate that gender is not only increasingly central to the academic study of IR, but is also very much a part of the day-to-day practice of international politics.

Conflict and violence

Feminists point to the intimate connections between the state and the prevalence of violence in international relations. Historically, the state has armed men and disarmed women, who have been constructed as the 'protected'. In the 1980s the feminist anti-war movement often treated the state's military apparatus as an expression of male aggression and destructiveness. Activists in the peace movement have long argued that rape should be viewed as an accepted part of the code that governs the fighting of wars rather than as an individual act of wrongdoing. For these reasons, feminists refuse to view violence as individual and isolated acts committed by states. Feminists see such violence as part of a complex which involves institutions and the way they are organised.

Feminists argue that violence is not endemic to international relations because of conditions of 'anarchy' or because states constantly face real threats to their security from hostile foreigners, as realists would contend. At the very heart of the state are discourses and practices of violence. Acts of violence are deeply embedded in power inequalities and ideologies of male supremacy. The most obvious manifestation of this is militarism.

This phenomenon of women being 'allowed' to take on 'men's' roles at times of emergency only to lose that 'privilege' once the fighting has ceased has been a common feature of twentieth-century conflict. Women's football for instance was massively popular during the Second World War.

CONCEPT BOX

Militarism and structural violence

Feminist scholars have also pointed out that our understanding of 'violence' should not be limited to direct acts of violence between states. Violence can be structural, embedded in unequal social relations which determine access to resources. Like direct violence, structural violence does great harm to people, and might also lead to premature death. Feminists claim that militarism and structural violence are linked. The higher the levels of military expenditure worldwide, the fewer resources are spent on food and welfare. Feminists also argue that the transfer of resources from the military to the civilian sector of the economy would, in all countries, reap social and economic benefits for all people, but especially women. Resources devoted to arms expenditure could be spent on health, education, development and in this way the most vulnerable people would derive immediate benefits. In this view, therefore, rather than providing protection from the violence of excluded 'others', the military-industrial complex actually does great harm to the 'vulnerable'.

AUTHOR BOX

Jenny Pearce – *Promised Land: Peasant Rebellion in Chalatenango, El Salvador*

There are some interesting connections between conflict, violence and the position of women in society. Jenny Pearce of the University of Bradford wrote a book in the 1980s about her experiences living with the resistance forces of the Frente Farabundo Marti para la Liberación Nacional (FMLN) in El Salvador. Conducting research which would have failed any kind of 'risk assessment', Jenny lived with the guerrilla forces of the FMLN while they fought a bloody civil war against a highly repressive state and army backed by the USA.

Many women fought in this struggle which sought to free the Salvadoran population from decades of military repression and human rights abuses. Although not a dominant strand of debate – given the necessities of violent struggle in terrain hardly perfect for a guerrilla force – some attention was given to the question of whether women's liberation would occur as a result of the revolutionary struggle or whether it should be a priority and precede it. In the case of both post-war El Salvador and post-revolutionary and nearby Nicaragua, women appear to have lost gains as traditional machismo society has returned and women have been forced to re-adopt accepted roles in society.

Figure 6.3 During the Second World War, women's football became very popular, but soon disappeared again once the war was over. This is just one example of women 'being allowed' to play 'men's' roles in wartime.

Source: Hulton Collection/Corbis.

Summary

1. Feminism is a broad church with many different strands. There are important differences in feminist theories, but also commonalities.

2. Contemporary feminist theory does not focus solely on the lives of women but is an analysis of the socially and culturally constructed category 'gender'.

3. A great deal of feminist scholarship is concerned with practices of discrimination and exclusion. However, feminists do not regard women as 'victims'. Feminism is also concerned with uncovering and highlighting ways in which women are empowered to achieve positive changes in their social position.

4. Contemporary feminism does not regard 'women' or, indeed, 'men' as a single category, but is sensitive to the nuances of gender identities. Given the great variety of women's experiences and gender relations it is clear that oppression takes many forms.

5. Feminism has gained influence in International Relations theory since the 1980s, though the scholarship which informs it has a much longer history.

6. Feminist scholarship has made a valuable contribution to very many areas long held to be central to international relations.

7. Some (male) commentators argue that the gender 'variable' can be incorporated into mainstream IR research agendas. At the same time, feminism challenges conventional ideas about what is central or marginal, important or unimportant in IR; in effect what constitutes a 'mainstream agenda'.

8. The central insight of feminism is, perhaps, the way in which the notion of a clear private/public distinction renders invisible a particular set of power relations. From a feminist perspective, the private is not only political, but increasingly international or global.

Criticisms

One criticism which could be levelled is that, while ostensibly concerned with gender relations, feminists tend to concentrate on women, in their empirical work particularly. This is probably an accurate observation in relation to the first wave of feminist writing in IR, but more work is now appearing on masculinities in IR. Many feminists would counter that they are interested in gender relations because these explain how women are locked into unequal relationships, or indeed, how ideas about gender are used to legitimise the unequal status accorded to women. Concentrating on women is thus consistent with the desire to look at the world from the 'bottom up'.

Another potential criticism is that, while offering important insights, feminists have failed to construct a coherent account of the nature of international relations, akin to, say, realism or liberalism. Certainly, there is no one 'feminist paradigm' or feminist theory of IR. However, many poststructuralist feminists working in the field would contend that the construction of one coherent world view is neither possible nor desirable (see chapter 5).

It might also be argued that feminism does not take into account other major divisions between women based on, say, social class or ethnicity. This is a criticism which has been levelled at liberal and radical feminism particularly, and with some justification. Most contemporary approaches to gender attempt a more nuanced analysis which explores the ways in which culture, class, race, and so on intersect and cut across gender divisions.

Another possible criticism is that feminism relies ultimately upon the notion that there is a universal category 'woman' and that women share certain common experiences or interests. In reality, gender relations, 'women's experiences' and the social meaning ascribed to gender difference differ from society to society and from culture to culture. This criticism is central to postcolonial and post-structuralist critiques of Western feminism. Again, the response has been to try to develop a more nuanced understanding of how female (and indeed male) subjectivity is constructed. However, while accepting that difference must be taken seriously, many feminists in the critical and standpoint traditions maintain that this concern with difference should not obscure the continuing existence of stark gender inequalities and the degree to which women are discriminated against in all cultures and societies.

Common misunderstandings

1. *Men cannot be feminists.* As we noted above, to adopt a feminist lens or gender lens is a political act. Most feminists in IR would probably regard male scholars (and students) as 'good feminists' when they engage seriously with feminist ideas and arguments and incorporate feminist concepts and analyses into their own work. Liberals would hold that feminism is a demand for equal rights, and would be happy to attach the label 'feminist' to men who support the cause of equal rights for women. However, some feminists hold that ultimately one's identification with feminism arises out of personal experiences of discrimination and a feeling of empathy and solidarity with other women. In this view men cannot be feminists, but only sympathisers and supporters.
2. *Gender is the same as sex.* No. Sex describes the anatomical, or biological differences between men and women. Gender describes the social significance or meaning ascribed to those differences.
3. *The study of gender in IR is about women.* Although many feminists tend to concentrate on the position of women (see above), the main focus of contemporary feminism is in gender identities and gender relations. The position and status of women cannot be understood without some reference to prevailing ideas about gender and how gender relations are organised in specific societies.
4. *All feminists are lesbian man-haters.* This unwarranted and abusive 'criticism' is sometimes levelled at feminists by those who for whatever reason – ideology or personal insecurity perhaps – are strongly opposed to feminist beliefs and practices. For example, one-time US Presidential candidate Pat Robertson famously, or infamously, described feminism as 'a socialist, anti-family political movement that encourages women to leave their husbands, kill their children, practise witchcraft, destroy capitalism and become lesbians!' The equation of all feminism with lesbian separatism and/or man-hating is without foundation. Feminism is above all about understanding and combating specific aspects of power and inequality rather than closed-minded condemnation.
5. *The study of gender and IR is only of interest to women.* No. The study of gender in IR requires men to reflect on questions of masculinity, masculine identity and power as well as female identity, femininity and inequality. Many feminists would argue that the often trite dismissal of feminist analysis as 'marginal' or a 'women's issue', both reflects and reinforces the dominant social position of men and their refusal to engage with any discourse or practice which threatens their privileged position.
6. *Feminism is another world view or paradigm.* No it is not. See above.

Further reading

Key texts

Chowdhry, G. and Nair, S. (2002) (eds), *Postcolonialism and International Relations: Race, Gender and Class*, London: Routledge.

Enloe, C. (1989), *Bananas, Beaches and Bases; Making Feminist Sense of International Relations*, London: Pandora (along with the special issue of Millennium – below – generally regarded as one of the first and most influential feminist text in IR).

Jabri, V. and O'Gorman, E. (1999) (eds), *Women, Culture, and International Relations* (series: Critical Perspectives on World Politics), Oxford: Lynne Rienner Publishers Inc.

Lee, Y. L. (2009) (ed.), *The Politics of Gender: A Survey*, London: Routledge.

Pease, B. and Pringle, K. (2001), *A Man's World: Changing Men's Practices in a Globalised World*, London: Zed Books.

Peterson, V. S. and Runyan, A. (1993), *Global Gender Issues*, Boulder, CO: Westview Press.

Pettman, J. J. (1996), *Worlding Women: A Feminist International Politics*, London: Routledge.

Shepherd, L. (2009) (ed.), *Gender Matters in Global Politics. A Feminist Introduction to International Relations*, London: Routledge.

Special Issue: 'Women in International Relations' (1988), *Millennium: Journal of International Studies*, Vol. 17, No. 3 (one of the first collection of articles from UK-based feminist scholars that ask 'where are the women in IR?').

Steans, J. (2006), *Gender and International Relations: Issues, Debates, Future Directions*, Cambridge: Polity Press.

Sylvester, C. (1994), *Feminist Theory and International Relations in a Postmodern Era*, Cambridge: Cambridge University Press.

Sylvester, C. (2002), *Feminist international relations: an unfinished journey*. Cambridge: Cambridge University Press.

Tickner, J.A. (1992), *Gender in International Relations: Feminist Perspectives on Achieving Global Security*, New York: Columbia University Press (a re-visioning of security written from a feminist standpoint position).

Whitworth, S. (1994), *Feminist Theory and International Relations*, Basingstoke: Macmillan.

Zalewski, M. and Parpart, J. (1998), *The Man Question in IR*, Oxford: Westview Press.

Additional reading:

Ackerly, B. (2001), 'Women's Rights Activists as Cross-Cultural Theorists', *International Feminist Journal of Politics*, 3, 3, pp. 311–46.

Mazurana, D., Raven-Roberts, A. and Parpart, J. (2005) (eds), *Gender, Conflict and Peacekeeping*, Plymouth and Lanham MD: Rowman and Littlefield.

Meyer, M.K. and Prugl, E. (2000), *Gender Politics in Global Governance*, New York: Rowman and Littlefield Publishers Inc..

Rai, S. and Waylen, G. (2008), *Global Governance: Feminist Perspectives*, London: MacMillan.

Special Forum Section, 'Negotiating difference/negotiating rights: the challenges and opportunities of women's human rights', *Review of International Studies*, January, 33, 2007.

True, J. (2003), 'Mainstreaming Gender in Global Public Policy', *International Feminist Journal of Politics*, Vol. 5, Issue 3: 368–96.

Weber, C. (1994), 'Good Girls, Little Girls and Bad Girls: Male Paranoia in Keohane's Critique of Feminist International Relations', *Millennium: Journal of International Studies*, Vol. 23, Issue 2: 337–49.

Whitworth, S. (2004), *Men, Militarism and UN Peacekeeping: A Gendered Analysis*, London and Boulder, CO: Lynne Rienner.

Yuval-David, N., Anthias, F. and Kofman, E. (2005), 'Secure Borders and Safe Haven and the Gendered Politics of Belonging: Beyond Social Cohesion', *Ethnic and Racial Studies*, Vol. 28, Issue 3: 513–35.

7 Social constructivism

Introduction

Social constructivism is one of the youngest 'major' theories in International Relations. As we will see, its main attraction as well as its main difficulty is that it tries to occupy the 'middle ground' in International Relations. Its proponents thus accept the influence of both structures and agency, and focus on how they influence each other. Social constructivists attempt to find a practical answer to the postmodern challenge to scientific knowledge in order to be able to conduct empirical research. In addition, they are interested in the interplay of interests and ideas, as well as in the impact of norms, culture and institutions on international politics. Typical themes addressed by social constructivist work are, therefore, the construction of national interests, the spread of human rights, the impact of international organisations on state identities (and vice versa), or the development of different forms of international society.

> **Social constructivism** attempts to find a practical answer to the postmodern challenge to scientific knowledge in order to be able to conduct empirical research. It focuses in particular on the interplay of structure and agency, and of ideas, norms and interests.

Before we start to present and discuss the core features of social constructivism at greater length, it is worthwhile reflecting shortly on why this approach is called 'social constructivism'. 'Constructivism' here means that these authors do not accept any social features of life as given. Instead, while they acknowledge that human beings are always situated in particular contexts which inform their actions, they also reproduce, or construct, their 'world' through their actions. The world we live in is therefore always contextual. This is in stark contrast to neo-realism, which argues that the basic features of the international system are universal, and have been operating in history as well as at present, in the ancient Greek system of city states as much as during the Cold War. The process of construction, in turn, is a 'social' process – it cannot be done by one person alone, but only in the engagement with others. The term 'constructivism' therefore does not imply voluntarism. Individuals are always part of broader settings which they can shape, but only within the specific context.

'Social' also clarifies a contrast to the focus on language in postmodernism: the construction we are talking about in this chapter is one that can be observed in the many different practices of actors engaged in international politics, rather than the construction of our understanding of reality through language, which is one of the starting points of postmodernism, as we have seen in chapter 5. This does not mean that social constructivists are not interested in discourse – in fact, it is a central category which helps them to explain, for instance, foreign policy.

As you will see in more detail in this chapter, social constructivists:

■ analyse the interplay between structure and agency in international politics;
■ are interested in the role of ideas, norms and institutions in foreign policy making;
■ argue for the importance of identity and culture in international politics;
■ do not deny the role of interests in policy making, but try to understand how these interests are constructed;
■ accept that social science cannot operate like the natural sciences, but nonetheless insist on the possibility to theorise and empirically analyse international politics as a reality.

But we are running ahead of ourselves. To understand social constructivism, it is best first to have a closer look at how it developed in International Relations, and how it has become established as the 'middle ground' of the discipline.

Origins

During the second half of the 1980s International Relations as a discipline was dominated by what is sometimes called the 'third', sometimes the 'fourth' debate. This debate is covered in more detail in the concluding chapter. The numbering was not invented to confuse students, although confusing it is. There is no dispute about the first two debates that shaped the study of international politics, although these, too, neglect a lot of other work going on at the time. The first one was between realism and idealism. It essentially asked ontological questions – questions about the nature of international politics, and, indeed, the nature of human beings, such as whether humans are inherently bad and peace therefore difficult to achieve.

The second debate was between behaviouralists and traditionalists. This one was about methodology: the behaviouralists, mostly from American universities, wanted to turn IR into a 'proper' science, and focus on the formulation of universally valid theories that explain outcomes in international politics on the basis of causal relationships between observable behaviour (thus the name). Traditionalists, in contrast, argued that international politics cannot be studied like the natural sciences. In particular, they cast doubt on the possibility of formulating universally valid theories in IR. Instead, they suggested that the traditional (philosophical) methods of historians in particular were more adequate to understand international politics.

Hedley Bull was one of the outspoken representatives of traditionalists in the 1960s and 1970s and, although Australian, he is seen as one of the core figures of the so-called 'English School' of IR, on which more in the 'Themes' section of this chapter. To this date, the approach taken in many universities in Britain towards the analysis of international politics and the teaching of IR is sceptical of the possibilities of a 'science' of IR, and there is an emphasis on the contextual understanding of history, or the role of factors not readily observable, such as norms and ideas, or the pursuit of critical and normative theory rather than universally valid explanations.

In the 1980s both realism and liberalism (idealism) were revamped – you should be familiar with the debate between neo-realism and neo-liberalism from previous chapters. You should also have noticed that the so-called 'neo-neo-debate' between these two theories was a rather narrow one. It centred on questions such as whether states are pursuing absolute or relative gains, or whether power was predominantly military or economic. Both theories had accepted the central status of states as actors in international politics, the presumption of states as rational actors, and the focus on the international system rather than, for instance, domestic actors.

Indeed, the terms of the debate were so narrow that Yosef Lapid, in a famous article about the future of IR published in 1989, did not see it as one of the great debates of the discipline, and focused instead on the neo-neo-camp, or rationalism, and the various approaches that had started to criticise rationalism and to look for alternative ways to think about international politics. These included, for instance, feminism and postmodernism, which are covered in other chapters of this book. Their attack on rationalism operated on many levels: ontologically, they disputed the unquestioned status of states and the assumption of rationality; and methodologically, they sided with the English School and the traditionalists, and rejected the notion of science, which both neo-realism and neo-liberalism built upon. Indeed, many reflectivists went a step further and turned the methodological question into an epistemological one, which means that they started to reflect on the basis on which we can have knowledge about the world at all. The traditionalists might not have liked science, but they still thought it possible to approximate objective knowledge. Reflectivists disputed this, and consequently focused their research on the production of knowledge in IR and the consequences of constructing international politics in particular terms for the practice of international politics.

Ole Wæver, for one, counts the neo-neo-debate as the third debate, and therefore sees the debate between rationalists and reflectivists as the fourth one. He also argues that at the extremes of the fourth debate there was little to gain for the future development of IR. On the rationalist side, there was boredom: not much to discuss here. On the reflectivist side, there was the danger of nihilism: how can we say anything meaningful if all we say is a reflection of the particular discursive circumstances of our statement? Wæver's own answer was to adopt what initially looks like a paradoxical position, trying to combine elements of postmodernism and realism. This is not quite the path taken by social constructivists, but in their basic analysis, they agree with Wæver and his view of the fourth debate.

Between the two radical poles, social constructivists see themselves as occupying the middle ground. In an influential article, published in 1997 by the *European Journal of International Relations*, Emanuel Adler identified **social constructivism** as occupying the space between the individualist account of rationalism, which starts from the individual subject, and the holism of structuralism, which focuses on all-encompassing accounts of world politics; between the agency-oriented explanations of rationalism and the focus on structure in structuralism; and between the materialism integral to rationalism and the ideationalism in cognitive approaches (and, in Adler's, however mistaken, view, in many reflectivist works). In addition, social constructivism was to provide the *via media* by accepting some of the ontological insights of reflectivism, as well as respecting the epistemological concerns, but without giving up the aim to understand, and possibly even to explain, concrete outcomes of international politics.

Social constructivism should be viewed more as an approach to IR than a fixed perspective. In this section, we set out how some of the work produced thus far speaks to some of the themes identified in other chapters in this book.

CONCEPT BOX

Structure and agency in IR revisited

Most students of social behaviour face a fundamental dilemma when they approach their subject: on the one hand, individuals act, they do something, and this has certain effects; on the other hand, most of the time what individuals do is shaped by their environment, which in turn is influenced by what people do. As analysts, we need to start somewhere – but do we begin with the structures that influence the behaviour of individuals, or with the (more readily observable) acts done by individuals, or groups of people? Traditionally, most theories and approaches have focused on one side or the other of this structure-agency problem, often without explicitly reflecting on their own bias in this respect. A classic example is the explanation of underdevelopment: those who blame corrupt leaders focus on agency, those who explain underdevelopment on the effects of the colonial heritage or capitalism favour structure over agency. While most people will intuitively agree with social constructivism's project to overcome the structure/agency divide, this is much easier said than done when it comes to concrete empirical research.

As you might imagine, such an attempt to occupy the middle ground between very divergent poles produces a rather mixed bag of approaches. Indeed, as people like Steve Smith have pointed out, the church of what passes as social constructivism is so broad that one sometimes wonders whether it is any coherent church at all: the range of 'followers' span from those merely integrating ideas into a materialist-rationalist framework to those who focus on the analysis of discourse and operate, both theoretically and methodologically, close to reflectivism, and especially poststructuralism. In a review of social constructivist work on European integration, Thomas Christiansen, Knud-Erik Jørgensen and Antje Wiener have therefore used the image of an arch between the poles of rationalism and reflectivism to symbolise the 'middle ground'. In doing so, they wanted to indicate that, while sharing a few central assumptions, social constructivists predominantly define themselves by distancing them from both poles to various degrees.

AUTHOR BOX

Anthony Giddens

Many social constructivists in IR take their inspiration from the work of Anthony Giddens. Giddens is a sociologist who from 1997 to 2003 was the director of the London School of Economics and Political Science. One of the most influential parts of his work sets out the idea of structurationism: that action is influenced and constrained by social structures, which in turn are reproduced by agency. There have since been many critiques and variations of this theme, but for IR, Giddens' formulation still remains most important. The middle ground has not only been core to Giddens' academic work: he is also an influential political thinker, who helped formulate the (by now less fashionable) 'third way' as the ideology of New Labour in the United Kingdom.

Social constructivism can nowadays legitimately be seen as one of the mainstream approaches to International Relations – and, indeed, perhaps as the most important one. Yet is it a theory? In contrast to neo-liberalism and neo-realism, social constructivism does not put forward a set of coherent hypotheses that would form a unified theory in the narrow sense of the term. Instead, it operates with a series of core assumptions on the basis of which more specific hypotheses and arguments need to be formulated. We are therefore using the term 'approach' to describe social constructivism in this chapter, rather than 'theory'. Of course, the term 'theory' is often used much more loosely, to simply denote abstract reflection, and in that sense social constructivism is an approach that is part of International Relations theory. However, in contrast to the neo-neo-debate, social constructivism is not specific to IR at all – instead, it is an approach that crosses the disciplinary divides in the social sciences, and so it might well be that you have come across its central assumptions elsewhere in a way in which you would not have encountered, say, neo-realism in sociology.

> **REFLECTION BOX**
>
> Stephen Fry describes a compromise using the play on words 'a stalling between two fools'. In 'falling between two stools', does social constructivism get the best – or worst – of 'both worlds'?

Assumptions

1. While the rationalist neo-neo theories tried to explain certain outcomes in international politics, most social constructivists instead prefer to describe their task as 'understanding'. This refers back to the work of German sociologist Max Weber, who set out the task of sociologists to understand the subjective motives and world views of actors, which are important factors having an impact on our social world, but in a much less automatic and determining way than objective explanations based on clear causal relationships between readily observable phenomena.

2. As outlined in the section above, social constructivists try to bridge the gap between structure- and agency-centred theories and argue that structure and agency are mutually dependent. As a consequence, most social relations are relatively stable, but the continuous reproduction of structures brings with it the potential for change.

3. In order to account for structures which are not readily observable, social constructivists often draw on so-called 'critical realism'. This 'realism' has nothing to do with the realism or neo-realism of IR, but is instead an epistemological point of view that argues that we can deduce the existence of structures from their effects, which they influence but do not necessarily determine.

4. Social constructivists emphasise the role of norms in people's behaviour. Foreign policy, for instance, is not only a matter of national interest, but also of acceptable behaviour in the international society. Some social constructivists also stress ideas. These are often treated as individual beliefs, whereas norms have a much more social quality, i.e. they exist beyond the individual. The study of ideas as beliefs is therefore more adequately seen as a cognitive approach, which was popular already in the 1970s in foreign-policy analysis. Social constructivism properly speaking is less interested in such individual beliefs than in the influence of societal norms.

5. Apart from norms, social constructivists emphasise the role of institutions. Again, while the basic idea behind this is simple and easy to understand, the way in which the term is employed in concrete studies is often confusing. The reason for this is that institutions can be formal or informal. Formal institutions are based on written or explicitly acknowledged principles, rules and norms. the university, the state, the football club, etc. Informal institutions are merely stable patterns of practice. In this sense, particular roles within a family are treated as social institutions. They are not just based on random behaviour or an individual incidence, but on a repetition of the same behaviour over a longer period of time. While a formal, narrow understanding of institutions brings the concept close to the notion of an organisation, the wide, informal understanding makes it often difficult to distinguish between norms and institutions.

6. In line with their interest in the relationship between structure and agency, social constructivists analyse institutions with a particular focus on processes of institutionalisation, i.e. the development of a pattern of practices, and on socialisation, i.e. the adoption of norms and patterns of behaviour by actors new to institutions. For instance, when analysing European integration, social constructivists are interested in the development of further integration not only in the formal sense but also through the establishment of routines among officials in the European

Commission or in national ministries in day-to-day practices. In addition, social constructivists are interested in finding out to what extent new member states are becoming socialised into the existing institutions of the European Union, or whether and how they are altering them.

7.   The focus on norms and institutions does not mean that social constructivists disregard the role of interests (remember: they situate themselves in the middle ground!). There are two ways in which interests enter social constructivist research. First, they are not taken for granted. Instead, social constructivists concern themselves with how interests are formulated, and in particular the role of institutions, norms and ideas in this process. Second, social constructivist work often analyses the interplay between ideas and interests. In other words, they are not only concerned with the impact of institutions, norms and ideas on interests, but they also ask to what extent interests account for particular ideas (or institutions), and how they in turn are shaped by them.

8.   Discourse plays a central role in the work of social constructivists. For them, discourse is more or less a synonym for communication. As such, it is necessary to reach understandings about identity and interests and to reproduce institutions and norms. Indeed, all of these are only 'visible' through communication, and discourse becomes the core material on which social constructivists base their work. Discourse is also central to achieving so-called 'intersubjective understandings'. This is the category social constructivists take from the work of Jürgen Habermas. The meaning of social reality is not an objective category, but relies on conventions that are widely accepted. Such conventions are, however, not purely subjective either: they are not dependent on the individual, but on understandings shared by a number of individuals. This is why they are called 'intersubjective'.

CONCEPT BOX

Logic of appropriateness

Sociologists James March and Johan Olsen developed the notion that action is driven by different kinds of logics. In particular, they distinguish between the logic of consequentiality and the logic of appropriateness. When people act according to the logic of consequentiality, they pursue particular interests and assess the utility of a possible action in terms of their preference order at a given point in time. In other words, they assess the consequences of their actions for their interests. In contrast, if actors follow the logic of appropriateness, they do not make such rational calculations of interests, consequences, and utility. Instead, they do what seems appropriate in a particular context because there are (often unwritten) norms that prescribe a particular kind of behaviour. As with most such oppositions, the two logics are ideal types, and in practice, action will often be informed by a mix of logics. To complicate things further, whether or not one sees the logic of appropriateness at work depends not so much on empirical observation as on ontological assumption: those who start from rationalist premises will argue that we follow norms because it is in our interest to do so, and therefore refer back to the logic of consequentiality. In the concrete study of international politics, whether one logic prevails over another is difficult to demonstrate. However, at least from a social constructivist point of view, it is important not to underestimate the impact of norms, even if they are frequently broken – indeed, that they are broken only demonstrates their existence, as we would otherwise not know that such a norm exists. It is like crossing the street on the red light: there is a norm that one must not do so (even though it might be in the interest of a particular person at a particular moment to cross the street), and we recognise the existence of the norm, yet most of us will have crossed a street despite the red light at some point in our life.

| Figure 7.1 | Playing a board game illustrates a number of social constructivism's main features. Kids playing a game act according to rules and norms that they accept in the 'world' of the game without questioning their rationality. They also become socialised into this 'world' to the extent that, for the duration of the game and sometimes beyond, they often identify with the roles that have been allocated to them or their figures. |

Source: Sipa/Rex Features.

CONCEPT BOX

Neo-institutionalism

The study of institutions is, unsurprisingly, called 'institutionalism'. Traditionally, the so-called old institutionalism was mostly interested in the description of formal institutions and how they worked. With the rise of behaviouralism, the interest in institutions subsided. Since the 1980s in particular, however, institutionalism has undergone a renaissance. This new, or neo-institutionalism takes a broader view of institutions, is especially interested in their role within society, but also tries to formulate a theory of institutions as such. While many new institutionalists can be classified as, or explicitly see themselves as, social constructivists, this is not true for all of them. In fact, many authors distinguish between two or three institutionalisms. On the one hand, rational institutionalists are more or less what we in IR know as neo-liberals: they acknowledge the importance of institutions to regulate behaviour, but these institutions are set up and maintained because they are in the interests of those that participate in them. Sociological institutionalism, on the other hand, stresses the independent role of institutions in shaping the behaviour of their members. A third kind of institutionalism, close to the sociological version, is so-called 'historical' institutionalism. Here, actors are enabled and constrained in their actions by past actions, which have since become institutionalised. A famous example of this is the set-up of the QWERTY keyboard. The arrangement of letters on our keyboard was developed to make it less likely that the hammers on a mechanical typewriter got entangled. While this is of no concern to those of us using computers, we still operate on a QWERTY keyboard because this has become the standard of keyboards with which we grow up and on which we train – to change the set-up would therefore require a huge effort to change our practices, even if it would ultimately lead to quicker ways of typing.

ANALOGY BOX

Joining the club

Socialisation is something that we have all experienced at some point in our lives. Whenever we join a club, an organisation, an established group of friends, or even a new workplace, we are confronted with a set of rules and norms, and 'ways things are done here'. Some of these might be written down, and we will have to sign that we will conform to these rules. Others will be informal – and we soon realise that we stick out if we don't abide by them too. Quite often, we encounter norms and practices that we don't agree with. Perhaps we stage a fight to change them. More often than not, however, after a few months, or perhaps years, we find ourselves following the same patterns – and very often defending them. Our change in behaviour would then be an excellent example of successful socialisation.

CONCEPT BOX

Strategic and argumentative behaviour

Some social constructivists argue that there is a third logic of action, other than the logic of consequentiality and the logic of appropriateness covered in the concept box above. Drawing on the work of Jürgen Habermas, they propose that actors not only act strategically or appropriately, but also argumentatively (see earlier discussion in chapter 4). This means that an actor does not want to impose his or her personal interest, but neither does he or she blindly follow a given form. Instead, actors argue with each other to find the best course of action. A core article in *International Organization*, written by Thomas Risse, was programmatically titled 'Let's Argue!'. Habermas' work should be known to you as one of the reference points of Critical Theory. Indeed, Critical Theorists such as Andrew Linklater use Habermas' formulation of discourse ethics as a cornerstone for the democratic development of political communities beyond the nation-state. Discourse ethics prescribes the approximation of an open dialogue that is guided by the search for truth, and not for power. This sounds a lot like argumentative behaviour, but how do we get from the formulation of an ethics to the development of an analytical category to observe social behaviour? The clue to this lies in the argument that the so-called 'ideal speech' situation on which discourse ethics is founded, i.e. a situation in which speakers can participate freely and reason with each other without the inhibitions imposed by domination, is not a utopian ideal, but is in fact implicitly presupposed in many day-to-day conversations. If this were not the case, we would experience a continuous breakdown of communication. Consequently, while there is no doubt that actors do act strategically and according to the logic of appropriateness, they also, at least sometimes, behave argumentatively.

REFLECTION BOX

Constructed knowledge?

Both social constructivists and postmodernists place a heavy emphasis on 'discourse' in their work. Indeed, methodologically, a lot of what scholars from both approaches do in their work can be described as 'discourse analysis', and to those new to the field, their analyses look much more similar than the authors say they are. So what's the difference?

Postmodernists and social constructivists follow different purposes in their work. Social constructivists want to understand, and possibly explain specific aspects of international politics. Postmodernists, in contrast, think explanation is problematic because they do not think that we can have an 'objective' access to 'reality'. Therefore, their main purpose in theorising is the critique of prevailing concepts and assumptions in theory and practice, and their political consequences.

Whether or not you find social constructivism convincing as an approach to the analysis of international politics will depend on your view of one crucial problem among others. Social constructivists agree that reality is not a fixed given, but that it is produced in the interplay between structure and agency. States, for instance, exist because of specific historical developments, and while the existence and a specific understanding of states heavily conditions foreign policy making, for instance, the nature of states is constantly changing, not least through foreign policy.

Yet what about knowledge? Would the same argument not apply to the production of knowledge, which should then also be seen as context-specific? And on what basis can we then make observations about international politics, and understand and explain it? If you think all of these questions are irrelevant, you are probably not even a constructivist. If you think they are relevant, but that they do not prevent you from analysing, for instance, the impact of institutions and identities on foreign policy, you have accepted a core assumption of social constructivism. If, however, you think that the answers to the questions above make it impossible to see International Relations as a social 'science', you will probably find postmodernism most convincing. And if you cannot really decide because you see the argument, but still want to say something meaningful about the world, you are not alone – many social constructivists feel the same way.

Themes

The state and power

For social constructivists, international politics is not adequately captured in an analysis of the international system, which is central to neo-realism. Remember that in neo-realism the international system has quasi-mechanistic features: the structure of the system forces states to behave as they do. From a social constructivist perspective, there is nothing universal or automatic about this. Instead, states behave in the way they do because they are socialised into the institutions of international politics. It follows from this that international politics is not governed purely by power and interests. There are fundamental norms in international politics, even though they might be such basic ones as sovereignty and non-intervention. The balance of power, for instance, could then be seen not as a law of the international system, but as a norm that states come to accept over time and act accordingly.

As discussed above, the fact that norms are broken does not mean that they therefore do not exist – instead, this proves their existence. Take the norm of non-intervention as an example. Of course states have always broken this norm, and sometimes very blatantly so by invading other states. At the same time, however, such invasions have regularly been condemned by other states, and sometimes justified military interventions to return to the status quo before the invasion. Even the governments of the invading states are often at pains to justify their violation of the norm of non-intervention, for instance, by making historical claims about the territory occupied, or by reference to security concerns. If the norm of non-intervention did not exist, there would be no need to go through the motions of justifying such an occupation.

National interest is a category often applied by politicians to justify, and by realist analysts to explain, policies. In these cases, national interest often appears to be an objective property of a state, and can be deduced from a state's geographic position, its natural resources, or other such factors. More critically minded students of international politics, in contrast, see the national interest as much more problematic and ask whose interest it actually is, recognising that the nation is itself not a unitary actor, but consists of many different groups and people who are likely to define the national interest in different ways. We return to the concept of national interest below.

Institutions and world order

International society

Because of the existence of norms and institutions on an international level, social constructivists prefer to speak of an international society rather than an international system. A society is characterised by the existence of mutually agreed norms and common institutions, while a system can exist without any of these and operate purely according to mechanical laws. In this, social constructivists are similar to an older approach to International Relations already mentioned above when we discussed the second great debate of IR: the so-called 'English School'.

CONCEPT BOX

A 'society' of states?

Already in the 1970s the English School differed from US-dominated neo-realism not only in its methodology, but also regarding the question of the role that norms, and in particular international law, play in international politics. On both accounts, the English School displays clear social constructivist characteristics. Indeed, the methodological and substantive arguments are not unrelated. Searching for a social, scientific and universally applicable theory of international politics makes one biased towards finding 'mechanistic' laws, rather than much softer and changeable societal norms. Furthermore, just like social constructivism, the English School is a rather broad church. Hedley Bull, its most famous proponent, for instance, is often accused of realism, because states play a central role in his work. Similarly, Alexander Wendt, one of the most prominent social constructivists in IR, does not problematise the existence of states as such. At the other end of the spectrum, authors such as Iver Neumann and James Der Derian come from an English School background, but their work is much closer to postmodernism in that they analyse the discursive practices that constitute states, or the transformation of international politics through technological developments in a digital age.

AUTHOR BOX

Hedley Bull

An Australian by birth, Bull was appointed Montague Burton Professor of International Relations at Oxford University in 1977, having previously been professor at the Australian National University for ten years. Bull was a crucial figure in the second debate, when, in 1966, he engaged in a debate with Morton Kaplan, and argued against a 'scientific' treatment of international relations, and in favour of traditional methods. The publication of his most famous work however coincided with his joining Oxford. In 1977 *The Anarchical Society: A Study of Order in World Politics*, was published. In this book Bull sets out his idea of an international society and its main norms and institutions. He agrees with the realists that modern international society is anarchic in the sense of not being governed through formal hierarchies, but insists that this does not mean that there are no norms, and that therefore there is a societal aspect to international politics. The five main institutions of the international society, according to Bull, are the balance of power, international law, diplomacy, war and the existence and role of great powers. To him, these institutions and norms such as sovereignty and non-intervention were guarantors of order, and he was rather sceptical of the possibility, as well as the desirability, of this order being fundamentally changed. Human rights, therefore, had to be balanced against sovereignty and non-intervention. One force that Bull identified as a potential challenge to the society of states was European integration, but he argued that it was most likely that, eventually, this would lead to a European state that would not challenge the basic principles of international society, rather than a new form of governance. Ironically, he coined the term 'new medievalism' to describe the overlapping forms of governance that he saw emerging in Europe, but which to him were of a transitional nature until the new European state was established. Today, many European integration scholars take the EU's challenge to the society of states much more seriously, and 'new medievalism' has become a common term to use in this context.

One of the debates within the English School, which is also relevant to social constructivism, concerns the role of states and that of individuals in international relations. Against the concept of an international society as a society of states, scholars such as John Vincent have stressed transnational norms such as human rights, where the reference point is not the state but the individual or non-state groups. Barry Buzan has characterised this debate as one between international and world society. Both share a concern with the role of norms beyond the state, but because of their different reference points, there is a tension between them that is crucial to many debates in international relations. In the traditional society of states, human rights are guaranteed through the state, although in principle they should also protect against the state. If human rights are universal, however, the state as the guarantor of human rights is insufficient, and human rights become the grounds on which the norm of non-intervention is broken. This has become particularly relevant after the Cold War, with cases such as the international interventions in Somalia and Kosovo and the institutionalization of the International Criminal Court. These developments possibly indicate a change in the predominant norms of international society. At the very least, the balance between international and world society is being renegotiated, even if this does not mean that the norm of state sovereignty is dead.

REFLECTION BOX

Who defines human rights?

One of the core problems of the universality of human rights is 'who actually defines these rights?' The pluralist society of states guaranteed, among other things, that different world views are protected within different state borders, and no state could easily force another to accept its own ideology. On the downside this also meant that diversity within the state was severely constrained, and that dictatorial regimes justified their often violent actions with reference to different cultures. Within the English School some have suggested the notion of a 'solidarist' society of states, which would be based on more shared norms such as human rights than the pluralist version. Some have argued that, with the increased attention to human rights and more interventions in the name of these rights, the international society is indeed becoming more solidarist. Yet this does not solve the major problems of the definition of human rights. The tension between international and world society therefore seems to be one that is very difficult, if not impossible, to settle, and which needs to be renegotiated in different cultural contexts and historical epochs.

Different types of anarchy

As in the case of the English School, social constructivist authors do not dispute that the modern international society is anarchical. As discussed above, this does not mean that international politics is completely chaotic and violent – it simply means that there is no single, hierarchical government as we find it within states. Neo-realism takes this characteristic of anarchy to be universally valid across different times and cultures. In principle, the system of the Greek city-states operated according to the same logics as the modern international state system, and anarchy is the basis for these logics. Yet, even a cursory look at the way international politics operates at present will reveal that this universal validity of the concept of anarchy is problematic.

First, on a regional level, the European Union (EU) stands out as a case in which a regional system of states is now governed in part by hierarchical relationships. The *acquis communautaire*, the set of rules and laws within the EU, has direct effect in all member states. What is more, many of these rules and laws are now decided by what is called 'qualified majority voting'. This is a voting system among the member states, according to which a certain number of votes is sufficient to pass EU legislation (although the European Parliament will also have a say). The significance of this is that a member state that is outvoted by this system will nonetheless (be obliged to) follow and implement the agreed legislation. In essence, this has introduced a considerable degree of hierarchy within the EU, although it is not quite/yet the same kind of centralised government as we find it within the state.

Second, on a global level, international law, despite being 'soft' law, has gained more and more relevance in international relations, especially after the Cold War. Furthermore, within the United Nations the Security Council does have the power to legitimise the use of force against a state that has violated international law. While this degree of hierarchy is no doubt weaker than it is in the case of the EU, it is nonetheless an important qualification of the supposed anarchy within the international system.

AUTHOR BOX

Alexander Wendt

One of the most prominent social constructivists in IR is Alexander Wendt. Wendt became famous with a series of articles in the late 1980s and early 1990s, the most famous of which is 'Anarchy is what states make of it', published in the journal *International Organization* in 1992. In this piece Wendt sets out the consequences of Giddens' structuration theory for the analysis of international relations. He argues that anarchy is not simply a given, but is moulded over time through the behaviour of states. In his main book, *Social Theory of International Politics* (1999), Wendt argues that there are 'three cultures of anarchy', which he labels Hobbesian, Lockean and Kantian. The Hobbesian culture is closest to the neo-realist image of anarchy, in which power and interests dominate, whereas in the Lockean version states, although rivals, recognise each other's sovereignty, and therefore submit to a minimum standard of common norms. In a Kantian system, the scope of shared norms is much more extensive, and states no longer see themselves primarily as rivals.

In short, anarchy is a very broad category, and although the Greek city-state system and the post-Cold War global international system might both be characterised as anarchical, there are indeed important differences between them. The concrete type of anarchy is therefore context-specific: it changes over time, and according to region. Following the logic of structure and agency in a social constructivist view, states shape anarchy through their interactions, and the concrete form of anarchy prevalent in a given historical and spatial context shapes the nature and behaviour of states.

International regimes

One of the ways in which international relations become more regulated is through international regimes. These regimes are commonly defined as sets of norms, rules, principles and decision-making procedures. They are instruments for states to cooperate in order to achieve common aims without setting up a formal organisation. As such, they have been a prominent focus of neo-liberalism (see also the entry on 'regimes' in the Glossary of key or problem terms).

Neo-liberals have a very rationalist and instrumental view of regimes. According to this view, states enter into a regime because it is in their interest to do so. Typically, this is because the problem to be tackled is of a transnational nature and cannot be successfully addressed by a state on its own – environmental issues are typical of such a problem. By setting up a regime, states can coordinate to agree on common policies. They gain more information about the problem as well as about each other, thus reducing the chances of being caught by surprise by another state's actions. They also reduce so-called 'transaction costs' that would be entailed in having to make bilateral agreements, or engage in day-to-day cooperation.

Take the example of the General Agreement of Trade and Tariffs (GATT): states agreed on the principle of liberalising international trade in order to gain economic benefits; they also agreed on fundamental norms about how international trade should function, on specific rules that they would abide by in the future, and on decision-making procedures in the form of a series of meetings to review the progress of liberalisation and the set of rules decided in the last round of talks. If each of the participant states had had to negotiate trade agreements on a bilateral basis with each other state, the whole enterprise would have been much more labour-intensive, and fraught with the danger of states agreeing more beneficial terms with one partner than with another. Indeed, GATT was so successful that its members have now turned it into the World Trade Organisation, thereby further formalising the institution.

Neo-liberals explain the persistence of regimes with the absolute gains states make through their participation in regimes. To social constructivists this is insufficient. They focus instead on what we have above called 'processes of socialisation'. A regime is like a club: the longer and the more successfully it runs, the more will its underlying norms and principles become part of the identity of its members. Neo-liberals tend to underestimate this identity-changing effect of regimes. Social constructivists draw our attention to the fact that a state's identity and its interests cannot be held stable over time within a regime. In the case of GATT, while there has been a general trend towards neo-liberal (in the economic sense) policies since the 1980s, the regime might well have contributed to this change, and bolstered the neo-liberal outlook of its members.

REAL WORLD EXAMPLE

The Diplomatic Community

The world of diplomats is generally seen as the arena in which states represent themselves and so as an expression of the intergovernmental nature of international politics. Yet this is a very simplistic view. Diplomats work within an institutional context that has grown over centuries and entails a long set of rules, norms and codes. These circumscribe the sovereignty of states as much as they make it possible: states (or rather, their representatives) cannot behave in whatever way they see fit, but at the same time the existence of a more or less ordered society of states relies on these common rules being observed. In addition, diplomats are concentrated in the capitals of states and the seats of big international institutions where their fellow diplomats are often among the main points of contact, and where they frequent the same restaurants, cafes or bars, at least for the temporary period of their posting. This allows for much closer relationships to form, and has an impact on the identities of diplomats which they quite often have to reconcile with the demands and views of 'their' capital.

Identity and Community

The importance of identity

To social constructivists identity is a crucial concept not only to explain national interests. Rather, they argue that identities in themselves matter for policy making, and not only through the definition of interests. This is a consequence of assuming the logic of appropriateness: an identity will provide actors with a particular role in international relations, and they will try to act in a way they see as appropriate to that role. Several studies have, for instance, shown that the belief in European integration in post-war Germany, and the self-definition of Germany as a European state has led to policies that are very different from the much more Atlanticist self-definition of Britain, or the social democratic nationalism of Denmark.

Because identity is such a core concept to social constructivists, they are also interested in the construction of identities, and how they change. In a similar way to postmodernists, they refer to processes of 'othering' when they analyse the construction of identities. This is based on the insight that every identity requires an other against which it is set. If there were no other, there would be no identity, as everything would be the same. In contrast to postmodernism, however, social constructivists do not derive this argument from linguistic philosophy, but from social psychology. Research into group behaviour has shown that groups tend to distinguish between insiders and outsiders, and gain their identity from this distinction. There are lots of examples for such more or less successful identity constructions in international relations: the construction of British identity versus Europe, of European identity versus Islam or (the United States of) America, US American identity versus terrorism, and so on. As already indicated, this argument is also taken up in chapter 5 on postmodernism.

Given that identities are so important, it comes as no surprise that social constructivists are also interested in their change. This is however a much more tricky area. Constructivists normally assume that identities are 'sticky' – they do not change easily. Indeed, if they did change easily, they would be rather less useful as a category in understanding international politics. But how and why do they then change at all? One straightforward answer has already been given above: states enter into new relationships, and become socialised in the process. Indeed, research on state identities and European integration has shown that identities on that level are rather stubborn, and that socialisation is a very long process.

HISTORICAL BOX

Transforming NATO

NATO's roots are as a military alliance to safeguard 'the West' against the communist threat posed by the Soviet Union and the expansion of its sphere of influence. When the Cold War ended, and the Soviet Union collapsed in 1989–90, many predicted that NATO would have come to an end, too. Indeed, neo-realists in particular still forecast that NATO will not survive for much longer, and some have taken the splits within NATO over how to deal with the threat that the Iraq of Saddam Hussein posed in the eyes of the Bush government in the USA as evidence of NATO slowly falling apart. There is no doubt that NATO needed to reinvent its identity. It did so by refocusing its aim to protect and spread liberal democracies, taking on board the liberal argument that democracies do not fight each other (see chapter 1 on liberalism). This was partly creative policy making, but it was also due to already existing aspects of NATO's identity and therefore an instance of path-dependency. After all, NATO's existence as a military alliance could already be interpreted as a means to safeguard liberal democracies – that not all of its members had always been democracies is a historical detail conveniently forgotten in this context. A matter of debate however is whether the new identity is as strong a kit as the old Cold War self-understanding.

For identities to be changed radically, there has to be an 'external shock': something must happen that challenges them fundamentally. The Second World War was such an event for Europe; the terrorist attacks of 9/11 might prove to be such an event for the USA. Such events go to the heart of the self-understanding of a state, and its core norms. Eventually, these norms and self-understandings might well be strengthened as a result of the challenge. Alternatively, however, the perception of a misfit between them and the outside world is stronger, and they need to be adjusted.

Normative entrapment

One of the core processes in the interplay between norms and interests is what one might call 'normative entrapment'. This refers to situations in which actors make promises which it seems opportune or in their interest at the time to make, but which they never actually intend to keep. These promises come back to haunt them at a later time, when those to whom promises were made eventually call them in.

CONCEPT BOX

The Spiral Model

The move towards the acceptance of human rights is a crucial instance of domestic regime transformation. This is a complex process and involves many different actors. Thomas Risse, Stephen Ropp and Kathryn Sikkink have suggested that the process of such domestic regime transformations can best be captured by their so-called 'spiral model'. In this model, authoritarian rulers who violate individual human rights agree to respect these rights in the future in order to achieve economic aid or other benefits. They do not take this commitment seriously, as to them it is only written on paper. Yet the fact that they have signed up to respect human rights enables opposition actors to make claims towards the ruler. This and transnational community of governmental and non-governmental organisations supporting the opposition and adopting a strategy of shaming, strengthens their claims, and ultimately this may lead to a new government. For the transformation to be really successful, however, human rights need to be 'internalised' as a norm. It is often only when a new generation of political leaders has been socialised into an environment in which the acceptance of human rights is the norm, that the transformation process can be seen as complete. The 'spiral' of domestic change starts therefore with the initially purely rhetorical commitment to human rights, and ends with the socialisation of a new generation into a world where human rights are without doubt regarded as the norm.

From a realist perspective there is no obligation to fulfil the promises at a later stage. Yet, even a closer inspection within a rationalist framework makes the choice appear rather more difficult. The state representatives who made the promises might not want to be seen as lying, especially if they think that their state may want something from the state to which the promises had been made to in the future. As the spiral model of the spread of human rights shows, the promises made might also lead other actors to put increasing pressure on the promising actor, whose initial stance might eventually become untenable. From a social constructivist perspective, however, we also need to take into account the logic of appropriateness. States will fulfil at least some promises because they see it as appropriate to do so. They might not initially have thought that they will ever have to keep their promises but, especially if the promises have become part of the self-understanding of a state (or other international actors), it would require a significant challenge to the state's identity not to do so.

HISTORICAL BOX

EU enlargement

It is widely agreed that it is difficult, if not impossible, to explain the European Union's enlargement to the East in May 2004 within a purely rationalist framework. The EU was involved in a difficult process of consolidating its institutions internally when the decision was made, and the addition of more members did not make this task seem any easier. Furthermore, most of the prospective new members were much poorer than the old member states and had a large, uncompetitive agricultural sector, requiring substantial financial transfers as part of the Union's Common Agricultural Policy and its structural funds. So why did the EU members decide to take in their neighbours to the East? One explanation given for this is that during the Cold War European Union politicians often made references to Europe being split, and explicitly or implicitly set out the future of a European Union spanning the whole continent. Given the perceived permanence of the Cold War at the time, only a few visionaries probably believed that such a Union would indeed come true at some point. For the others, following the logic of appropriateness, it was little more than what one was supposed to say. When Central and Eastern European political leaders reminded their Western counterparts of their promises, and referred to Europe's identity as a single unit, there was, *de facto*, little choice than to pursue enlargement.

Peace and security

Cultures of security

Social constructivists also address security issues. There are three areas in which they have conducted research. First, following on from the research on identities, norms and policy, several authors have analysed the culture of security prevalent in particular countries, and how this culture shapes and is reproduced by security policy.

Second, a group around Emanuel Adler and Michael Barnett have taken up the concept of security communities developed in the 1950s by Karl Deutsch. Security communities are said to exist when a group of states share a sense of community and develop institutions for a stable peace between them. On the far end of the spectrum, so-called 'amalgamated security communities' are essentially autonomous political communities of their own. More common in international relations is the case of a pluralistic security community, where states retain their identities, but nonetheless share a deep sense of identity. The research around security communities centres on the themes we have already explored above: how do the norms and institutions of security communities influence the security policies of a state that is part of such a community? How do states get socialised into a security community? How do these communities change?

Finally, constructivists have participated in the debate about the widening of the concept of security. Traditionally, security is very much seen in military terms. It was Barry Buzan who in the early 1980s suggested that security should be analysed in different 'sectors' of society, including the economic and what he called the 'societal' sector, the latter pertaining to questions of identity. At the same time Critical Security Studies aimed at changing the main reference point of security from the state to the individual and developed the concept of human security, which has also become very influential in policy making at the United Nations. Against this, traditionalists wanted to keep a narrow definition of security. Their main argument was that the concept would otherwise lose its analytical value and could no longer be distinguished from any kind of politics.

Together with his colleague Ole Wæver, Buzan from the late 1980s onwards became the core of the so-called 'Copenhagen School' of security studies (see chapter 4). Here, they proposed that security should not be defined substantially. Paraphrasing Wendt's argument about anarchy, one could summarise their argument as 'security is what actors make of it'. In other words, they argued that security is defined through discourse, and its meaning will depend on what in a particular societal and historical context is accepted as security. In their own definition they therefore focused on the formal criteria that turned something into a security object. They specified these criteria as the representation of something as an existential threat to a particular community, justifying measures that would otherwise not be seen as legitimate – war would be an extreme case. With this discursive definition of security we have, however, moved far to the reflectivist pole of the constructivist spectrum.

Summary

1. Constructivism is not one single theory. It is better characterised as a range of different approaches that share scepticism towards any kind of ontological givens. Instead, it argues that our world is continuously reproduced by the interplay of structure and agency.
2. Social constructivism can be distinguished from more radical forms of constructivism by its separation of epistemological from ontological questions. In contrast to poststructuralism, social constructivism does not question the possibility of knowledge.
3. Therefore, social constructivism is often seen as constituting the middle ground in International Relations between rationalist and reflectivist theories.
4. Social constructivism draws on sociological theories and consequently stresses the societal aspect of international relations, as opposed to the mechanistic qualities of the international system in neo-realism. In doing so, social constructivism has an affinity to the so-called 'English School' of International Relations.
5. Social constructivism focuses on the role of norms, institutions, identity and culture in international relations. This makes it different from interest-based theories such as neo-realism and neo-liberalism.
6. Norms and institutions are crucial in the process of socialisation. Social constructivists argue that, just like individual human beings, states become socialised into particular forms of international society.
7. One of the core authors of social constructivism is Alexander Wendt. Wendt's primary contribution to the study of international politics is his analysis of the changing nature of the international system in history.
8. For social constructivists, national interest is a category that needs to be explained, rather than being treated as an explanatory factor. They are interested in how interests and norms and institutions interact – for instance – in the making of foreign policy.
9. Many social constructivists distinguish between different types or logics of action, such as strategic and argumentative (or 'communicative') behaviour, or the logics of consequentiality and appropriateness.
10. Methodologically, a social constructivist approach normally stresses historical processes, because it is otherwise unable to demonstrate the interplay of structure and agency.

Criticisms

As one would imagine, social constructivism is criticised by both the rationalist and the reflectivist end of the spectrum of the fourth debate for being inconsistent or not radical enough. The rationalist critique focuses on the empirical evidence for the proposed arguments. They argue that most of the puzzles addressed by social constructivism can be adequately explained by interests and other 'material' factors, and that the impact of such things as norms accounts for, if anything, a very small portion of the variation in state behaviour. Some also find the very notion of identity or norms as explanatory factors problematic, as they cannot be readily observed. This criticism is difficult to counter – in the end, it boils down to the question of whether or not one accepts the critical-realist epistemological foundations of most social constructivist work. What we hope we have shown in this chapter is that social constructivism does add some valuable insights to the analysis of international politics that either cannot, or only with some difficulty, be brought into a rationalist framework.

One further counter-argument to the rationalist criticism is that it misunderstands the whole social constructivist project, which is not to explain outcomes through recourse to independent variables, but rather to show that there are no really independent variables in social relations, and that we need to approach international politics with the aim of understanding actors' behaviour from the 'inside'. Similarly, the criticism that social constructivism is not really a theory can be rebutted by pointing out that it does not want to be a theory in the universally applicable sense of, say, neo-realism.

Nonetheless, some major problems remain. One is that a lot of the concepts that social constructivists operate with are rather unclearly defined. Some analyses, for instance, talk about identity, culture, norms and institutions, and it can be rather difficult to separate them. Needless to say, this problem becomes more important the further social constructivist work gets to the rationalist pole and does indeed want to explain. Similarly, nearly all attempts to distinguish empirically between different logics of action have run into severe difficulties. The reason for this is that, while the differentiation, for instance, between strategic and argumentative action might make a lot of sense as an abstract ontological theorisation, unless we find a means to look into a policy maker's head, we cannot determine whether s/he does the things s/he does because s/he is motivated by interests, norms or the search for the best argument.

One criticism that is shared by many rationalists and reflectivists is that most social constructivists, despite their emphasis on the interplay between structure and agency, focus their analyses on structures such as identities, institutions, cultures and norms. This is indeed true, and is accepted by many social constructivists. The reason for this bias is that most of the empirical work done by social constructivists starts from a critique of rationalist explanations, which in turn focus on agency. Scholars such as Jeffrey Checkel have, however, started to address this problem by focusing more on what drives individual agency.

There are also several criticisms from the reflectivist camp. When introducing Hedley Bull's work we have already indicated that he shares with social constructivists like Alexander Wendt a considerable state-centrism. In a lot of mainstream social constructivist work the state is taken as an unproblematic category and is treated as the central actor in international relations. Both Critical Theorists and postmodernists disagree with this, as should be clear from the chapters where we introduce these two perspectives.

Another common criticism especially from postmodernists is that social constructivists do not take language seriously enough. While they acknowledge the importance of discourse, their understanding of it remains shallow, and very few social constructivists, located towards the postmodern end of the spectrum, recognise the power of language in its own right, rather than as a transmitter of norms and a means of socialisation.

Finally, we have already drawn your attention in the reflection box on p. 191 to the problem of inconsistency, and the question of whether a social constructivist position in the middle ground is actually tenable without running into contradictions. Can one argue that reality is socially constructed without having to make the assumption that science and knowledge, and consequently one's own work, is socially constructed, too? If so, what then is the significance of this work?

None of this should detract from the critical insights that social constructivism has provided us with since the 1990s. Also, perhaps one should also be grateful that social constructivists have not stayed in the corners of the fourth debate but opened up a space between the poles where dialogue is possible, if not necessarily and always easy.

Common misunderstandings

1. *Constructivism means that people can simply make up their own world.* On the contrary, social constructivists stress how anything we do is embedded in and influenced by structures such as institutions and cultures. However, they also reject the notion that these structures are fixed for all time. Instead, they point to the fact that these structures need to be reproduced through our actions, and that they are therefore always subject at least to the possibility of change.
2. *Social constructivism is an abstract theory that has nothing to say about the real world.* Much social constructivist work can indeed seem a bit abstract. This has largely to do with the fundamental epistemological and ontological issues social constructivists need to address within the fourth debate to develop their own position. However, there is a lot of very empirical social constructivist work around, and because social constructivism is an approach rather than a theory, its real value in many ways can only be appreciated in the context of concrete empirical research.
3. *Social constructivism is full of difficult words no-one understands.* This mixes social constructivism up with postmodernism (or, more accurately, poststructuralism – see chapter 5), which is sometimes seen as a 'radical' constructivist perspective because it acknowledges that our knowledge is also socially constructed, and that language plays a crucial part in this construction.
4. *Social constructivists are idealists who have no sense of the hard issues of international politics.* Locating themselves in the middle ground, many social constructivists stress the importance of interest and strategic considerations. However, they insist that these are not the only important factors influencing international relations. Because rationalists focus on the role of interests, many social constructivists tend to concentrate on the influence of ideas, identities or norms, but that does not mean that they deny the importance of interests.

Further reading

Adler, E. (1997), 'Seizing the middle ground: constructivism in world politics', *European Journal of International Relations*, Vol. 3, No. 3, pp. 319–63 (this core article outlines social constructivism as the middle ground between rationalism, reflectivism and structuralism).

Bull, H. (1977), *The Anarchical Society: A Study of Order in World Politics*, Basingstoke: Macmillan (a core work of the English School, in which Bull sets out clearly the organising institutions and norms of international society).

Checkel, Jeffrey T. (eds) (2007), *International Institutions and Socialization in Europe: An International*

Organization Reader, Cambridge: Cambridge University Press (a collection of essays that focus on the impact if institutions in one of the most densely institutionalised world region).

Christiansen, T., Jørgensen, K.E. and Wiener, A. (eds) (2001), *The Social Construction of Europe*, London: Sage (a very valuable and influential collection of essays from all parts of the social constructivist spectrum on European integration and governance).

Hopf, T. (2002), *Social Construction of International Politics: Identities and Foreign Policy, Moscow, 1955 and 1999*, Ithaca, NY: Cornell University Press (an exemplary study demonstrating the use of a constructivist framework for the analysis of foreign policy, but also making a good read of great historical moments of the twentieth century).

Onuf, N. G. (1989), *World of Our Making: Rules and Rule in Social Theory and International Relations*, New York: Columbia University Press (Onuf was one of the first social constructivists in International Relations. Many constructivists have been influenced by this book).

Risse, T., Ropp, S. and Sikkink, K. (eds) (1999), *The Power of Human Rights: International Norms and Domestic Change*, Cambridge: Cambridge University Press (this has become a classic empirical work from a social constructivist perspective. The 'spiral model' of the impact of human rights on domestic change is outlined and applied to several case studies).

Wendt, A. (1999), *Social Theory of International Politics*, Cambridge: Cambridge University Press (Wendt is widely regarded as the most influential social constructivist. In this book, he summarises his ideas about institutions, norms, culture and anarchy in international politics).

8 Green perspectives

Introduction

Context

The first edition of this book was published in 2001 and written over five or six years previous to that. The very first version, written exclusively for a course at Nottingham Trent University, did not have a separate chapter on the environment, although it used environmental political issues in providing examples of different facets of international affairs. Despite the omission of a specific chapter, environmental issues were increasingly on the agenda of international relations in ways which this chapter will describe. A separate chapter became unavoidable as publication neared.

It simplifies too much, and is certainly not this neat, but one might even argue that decade by decade over the past 50 years, something qualitative has changed in terms of human perceptions of the environment and the way in which it has reached many people's agenda. The 1960s saw an initial and then more widespread consciousness of the interconnections between human life and nature, epitomised by Rachel Carson's book *Silent Spring* which documented the dangers of pesticides accumulating and travelling in ecological systems. It was a decade of rejecting much of what had previously been regarded as normal in terms of human assumptions about the environment, and this included the pollution associated with contemporary societies.

The 1970s saw the international community of states become more involved in the idea of 'the environment'. Rather than simply seeing it as a 'hippy' fad associated with committed groups and individuals, nation-states started to become involved in thinking about the connections between environment, development, resources and population. In 1972, for instance, 114 countries met in Stockholm for the United Nations Conference on the Human Environment (UNCHE). The 1970s might be seen as the decade of an argument framed as environment *versus* development, which suggested a trade-off between the two: that is, if we save the environment we have less development and if we have more development we inevitably destroy the environment. While it can be very tempting at this particular point in history to see the story of humanity as one of 'progress', we should not too easily dismiss the currents of the 1960s and 1970s as we might their fashions or level of technology. There are still very strong arguments that humanity has lost sight of its intimate connections with nature through modern living. Also, while seeing environment and development as mutually exclusive has proved to be politically unpalatable (as we shall see below), it might yet prove to be a particularly important insight if capitalism enters a more profound period of 'crisis after crisis'.[1] There must ultimately be *Limits to Growth* if growth is defined quantitatively.

---

[1] Song Title: *The Coathangers* (Shambrook/Pettiford, 1985).

That said, the message of environmentalism as 'reorientation' or 'restraint' proved difficult to swallow for many actors and interests. After the Second World War, economic recovery picked up through the 1950s and 1960s in the Western world. This was also a period of widespread decolonisation (see chapter 3) and optimism that developing countries might mimic the path taken by richer countries. Despite the world economy hitting choppier seas in the 1970s, it was clear that material standards of living were a key political aim under almost all political systems. In the Western democracies politicians found it difficult to embrace environmental policies which would sacrifice short-term development for ill-defined aims of long-term ecological stability. For the communist (East) side in the Cold War, initial promise in the 1950s that their command economies could outperform the West looked increasingly shaky as the 1960s brought slow-down and the 1970s stagnation; their politicians too needed more development and material prosperity, not less. Less developed countries were determined to raise living standards through development; any thought here about the environment could easily be dismissed by the idea that those who had caused the problems – the richer countries – ought to be sorting them out.

Into this context the 1980s saw the term 'sustainable development' come to the 'rescue' – although not, as we shall see, of the environment. Although infinite growth in a finite system is impossible, leading some to dismiss sustainable development as inherently contradictory (an oxymoron), sustainable development was able to appeal to everyone. Essentially it resolved all the issues above by admitting that development was crucial (rich countries tend to have better environments after all), but arguing that it could take place within a system/context which was sensitive to the importance of the environment/nature. This chapter considers this key idea in more detail, but by way of introduction we argue that sustainable development was a political success more than an environmental one. Just as many states have appropriated the label 'democratic' despite being, in practice, undemocratic, all kinds of actors raced to embrace sustainable development for all kinds of reasons which had nothing to do with the environment. Sustainable development was 'good PR', 'a solid marketing message' and a 'vote-winner'. In effect, one could argue that 'business as usual' was given a 'green-wash'; a look of concern often substituted for genuine action.

Despite the undoubted problems with sustainable development, the 1990s were effectively a period of consensus building around its importance. Like the emperor's new clothes everyone had to agree that sustainable development was a fine thing indeed. Some have argued this period of green limbering up was actually a necessary 'stage' in addressing environmental concerns – that is, that high-sounding ideas like 'greening spirituality' (see below) need to be preceded by small lifestyle changes which come from allowing the environment onto the agenda beforehand through sustainable development. As these changes become 'normal' – and the environment continues to get worse overall – people are persuaded of the need to make/support more fundamental changes. In parallel, supporting scientific evidence about the negative effects of human behaviour on the environment also began to grow, reinforcing perceptions that the nature of consumer society may need to be reconsidered.

Many environmental currents and concerns came together in the 1992 Rio Conference (United Nations Conference on Environment and Development) which produced a wide-ranging, 800-page document called Agenda 21. Despite the name, Agenda 21 was actually more like a list of problems or state-of-the-planet audit. Nonetheless it was a starting point. However, the overall outcome of Rio was the dominance of a politically acceptable, business-focused version of sustainable development, aka 'green-washed' continued/continuous growth. Accordingly, by the 1997 New York follow up to Rio (Rio +5) delegates were able to note that little progress had been made against a whole range of environmental indicators, while development – with all its inherent destruction and injustice – continued apace. What went unsaid at UNCED by those with power was that the environment was still way down the priority list after words like growth, jobs, defence and so on.

So far, this context section has suggested a development of environmental consciousness. While this may be a reasonable way to recount the narrative, it is important to note that this by no means suggests that this is an easy journey with an inevitably happy ending. The end point is very much in doubt, and there are enough vested interests associated with life-destroying practices for us to doubt that humanity will find a way to act upon the many warnings it has received. Wallerstein's projection that the collapse of capitalism will be followed by socialism *or* barbarism is worrying, even for those who might regard socialism as a positive development. Having noted the need for tentativeness in regarding the environmental crisis as a Hollywood script which will play itself out by 'man' and 'nature' living happily ever after, we can notice further developments in the most recent decade.

If we were to characterise most of the decade since the first publication of this book in 2001, one might say that the consensus on the importance of environmental problems finally came to dominate and won the debate, at least *theoretically*. However, practice has been, and is, slow to catch up. What does this mean? Well, for example, most scientists now accept that global temperature has been steadily rising for perhaps 100 years, with a steeper rise in recent years. What is more, the public at large have also largely got the message. In the UK, for example, where once people joked about global warming being a good thing, there is now more seriousness among a large proportion of the population about the need to address it. Of course (just when Brits thought the weather couldn't get any worse) this may have something to do with climate change meaning, above all, climate instability and disruption; for the UK this may well not mean much warming at all, but the disruption of ocean currents and coldish dry winters and (even) wet(ter) summers.

However, despite the environment now being taken seriously, the political pressures – particularly of democracy – seem to have continued to prevent concerted action on a necessary scale. Many fear the consequences of inaction. Just as there comes a point when it is too late to make an oil-tanker change direction to avoid collision with the cliff it is moving towards, so many Greens argue that we may already have stored up too much damage which will be played out through self-reinforcing mechanisms with disastrous consequences, whatever we decide to do in the future. One example would be melting ice-caps and the link with rising temperatures; as they melt they become smaller and reflect back less heat into the atmosphere, so that more heat is absorbed and even more ice melts.

Although this neat division into decades of changing attitudes is almost certainly too simple and contains significant overlap, as this book approaches its third edition, we might be seeing the beginnings of another shift. This time it seems that our experience of life on earth may be about to reinforce that which we know theoretically; in other words, demands for a green new deal may finally be taken seriously because the cracks in the old system become too great. So, for instance, at the time of writing the world is entering a significant economic downturn with many and complex roots; avoiding questions about carrying capacity, energy dependency, food security, climate change and so on may no longer be possible.

We hesitate to make predictions, but if you are reading this between 2010 and 2015 there is a strong likelihood that you are living a time of significant economic turbulence and a fluctuating oil price; periods of growth will likely be checked by increased demand for oil above what is possible to produce and, in consequence, an increase in oil prices leading to contraction of the economy, lower demand and reduced oil prices leading to a recovery. Even if the above scenario fails to materialise, a number of things remain true. The established fact of '**peak oil**' is reinforcing resource/energy scarcity fears and putting the environment at the forefront of the practical as well as theoretical agenda. Beyond the central issue of oil, melting ice at the poles and unusual climatic impacts (including frequency of 'natural' disasters) are amongst those things giving people a very real local *and* global sense of (environmental) crisis. In previous decades oil tankers ran aground or chemical factories exploded, but now there is a much clearer sense of holistic perspectives on the environment being evidenced by global events of one sort or another.

Peak Oil: The idea behind 'peak oil' is that oil production will typically follow a bell shaped curve on a graph. The peak of production will occur when approximately half of the oil has been extracted. There is evidence, with exceptions to prove the rule, that this applies for individual wells, oil-fields, etc. The reasons are to do with oil becoming more difficult and expensive to extract over time. The bell curve applies to oil discovery and oil production, with the former ahead of the latter. World oil *discovery* peaked in the 1960s and today humanity consumes around four times as much oil as it discovers. Looking at total oil production, there is every reason to believe that we are at or near 'peak oil' now or in the near future. Entreaties to boost oil production to lower prices which have come from some leaders such as Gordon Brown in the UK have either been ignored or are, more likely, not possible. Economic superpowers in the making such as India and China seem to suggest that demand will continue to rise; the political and economic instability which is threatened might finally provoke action from politicians on environmentally sustainable ways to cope with the industrial societies we have created.

Ultimately, despite wise warnings spanning whole decades, humanity has acted like the child who eats all its sweets (candy) today even though it has been warned to save some for the rest of the week. As the impact of our behaviour is brought ever more sharply into focus, this chapter (once nearly excluded) seems more central to the future of international relations than ever. Apologists for industrial society arguing against the idea of limits to growth have frequently posited that there was no need to worry because our wisdom and technology were coming together. It is to be hoped as we enter the second decade of the millennium that our wisdom now recognises that technology can be a part of the solution but will also be a part of the problem in particular forms of society; beyond this it seems certain that environmental and resource issues will force us to act in various practical ways in the near future, regardless of philosophy or theory. Nonetheless, understanding philosophy and theory can be important to students of IR in understanding the chances of action and success, either within or without capitalism. So, while the practical challenges of environmental politics merit the attention of students of international relations, a sense of theory is as important to them here as it is in looking at military power, economic cooperation of social justice; indeed all of these elements are woven into the analysis of green perspectives.

Introducing Green Theories and Perspectives

Especially given the complexity and range of issues connected to the environment, we do not consider that there is a separate 'Green' perspective in International Relations. However, as an issue area, the environment has become extremely important over the past 50 years (see above). We think it is important to think about different green perspectives and how they relate both to IR theory and world politics. The linkages between environmental practice, green philosophy and politics are significant. All political and economic positions have – even if only implicitly – a base in some or other ecological ethics. Similarly, any ecological position must imply political decisions about the way it can gain acceptance and be put into practice. Thus, different political (and theoretical) positions may relate to environmental concerns and ecological ethics in different ways.

Specifically on the issue of the environment's increasing importance in international relations, there has been growing awareness of problems of resource scarcity, acid rain, ozone depletion and **global warming**.

Global warming: Global warming is taking place through what is most easily understood as a 'greenhouse effect'. Gases are being produced (particularly carbon dioxide) through industrialisation and particularly motor and air transport. Such gases can be absorbed by vegetation, but deforestation means there is less forest and they are accumulating in the atmosphere. Greenhouse gases let heat in, but not out again, leading to a warming effect.

A number of **ozone-depleting substances**, produced through industrial production and consumption processes, are attacking the earth's protective layer of ozone, leaving us potentially exposed to the more harmful of the sun's rays. The problem has received attention and action internationally, but a hole in the ozone remains which will take many decades to repair itself even if use of ozone-depleting substances is halted completely – which it has not yet.

Environmental concerns have begun to permeate International Relations because of these big, and complex, issues. Perspectives in this book have sometimes had adherents who develop positions on the environment. In this chapter we make a distinction between incorporating environmental issues into existing perspectives in this way and deeper philosophical positions focused on ecology.

Figure 8.1 These statues on Easter Island are all that remain of a once thriving, but alas, ecologically destructive, society. What characterises the contemporary world is not the ecologically destructive tendency of humanity but the fact that it has now become global in scale.

Source: Bettman/Corbis.

In thinking about how the environment has become problematised in IR, we make the distinction between 'thinking green', often **anthropocentric** in the sense of incorporating environmental issues or concerns into existing perspectives, and Green Thought, often **ecocentric**. Green Thought we see as a radically different way of thinking about the human–nature relationship, the problematic nature of modern forms of life and contemporary social practices, and the limitations of scientific knowledge in 'solving' human problems.

> **Anthropocentric:** human-centred. In terms of the environment it describes a world view which sees environmental problems purely from the perspective of humanity.
>
> **Ecocentric:** nature-centred. Strictly speaking, it would be impossible for human beings not to be anthropocentric to some extent, but ecocentrism describes the attempts to prioritise and privilege nature in arriving at prescriptions for the ordering of societies and international relations.

Although we contend that nowadays one can draw the distinction between tacking green issues on to other theories and regarding nature as central, this is a relatively recent development in studying IR. Despite the influence that various environmental events, reports and books were having amongst the public at large from the 1960s onwards, in the very tense times of the Cold War all this had little impact in IR, which was dominated by a concern with power politics (realism) and later the success of the international economy (liberal pluralism) and its failures such as debt (structuralism). It was not until the end of the Cold War in the late 1980s and early 1990s that IR really began to think about environmental issues and environmental philosophies in a more serious way.

So, environmental concerns like acid rain, resource depletion, soil erosion, food shortages and global warming can be viewed as simply 'issues' which are now pushing their way onto the international agenda, or 'problems' which can be 'solved' by international cooperation. Realists now discuss ideas such as 'water wars'. For others, the environment is viewed as an aspect of North–South relations; so, neo-Marxists (structuralists) might focus on the close links between poverty, inequality and ecological breakdown, or suggest that a consideration of the environment raises problems for orthodox liberal economic theory. Liberal pluralists, on the other hand, have drawn attention to the complex interactions surrounding environmental regimes and the role of non-governmental organisations.

CONCEPT BOX

'Thinking green'

With regard to what we have termed 'thinking green', perhaps the only shared assumptions are that:

■ the world faces serious environmental problems;
■ the environment is important because, in some sense, continuing resource depletion, global warming, environmental degradation and pollution, all constitute a threat to the well-being of the human race;
■ given the global nature of many environmental 'problems' or 'issues', it is appropriate that they are addressed by International Relations scholars;
■ global environmental problems can be solved, or at the very least managed, through cooperation in existing, or reformed, forums including global institutions.

In a broad sense, all of the above might be pointed to as examples of 'thinking green'. In this chapter, we will spend some time considering such ways in which focusing on the environment as an issue can enrich our understanding of some quite 'traditional' areas of concern such as the state, power and so on. Accordingly, sections of this chapter are closely interlinked with earlier chapters.

However, we also move on to Green Thought (ecologism). This represents a fundamental challenge to the 'issue' or 'problem-solving' approach to the environment/IR. From such a perspective, the contemporary state-system, the major structures of the global economy and even global institutions are seen as part of the problem. In addition, modern science and technology, which is drawn upon extensively in 'problem-solving' approaches to the environment can, to some degree, be viewed as much as a cause of global environmental degradation as offering a solution.

Since the 1960s there has been a more serious interest in the environment, among academics in the West at least. At the heart of such interest has been a (re)consideration of the 'human–nature' relationship. Put simply, academics with green sympathies have looked to challenge a view of nature as something external, hostile and dangerous to human beings: a view which suggested that our natural environment should be conquered and subdued rather than respected and lived with. From these deliberations on the human–nature relationship, a more critical perspective has emerged. For our purposes, we will use the term 'Green Thought' to distinguish such critical approaches to the human–nature relationship, from more limited and reformist forms of green.

For 'Green Thought' the inherent optimism of some 'problem-solving' approaches is rejected and the argument made that the relationship between human beings and nature largely explains the current environmental crisis. Furthermore, various facets of that relationship need to be restructured, if we are to enjoy a secure future. Such a position has at its heart a belief that the world is composed of a series of interrelated **ecosystems**.

Ecosystem: an interrelated ecological web. Many creatures and organisms are connected to each other. Remove any one and the whole thing may collapse like removing a brick in a game of Jenga.

Human beings are also embedded in ecological relationships. For this reason it is not possible to make a real distinction between human beings and other living things. Green Thought offers a **holistic** world view which highlights the intimate connection between human life and the global ecosystem. We discuss how Green Thought encourages a fundamental shift from a focus on the 'international realm' to a conception of the 'global' in contemporary theory.

Holistic: human beings in 'scientific mode' are often accused of breaking problems down into manageable chunks – atomism – as a way to solve them. Greens very often offer a more holistic approach which sees that we must look at the 'whole' given its intimate connections.

HISTORICAL BOX

First pictures of the earth from space

The first pictures of the earth from space had a profound influence on people's perceptions of the planet. From space the earth is clearly whole: a blue/green planet. In this view invisible political and territorial boundaries somehow 'appear' insignificant. These images also brought home the global nature of many environmental problems which have no respect for state boundaries and the finite nature of the world, however 'infinite' it might feel.

In summary, Green Thought demands radical changes in forms of socio-political organisation and respect for non-human species. As its proponents have pointed out, Green Thought need not be a fixed position but generally involves:

- a rejection/renegotiation of anthropocentric world views;
- the belief that human interference in the natural world is currently threatening the survival of both humankind and other species;
- an insistence on the need for fundamental changes in social, economic and technological structures and ideological/value systems;
- a distinction between vital and non-vital needs;
- a rejection of development strategies which encourage economic growth above quality of life;
- an ethics based on a 'green theory of value' which places an intrinsic value on non-human life;
- an active commitment towards implementing the changes necessary to achieve a genuinely green future, which includes promoting alternative lifestyles, values and a decentralisation of power.

Origins

Looking at the origins of all types of green thinking we see a mixture of influences, which we divide into three specific areas: scientific/technological, philosophical/ethical and political. Scientific/technological origins refer to knowledge about, and awareness of, a problem. Philosophical/ethical origins refer to speculations about the relationship between human beings and the natural world; human behaviour has contributed to environmental problems *and* raised awareness of the need for different ways of thinking. Political origins refer to prescriptions for the development of action to overcome a perceived crisis. These distinctions should help to make sense of the narrative offered below.

In terms of current interest in the environment, it is almost a convention to cite its beginnings as Rachel Carson's highly influential book *Silent Spring* (1962). Though the book postdates a lot of environmental concerns, going back to the industrial revolution, and predates a lot of serious ecological philosophy, it is since this time that the environment has become perceived as vital to the existence of humanity rather than a limitless, often hostile and external, resource to be exploited for the production of human material wealth. In other words, this book did much to encourage the view that human beings should be living with nature, rather than triumphing over it.

Various factors have subsequently contributed to growing public awareness of environmental issues. These factors include environmental disasters such as the meltdown of the nuclear reactors of Three Mile Island, USA in 1979 and Chernobyl, Ukraine in 1986, as well as the human tragedy caused by gas-leaks at the Union Carbide factory at Bhopal, India in 1984. It is only relatively recently that people have had genuinely to worry about immediate environmental threats to the existence of the species such as nuclear weapons, greenhouse gases and holes in the ozone layer.

Many would date Green Thought itself from the publication of various doom-laden predictions about the future, most notably the Club of Rome's *Limits to Growth* report, published in 1972 (see the Literature Box below). *Limits to Growth* was significant in stimulating discussion, debate and research and in offering an alternative to humanity's predominantly growth-orientated attitude. To some degree, the 'limits to growth' argument, combined with a rejection of anthropocentrism, can be seen as the very essence of Green Thought.

LITERATURE BOX

The *Limits to Growth* Report (1972)

Researchers used computer modelling techniques to 'prove' their findings that environmental factors would soon place restrictions on growth and/or lead to disaster. Exponential economic growth and population growth were producing a set of interrelated crises, they said. The world was rapidly running out of resources to feed people or provide raw material for industry. Finally the ability of the environment to actually absorb the waste products of human consumption and industrial output was being exhausted. Human society would collapse before 2100, they predicted. *Limits to Growth* forms part of what has been called a 'Survivalist' discourse, which emerged to challenge the belief that humanity's ingenuity would always find ways around environmental problems.

We can also identify a distinctly 'reformist' strand of environmental thinking which owes much to the utilitarianism of Bentham, discussed at greater length in chapter 1. Utilitarian approaches to the environment prioritise the 'pleasure principle' and the maximisation of individual human material gain. Similarly, it is possible to identify a rather authoritarian strand of environmentalism which evokes Hobbes in calling for a 'green Leviathan' – a centralised power to overcome the ravages of 'natural' economic competition (see chapter 2). Some contemporary Green thinkers and activists undoubtedly have affinities with anarchism. Some versions of anarchism evoke images of people living in small-scale communities, which provide for basic needs while eschewing materialism, and finding peace and contentment in this simple lifestyle, which allows them to live comfortably without destroying the environment or exploiting other human beings. Many Greens advocate the devolution of power and decision making away from the impersonal, bureaucratic structures of central government, to the local community. Here we find echoes of Rousseau's belief in direct, participatory democracy.

Despite such complex and historical origins, we need to follow a different path in order to really appreciate the contemporary crisis and efforts to theorise it. The term 'ecology' itself is, in effect, a nineteenth-century invention, first appearing in the work of Ernst Haeckl. Haeckl's work is important because it is from this that we get the image of ecosystems as interrelated and of nature as alive. But why would it be necessary to articulate such a view of nature or the environment in the first place? To answer this question, we need to understand Western political and social thought from the sixteenth century onwards, and how modern science in particular has represented the relationship between humanity and the natural world. Indeed, having acknowledged the influence of a wide range of diverse thinkers in different strands of 'thinking green', perhaps the most useful starting point for understanding the origins of Green Thought is in a critique of the project of modernity.

The idea that human ingenuity and scientific reason could be used to subdue nature and resolve a multitude of problems came about with modernity and, subsequently, the Enlightenment. Prior to this modern period, religion played a much more important role in understanding and 'explaining' the nature of human life, forms of social organisation and the relationship between human beings and their 'environment'. For example, in Judaeo-Christian thought, human society was thought to be ordained by God and organised according to His will. This is not to say that religious belief systems necessarily preclude the domination of nature. Indeed, the Old Testament outlines in some detail a 'natural' hierarchy which justifies, to some extent, the exploitation of the natural world. However, this is in the context of an all-embracing moral philosophy which encourages respect for all of God's creations and a degree of humility in the face of His omnipotence.

As we saw in earlier chapters, one characteristic of modernity is that secular thought, frequently legitimised by appeals to rationality and scientific 'evidence', played a key role in challenging religious influence in political life. The Enlightenment rested on the belief that the application of science to a range of human problems would much improve the material well-being of humankind. At the same time, the capacity of human beings to understand rational principles would allow for the reorganisation of social, economic and political life. Together, these innovations would allow human beings to continue on an onward and upward path, towards a 'better' life. The 'buzzword' of modernity and the Enlightenment was 'progress'. This new found 'faith' in rationality and science also encouraged a view of humankind as master of, if not the universe, then certainly the Earth.

Environmental problems facing us today have much to do with such optimism. Before looking at the contemporary period, therefore, we need to look at two particular people who were absolutely crucial in changing attitudes from the almost deferential and timid in the face of nature, to the domineering and confident. Francis Bacon's role in shifting images of nature from the pre-modern to the modern is highly significant. Bacon justified scientific analysis in terms which fitted the religious orthodoxy of the time. For example, he argued that not to look more closely at the world that God had created was actually an insult to God and that scientific method was, therefore, imperative. In suggesting that science was discovering the complex wonders of God's creation, Bacon was able to construct important 'loopholes' in religious doctrine which then allowed the development of science.

However, intellectually, far greater credit in this process is due to René Descartes. From Descartes, we can call the anthropocentric view of the human–nature relationship a 'Cartesian' view.

AUTHOR BOX

René Descartes

Descartes established two premises of profound influence in Western philosophy. The first was that there was a clear distinction between mind and body, and the second, crucial in this context, that the natural world is a machine. In effect, he argued that the understanding of natural processes can be achieved by reducing them to mechanical laws. To Descartes, and those subsequently influenced by him, nature is merely matter in motion. As such it is 'dead'. There is no moral dilemma in using nature for our own purposes and no need to look upon it with mystical awe. The view that nature exists for the benefit of human beings and has no intrinsic value is known as 'anthropocentrism' and has characterised the organisation of human societies in the West ever since. In other words, it was discovered that human beings could use nature for their own benefit, that it was not necessary to live in fear of nature and that science had the potential to transform societies.

Cartesian anthropocentrism is now subject to conscious reflection given that the physical effects of human beings losing sight of how humanity is a part of nature are becoming increasingly apparent. The debate over whether to resolve a perceived environmental crisis by utilising an adapted anthropocentrism or by replacing it with an ecocentrism (ecologism) is at the base of Green theoretical arguments and debates.

LITERATURE BOX

Carolyn Merchant's *Radical Ecology*

This book locates anthropocentrism in the birth of modernity. Anthropocentrism is inextricably bound up with the emergence of instrumental rationality, the subordination or domination of nature (as Merchant puts it 'the death of nature') and the institutionalisation of patriarchal social relations.

We should also note at this juncture that modern discourses about the nature of man as an autonomous, rational being and calls for a more rational or scientific outlook were challenged. As pointed out in our discussion of feminism (chapter 6), the Enlightenment generated a number of 'counter-discourses'. Much utopian thinking of the time was not concerned with material advancement, but with spiritual matters. However, with the scientific revolution, which sprang from Enlightenment thinking, increasingly the eternal human quest for the 'good life' became associated with conquest of, and dominion over, the natural world in the service of material advancement. In the light of this, many Greens today hold that in the contemporary world, global consumerism, which is destroying the environment, is rooted, ultimately, in an anthropocentric view of nature.

What is distinctive about Green Thought on justice, morality and ethics is that it attempts to think beyond the boundaries of most discourses, by broadening the concept of 'community' to include animals and other non-human living beings. In many cases, this has essentially involved taking up the theme of egalitarianism from other modern philosophies but applying it to all species, as in animal-rights discourse.

REFLECTION BOX

In terms of attitudes towards the domination of nature for human ends, how does Green Thought differ from Critical Theory?

Figure 8.2   Animal Aid demonstration outside Unilever office in Blackfriars, London, Britain, 1997: animal rights protest against cruelty in laboratory testing at Unilever.

Source: Tony Kyriacou/Rex Features.

Although arguments about vegetarianism have tended to be couched in moral terms and evince a distaste for the idea of feeding on the flesh of another sentient being, this is another example in which the contemporary situation may introduce a practical reality more convincing than the theoretical arguments such as those made by Singer (see below). These practical arguments are over the misuse of resources. Livestock production is contributing nearly 20 per cent of all greenhouse gas emissions from human activities, for instance, including a third of methane (many times worse than carbon dioxide in terms of its potential for global warming) and two-thirds of nitrous oxide (which is 265 times worse). Vegans (and vegetarians) are pumping dozens of tons less carbon dioxide into the atmosphere over the course of their lifetime than those who consume meat (and dairy). In a world of hunger the arguments go beyond climate change; high proportions of meat (bones, fat, past sell-by date) gets wasted and five or six times as many people can be fed by land producing vegetables, fruits, cereals and vegetable fats than if production is of meat, milk and eggs. Chris Brazier suggests that, in a world where affluence is still translated into greater meat consumption, at an individual level altering our diet may become as much of a necessity as insulating our homes or reducing our air travel.[2]

CONCEPT BOX

Animal rights

Ecocentrism is arguing for the intrinsic rights of all nature, but is there any reason then for making the distinction between biting a banana and kicking the cat? The answer is yes because the cat is sentient: that is, a cat is a type of being which is conscious of pain. Since the cat can experience pain and suffering, we have a moral obligation towards it and it therefore has rights.

Peter Singer is famous for developing the notion of animal rights, beginning his journey through the observation of various farm animals. He applied their situation to the 'pleasure-pain' principle of philosopher Jeremy Bentham which suggests that an act is immoral if it results in an overall increase in pain. Singer thus retains 'the individual' as the focus – the morally relevant unit – but extends the boundary of the community to sentient creatures beyond humanity.

So far our discussion of 'origins' has been confined to Western traditions. However, it is important to note that Green Thought also draws upon a number of non-Western philosophies. Arguments here often focus on environmentally destructive development as part of Western culture and the alleged respect inherent in some other cultures for the natural world. For example, the Gaia notion of the earth as a living being, complex and wondrous, and not just as a source of satisfaction of infinite wants has important spiritual and moral implications. Not only does Gaia (earth) deserve protection, but also we might be signing our own suicide note by continuing with current practices of development based on ever-expanding growth and consumption. Greens have engaged with a number of holistic philosophies which start from the premise that the best knowledge comes from understanding entities not as various parts, but as whole systems with parts that interact. The recognition of non-Western influences is important because the Green call to 'think globally and act locally' involves a serious appreciation of how local indigenous knowledge systems have allowed human beings to live successfully with nature for many years and are similarly threatened by the so-called 'progressive' forces of modernisation and globalisation.

---

[2] Information in this section has been modified from the December 2008 issue of *New Internationalist* magazine and particularly Chris Brazier's 'Meat's too expensive', pp.14–15. He notes that his statistics are drawn from a lecture by Dr Rajendra Pachauri, 'The impact of meat production and consumption on climate change', 8 September, 2008. Dr Pachauri is Chair of the Intergovernmental Panel on Climate Change.

Figure 8.3 Global warming.

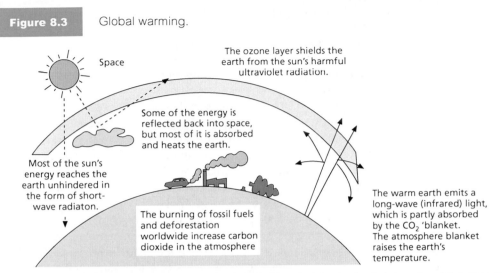

Space

The ozone layer shields the earth from the sun's harmful ultraviolet radiation.

Some of the energy is reflected back into space, but most of it is absorbed and heats the earth.

Most of the sun's energy reaches the earth unhindered in the form of short-wave radiaton.

The burning of fossil fuels and deforestation worldwide increase carbon dioxide in the atmosphere

The warm earth emits a long-wave (infrared) light, which is partly absorbed by the CO_2 'blanket. The atmosphere blanket raises the earth's temperature.

Source: B. Hocking and M. Smith (1995), *World Politics: An Introduction to International Relations*, 2nd edn, London: Prentice Hall, p. 141.

Assumptions

With regard to Green Thought, it is possible to identify a coherent set of related assumptions:

1. Greens emphasise the global over the international. For example, the importance of global community is recognised as well as the rights of local communities to control their own resources. Bio-regional communities are seen as the basic building blocks of the earth.
2. Greens begin from the implicit understanding that current human practices are in some way or other 'out of sync' with the non-human world.
3. Greens stress that modern practices, underpinned by anthropocentric philosophical belief systems, have been critical in causing the environmental crisis.

> **REFLECTION BOX**
>
> What are the prescriptive implications of this approach? That is, what does it suggest we do, and what might be the consequences of such action for how we live?

Themes

The state and power

There is no one single Green theory of the state. However, within IR, there have been discussions about the implications of environmental problems for sovereign states. For example, is the autonomy/legitimacy of the state being undermined by the need for global responses to these problems? If sovereign power must be conceded to global institutions, does cooperation mean that we need to rethink the distribution of power among states and other actors? Is our notion of sovereignty changing? If the state is facing multiple challenges, is this a good thing? In the 1970s liberals linked the environment to emerging interdependence among states. They argued that this was likely to alter the state-system fundamentally by eroding sovereignty. Today some liberals contend that environmental problems like ozone depletion and global warming are compelling states to engage in more cooperative strategies, thus undermining the principle of sovereignty. Environmental practices may be leading to new norms of sovereignty.

Litfin argues that political responses to global environmental problems modify the rights and capacities of states. Many Third World states lack the capacity to enforce environmental standards; the establishment of international environmental institutions and the activities of transnational environmental actors, particularly NGOs and epistemic communities (knowledge communities, or 'experts' such as scientists), create new forms of governance and authority. These may not be replacing the state, but they are modifying the character of sovereignty. Similarly, discourses of sustainability (however unsatisfactory) compel the state to incorporate some sense of ecological accountability. The growing citizen activism manifested in the proliferation of NGOs and social movements also encourages 'sovereign bargains' to be struck in the form of environmental regimes. NGOs and social movements are, of course, about politics beyond the nation-state, in so far as they provide alternative channels of control and authority and reshape social meaning and beliefs. The cumulative effect of all of these developments may be to alter the norms and practices of sovereignty and create alternative and legitimate channels of political activity. Furthermore, the legitimacy of institutions of the state can be seriously undermined by social divisions and conflicts which are, in part, a consequence of deteriorating environmental conditions.

The increasing scarcity of resources can work to increase the state's vulnerability because it weakens the bonds between the state and society. At the same time, the failure of, for example, agricultural crops can increase the demands made on the state by particular social groups. A recent study by the Project on Environment, Population and Security (EPS) concluded that environmental scarcity increases society's demands on the state while simultaneously reducing the ability of the state to meet those demands.

WORLD EXAMPLE BOX

Can states help the environment?

States *have* sometimes gone against accepted economic rules by seeking to limit imports of dolphin-unfriendly tuna and unsustainably harvested timbers on environmental grounds, but the pressures of the liberal free-trade system make such resistance difficult. Furthermore, the pressures of the state system and global economy make getting the most out of natural resources essential; thus states such as Indonesia, Malaysia and Brazil maintain their sovereign rights to chop down their own trees. International groupings of states, meeting in various forums to address resulting issues, have had only limited success in putting a curb on state behaviour.

These are some of the ways in which 'thinking Green' challenges conventional understandings of the state and sovereignty in IR, but is there a uniquely Green perspective on the nature and role of the state? The answer is 'no'. As we suggested in our discussion of origins, there have been strong anarchist influences on Green Thought. These have objected to the state because it is a hierarchical institution which consolidates all hierarchical institutions. Paterson has drawn attention to the state support of patriarchy and other non-egalitarian social relations. The state also supports technological developments and forms of economic organisation that damage the environment; accordingly an influential strand in Green Thought advocates the decentralisation of power to small-scale communities or larger bio-regional communities.

In response to the debates about sovereignty alluded to above, realists might counter that, whatever the challenges are to the contemporary state, it nevertheless remains the only body which has sufficient legitimacy, resources and territorial control to enforce environmental rules. Only states can formulate foreign policy; international law bolsters the principle of sovereignty, so environmental agreements fortify and reproduce the principle of sovereignty and hence bolster the state system. Furthermore, the state system can actually work to contain economic forces which are encouraging the reckless and relentless destruction of the environment.

While Greens reject the assumptions and prescriptions of realism, some have nevertheless supported the idea of a strong state that has the power to negotiate at the global level. The state can also play a role in redistributing resources from the rich to the poor regions of the world. Indeed, many Greens argue that the environmental crisis is such that reforms must be 'marched through' as a matter of urgency. Only the state can promote effective international action. So, while holding somewhat ambivalent views of the state, some Green thinkers nevertheless regard the state as a necessary 'evil'. At the same time Greens see an urgent need to devolve power down to local communities and also to centralise power up to the regional and global level. The nation-state is seen to be both too big and too small to deal effectively with environmental challenges and to fully coordinate responses.

AUTHOR BOX

George Monbiot: Is the state a 'necessary evil'? (Excerpts from a *New Internationalist* interview, *The Action*, Winter 2008)

Although quoting out of full context is sometimes unfair that is not the intention here. The intention is to demonstrate that an environmental campaigner such as George Monbiot will not automatically be pro-anarchist and anti-state, even if this is for pragmatic/instrumental reasons. But since these words are taken out of full context, it seems only fair to urge you to take a look at some of Monbiot's very accessible work which appears in a range of publications, electronic and otherwise.

'Claiming that anarchism is the only means of tackling climate change is a very good way of discouraging people from getting involved ... We have to use all the resources available to us now and [...] that includes the state and corporations ... This is the only system we've got right now ... if [it] is really about stopping climate change, those of us involved have to take a pragmatic view ... my worldview has become quite Hobbesian ... We have to use every means at our disposal [...] to put intolerable pressure on the Government'

Conflict and violence

If realists, and indeed other theorists of IR, have displayed little interest in the environment, perhaps they should. The aforementioned EPS project suggests that global warming and ozone depletion are unlikely to be the immediate cause of violence, but over a longer period they might interact with other environmental and demographic pressures and add to tensions.

For instance, although globally there is more than enough fresh water to meet human needs, many parts of the world already face water shortages. Poor water resources increase the risk of waterborne diseases like malaria. In parts of Asia and Africa there is a scarcity in good quality crop land, while in many places around the world overexploitation of fisheries not only threatens ecosystems, but has already produced unemployment and economic hardship. The EPS report concludes that environmental scarcity could interact with factors such as these to cause significant social effects; environmental scarcity can exacerbate social divisions or create new forms of social segmentation, increasing class and ethnic conflict.

Although the report explored the links between the increasing scarcity of renewable resources and the rise in violent conflict *within* countries, it has significant implications for relations between states. As we will see below, the scarcity of resources can generate conflicts between states, particularly where there are existing disputes about territory, and 'ownership' and control of resources. Poverty in turn adds to migratory pressures; people will move to areas where environmental resources are more plentiful, or to other countries. Migration can generate ethnic tensions, especially where resources are already scarce. Where the ethnic mix of a country is delicately balanced, an influx of migrants can both increase tensions and further undermine the stability of the state.

Of course, one does not have to be a realist to recognise the existence of conflict and violence in human relations; feelings of relative, as well as absolute, deprivation fan the flames of conflict. This is exactly the kind of conflict that military institutions find very difficult to control, never mind resolve. In many parts of the developing world, where civil society is weak and democracy fragile, worsening environmental conditions can further undermine the legitimacy of government and social institutions. If the political opportunities available to people to change their situation decline, then political violence is much more likely.

It would be appropriate to finish this section by mentioning how Green Thought actually challenges our perception of the meanings of terms like conflict and violence, though this is not exclusive to Green Thought. Conflict need not imply only physical violence; conflict means differing points of view, each committed to resolving a difference in its favour. In this sense there exists a fundamental conflict in human societies between advocates of an environmentally destructive industrial society (a growth paradigm) and those who would challenge this way of organising society (a limits-to-growth paradigm). According to such an interpretation, what has been called the 'mega-machine' of industrial society (capitalist or socialist) has been inflicting great violence to the planet.

Institutions and world order

In this section we outline briefly some of the ways in which environmental problems have led to the setting-up of new regimes or have forced their way onto the agenda of international organisations like the UN. We then attempt to go beyond this narrow concern with green issues and institutions, and consider briefly how Greens critique the existing world order and attempt to re-vision a world order based on environmentally sound principles and practices.

Since UNCHE in 1972 (see introduction to this chapter) the environment has been regarded as another manifestation of interdependence in international relations and another reason why states are compelled to engage in cooperation to 'manage' the problem. Put simply, the message of the Stockholm conference was that how countries got rich (or stayed poor) could have environmental consequences. Until relatively recently the solution to environmental problems has been founded on a basic faith in the possibilities of development. Liberals, for example, were highly optimistic about the possibility that guarding against environmental catastrophe and safeguarding natural resources were examples of common interests that could lead to cooperation in the search for solutions. Liberals were the first to suggest that environmental regimes could be used to work out win–win scenarios in order to correct environmental imbalances (see chapter 1).

The notion that the environmental consequences of development, industrialisation and growth can be 'managed' has been criticised by radical Greens. They believe that many of the UN conferences and the regimes and institutions which have grown up in consequence all start out from the basic premise that the effects of industrialisation can be dealt with, allowing human society to 'progress' in much the same way that it has been doing. This managerialism assumes that development is not a problem in itself, but that modifications to development strategies are needed. To draw a simple analogy, a car engine which is perfectly designed but which has a small oil leak will blow up sooner or later if action is not taken to correct the leak, but such action is entirely possible. 'Shallow' environmentalism is frequently used to justify reforming existing relationships, whereas some Greens argue for a radically decentralised, non-hierachical form of social organisation.

The reformist concept of 'sustainable development' (see introduction to this chapter) which came out of the Rio Summit assumed that the fundamental tenets of the development discourse did not have to be rethought, but needed to be managed rather differently. Sustainable development was popularised in 1987 when the World Commission on Environment and Development (the Brundtland Commission) defined it, broadly speaking, as development which meets the needs of the present without compromising the needs of future generations. This definition is vague, and open to such a variety of political interpretations.

This **shallow environmentalism** manifested itself in International Relations theory in a number of ways. For example, liberal economists conceded that their failure to incorporate environmental factors into their analysis was a weakness in classical economics. However, they do not argue that this weakness invalidates their basic premises; simply that as with other inputs and outputs a price must be attached to environmental goods if they are to be used efficiently. Liberalism is anthropocentric when dealing with the environment. It does not question the goal of human progress, or even the basic means to achieve this; it merely suggests, returning to the car analogy above, that we fix the leak. Similarly, contemporary liberal theories assume that the states can respond effectively through the facilitation of regimes and institutions.

Shallow environmentalism: A term which describes the view that environmental problems can be resolved within the current systems of human social, political and economic organisation.

Deep environmentalism: Variously known as deep ecology, ecologism or a deep green perspective, deep environmentalism suggests that ecological decay is inherent in current patterns of production and consumption and that the only way to safeguard the future of humanity *and* other species is to radically alter social, political and economic structures in human society.

INFORMATION BOX

Agenda 21

This is the shorthand term used for the extensive framework document adopted at the Rio Earth Summit to guide policy makers into the twenty-first century. It is 800 pages long, partly as a result of the complexity of the issues it is addressing, but also because it seems to many like a very long wish-list about what might be different in the world. Critics have suggested that rather than a radical blueprint for action it is simply a detailed list of those problems which exist and which we would like to resolve. Agenda 21 makes no attempt to answer the politically contentious issue of which problems are most important and therefore in what order we should go about resolving them. However, on a practical level in response to Rio and Agenda 21 new institutions have been set up to manage environmental problems.

Greens argue that there is a need to challenge this view and reclaim a set of beliefs about the nature of the ecological crisis; to suggest that radical changes are necessary in order to respond to problems. From a Green Perspective, world order, as it is currently constituted, is based upon capitalism, industrialisation and a consumer culture. These dominant forms of social and political organisation are built upon and perpetuate oppressive social relationships – class inequalities, patriarchy and the destruction of indigenous peoples and communities. Modern social practices and forms of organisation across the globe are also damaging to the environment.

In making us aware of physical limits, ecocentric perspectives are urging us to think beyond mental barriers and towards a fundamental transformation of our spirituality regarding the planet. This would include de-emphasis on material things and liberal individualism and a (re)emphasis on living within limits. Over time, populations would have to drop, and peoples would live in sustainable decentralised communities, similar in some respects but culturally diverse.

We do not necessarily have to accept green positions as a dichotomy between the optimistic tinkerers and the revolutionaries. The 'shallow' lifestyle changes made by many ordinary people (recycling, car-sharing and so on) could be regarded as part of a broader movement towards popular involvement in politics as well as the beginnings of the development of a deeper ecological consciousness. Initiatives like Agenda 21, it might be argued, can play an important role in raising consciousness among people at the local level so that these people go on to make important connec-

Figure 8.4   Rising temperatures since 1860.

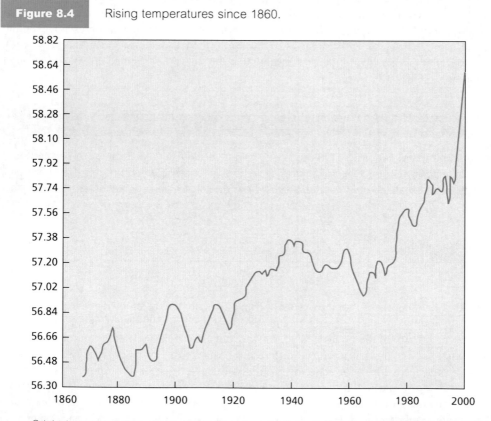

Original sources: Adapted from World Resources Institute, R. Repetto and J. Lash (1997), 'Planetary roulette: gambling with the climate', *Foreign Policy*, 108 (Fall), p. 108; and L. Brown *et al.*, *Vital Signs*, New York: Norton.

Taken from: C.W. Kegley and E.R. Wittkopf (1997), *World Politics: Trend and Transformation*, 7th edn, New York: St Martins, p. 381.

Climate change is one of the biggest challenges for Agenda 21. This graph shows increasing temperatures since 1860 based on five-year averages.

tions between the everyday practices of their locality and the global nature of environmental problems.

Although Greens do recognise that advances have been made through initiatives like Agenda 21, they also believe that it is important to continue to develop a critique of the shallow environmentalism inherent in such approaches. Greens adopt a strategy of lobbying political élites at local, national and global levels in an attempt to influence decision making, but they also believe that it is important to avoid cooption by maintaining a critical distance from élites and existing institutions. In making sustainable development a self-evident truth and reducing the Green movement to a friendly, yet wagging, finger, shallow environmentalism might be seen as having robbed the overall Green movement of its critical potential.

Peace and security

Earlier in the book, we drew a distinction between positive and negative conceptions of peace and security. Since the birth of International Relations as a discipline, scholars have recognised that security involves more than simply the absence of war. Liberal idealists believed that security required the construction of institutions and the conduct of international relations according to principle not power. In the 1970s and 1980s liberals argued for a strengthening of institutions and forums in order to bring much needed stability and facilitate cooperation in our dangerously interdependent world. Despite the long period of Realist domination in the discipline, and the scepticism and cynicism of the Cold War era, this view of security has re-emerged from time to time.

A turning point in the history of East–West relations, for example, was Mikhail Gorbachev's call for a new conception of security which recognised the interdependence of all peoples, economies and environments. This proclamation of interdependence, which implied an urgent need to move beyond the nation-state and achieve global security through extensive cooperation, ended the Cold War rhetoric of 'two camps' and inevitable ideological, political, economic and military conflict between capitalism and communism.

In earlier chapters we argue that both structuralists and feminists have developed important critiques of militarism and 'negative' conceptions of security/peace which inevitably fuel militarism. Consciousness of environmental degradation has encouraged research which measures the impact of militarism on the environment, and covers both the aftermath of past wars and the ongoing problems caused by current conflicts. The diversion of resources from social groups to the military can exacerbate poverty, which in turn has a negative impact on how scarce resources are utilised. The crisis of legitimacy which many states currently face is also destabilising. Conflicts cause both biological and physical damage to the earth, as does weapons testing, including nuclear testing in peace time. The proliferation of nuclear technologies and the development of chemical weapons all threaten potential disasters in the future.

Environmental disasters resulting from the first Gulf War pushed the environment as an 'issue' onto the security agenda. It has become increasingly apparent that in addition to 'war', environmental risks are associated with the current way in which the global economy and societies are organised. Rising sea-levels threaten many small island-states who have contributed little to the problem. More generally, we are all vulnerable to a wide range of risks, including environment-related ones, over which we have no control.

Greens share ground with feminists and some Liberals in arguing for a positive conception of peace and security. Some Greens have explicitly adhered to principles of non-violence, or suggested that violence emerges from environmentally destructive ways of organising societies. Furthermore, debt and development are very relevant to debates about security and, for this reason, Green thinking about security also involves a critique of dominant modes of political economy. Capitalist economies assume and require ongoing economic growth, and this has profound implications for ecological systems. In short, there can be no lasting peace unless oppressive social practices are ended and injustices eradicated. In developing a critique of capitalism, Greens share overlapping concerns with structuralists, critical theorists and feminists. For Greens, though, peace also involves establishing a harmonious relationship between human beings and other living entities. From a Green perspective, therefore, achieving 'security' requires a change in world view.

ENVIRONMENTAL DEGRADATION AS VIOLENCE?

If we define violence as an act or process which prevents people from realising their potential then environmental degradation can clearly be seen as violence. As such it is helping to prevent the achievement of 'positive peace' which is a situation where there is not just the absence of war, but the presence of justice.

Figure 8.5   Indonesia: deforestation outside the Gunung Leuser National Park, Sumatra, Indonesia.

Source: DCY/Rex Features.
Poor countries frequently have to exploit their resources any way they can to try and 'develop'. Around the globe this has led to widespread deforestation, both for the timber itself and to clear land for other productive activity such as cattle ranching to feed the developed world's seemingly insatiable appetite for cheap meat.

The links between some structuralist writing and deep-green critiques are apparent. A focus on political economy and the theme of inequality is clearly important in Green Thought. For example, they share a common concern with 'overconsumption' of resources by the North. But, in what ways do they differ?

Inequality and justice

Inequality tends to exacerbate environmental problems and ending unjust and oppressive relationships is a fundamental tenet of Green Thought. It follows that engaging with Green Thought necessarily entails addressing issues of inequality. Although environmental degradation of various kinds brings about a general decline in the quality of human life, clearly the weight of hardship is not carried equally by people across the world, but felt disproportionately by those who are already disadvantaged.

The 1992 United Nations Conference on Environment and Development explicitly linked the environment and development, based on scientific evidence that environmental degradation linked to absolute poverty put pressure on marginal land and advanced desertification. Reduced agricultural output and economic production can be a cause of social deprivation and also increase already existing social inequalities. The enclosure of agricultural land during development processes concentrates more resources and power in fewer hands. Since Rio the link between the environment, sustainable development and inequality has continued to be emphasised. This immediately raises questions of social justice – how do we decide how resources are distributed?

Dobson has argued that we cannot assume that justice and sustainable development are complementary. That is, a government could devise an ecologically sustainable society but one which was based on inequalities or where some people had less than the most basic needs. Similarly, we can envisage 'just' societies which are heading towards environmental collapse because everyone is consuming too much.

Problems of justice at the international level are not obvious. Let us take the specific example of global warming. At first sight, this seems to be a relatively easy problem to identify and, with sufficient political will, to solve. Identify the 'culprits' and compel them to make amends for their wrongdoing. What at first appears to be a readily identifiable solution, is on closer inspection, rather more complicated. First, we have to establish whether there is indeed a problem; some scientists have strongly disputed this 'fact'. Even if we assume that global warming may contribute to climate change, is that necessarily a problem? Assuming that we agree that it is a problem, we have to decide whether, ultimately, we value material goods over the risks of global climate change, or coping with the consequences of pollution? Second, if we accept that the rich nations of the world have contributed most to this problem this still begs the question of whether they should rectify the damage which has already been done. Is justice, in essence, about righting a wrong?

At the same time the drive for just solutions raises many potentially divisive issues. For example, Dobson argues that protecting the environment might ultimately mean less development, but this is likely to have a much greater impact on the poor countries of the world. This raises the question of whether the interests which poor countries would be expected to sacrifice are of a different order to rich nations. Action to tackle environmental problems is being debated in the context of a world where disparities in wealth and awareness of those disparities is increasing. Therefore, it is clear that the issues of development, resource depletion and environmental destruction must be viewed in the context of much more profound issues of international distributive justice. In the past few decades an array of institutions, regimes and forums have grown up that, potentially, allow some mechanism to redistribute wealth, income and resources across the globe, but if these mechanisms are to succeed, all participants must accept that they are legitimate.

There have been numerous attempts to apply basic principles of justice to global environmental problems. For example, in relation to global warming, some theorists have used the existing frame-work of international 'common law' to try to decide what constitutes a 'fair' and accepted level of carbon dioxide emissions with the global warming literature leaning towards the view that equity requires differential obligations between rich, industrialised nations and developing nations, including transfers from the former to the latter.

You might have noticed that so far our discussion of inequality and justice has been somewhat anthropocentric – that is, questions of justice have been confined to relations between human beings. Greens are, of course, seriously interested in issues to do with international redistributive justice because they recognise that very little will be achieved unless these divisive issues are tackled head-on. However, Green Thought goes beyond questions of 'who gets what'. The environment is seen to have its own value and Greens might want to include the 'needs' of the environment and the 'rights' of other living creatures in any assessment of what is a just order. Ecocentrism is based on an ethics that recognises the interests of the non-human community, the interests of future generations of human and non-human beings and adopts a holistic perspective, so valuing populations, species, ecosystems and the ecosphere as a whole.

Identity and community

One of the problems of attempting to think about questions of justice and ethical behaviour in an international context is that it assumes some notion of community. Communitarians say that ethical ideas are rooted in specific communities, and arguments about justice are only convincing within community boundaries. Cosmopolitan thinkers, on the other hand, get around this problem by extending the notion of community to the entire human race. Green Thought on community is distinctive because it, at one and the same time, requires us to think about community in global *and* local terms. That is to say, many Greens are seeking to expand the boundaries of 'community' to include all of the world's peoples and, indeed, non-human species, but at the same time, in questioning indus-trial society and development, Green approaches support diversity and resist the destruction of difference which is manifested in many cultures and communities.

Greens have been criticised for encouraging parochialism in their visions of community. Some Green Thought can be quite authoritarian – small-scale communities run along hierarchical, conser-vative lines aiming at self-sufficiency because freedom and egotism create problems. However, most Greens argue that there is not necessarily a contradiction here; while social and economic problems are global in nature, they can only be addressed effectively by the construction of small-scale com-munities and self-reliant economies. Hierarchical social relations are seen as a problem. Nonetheless, at the same time, we might need a degree of coercion to meet basic ecological responsibilities and guarantee human rights. However, this would be significantly less than the concentrated, coercive powers vested in the sovereign state. These same local communities might be linked in a global 'com-munity of communities'. Greens evoke a new image of 'community' (in the sense of universal ethics) as stretching across the globe, yet intimately connected to the locality.

From a Green perspective, of course, the problem of thinking about justice and community is made even more challenging by the insistence that conceptions of community must include non-human species. In terms of Green Thought on community, Mary Midgley's book *Animals and Why They Matter* (1983) was an important milestone. Midgley argues that questions of community, morality and ethics can be extended to animals if we accept that they are sentient beings. Animals might not possess the capacity to reason, in the sense that we commonly use the term, but they do have feelings. However, this view of community does not make meaningful connections between human beings and animals and the ecosystems that sustain them. All ethics is based on the idea that the individual is a member of a community of interdependent parts. From this we can extrapolate a land ethic – species and plant life should be preserved because it is a stockpile of genetic diversity – which allows for recreation, aesthetic pleasures as well as meeting needs, but this is essentially anthropocentric. The erosion of sovereignty might see the increasing importance of local identities and communities whose lives are much more closely intertwined with specific ecosystems. In order to re-vision community we must get away from the view of the world as divided into distinctive political spaces (like states) and, instead, conceptualise the Earth as being made up of integral bio-regions.

Greens argue, therefore, that the realisation of a secure Green future is not only a question of re-visioning community, but also entails a radically different understanding of self/identity and our relationship with 'others'. Eco-feminism has been very influential in Green Thought, particularly in relation to questions of self and identity. Eco-feminists have developed an important critique of the mind/body dualism which is fundamental to Cartesian thought, and offer an alternative conception of what Freya Matthews termed the 'ecological self'.

CONCEPT BOX

The ecological self

Mary Mellor (following Freya Matthews) has argued that breaking away from Cartesian dualisms involves re-examining the lower value accorded to the underside, the body, the senses, emotion, the imagination, the feminine and nature. It also involves problematising rigid boundaries and polarised conceptions of identity obtained through exclusion. The ecological self goes beyond the boundaries of mind/body, human/nature, man/woman, self/other, to a conception of the self as embedded in social and ecological communities, acting in solidarity with and caring for others, and recognising the 'other's' intrinsic value.

You will recall from earlier discussions, that Descartes has been a central figure in the story of modernity. Central to Descartes' conception of the self and modern identity is the notion that there is a clear and necessary distinction between the realm of the mind – rationality and critical reflection – and the body – the realm of the passions. The identity of the modern subject – who we think we are and how we relate to others – is intimately tied up with this notion of the domination of mind over body. The subordination of the passions is seen to be essential to the construction of the rational, autonomous individual. This mind/body dualism is also fundamental to the modern world view – the subordination of nature to rational control in the interests of human advancement. From a Green perspective, this self through processes of self/other dualisms is inherently problematic for many reasons. Fundamentally, the construction of self and identity is tied up with the exploitation and domination of nature.

REFLECTION BOX

How does the eco-feminist critique of the Cartesian world view compare with the postmodern critique outlined in chapter 5? How does the eco-feminist view of the ecological self compare with standpoint feminist views of the construction of self and identity, outlined in chapter 6?

Summary

1. Environmental issues have been taken up by IR scholars and so 'thinking green' and Green Thought have shaped the discipline in various ways.

2. 'Adding in' the environment has served to enrich many existing theoretical perspectives in International Relations and furthered our understanding of a range of areas and concerns such as the state, conflict, inequality, cooperation, institutions and governance.

3. However, 'adding in' is a problem-solving approach to the environment (see chapter 4), based on an anthropocentric world view. Contemporary environmental problems and disasters have shown the dangers inherent in adopting such an anthropocentric view. Environmental concern has developed as a result, especially since the 1960s.

4. It is possible also to identify a distinctive tradition of 'Green Thought'. Drawing upon Green Thought it is possible to construct a distinctive Green position or Green perspective on IR.

5. At the very heart of the Green perspective is a concern with the human–nature relationship.

6. Green Thought emphasises the change from pre-modern to modern world views as crucial to our understanding of environmental problems. Whereas in pre-modern times people were deferential towards/fearful of nature, modern perceptions have emphasised humanity's ability to conquer nature.

7. A Green perspective demands a restructuring of various facets of human organisation, from everyday practices like consumerism, to contemporary world order built on the exploitation of the natural world and the oppression or marginalisation of specific social groups.

8. While we should be careful not to overstate the similarities, Green Thought shares some similarities with feminism and postmodernism.

9. For 'Green Thought' the problems of going beyond critique and actually putting such suggestions into practice should not be underestimated. Nonetheless, it provides a powerful critique of the contemporary organisation of international society. Awareness not only of environmental problems but of the philosophical underpinnings of how human beings relate to nature may be crucial to the future of the planet.

Criticisms

Criticisms are offered of both shallow environmentalism (thinking green) and Green Thought, not as the final word on the weaknesses or flaws identified, but as a way into discussion.

On a practical level, shallow environmentalism seems very much to be dealing with the realms of the possible: asking what action we can take to minimise human impact on nature within current patterns of social, economic and political organisation. While this may seem sensible, the worry is that the possible may not be sufficient. Ultimately, the environmental lobby might only promote NIMBYism and short-term problem solving.

Shallow approaches have tended to urge the third world to do as the first world says rather than as it does. In encouraging 'sustainable *development*' shallow approaches tend to suggest the preservation of the vast resources of the South for Northern use. In this context 'sustainable development' may be more correctly interpreted as an attempt to protect the existing way of doing things against a critical tide of cultural, ecological and feminist arguments rather than as genuine environmental concern. Green Thought, on the other hand, acknowledges the role of the North and its high consumption practices as the primary cause of environmental degradation.

Figure 8.6 Rate of population growth across history.

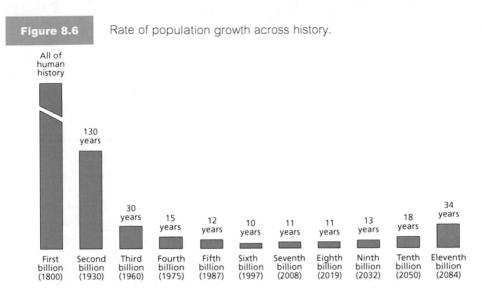

Original source: *A Citizen's Guide to the International Conference on Population and Development* (1994), Washington, DC: Island Press, p.14.

Taken from: B. Russett and H. Starr (1996), *World Politics: The Menu for Choice*, 2nd edn, New York: W.H. Freeman, p. 445.

Reflection – Deep Ecology would imply a sharp reduction in human population and a reversal of these trends. How likely, easy or desirable do you find such a prospect?

Different criticisms can be made of Green Thought; despite a radical tag they have been criticised for conservatism, or even authoritarianism. This is because of a concentration on the oppression of nature over other oppressions. However, there is much misunderstanding surrounding 'deep ecology', and such accusations are refuted partly by arguing that some humans dominating other humans is an effect of humans dominating nature. Moreover, eco-feminism, for example, is a very influential strand of Green Thought, which seems to suggest that Greens are attuned to the complex forms of social oppression and exclusion which exist. Fundamentally, the impossibility of growth in a finite system and the lack of respect offered the non-human world by the human, necessitates profound changes in *all* aspects of our social *and* political behaviour.

There are some very practical criticisms of ecocentrism. In the real world, wars may start over water, whales may be saved through the deliberations of an international regime and children may die because of contaminated water supplies – might the more established IR perspectives be considered more helpful in understanding the nature of these things? Furthermore, the dangers of actually attempting to dismantle current patterns of social, political and economic organisation are likely to be very great. To achieve a deep-green future is deeply problematical; it would require a complete reversal of the economic growth trajectory and a radically revised international system. In other words, deep ecological prescriptions frequently tend towards the unrealistic, especially given potentially short time scales (see George Monbiot above). Although this is not an unreasonable criticism, the current system does seem to miss out on environmental 'quick wins' for very short-term economic reasons; in an era of energy security worries, for instance, buildings could easily be not only energy efficient, but also net generators of power.

Common misunderstandings

1. *Green thought constitutes a unified position or ideology.* It ought to be very clear from this chapter that this is wrong. There are in fact many different sorts of green positions and these do not relate in a direct way to traditional political distinctions of right and left. In fact, green positions which favour humanity *and* those which want to centre our understanding on nature can rest on political foundations which are either left or right wing in orientation.

2. *Environmentalists hate human beings.* Just as feminists are wrongly berated for being men-haters, similarly taking a strongly green position does not imply hating humanity but may merely reflect a feeling that humanity ought – by virtue of its capacity for reason – to show more respect for the planet.

3. *Following the advice of groups like Greenpeace will inevitably save the world if only we would do it.* Not necessarily. Greens suggest it is in our own interest to preserve nature and our moral responsibility to other creatures and to future generations of humanity. But the 'random factor' in nature means we can only ever take reasonable precautions, not deal in certainties.

4. *Green thinkers are all 'anti-modern', 'anti-science' and 'anti-progress'.* This argument has been used as a tactic, especially by those with economic interests in preserving the current model of environmental destruction. In fact, all varieties of green thought actually offer a different version of progress which focuses on a sustainable future and a society more in tune with the needs of all other creatures, both human and non-human.

Further reading

Adams, W. M. (1990), *Green Development: Environment and Sustainability in the Third World*, London: Routledge (an excellent introduction to the origins of environmental thought in both Western development and northern environmental Discourses).

Carson, R. (1962), *Silent Spring*, Harmondsworth: Penguin (the seminal work in terms of stimulating a popular consciousness over the environment).

Dryzek, J. (1997), *The Politics of the Earth: environmental discourses*, Oxford: Oxford University Press.

Lomborg, B. (2001), *The Skeptical Environmentalist: Measuring the Real State of the World*, Cambridge: Cambridge University Press (if you are convinced by the environmentalist case, you had better make sure you have answers for the sceptical arguments put forward by former green Bjorn).

O'Neill, K. (2009), *The Environment And International Relations*, Cambridge: Cambridge University Press.

Paterson, M. (2000), *Understanding Global Environmental Politics. Domination, Accumulation, Resistance*, Basingstoke: Macmillan (an excellent and thorough analysis).

Sessions, G. (ed.) (1995), *Deep Ecology for the Twenty-first Century*, London: Shambhala (a good way to get into the more radical versions of ecological philosophy).

Conclusions, key debates and new directions

Introduction

In some books you can simply skip to the conclusion to get the main points. However, this concluding chapter is not a summary of all that has gone before, but a series of arguments and debates which emerges from a full understanding of it. This concluding chapter builds upon all the previous chapters and cannot be read profitably in isolation. Each chapter does contain quick summary information for those seeking it.

As is evident from our discussion of the multiplicity of perspectives that exist in IR, there is no simple answer to the question: what are we studying when we study 'International Relations'? Moreover, there is no easy answer to the question: what is the 'real stuff' of international politics? This is because theoretical perspectives conceptualise or construct the domain of international relations in distinctive and contrasting ways. Nor do scholars agree on the best way to conduct research in the field, on what methodology to adopt. It is equally evident that the status of the 'knowledge' generated through such activities is the subject of much dispute in contemporary IR theory.

For some scholars the critical and constructivist turns in IR theory since the mid-1980s, and the proliferation of perspectives like poststructuralism, social constructivism, Critical Theory, feminism and Green Thought, along with the blurring of boundaries between IR and other areas of the social sciences is a cause of not a little anxiety. These developments have been viewed as undermining the notion of International Relations as a distinctive 'discipline' – a branch of learning or discrete area of study concerned with the high politics of war, diplomacy and foreign policy – and so weakening its claims to be relevant to policy makers.

However, it may be that other theoretical perspectives are more helpful to policy makers. Positing that IR theory should provide a guide for policy makers to safeguard or further the national interest, for example, presupposes a state-centric world view. Liberals, structuralists, constructivists and critical theorists, in a broad sense of the term, would no doubt contend that this complaint is based on a narrow and partial view of IR. 'Politics' is not simply about the activities of government and the formulation and implementation of policy, but is more broadly concerned with the exercise of power and influences and so embraces a variety of 'actors', processes and interests. Should not theory also be useful as a 'guide to action' to NGOs or social movements like Greenpeace, Oxfam or the international women's movement? (This has been the subject of a debate between Wallace, Booth and Smith – see Further reading.)

One could argue that there has never been a consensus on the core concerns of the discipline. Although International Relations was born out of the human tragedy of war, from the earliest times there have been debates about what its main focus should be, disagreements about how to go about studying the world and contrasting views on the purposes this knowledge could serve. It is evident that at all levels – ontological, epistemological and methodological – IR is essentially contested. This concluding chapter aims to develop the implications of theoretical diversity and plurality in IR through a discussion of the so-called 'post-positivist' debate in IR and by pointing to some possible new directions in the study of IR.

The post-positivist debate

Contemporary IR theory has recently emerged from the throes of the so-called 'post-positivist' debate (sometimes referred to as the 'fourth debate'). Of course, debates within IR theory do not take place in a vacuum, and the post-positivist debate has to be understood in terms of its relation to a wider debate in the social sciences. For this reason we have included in the Further reading some key texts by authors who are not identified with IR directly, but whose ideas have been very influential in IR. We can broadly identify the main divisions or positions in the post-positivist debate as between those who argue that it is possible to understand the world objectively, and those who believe that interests, values and dominant power relations inevitably shape the activity of theorising and the claims that are made about the 'real world'.

There are a number of ways of categorising theories: for example, positivist and post-positivist; foundationalist and anti-foundationalist; explanatory and constitutive; and 'rationalist' and 'constructivist'. We will elaborate on different categorisation of theories and how they are pertinent to contemporary IR theory below. While these broad categorisations are useful, they can disguise differences between approaches that are broadly 'positivist' or fall under the general category of 'post-positivist'. We will make some finer distinctions within these categories in due course, but first it is useful to say something more about positivism in IR.

Positivism and critiques of positivism in IR

Positivism in IR

Positivism is associated with the methods and epistemological claims characteristic of the natural sciences. Within the social sciences positivists contend that the social and political world is amenable to understanding in just the same way as are the workings of the natural world. In a pre-modern age the world might have seemed mysterious to people – a creation of God perhaps – but with the advent of modern science the world became 'knowable' as science endeavoured to establish the laws of nature. Positivists in IR are hopeful that we can eventually establish the 'laws' that govern relations between states, in much the same way that we have discovered the laws of physics, for example.

REFLECTION BOX

The contention that democracies do not fight one another has been advanced as a 'law' in international relations, which has been established by empirical 'facts' (see chapter 1). Is seeking such laws a sensible way for IR to proceed? Is it possible to identify laws governing the social and political worlds (worlds of meaning) in much the same way that we might establish laws in physics?

In positivism a research method is viewed as a technique for – or way of proceeding in – gathering evidence. Evidence might be gathered through interviews with key actors; by observing phenomena/behaviour; or by collecting data and/or studying historical records. The precise choice of methodology is underpinned by a theory of how research should proceed, and this in turn is influenced by the dominance of particular perspectives or paradigms in specific 'scientific' disciplines. In the context of IR Robert Keohane has advocated the formulation of 'generalisations about international relations' that can be shown to be 'scientific because they are based on publicly known methods and checked by a community of scholars' (1998, p. 196). According to positivists, if theory is to generate useful knowledge about international relations, IR scholars must be willing to formulate their hypotheses in ways that are testable and potentially falsifiable with evidence.

You will recall from the discussion of whether 'gender is a variable' in chapter 6, that feminist IR has been criticised by 'mainstream' scholars on the grounds that the claims that feminists make about the world are asserted, but are not verified or proven. Keohane has sought to try to persuade feminist scholars (in a way that has been seen as rather patronising) that they should (re)frame their research agenda in ways that make their contentions amenable to scientific analysis. So, for example, the introduction of a gender variable might inform theories on causality or help us to quantify 'impacts' – for example, the degree to which men and women are differentially affected by the impact of armed conflict, or structural adjustment policies. The crucial thing is that, in order to test a hypothesis (that 'the security order is gendered and that this is detrimental to women particularly', for example), one would need to: first, identify a possible gender variable; second, collect the evidence – the necessary empirical data needed to test such a claim; and finally, test this contention by measuring impacts or outcomes.

However, most contemporary feminist theorists dismiss positivism and this kind of empirical research agenda as an 'add gender and stir' approach. Indeed, the exchange between Keohane, Weber, Tickner and others, alluded to in chapter 6, points to deeper 'problems' in positivism, notably its ontological and epistemological presuppositions.

Ontology is the branch of philosophy that deals with the nature of existence or being. Before we can say anything much about international relations, we have to decide what we think the world is like, who are the major actors in IR, what are the main processes and so on. In attempting to 'map the field' in this way, we need to decide whether entities have a real, material existence which we try to apprehend through our senses, or, conversely, whether through the process of conceptualisation and theorisation, we create or construct our 'reality'. Thus, a neo-realist assumes that states as key 'actors' have an independent existence and that 'anarchy' is an objective condition or 'fact' which states have to negotiate, regardless of what we might like to imagine. The activity of theorising should be directed towards gaining a better understanding of these real world conditions.

CONCEPT BOX

Ontological claims are rooted in the differing philosophical traditions of *foundationalism* and *anti-foundationalism* – which debate, among other things, whether entities – for example, sovereign states – have an independent existence, or whether they are in various ways, socially constructed. So, can we talk about anarchy as a real condition that exists independently of what we might like to imagine about world order? Or, on the contrary, is anarchy as the social constructivist Alexander Wendt holds, 'what states make it', an intersubjectively constructed and negotiated understanding of what contemporary world order is like?

In contrast, a post-structuralist would eschew any such ontological certainty. Post-structuralists contend that nothing exists outside discourse. This does not mean, as some critics contend, that post-structuralists do not recognise that there are real incidents in which the lives of real people are profoundly affected, like the attack on the twin towers in New York in September 2001, for example. Rather, post-structuralists contend that as soon as we attempt to move beyond the immediacy of an event or incident, to endeavour to understand and explain why and/or how it took place and what the consequences are – in effect when we start to make claims about the meaning and significance of an event – we are immediately thrown into the realm of language, of shared social meanings and discursive constructions.

In IR theory there may be a degree of consensus about what 'exists' in the sense that all theoretical perspectives seek to identify 'actors' such as states, international institutions, NGOs, social movements and multinational corporations, even if theorists disagree about the role, relative weight or significance of these 'actors'. However, we immediately run into problems when we try to understand the nature of the state (is the state a rational, autonomous actor, for example, or a *performance*), or identify the existence of structural inequalities between social groups or countries. Clearly, in all of these cases we are not dealing so much with real 'things' directly, but with intellectual constructs – ideas and concepts which help us read or construct 'reality' and thereby gain an understanding of the material world around us. Inevitably, this means that there are disputes about whether we can speak meaningfully of structural inequalities, observable cycles of economic booms and depressions, real balances of power, or manifest patterns or networks of cooperation. Moreover, as we have seen, there is something of a divide between those who view the world through an essentially state-centric prism and those who argue for a holistic approach to 'global (social) relations'.

As early as the 1970s it was evident that there was much disagreement among realists, liberals and structuralists about what the world was really like and what could be said to exist. These disagreements within IR have only increased with the proliferation of critical and constructivist perspectives. In seeking to identify certain core variables, positivists necessarily work with settled and rather essentialist categories. For example, in invoking a gender variable, positivists assume that 'women' and 'men' are stable categories. As we saw in chapter 6, feminist IR scholars are more likely to **problematise** universal and stable categories, as indeed are social constructivists and post-structuralists who believe that such categories are discursively constructed.

Problematise is one of a number of words often used in IR though not much in normal conversation. To problematise something is simply not to accept it uncritically and to ask questions of what we have previously taken for granted.

It is not necessary to elaborate any further here on ontology; suffice to say that it is not possible to separate ontological questions – what and who we think exists, the categories we employ – from how we construct knowledge about international relations.

Epistemology deals with how we can 'know' things and the nature and status of the knowledge claims we make about the world.

Positivists assume that the rigours of scientific analysis guard against the knowledge becoming tainted by ideology. We must put aside our own values and beliefs in an endeavour to establish the 'facts' about the world. So, a biochemist, for example, might study the function of bacteria in the human digestive system. In this case, his/her social, moral or political values – whether he/she supports the institution of marriage, believes that lying is sometimes justifiable, or votes for the Conservative Party – are unlikely to have any bearing on the task in hand.

Although we argue here that scientific analysis is unlikely to be affected by social, moral and political values, many scientists in the world are funded by governments or organisations which do have political agendas. Could the source of funding affect how the results of scientific research are presented? How? Would you accept as 'fact' research on the impact of smoking on health if you knew that the research was funded by the tobacco industry?

To positivists, the social scientist must endeavour to be as objective as possible when conducting research and must ensure that the objectivity of his/her research can be established, or refuted perhaps, by subsequent research projects. The test of science is that its claims are potentially falsifiable by new evidence. So, in the case of research on smoking and health funded by the tobacco industry (above), a positive might recognise the potential for bias to taint the results. However, the key point is that the research can be duplicated by independent entities and so is potentially falsifiable. The positive critique of interpretive approaches in IR is that their contentions cannot be replicated – the methodology employed precludes this possibility.

However, in attempting to free knowledge from ideological distortion, positivists risk presenting certain social phenomena as 'natural'. For example, if we 'establish' that major wars occur at regular intervals, or in 'long cycles', we do not necessarily need to understand the motives or beliefs of those involved to understand why wars break out. Human beings become 'objects' of study, because it is assumed that a social phenomenon (in this case war) can be understood without reference to the meanings which people ascribe to social situations. Moreover, while positivists tend to pursue empirical research in order to establish the 'facts' about the world, the evidence or data – presented as 'fact' – have to be interpreted (infused with meaning) and this raises questions about whether underlying social or cultural beliefs, or the specific motives that drive research projects might influence how the findings are interpreted and presented. So, if researchers are always men who have been raised in the West, no amount of replication will address the possibility of deeply rooted biases or culturally coloured interpretations of the data and results. The 'facts' do not speak for themselves, in other words; they are interpreted in various ways. Moreover, the prescriptions that flow from these interpretations can have profound political implications.

'Facts are meaningless. You can use facts to prove anything that's remotely true.' (Homer J. Simpson)

The feminist notion of 'feminist lenses' or 'gender lenses' points to the way that perspectives are politically grounded and that the construction of knowledge is linked to specific interests. Feminists argue that, historically, man and masculinity have been falsely presented as *the human case*. Gender is not an isolated variable, but a social relationship characterised by inequalities in power. Some feminists seek to improve or advance the position of women, who have historically been a subordinated group and make no apologies for the normative underpinnings or political bias in their work. Furthermore, as Weber has pointed out, we cannot isolate a gender as a variable because gender is something that pervades our very being and identity. We view the world from a culturally embedded and socially embodied perspective.

Is structuralism a positivist approach? To help you answer this question you might like to re-read the section on 'origins' in chapter 3.

Critical Theorists have contributed to the critique of positivism and neo-realism specifically within IR, but they do not reject scientific analysis out of hand. Critical Theorists hold that there are different forms or kinds of knowledge which serve different ends or purposes. So, for example, scientific and technical knowledge is in essence about the objectification of nature in the interests of human advancement, while the social and human sciences are, or should be, directly concerned with the conditions under which human beings achieve greater autonomy, control and freedom in their lives. If science can help us to gain a better understanding of ourselves, why we succumb to certain illnesses perhaps, or how we could transcend the limits imposed upon us by our physical bodies by discovering the laws of aerodynamics, then why not harness the potential of science in the service of human emancipation? There are certain spheres of human life where the pursuit of scientific knowledge and understanding is perfectly legitimate. The 'problem' does not lie in science *per se*, but the influence of scientism, or positivism, in theories which are to do with the meaning and purpose of human life.

Critical Theorists hold that knowledge about the social world is necessarily of a different kind from knowledge about the natural world. In science we might desire knowledge in order to subordinate or control the natural world, but knowledge about the human world is sought in order to foster greater freedom, rather than greater control – or at least it should be. The 'problem' is that we no longer regard science as one form of possible knowledge, but rather identify knowledge only with science. If emancipation is to remain a project for humanity then the influence of scientism, which has given rise to a tendency to regard all human problems as essentially technical ones amenable to technical solutions, must be countered. In this way, knowledge is generated which enhances autonomy and responsibility.

Before moving on, however, it is useful to attempt to clear up some common misunderstandings about positivism in IR. There is a tendency among students to view positivism in a wholly negative light, mainly because constructivist and critical theorists (including feminist) have tended to make the critique of positivism a point of departure in generating alternative approaches to the study of IR. It is important to recognise, though, that positivists might – and often do – regard their work as (potentially) progressive. This was certainly true of the early pioneers of social science who often saw themselves as socially progressive people who aimed to refute the claims of religion and challenge social practices and forms of organisation founded upon tradition and/or prejudice. Many of the early proponents of positivism in social science saw it as their mission to disprove the existence of God and so undermine the authority and sway of religious doctrine. During those days they were the radicals! In IR specifically we can identify many examples of scholars who employ positivist methods in the service of socially progressive ends. The work of the late Michael Nicholson would be an example of this.

Not all feminists are opposed to positivism, or empiricism, providing that more attention is paid to the position of women (in IR). Including women as researchers would go some way to addressing the under-representation of women in the academy, where male dominance might well create biases and so distort the findings of research. In her (limited) defence of feminist empiricism, Sandra Harding argues that 'bringing in' women to the field (of IR in this case) undermines the *male subject as human* case. This move can then create some space for a deeper critical analysis of the ways in which a culture's beliefs, what it calls 'knowledge', are socially situated. Research on women in IR (a discipline that has historically focused on states and security and foreign policies made largely by men) can produce empirical and theoretical results that are more balanced since they challenge the usual tendency to view women and their lives as insignificant or irrelevant in IR; although, as we noted above, for most feminist IR scholars 'bringing in' women is not enough to transform a thoroughly gendered academic discipline.

It is not uncommon for students to confuse positivism with state-centrism, but state-centric approaches are not necessarily positivist. For example, the English School is a state-centric approach to IR, but adherents of this school of thought do not regard the study of international relations as a scientific enterprise. Instead, they argue for a more interpretive approach and draw upon philosophy, law, history and political theory in their studies.

Sometimes positivism is equated with realism, liberalism and structuralism and post-positivism with critical theories like the Frankfurt School, feminism and poststructuralism, but again this is misleading. For example, there is some disagreement about whether realism should be regarded as a positivist approach. On the one hand, the 'Machiavellian strand' of realism claims to represent the world view of the statesman or diplomat who is forced to operate in an uncertain and dangerous world. Realism provides a guide to action based on the guiding principles of *realpolitik* in the interests of the preservation of the nation-state. In this view the 'balance of power' is a conscious strategy, or practice, pursued by statesmen, diplomats and military leaders to preserve the peace, or more accurately to prevent the dominance of one power and maximise the autonomy of individual nation-states. Clearly, realists invest value in the state, or they would not be so deeply concerned with problems of 'national security'. So, realist knowledge of international relations can be said to be constructed from the point of view of the interests of the state.

On the other hand, realists clearly believe that 'threats' are real threats; the world really is dangerous and uncertain, and that these conditions exist independently of what we imagine or what we would like to believe about the world. At different times, influential writers like Morgenthau and Carr have insisted that the study of International Relations should eschew normative concerns with justice or rights in the interest of discovering more about the realities of power, and both writers are known for making a plea for a 'science' of international politics (no doubt mindful of the dangers of ideology in international politics in the wake of Nazi aggression in the 1930s and 1940s).

This call for a science of international politics was taken a stage further in the 1960s, when the North American behaviouralist school insisted that researchers adopt the exacting standards of scientific analysis and research in their studies. Behaviouralists took key concepts from realism – the state, power, national interests – but developed a mechanistic model of the workings of the international system. For these reasons realism is frequently subject to post-positivist critiques, but you should be aware that realists are not necessarily unreflective about the values and beliefs which underpin their world view.

Neo-realism and neo-liberal institutionalism

Before turning to post-positivist perspectives in IR, it is helpful to distinguish between two approaches in IR that have been categorised as positivist because they share a common foundation in their research methodologies: neo-realism and neo-liberal institutionalism. Neo-realism, along with neo-liberal institutionalism can also be categorised as rationalist approaches to IR.

Rationalism avoids the problems of presenting outcomes in international relations in terms of natural 'laws', because it emphasises the need to understand how choices are made by cognisant actors. However, rationalists also assume that, through careful collection and analysis of the data, we can draw sound conclusions about how actors behave both individually and collectively. Therefore, we can explain certain policy outcomes and might even be able to predict how actors will behave according to the specific conditions and context in which decision making takes place. Waltz's neo-realism assumes that states behave rationally, albeit in the context of the constraints imposed on them by the anarchic structure of the international system.

As we noted in chapter 1, liberals believe that we are able to construct categories and concepts which collectively give us a picture of reality and help us to understand our world because we are capable of rational thought. For Kantians and contemporary idealists human beings possess the capacity for cooperative action in the interest of realising a better, more rationally organised world. Neo-liberal institutionalists draw upon a rather more utilitarian conception of rationality, which involves the ability to weigh up the costs and benefits of any course of action. Liberals start from the premise that individuals (or states) are essentially self-interested, but posit beneficial outcomes from competition, rather than presenting international relations as a continuous 'war of all against all'. Neo-liberal institutionalists argue that successful cooperation is dependent upon mutual interests to be gained through cooperation over a range of issues and areas. While the 'costs' and 'benefits' of cooperation are not necessarily distributed equally, (since states are absolute gains maximisers), cooperation is rational.

This view of rationality and the connection between rationality and the pursuit of interests is shared by neo-realists and neo-liberals. While neo-realism and neo-liberal institutionalism differ in important respects, they both: first, seek to identify certain phenomena that need to be explained, such as the conditions under which international cooperation is possible; second, identify the key actors; and, third, advance arguments about actor's preferences in the context of a range of possible outcomes. Being rationalist, both approaches, seek to demonstrate under what conditions an outcome or pattern of actions would emerge if actors were choosing rationally. These are common assumptions shared by all rationalist approaches, although there are clearly differences in what realists/neo-realists and liberals/neo-liberal institutionalists would see as an instance of rational decision making in IR.

Neo-realism as 'orthodoxy' in IR

The post-positivist debate opened up a multi-pronged attack on positivism and wide-ranging critiques of the neo-realist 'orthodoxy' in particular. Positivism has been the dominant approach or orthodoxy in the study of IR (especially in the USA). As we will elaborate below, from a constructivist (in a broad sense) perspective 'knowledge' in academic disciplines like IR is socially generated and socially bounded. That is to say, the knowledge generated in and about IR should be regarded as discourse, not truth or fact. Knowledge is generated through consensual understandings among scholars of what constitutes a distinctive 'discipline', which includes agreement on the dominant preoccupations of the field and how our knowledge of this particular domain can best be advanced. These fundamental assumptions and commitments shaped the kinds of questions asked and the particular modes of inquiry that are considered legitimate in the field.

'Orthodoxy' has been used to describe a perspective that has been so widely adopted that it becomes accepted as a 'commonsense' view of the world against which all other perspectives should be assessed and evaluated. For much of the post-Second World War period realism and later neo-realism served as a commonsense view of the world against which other perspectives could be measured. In the 1980s neo-realism particularly became the 'orthodoxy' in IR as both its fundamental assumptions and epistemological and methodological commitments increasingly shaped the kinds of questions asked and the particular modes of inquiry that were considered legitimate in the field. The propositions of neo-realism were widely accepted by IR scholars and served as a guide to empirical research projects and the construction of knowledge in the discipline.

REFLECTION BOX

Common sense?

We talk in this section about 'common sense'. To have such a thing is regarded as a very good trait in individuals; those without it do stupid things. However, the idea should be treated with caution. It was once regarded as 'common sense' that slavery was OK based on ideas of racial supremacy. Sometimes common sense may be 'wrong' even though it is the accepted way of thinking about things. This is why it is important to engage with a broad range of perspectives in IR: thinking about the world of IR from multiple positions engenders a critical and reflective disposition and encourages us to challenge phenomenon and 'facts' that might otherwise be taken for granted.

If, as post-structuralists contend, knowledge is discursively constructed, or, as Critical Theorists hold, is conditioned by the social, political and historical context in which the theorist operates as well as specific interests, this would suggest that at the very least there are multiple 'realities' and multiple perspectives on the world. Thus, neo-realism should be viewed as an ideology and not as an objective theory. It might be that realism/neo-realism retained its dominant position in IR theory even in the face of the emergence of competing perspectives like liberal pluralism and structuralism because it served as a useful lens through which to negotiate the politics of the Cold War period and as a justification for US military strategy and the pursuit of US foreign-policy goals. Moreover, the marginalisation of structuralism, particularly within the US academic community, probably had much to do with its Marxist underpinnings and political sympathies.

The end of the Cold War provoked a wave of criticism of neo-realism. For example, neo-realism was held to be a rather 'thin' or *parsimonious* theory because it of its oversimplified view of structure (anarchy) and agents (states) in IR. On a more fundamental level, neo-realism was criticised on the grounds that it presented 'structural anarchy' as a permanent or enduring feature of international relations, when the state system and 'anarchy' merely described a particular feature of world order at a particular time in history, which in turn reified that same world order and provided a powerful justification for the status quo (it might be helpful at this point to refer back to the discussion of the state and world order in chapter 4). The 'problem' with realism and latterly neo-realism is not that it is a particular and partial construction of a complex reality – all theoretical perspectives are particular and partial constructions of reality – but that it is often presented as 'commonsense' or 'objective reality', and its claims are used to marginalise or undermine the 'utopianism' of alternative positions. Realism/neo-realism as ideology potentially serves conservative political ends by providing a powerful legitimisation of power politics and denying the possibility of (radical) change.

Critical Theorists like Robert Cox have taken this one stage further by arguing that dominant paradigms (in effect neo-realism) are world views which attempt to identify and explain certain historically contingent phenomena – like the state-system, anarchy, power politics – but which both reflect and further the interests of dominant states, or influential groups within dominant states. From this perspective the ideology of realism/neo-realism constructs a particular model of the world which then serves to justify and perpetuate the kind of social and political order it describes.

CONCEPT BOX

The nature of paradigms

We might gain a better understanding of realism/neo-realism as the 'orthodoxy' in IR through a brief foray into an earlier debate within IR – the 'inter-paradigm debate'. A paradigm is a shared understanding and way of approaching problems which is accepted by a community of scholars and used to inculcate students with fundamental ways of 'knowing the world'. Thomas Kuhn, a historian of the natural sciences, believed that paradigms constituted the fundamental assumptions about the nature of the world and how it works that were generally accepted by scholars. Once established, they profoundly influenced the way that research projects were identified and carried out. For long periods of time the central beliefs or assumptions of a paradigm were not contested and could be used to define the field as 'not contested'. However, at particular periods in history dominant paradigms were subjected to challenge, perhaps because they were seemingly unable to explain new phenomena, or because more persuasive accounts emerged. For example, Newtonian physics had been the influential paradigm for a long time but was eventually displaced by quantum physics, influenced by Einstein, Bohr and others early in the twentieth century. For Kuhn, even in science, theory could not be seen as an activity designed to discover or establish 'truth'. However, the paradigm shifts that have taken place from time to time in science might mean that we are gradually moving away from falsity.

Within IR the insight that emergence from Kuhn's work on paradigms is that one must be sensitive to how disciplines develop historically, which paradigms are widely accepted and the consequences of this. The so-called 'inter-paradigm debate' from the mid-1980s was essentially a debate about the implications of competing paradigms in IR. What emerged out of the inter-paradigm debate was the insight that realism, liberal pluralism and structuralism, which were the three main paradigms in IR at the time, did not so much describe reality but rather constructed reality differently, deciding upon different areas for focus. Since these perspectives constructed – rather than described – reality differently, world views could not be compared in any meaningful way. Moreover, these different world views were ideological constructs, rooted in competing value systems and driven by different agendas. Paradigms in IR should not, therefore, be viewed as accurate representations or models of the 'real' world, but at best, prevalent and shared beliefs about 'reality' that existed among a community of scholars in any one historical period. As we have noted in earlier chapters, realism and later neo-realism became influential in the study of IR in the aftermath of the Second World War and during the Cold War period to the degree that, for a long period of time, the central beliefs or assumptions of (neo)realism were 'not contested'.

Post-positivism in IR

We do not have much difficulty in identifying post-positivist approaches in IR theory: social constructivism, Critical Theory, poststructuralism, feminism and Green theory can all be described as post-positivist. Although there are differences and distinctions between and even within these approaches, for some purposes they can indeed be usefully grouped together. Collectively, these approaches are regarded as post-positivist because they reject the fundamental premise of positivism – that the natural world and social world are similar entities and amenable to investigation using essentially the same research methods. Post-positivists are inclined to view the social world as a world infused with social and cultural meanings, constructed through language, which in turn invokes powerful symbols and imagery. In distinctive ways all of these approaches raise questions about how social values and practices have a bearing on research and scholarship in IR, influencing both what we choose to study, and how we interpret the evidence.

However, post-positivism is not all of one kind. There are important differences between each of the approaches. We have already devoted a considerable amount of space to setting out the main assumptions and preoccupations of critical and constructivist approaches throughout the book and have demonstrated above how, in distinctive ways, each of these perspectives offers a critique of positivism in IR. Below we simply set out briefly some of the key differences between these approaches.

Poststructuralism

Post-structuralists emphasise the importance of power and the functions of discourse in IR. As Foucault held, discourse is bound up historically with specific regimes of power and every society – or discursive community however constituted – produces its own 'truths' which have normalising and regulatory functions. Since we are always, in a sense, prisoners of our own discourses, we cannot hope to discover 'truths' or 'facts' about IR. However, critique and deconstruction are valuable tools in that employing these techniques exposes the presuppositions and assumptions that underpin theories and research projects in IR and points to how power relations are always implicated in the construction of knowledge.

Social constructivism

Social constructivists also acknowledge that power relations are implicated in discourse, although this is not such a prominent and critical concern in social constructivist research. Social constructivists believe that knowledge claims about the social world are rooted in the discursive power of the 'knower'. Theories help us to construct a picture of the world so that the world cannot be understood outside the particular conceptual framework and the theories we construct about it. Thus, social constructivists emphasise the central role of ideas in constructing social life. A further insight of social constructivism is that agents are socially constructed.

When applied to IR, social constructivism helps us to understand how social agents produce and reproduce and redefine the constitutive principles and structures in which they operate. For example, in international society states engage in practices such as recognition which serve to legitimise the state (converting power into authority) and consolidating the norms and principles that inform and regulate conduct among states. This is clearly different from positivism, since the allegedly 'objective' characteristics of the state – even territory – are seen to be malleable under changing social and historical conditions. Therefore, sovereign states cannot be ontologically privileged; presented as having an objective existence. Similarly, this emphasis on norms and rule governed behaviour undermines the view of international relations as fundamentally anarchic. As Wendt held, anarchy is 'what states make it'.

There are obvious similarities between social constructivism and poststructuralism. Poststructuralists also focus on discourse as bounded areas of social knowledge and argue that meaning is derived from the historical, social, cultural and institutional context in which *discourse* is conducted. Perhaps the key difference between social constructivism and poststructuralism is that social constructivists are not opposed to the rationalist project of attempting to 'understand and explain' outcomes in IR. While social constructivists deny the existence of an objective world outside of discourse, they are concerned to go beyond critique and try to identify when and where ideas/discourse matter in determining policy outcomes.

Social constructivism thus appears to mix some of the goals of rationalism – understanding the process of decision/policy making and policy outcomes, with key ideas from poststructuralism. Indeed, rather than presenting social constructivism as a distinctive approach to IR, social constructivists often represent their work as being somewhere on a continuum with rationalism at one pole and poststructuralism at the other. This also points to why social constructivism is increasingly being constructed as a 'middle ground' in IR theory, one which holds out the promise of bridging the gap between what, on the face of it, appear to be the incompatible theoretical positions (we return to this below).

Critical Theory

Perhaps the central theme of the 'post-positivist debate' has been that knowledge is never innocent. Critical Theorists believe that theory is, as Cox held, always for someone, or at least for some purpose, and so postulate a linkage between knowledge and interests. Marxist-inspired theories tend to see the genesis of human experience in social labour and the social reproduction of the species. Contemporary Critical Theory contests the notion that 'human nature' is fixed and immutable, but does not rely so heavily on ideas about labour and social class in the formation of consciousness or identity, preferring to link the formation of the human psyche or subject with the institutional framework of society. In contemporary Critical Theory in IR we can identify two strands: Neo-Gramscian and a second strand influenced by the Frankfurt School and, latterly, Jürgen Habermas. In distinctive ways both strands of Critical Theory emphasise the importance of the ideational dimension of IR (although neither neglects the need for an analysis of material factors and forces too).

Critical Theorists agree with social constructivists and post-structuralists that people develop a sense of identity and infuse their actions with meaning through language, but they make bolder claims about the relationship between knowledge and interests. In respect to social constructivism, Critical Theory, in principle at least, makes a clear distinction between strategic actions and communicative (discursive) action, although in practice it is not always clear whether this distinction actually holds in the 'real world'. One way in which Critical Theory differs from poststructuralism is by imputing interests to specific social groups (Neo-Gramscians particularly) and linking knowledge directly with a universal interest in human emancipation. Thus, Critical Theorists seek to rescue an emancipatory project in IR, whereas post-structuralists would be highly sceptical about such a goal.

Feminism

Not all feminist theory can be described as post-positivist. Liberal feminists want to 'bring in' women, by undertaking more empirical research on the status of women around the world, or, perhaps, by inquiring into whether the incorporation of women into the foreign policy making process, or conflict resolution negotiations, for example, would make a difference in IR. Such a project does not fundamentally challenge the mainstream of IR, either in terms of what we chose to study or how we go about doing our research.

However, most feminist scholars working in IR would describe themselves as post-positivists of one kind or another. Post-structuralist feminists denounce all forms of foundationalism and point to the impossibility of achieving a neutral or objective stance. However, from a post-structuralist perspective, epistemological claims made in the name of 'women' are also problematic, since 'women' are similarly constructed through discourse. A major focus of post-structuralist feminism is, therefore, deconstruction and critique, which embraces the need to continually make 'interventions' in order to question universal categories like 'women' and 'men' and which problematises gender as a stable category of analysis.

Feminist IR shares some common ground with social constructivism in that gender can be viewed as socially or discursively constructed. Moreover, Cynthia Enloe, for example, is interested in going beyond the aim of feminist critiques of existing discourses in IR like realism, to explore the effects of gender in international relations. Post-structuralists are likely to be circumspect about the usefulness of tracking causalities or perhaps charting outcomes in this way, seeing more value in (re)telling gender(ed) stories in IR, and experience no anxiety or desire to justify their knowledge claims.

Critical feminists (those whose work owes much to historical materialism and who have affinities with Critical Theorists) attempt to rescue 'women' and 'gender' as categories of analysis in IR, but reject positivism because they see all knowledge claims as rooted in concrete experiences and interests (in this case gender experiences and interests). However, knowledge is also a *moment* of emancipation, since feminist knowledge challenges gendered ideologies that legitimise unequal social relationships between men and women. Along with Critical Theorists, some feminists are also interested in exploring the institutional frameworks in which gender relations are constructed and reproduced.

Standpoint theorists also reject the neutrality of 'facts' in favour of subjective epistemological positions, but take this epistemological claim further than even critical feminists, arguing that women and men occupy radically different life worlds. The essentialism (and ontological certainty) inherent in a standpoint position can be justified in terms of biological/sexual differences and/or social experiences, most often the latter. However a 'standpoint' is sometimes adopted merely as a strategic ploy, at which point the distinction between standpoint and poststructuralist feminism begins to break down.

Green theory

Not all the literature on environmental issues in IR falls under the category of post-positivist IR. Indeed, much of the work on environmental regimes is focused on decision-making processes and might even employ the language of rationality. The burgeoning Green literature in IR embraces scholars who adopt differing positions, some of which are in sympathy with poststructuralism (particularly in terms of the critique of modernity and modern society), while others are closer to Critical Theorists (undertaking a critique of capitalism and consumerist practices, for example). There are social constructivists among Green scholars in IR. It is also probably accurate to say that, across the entire range of perspectives and approaches in IR, it is Greens who have engaged most seriously and reflectively with feminism.

Ultimately, we can justify the labelling of Green theory as 'post-positivist' because of the sophisticated critique that Greens develop of the modern subject and modern societies. At the heart of Green theory is a reflective reconsideration of the 'human–nature' relationship. The 'ecological self' is not understood in terms of separation, difference and domination over nature, but rather in terms of connection with nature. This notion of the self as 'embedded' or connected is not uncommon in non-Western philosophies like Buddhism as well as having something in common with various constructivist and critical positions.

REFLECTION BOX

Science and deep ecology

Greens believe that far from (or as well as) helping human beings, scientific knowledge and attempts to achieve more and more control over the natural world have done a great deal of harm to the planet and all the creatures that live on it. Greens also believe that the emergence of the modern period, and the triumph of science, helped men to establish their power over women and legitimised the domination of the West over the rest of the world. Therefore, knowledge cannot be considered value-free and objective. Greens also argue for a fundamental change in how we understand ourselves and our relationship with nature. At the same time, at least some part of the Green perspective relies upon scientific evidence – the hole in the ozone layer, for example, or the damage caused to forests by acid rain. Are these two positions compatible, do you think?

If knowledge is never disinterested, impartial or 'objective', you might conclude that all perspectives are equally valid or, conversely, equally 'wrong'. Moreover, if knowledge is generated only within the framework of existing paradigms or perspectives or is discursively constructed, there is surely no such thing as a 'correct' or 'final' understanding? You might conclude that ultimately theoretical diversity and plurality in IR demonstrates the relativity of knowledge claims so that it does not actually matter which perspective you adopt.

Clearly, our choice of perspective *is* important to us. Moreover, most IR scholars believe that on some level their work is making a difference – adding something to our understanding of the world in which we live. As noted above, both rationalists and social constructivists believe that they are able to do some 'explaining' in IR. At the very least, we need to be reflective about the consequences of adopting one approach rather than another; it matters because it involves making judgments about what is significant and insignificant, central or marginal, enduring or ephemeral in IR.

As is evident from our discussion of feminism, these choices are not innocent, but profoundly political. Feminists claim that if we choose to focus solely on the male-dominated world of states and foreign policy, for example, we effectively marginalise the study of women/gender in IR. More important, such analysis presupposes a public/private division and thus disguises the profoundly gendered nature of international politics. From this point of view, failing to highlight issues of gender in both the theory and practice of international relations further perpetuates the invisibility of gender and the marginalisation of women specifically in the field. It is a political choice and has political consequences.

Post-structuralist scholars are generally keen on the project of generating different understandings of the world by adopting different lenses or 'perspectives' on IR. However, this is because in this way we undermine the idea that there is a fundamental 'truth' to the world which we might discover. From this perspective there are many stories which we could tell about the world and these are certainly not limited to the eight broad perspectives we have outlined in this text. Discourses of IR and the existence of competing knowledge claims also serve to undermine dominant power/knowledge relations and empower, to some degree, previously marginalised groups.

Critical Theorists, especially those who follow Habermas, reject the theoretical, pluralism advocated by poststructuralism, and cling to the belief that, while there are no undisputed 'facts' about the world and no disinterested positions, we can nevertheless adjudicate between different claims. Through dialogue, different claims can be assessed for their comprehensibility, 'truthfulness' and 'correctness,' providing that due regard is paid to questions of procedure so that certain groups and voices are not excluded from the discussion. In this way we grapple towards intersubjectively negotiated agreement on major issues and concerns – for example, the nature and substance of human rights. Moreover, while theory cannot in itself adjudicate and justify action, it can create reflective agents capable of full participation in decisions concerning action.

As we suggested in the introductory chapter, there are also practical consequences which flow from adopting certain theoretical positions. Theory should not be seen as something which is separate from the world of international relations (the practice of international politics), but as intimately connected with that practice. The actions of 'practitioners', be they diplomats, politicians or NGOs, are informed by their underlying beliefs and assumptions about how the world works. Similarly, the prescriptive implications (in effect, recommendations) of our 'theory' might be revolutionary. That is to say, we might be forced to conclude that the only solution to the problems that beset humankind is fundamental change in the way societies – including societies of states – are organised, and a radical alteration in the way people behave. In the case of Greens, for example, it may require that we fundamentally rethink our relationship to the natural world and so have a profound effect on how we think about ourselves, our relations with others and our day-to-day practices. As is evident from our earlier discussion of poststructuralism, we need to be alert to the way in which discourses justify and legitimise certain practices (as well as how these are contested).

Critical theories and problem-solving theories

In an influential article first published in 1982 Robert Cox made a crucial distinction between critical theories and 'problem-solving' theories. Problem-solving theories take the historical context as given and concentrate on providing solutions to problems which arise in that given 'reality'. So, for example, nuclear deterrence strategies are an attempt to think about the specific problems which nuclear weapons pose for the security of states. Deterrence theory takes for granted the existence of the state system and the security dilemma which arises under conditions of anarchy.

In contrast, Critical Theory is reflexive about the nature of 'reality'. Critical Theorists ask deeper questions, about how 'problems' are constructed in the context of dominant political, economic, social and ideological forces at work in the global order. Moreover, we have to grasp the historical specificity of certain sorts of social relationships. So, Critical Theorists might ask how human beings came to be divided up into nation-states and how the historically contingent condition of 'anarchy' has led to perceived security threats, and so on. Critical Theorists emphasise that world order might be changed through political (and ideological) interventions. There is an emancipatory project at the heart of Critical Theory that goes beyond the immediate preoccupations and problems of statesmen.

Critical Theorists argue that theory and practice must be seen as intimately connected. Critical Theory encourages us to think critically and reflectively about how particular values, assumptions and concepts are used to describe the current social 'reality' and possible alternatives. Theories prescribe what can be thought, and consequently, courses of actions which can be taken and can be adjudged according to the degree to which they either open up or close off the possibilities for human emancipation. At the same time, as we noted earlier, our action changes existing 'reality' and has an impact on what we and others come to think of as 'possible'. From this perspective, knowledge is generated through self-reflection, which provides the impetus to achieving self-understanding and autonomy of action and, so, emancipation.

The next stage in IR theory?

In chapter 4 we discussed a debate that emerged in IR in the 1980s in the wake of what appeared to be a theoretical impasse. Hoffman argued that IR should embrace Critical Theory, because this approach was at once materialist, historical and reflective about the ideological nature of knowledge claims. Critical Theory was championed as the 'next stage' or future of IR. Since Hoffman championed Critical Theory within IR, much interesting work has been done that draws upon Habermas' ideas particularly (see Further reading).

Feminist scholarship in IR has also developed significantly during the same period. Since the late 1980s feminists have produced work on: war and conflict; peace and security; ethics and human rights; identity politics; institutions, foreign policy and political economy. In so doing, feminists have succeeded in carving out a space for their work within what has historically been a gender-blind discipline. While exchanges between feminist scholars and those in the mainstream have been rather unproductive, feminist IR has shaped the contours of debate within critical and constructivist IR more broadly.

However, it is probably accurate to say that in recent years it is social constructivism, rather than Critical Theory, poststructuralism or feminism that has assumed 'centre stage' in IR theory. Indeed, social constructivism has been portrayed as occupying a newly constructed 'middle ground' in IR between the claims of rationalism, with its emphasis on decision making and rational choice, and poststructuralism, which emphasises the centrality of discourse in explaining outcomes in IR.

The growing popularity of social constructivism has encouraged yet another debate in IR in the interests of generating a productive engagement across the positivist/post-positivist theoretical divide. Rather than putting forward a dichotomy between more rationalist or constructivist approaches, it has been suggested that rationalism and constructivism can be combined. For example, if we locate 'rational choices' in a world of social meanings, it is possible to combine the insights that arise from both rationalism and social constructivism and bring together specific arguments to gain a more complete understanding of social reality. In this debate, rationalism and social constructivism are portrayed as lenses for looking at social reality or as analytical tools with which to theorise about world politics. However, it seems that projects that embrace theoretical and methodological pragmatism must in the final analysis concede the point that there are no uncontested, 'objective' facts about the world and instead move towards a model that favours the intersubjective negotiation of truth claims.

As was noted in earlier chapters that engaged with ideas on intersubjectivity and dialogue, it is clear that the politics of knowledge claims will once again come into play here. Post-structuralists and (some) feminists decry this attempt to establish an intersubjective consensus on the substance of IR or on methods and approach, not because they are unsympathetic to the notion of intersubjectivity or the negotiation of 'truths' but because, on the evidence of the theoretical conversations that have taken place thus far in IR, some voices and perspectives will inevitably be marginalised. It is better that we embrace theoretical pluralism in IR, because this has the effect of weakening the truth claims of powerful groups and empowering those previously marginalised in the study of IR.

In so far as IR theorists are now beginning to reflect more deeply upon the profound implications of social practices, culture and, crucially, power relations, in the construction of knowledge about the world, IR (what Mervyn Frost and Jim George has each labelled the 'backward discipline') is beginning to 'catch up' with trends in other branches of social sciences. In a sense, the positivist/post-positivist debate has seen IR theory come full circle, in that normative questions are once again at the very heart of the discipline. Mervyn Frost claims that, in drawing attention to the embedded nature of human beings in social structures and introducing questions of agency, how structures change over time, the post-positivist debate has focused attention once again on normative issues. However, Frost is somewhat equivocal about the long-term impact of post-positivist approaches in IR, since all appear to fall some way short of providing answers to the most pressing question which similarly preoccupied the early idealist pioneers: what would constitute a just world order?

If, all in all, this still seems difficult, you might take some consolation from the oft quoted remark that we become truly 'enlightened' only when we fully realise that we 'know' nothing. When studying IR (a discipline which sometimes appears to be dealing with everything) it can, at times, feel like you will never know *anything* at all; that there are simply more questions, but not any final answers. However, with perseverance, the study of IR is well worth the effort. IR raises questions about, and provides a window on, all aspects of international political life and, more importantly, embraces peoples across the world. We hope that this book helps to open a window on that world a little, making you aware of how your own practices impact on this world, and how ideas about the world have impacted on and influenced you. The words of Homer Simpson, or indeed anyone, will never be the same again.

Further reading

For a full list please see the further reading section at the end of the book.

Glossary of key or problem terms

This list of simplified definitions is designed to aid your understanding. However it is not comprehensive. Some words are not included because they are covered sufficiently in the text itself; you should use the index to clarify the meaning of any such word you do not understand.

Actor   If the world is regarded as a stage then actors in international relations can be understood in much the same way as actors in a theatre. An actor in international relations is an entity that can be said to have agency. This notion of an 'actor' can be applied to entities that are recognised under international law, so in this sense states are actors, but not individuals. In this view actors might be states, multinational corporations, international organisations, social movements, or in exceptional cases, influential individuals.

Agency   An actor (see above) is said to have agency when they are able to exert influence, or affect the outcome of any given process or event in some way. It is perhaps easiest to contrast 'agency' with the idea of 'structure' (see below). For those people who believe that 'structure' is highly important in international relations, human agency is limited; actors are unable to greatly influence individual events or the general course of history, because they are constrained by the structure of the international system or world-system.

Alienation   A term used by Hegel, Marx and Freud among others, the word alienation is similar in meaning to the idea of estrangement; to feel left out or somehow apart from another person, or social group. The term can be used in a stronger sense to denote a feeling of exclusion which generates feelings of anger or antipathy towards society.

Anarchy   (This term is discussed extensively in the text itself) A term used to describe a situation in which a central government is absent. Anarchy should not be conflated with chaos or disorder. English school scholars (see below) argue that in international relations, order, rather than chaos, is possible in a situation of anarchy on the basis of informal rules which are accepted by most states, most of the time. Such rules might derive from international law (see below).

Anthropocentrism   This simply means human-centredness. In the context of environmental debates it refers to the argument that nature is a resource which exists to be exploited by humans for satisfaction of their needs and wants. As such, nature does not have rights and can therefore be used by humans as they see fit for their own ends.

Asylum   An asylum is a place of refuge. In international law/international relations it refers to the process by which states grant asylum to citizens of other states who have a well-grounded fear of persecution in their home country. Asylum seekers should be distinguished from refugees, who have been temporarily displaced from their homeland (although refugees might subsequently seek asylum in the host country if they have a well-grounded fear of persecution upon their return).

Atomism   See **holistic**.

Autarky   Autarky means the condition of being independent or self-sufficient. In the contemporary world Cuba – subject to a US economic blockade and constant political pressure – provides an example of what might be described as 'enforced autarky'.

Autonomy   The ability to formulate and pursue goals independently. Questions of autonomy most often arise in relation to states, but can be applied to other actors (see above). It is frequently argued that autonomy is increasingly rare in a world characterised by interdependence. Autonomy should not be confused with **sovereignty** (see below).

Billiard-Ball Model   This is an image often used to present the (classical) realist world view. The billiard table represents the world and the balls are states. The analogy/metaphor suggests that states have very clear boundaries – a 'hard shell' – so that domestic politics is not directly affected by international politics. However, states do come into contact with each other, and just as a with a billiard ball hit at speed, they sometimes have a big impact on each other's behaviour. In this view, international relations is, in essence, about such inter-actions. The billiard-ball model usually allows for different sizes of balls (unlike the game) to represent the fact that some states have more power than others, and some states make a greater impact than others.

Bourgeoisie   First used to describe the emerging middle class in revolutionary France who challenged the political dominance of the aristocracy (*ancien régime*), the term is now more usually associated with Marxist thought. In Marxism the bourgeoisie is the class constituted by the owners of the means of production, in contrast to the proletariat, or working class who are wage-labourers. Whether enlightened and philanthropic or downright oppressive, the bourgeoisie, according to orthodox Marxist thought, is destined to fall along with the supporting economic system of capitalism because of the latter's internal contradictions (see below).

Capitalism   A social and economic system which is founded on the principles of private property and free – voluntary – contracts. In a capitalist society market mechanisms (the forces of supply and demand) ultimately determine the allocation of resources, the production of goods and services and distribution of 'rewards' (wages and profits). The nature of capitalism – whether it is socially beneficial and progressive or divisive and harmful – continues to be debated. For example, liberals typically claim that, though based on the selfishness of individuals, this system of social and economic organisation ultimately works to ensure the greatest good of the greatest number. In contrast, socialists complain that capitalism generates social inequality, encourages materialism and rampant consumerism and is ultimately wasteful in terms of both human and natural resources.

Civil Society   Civil society refers to those areas of human life where individuals engage in collective action and activity, but which are outside the realm of state action or not directly within the purview or control of the state.

Contradiction   A Marxist term used to express the idea that capitalism generates the contradictions which will ultimately cause it to collapse. In economic terms, the contradictions of capitalism are a tendency towards monopoly, and to forcing down wages, while at the same time encouraging overproduction in the drive to increase profits. In social and political terms, while ostensibly based on a system of free contract and individual choice, capitalism leads to the progressive impoverishment of the proletariat (see chapter 3). The system of economic organisation also creates the conditions in which workers are able to act collectively to throw off the chains of oppression.

Core–Periphery Model   This is the name given to the idea that the world is fundamentally divided into the haves and have-nots, privileged and victimised, powerful and controlled. Basically the core–periphery model describes how the structure of global capitalism (see above) as an economic, social and political form of organisation, inevitably divides the world into winners and losers. This system operates and is perpetuated by linkages between élites in core (rich, industrialised) countries and élites in the (underdeveloped, dependent) periphery, who have shared interests in supporting a system which guarantees their privileged position. The core–periphery model is a stark contrast and, perhaps, an important antidote to liberal views of a free-trade system or interdependent world. (See chapter 2).

Deconstruction   A philosophical approach implying a thoroughgoing critique of the way in which knowledge is constructed. Deconstruction questions the idea of truth by exposing the assumptions, and presuppositions in a 'text' (see chapter 5). It has its origins in literary studies (literary critique), and is particularly associated with the work of Jacques Derrida.

Deep Ecology   Also known as 'deep green', a deep ecological approach is one which rejects the idea of **anthropocentrism** (see above). Nature is viewed as alive and living creatures as deserving of respect. Some deep green thinkers even argue that we should assign rights to nature. It does not, as some of its critics claim, suggest that, for instance, anthrax spores are as morally considerable as humans. Deep ecology is a philosophy tied to bio- or **ecocentrism** (see below).

Deterministic   A theory is said to be deterministic when it implies that actors have little room to manoeuvre (agency); that their behaviour is pre-determined (as in biological determinism) or profoundly shaped or constrained by social structures (as in economic determinism). Thus, determinism denotes the idea that human choices have little bearing on social and political arrangements which are somehow inevitable/would happen anyway.

Development   'Development' is a good example of a '**discourse**' (see below). Development began to attract the attention of social scientists in the 1950s and 1960s, at a time when many former colonies were moving toward independence and needed to simultaneously build stable political institutions and achieve economic growth and diversification. For a long time the concept of 'Development' expressed the idea that all countries of the world follow a similar path towards industrialisation and modernity. Poorer countries, if they followed the right path or strategy, would pass through a series of stages until they reached the same position as rich, developed states. In more recent years the entire concept of development as economic growth and modernisation has been challenged by green and postmodernist thinkers, among others, on the grounds that it can be considered another manifestation of Western domination.

Discourse   In simple terms discourse means the way in which we use language to construct meaning or the way in which we infuse words with meaning or significance. In post-structuralist thought discourse has a rather more precise meaning. Poststructuralism and social constructivism, discourse refers to bounded social knowledge, shared by a community, however constituted. Post-structuralists argue that nothing exists outside of discourse. That is to say that the only way in which we can understand our world is through the 'conversations' that we have about it. Through discourse categories are constructed that are then assumed to have ontological status – i.e. are said to 'really' exist. Though this is a tricky idea it is discussed extensively in chapters 5, 6 and 7.

Ecocentrism   This simply means nature-centredness. In the context of the environmental debate, it refers to the argument that humans should not have free rein to exploit the planet's living and inert resources exactly as they please but should recognise the intrinsic value of the non-human world.

Ecosophy/Ecosophies   A nice abbreviated word used by the Norwegian deep ecologist Arne Naess and meaning an ecological philosophy.

Eco-system   An interrelated ecological web. Many creatures and organisms are connected to each other. Remove any one and the whole thing may collapse like removing a brick in a game of Jenga.

Egalitarianism   A belief in equality as a value or principle, from which follows the idea that inequality signifies injustice.

Egoistically   This word appears frequently in international relations literature and implies that states, like human beings, are essentially self-interested and act as maximisers of their own well-being or interest.

Emancipation   In popular usage, to emancipate is to liberate or set free, as in the case of the freeing of slaves. In Western philosophy and in Critical Theory particularly, emancipation means the achievement of autonomy, the ability to act independently. To be emancipated does not mean that one is free of all constraints and obligations towards others, only those which are deemed oppressive or unnecessarily confining.

Empirical   To be empirical is to favour modes of investigation or study which are derived from experience rather than relying on theoretical analysis and explanation. Empiricism thus denotes the belief that all knowledge of the world derives solely from experience. This should be distinguished from **positivism** (see below).

Empowerment   To empower is to give a person or group the capacity to act effectively to realise self-defined aims and objectives. Empowerment is thus distinct from liberty, which means the mere absence of unnecessary constraints, and implies some positive form of enablement, or facilitation, through perhaps access to resources or decision-making structures.

English School   The term 'English School' denotes a school of thought or collection of works which explore the nature of '**international society**' (see below) or the 'society of states'. Both facets of the English School are encapsulated in the phrase 'anarchical society' made famous by Hedley Bull, ironically an Australian! The English School is sometimes regarded as a variant of realist thought (both appear to be essentially state centric), but it is not. The intellectual influences are more varied, drawing upon liberal and rational strands of IR thought and other disciplines like sociology and international law.

Enlightenment   Period of human history (around the sixteenth and seventeenth centuries) when people moved from an age of superstitious medievalism to a belief in human reason and moral (and material) advancement.

Epistemology   Pertaining to knowledge. How do we know, what we know? Epistemology can be distinguished from the idea of ontology (which deals with the realm of what exists) in the sense that it concerns how we know things; what grounds we have for making knowledge claims.

Ethnocentric   Not to be confused with racist. In the broad context of international relations, ethnocentrism involves the tendency to regard one's own experience as normal, one's own way of thinking as rational and right and to suppose, therefore, that others will think similarly and will understand your motivations and actions.

Frankfurt School   The name given to a school of Critical Theory emerging first in Germany in the 1920s. The Frankfurt School was important in breaking away from orthodox (deterministic) schools of Marxist thought (such as Marxism-Leninism) drawing instead from the work of early 'humanistic' Marx, rather than the later 'economistic' work for which Marx had become more famous.

Genealogy   Term associated with the work of Michel Foucault. In everyday usage genealogy means to trace back a lineage, family or origins. It has a similar usage in poststructuralism where it describes a method of study which traces back the historical origins of ideas and concepts of theories. However, unlike history, which uses sources and evidence from the past to construct a coherent account or story about the present, genealogy demonstrates the ways in which dominant ideas and concepts have been used to construct particular power relations and in which dominant discourses have been contested.

Global Warming   Global warming is taking place through what is most easily understood as a 'greenhouse effect'. Gases are being produced (particularly carbon dioxide) through industrialisation and 'particularly' motor and air transport. Such gases are actually absorbed by vegetation but deforestation means there is much less forest. Such gases are actually accumulating in the atmosphere where they let heat in, but not out again, rather in the manner of a greenhouse. This is a 'separate' issue from ozone depletion in the view of atomised 'science', but all part of the same crisis of industrial society in a more holistic environmental view.

Hermeneutics   A method which is about interpretation rather than science.

Heuristic   An heuristic device is one which is used to aid understanding of something more complex by allowing the learner to discover for themselves. The device may not be a comprehensive explanation in itself, but allows one to go beyond it through analysis and reason.

Holistic   A holistic approach is one which studies things as a whole rather than breaking them down into constituent parts (which could be termed an 'individualistic' or 'atomistic' approach). A holistic approach to the environment believes that it is linked in numerous complex ways and should be studied as such. An atomistic approach might believe it possible to study a problem, such as deforestation, without reference to broader social, economic, political and ecological structures.

Ideological   Ideology literally means the science of ideas, but has come to denote all-embracing belief systems, which relate to the nature of society, and economic and political relationships. Ideology is sometimes contrasted with 'science' or 'truth' which claims to describe a 'reality' which exists independently of our beliefs about the world. However, it is not at all clear that science, 'truth' and ideology can be contrasted in this way, since all truth claims are rooted in fundamental beliefs or **normative** (see below) visions, while science does not so much consist of undisputed 'facts', but rather our best beliefs about 'facts' and 'reality' in any given historical period.

International Law   In essence international law is no different from domestic law. It governs relations between states (and other internationally recognised actors) on the basis of agreed principles and according to binding rules (such as those outlined in Treaties or Covenants), which can, in theory, be enforced through the Courts. However, international law is interesting because, in the absence of centralised authority (a condition of anarchy), there is no effective government or 'police force' to enforce the rule of law. Consequently, much of what is agreed is on the basis of consensus and cooperation. Moreover, states are only bound by agreements that they actively sign up to or by principles which they can be shown to have adhered to in their relations with others – state practices (customary law). Critics argue that the lack of sovereign government means that ultimately international law is not really law (a positivist view of law as the command of a sovereign) or that lack of effective sanctions or enforcement mean that international law is not effective. However, despite the absence of a sovereign power, states do obey international law most of the time. Thus, international law can be viewed as a way of expressing what states will normally do in a given situation and a codification of what it is useful for them to do (see also **Laws**).

International Society   The notion of International Society should be distinguished from the idea of an international system. International system denotes the idea that states interact with each other in various ways. However, in a society behaviour is 'rule governed'. Rules and norms of behaviour develop among states and, consequently, states come to have some notion of obligations to and expectations of each other, the most basic of which is the recognition of sovereignty.

Intersubjective   Intersubjective meaning is that established (or constructed) through the interaction of '**subjects**' (see below). The idea implies that 'things' have no independent 'meaning' outside that which is established through interaction or dialogue between conscious subjects.

Laws   The word 'laws' can be used in a scientific and legal sense. A scientific law is a regularity in behaviour (the law of gravity suggests that a cricket ball will fall if dropped); this type of law is comparable to a 'truth'. In IR there are few 'laws' of this type, although the proposition that democracies do not fight one another is sometimes held to be close to an established 'law'.

Liberal Internationalism   The belief that political activity should be framed in terms of a universal human condition rather than in relation to the particularities of any given nation.

Marginalisation   The process whereby some are considered to be of less significance or are neglected: that is, often those with little economic or political power, at local, national and global levels. Thus the Third World is marginalised in the global economy and international politics, the poor are marginalised in national economies and women are marginalised in many ways in socio-economic and political terms throughout the world.

Material   Something material is something made of matter or which is 'real', tangible/has substance. There has been a long, ongoing debate in social theory about the relative importance of material forces and ideas and the relationship between the two. Materialism is often contrasted with idealism, which holds that 'reality' is essentially a construct of the mind. In contrast, materialism holds that real material circumstances shape our consciousness (ideas) of the world.

Military Industrial Complex   A phrase originally used by US President Eisenhower to signify the close relationships existing between politicians, business and the military which operate to keep military/defence spending at high levels. Such close relations were reinforced by the revolving-door phenomenon where soldiers become politicians, politicians become businessmen and vice versa.

Misanthropic   A misanthrope is one who hates human beings; hence misanthropic. In the context of this book, some Deep Greens have been accused of misanthropism for their 'privileging' of the natural world over the human world. The counter-argument is, of course, that since human beings are part of nature, privileging nature cannot be considered misanthropic.

Modernity   This is the period of history associated with a belief in the ability of reasoned thought (and especially science) to achieve breakthroughs leading to human (**material** – see above) progress. A belief in the possibility of modernisation (and progress) is still very prevalent today, despite wide-ranging criticisms of modern, Western thought made by postmodern and post-structuralist thinkers.

Nihilist   A nihilist is one who believes in nothing. The reason for believing in nothing is a 'belief' that society is founded on lies and that truth is therefore not possible in this context.

NIMBYism   NIMBY is an acronym signifying 'not in my back yard'. NIMBYism in an environmental context is the tendency to be concerned about environmental issues only in so much as they affect oneself; for instance campaigning for or against a bypass scheme.

Normative   In everyday usage the term 'normal' or the 'norm' is used to describe a practice which conforms to the standards of a given society. The term 'normative' can be used to describe practices which obey the laws of 'normal' behaviour, or which conform to the norms of society, deviations from which might incur some form of sanction. The realm of normative action then encompasses values, ideals and judgements; it is about what is expected of us, what we should do. In IR the term normative is used in a similar way. An example of normative IR theory is that concerned with the role of moral codes, norms of behaviour or laws in the 'society of states'. A theory can also be considered normative if it raises, explicitly, questions or judgements which are founded upon certain ideals or moral standards: for example, theories which are concerned with inequality or justice between states, or social groups.

Otherness   Associated particularly with post-structuralist thought, otherness is that which is deemed as opposed to the self, that which is excluded or outside the self.

Patriarchal   Patriarchal society is a society in which men's dominance over women is institutionalised. Male domination is multifaceted, and both structural (embodied in institutions like marriage and the family) and ideological through perhaps the celebration of masculine, rather than feminine traits and values.

Pedagogical   Pedagogy is the science of teaching, so pedagogical means relating to the theory of teaching. Hence there is a pedagogical rationale behind exams in terms of the learning that they are said to demonstrate.

Polemical   To be polemical is to be argumentative or controversial. In the context of this book the use suggests that a debate has been conducted at the level of insult and 'mud-slinging' rather than as a genuine attempt to discuss problems.

Positivism/post-positivism   Positivism suggests that there are 'facts' about the world which can be established by observation and that such observation is neutral/independent or 'value free', i.e. not dependent on the 'position' of the observer as a part of the social world. Though positivists obviously favour an **empirical** approach (see above), one does not have to be a positivist to be an empiricist. Post-positivists and postmodernists particularly eschew grand theory in favour of empirical studies of specific societies, but reject the idea of value-free knowledge.

Postcolonial   If colonialism was the time when countries like Britain ruled others as possessions, the time after these countries gained independence (e.g. Zimbabwe) is known as the postcolonial period. Since the 1980s postcolonial writing has provided an important and influential critique of the West, and the construction of postcolonial societies as 'other': that is, different from and inferior to the West (see **Otherness** above).

Realpolitik   A German word popularised by the policy of Chancellor Otto von Bismarck (1815–98). It means realism about what is possible and a preparedness to use force where necessary. The latter has led to its association with 'lack of principle' or 'ruthlessness'.

Regime/s   The term regime has been around in IR theory since the 1970s and several classic definitions have emerged. Regime might be used to signify the leadership of a state (e.g. Saddam's regime). However, in contemporary IR, regime is most frequently used to refer to a set of rules and procedures concerning a given issue area which governs the behaviour of a particular group of actors – who are said to make up the regime which then makes decisions on the basis of this consensus. The International Whaling Commission is thus an example of an international environmental regime, though not an effective one. There is a more coherent international trade regime expressed in the World Trade Organisation.

Republic   A term use to describe a secular state in which there is a separation of powers in government and in which citizens are ruled by law and have some constitutional rights (in theory at least).

Securitisation   Denotes the process whereby an issue comes to be constructed as a security concern or issue.

Shallow Environmentalism   This is a view of the environment that, while it recognises that there is a problem and that action needs to be taken, also suggests that our solution need not fundamentally alter the way human societies are organised. It suggests, in effect, that we can amend our behaviour to ensure that we live in harmony with nature so that nature may continue to provide for us.

Sovereignty   To be sovereign means to have power or control. Most often, a state (to be sovereign) needs control within its own territory and the power to act independently in the international system, although there are numerous examples of states which do not have this capacity to act (due to, say, civil strife), but nevertheless remain sovereign. In these cases, continual recognition by the international community of states is crucial to their survival as sovereign, independent state actors.

Structural Adjustment   The name given to policies 'negotiated' between indebted developing countries and the IMF. Structural adjustment is a condition for receiving money. The money was needed in the wake of oil price rises and debt crisis in the 1970s and 1980s. Structural adjustment programmes (SAPs) meant countries spending less (fewer hospitals, scaling down government jobs, etc.) and earning more (growing more crops, for example). The effects of SAPs have sometimes had the desired effect in terms of raw economic data, but in removing peasants from subsistence land (in order to grow for export) and in reducing social expenditures, SAPs have also had serious effects in terms of hardship for already poor groups.

Subject   In everyday usage the subject is 'who' or 'what' an account, story or narrative is about. In contemporary post-structuralist theory, the term is used in a similar way. However, the subject is that thing or entity which 'acts'. Thus, discourses like realism construct the 'state' as the central actor which has concrete interests and acts to further the national interest, thereby investing the state with subjectivity.

Substantive   Coming from the word substance, substantive means real, or genuine. A substantive argument is therefore one over real, important issues; a genuine exchange of ideas rather than insults and contradictions (see/compare **Polemical**).

Sustainable Development   Often given a bland definition such as 'development which meets the needs of present generations without compromising the needs of the future'. However, sustainable development is highly controversial. Some critics have suggested that it is a contradiction in terms; others that it requires much more serious changes than politicians currently propose.

Teleological   Modes of thought which construct explanations, or prescriptions for action premised on some notion of an ultimate end or desirable goal.

Universalism   The idea that politics can be guided by universally valid principles, rather than being conditioned by particular local conditions. A doctrine is universal when it is said to apply to all human beings regardless of creed, colour or nationality, or other 'superficial' differences.

Utopian   A Utopia is a vision of the perfect social and political system. To be Utopian is therefore to be visionary and to believe in the possibility of improving human society until Utopia is reached. Oscar Wilde is reputed to have said that a map of the world without Utopia is not even worth looking at, though many IR scholars have disagreed (see chapter 1).

World Systems Theory   A variant of structuralism that conceptualises world order as being structured into a (rich, developed) core, (poor, underdeveloped) periphery and a number of intermediary or semi-peripheral states (see chapter 3).

Zero-sum   A 'zero-sum' game is one in which the answer is always 0. What does this mean? It means that if I gain something, you must lose a similar amount. Thus in war, a gain in territory by one side is automatically a loss by the other. Most closely associated with realism, not all international relations can be characterised in this way. For example, liberals hold that trade brings benefits to all, and international environmental agreements suggest that all humanity will benefit from their adoption. In these cases the answer is more than zero (i.e. everyone gains) and can be called a positive-sum game.

Further reading

These books and articles are referred to either explicitly in the text, or are useful in elaborating on the key arguments and themes that we cover in the text. As such, this extended list of references will complement what you learn from this book and will also provide a useful source of further reading when you come to write essays and research papers. **The texts in bold are the ones which appear with brief explanation of their importance at the end of each chapter.**

Introduction

Baylis, J. and Rengger, N.J. (1992), *Dilemmas of World Politics*, Oxford: Clarendon Press.
Baylis, J. and Smith, S. (eds) (1997), *Globalization and World Politics*, Oxford: Oxford University Press.
Berridge, G. (1992), *International Politics* (2nd edn), Harlow: Prentice Hall.
Bretherton, C. and Ponton, G. (eds) (1996), *Global Politics: An Introduction*, Oxford: Blackwell.
Brown, C. (1997), *Understanding International Relations*, London: Macmillan.
Burchill, S. and Linklater, A. (1996), *Theories of International Relations*, Basingstoke: Macmillan.
Calvocoressi, P. (1991), *World Politics Since 1945*, Harlow: Longman.
Evans, G. and Newnham, J. (1991), *The Dictionary of World Politics*, Harlow: Prentice Hall.
George, J. (1994), *Discourses of Global Politics: A Critical Re(Introduction) to International Relations*, Boulder, CO: Lynne Rienner.
Goldstein, J. (1996), *International Politics* (2nd edn), New York: Harper Collins.
Hocking, B. and Smith, M. (1995), *World Politics: An Introduction to International Relations* (2nd edn), Harlow: Prentice Hall.
Hollis, M. and Smith, S. (1990), *Explaining and Understanding International Relations*, Oxford: Clarendon Press.
Jackson, R. and Sorensen, G. (1999), *Introduction to International Relations*, Oxford: Oxford University Press.
Kegley, C. and Wittkopf, E. (2001), *World Politics: Trends and Transformation* (8th edn), New York: St Martin's Press.
Kennedy, P. (1994), *Preparing for the Twenty-first Century*, London: Fontana.
Little, R. and Smith, M. (1991), *Perspectives on World Politics*, London: Routledge.
Nicholson, M. (1998), *International Relations: A Concise Introduction*, Basingstoke: Macmillan.
Russett, B. and Starr, H. (1996), *World Politics: The Menu for Choice* (5th edn), New York: WH Freeman.
Woods, N. (1995), *Explaining International Relations Since 1945*, Oxford: Oxford University Press.

Liberalism

Brewin, C. (1988), 'Liberal States and International Obligations', *Millennium: Journal of International Studies*, Vol. 17, No. 2, pp. 321–38.
Claude, I. (1956), *Swords into Plowshares: The Problems and Progress of International Organisation*, New York: Random House.

Donnelly, J. (1993), *International Human Rights*, Boulder, CO: Westview Press.

Doyle, M. (1983), 'Kant, Liberal Legacies and Foreign Affairs', *Philosophy and Public Affairs,* Summer/Fall.

Doyle, M. (1986), **'Liberalism and World Politics'**, *American Political Science Review*, **Vol. 80, No. 4, pp. 1151–69**.

Ferguson, Y.H. and Mansbach, R. (1997), 'The Past as Prelude to the Future? Identities and Loyalties in Global Politics', in Y. Lapid and F. Kratochwil, *The Return of Culture and Identity in IR Theory,* Boulder, CO: Lynne Rienner.

Fukuyama, F. (1992), *The End of History and the Last Man*, New York: Free Press.

Hawthorn, G. (1999), 'Liberalism Since the Cold War: An Enemy to Itself?', *Review of International Studies*, Vol. 25, Special Issue, pp. 145–60.

Hoffman, S. (1995), 'The Crisis of Liberal Internationalism', *Foreign Policy*, Vol. 98, Spring, pp. 159–79.

Hurrell, A. (1990), 'Kant and the Kantian Paradigm in International Relations', *Review of International Studies,* Vol. 16, No. 3, pp. 183–205.

Kant, I. (1991), *Political Writings* (ed. Hans Reiss), Cambridge: Cambridge University Press.

Kegley, C. (ed.) (1995), *Controversies in International Relations*, New York: St Martin's Press.

Keohane, R. (1984), *After Hegemony: Cooperation and Discord in the World Political Economy*, Princeton, NJ: Princeton University Press.

Keohane, R. and Nye, J. (1977), *Power and Interdependence: World Politics in Transition*, Boston, MA: Little Brown.

Latham, R. (1993), 'Democracy and War-Making: Locating the International Liberal Context', *Millennium: Journal of International Studies*, Vol. 23, No. 2, pp. 139–64.

Luard, E. (ed.) (1992), *Basic Texts in International Relations*, London: Macmillan.

Mitrany, D. (1948), 'The Functional Approach to World Organization', *International Affairs*, Vol. 24, pp. 350–63.

Morse, E. (1976), *Modernisation and the Transformation of International Relations*, New York: Free Press.

Ricardo, D. (1971), *The Principles of Political Economy and Taxation*, Harmondsworth: Penguin.

Smith, A. (1910), *An Inquiry into the Nature and Causes of the Wealth of Nations* (with an introduction by Edwin Seligman), London: J.M. Dent.

Realism

Aron, R. (1966), *Peace and War: A Theory of International Relations*, London: Weidenfeld and Nicolson.

Beard, C. (1966), *The Idea of National Interest: An Analytical Study in American Foreign Policy*, Chicago, IL: Quadrangle.

Carr, E. H. (1946), *The Twenty Years' Crisis 1919–1939: An Introduction to the Study of International Relations*, London: Macmillan.

Clausewitz, C. Von (1968), *On War* (ed. with introduction by Anatol Rapoport), Harmondsworth: Penguin.

Evans, G. (1975), 'E.H. Carr and International Relations', *British Journal of International Studies*, Vol. 1, No. 2, pp. 77–97.

Herz, J. (1951), *Political Realism and Political Idealism*, Chicago, IL: University of Chicago Press.

Hobbes, T. (1904), *Leviathan* (ed. A.R. Waller), Cambridge: Cambridge University Press.

Jervis, R. (1988), 'Realism, Game Theory and Cooperation', *World Politics*, Vol. XL, No. 3, pp. 317–49.

Kaplan, M. (1966), 'The New Great Debate: Traditionalism vs Science in International Relations', *World Politics*, Vol. XIX, No. 1, pp. 1–20.

Keohane, R. (1986), *Neorealism and its Critics*, New York: Columbia University Press.

Kissinger, H. (1964), 'Coalition Diplomacy in a Nuclear Age', *Foreign Affairs*, Vol. 42, No. 4, pp. 525–45.

Krasner, S. (2001), 'Rethinking the Sovereign State Model', *Review of International Studies,* Vol. 27, No. 1, pp. 17–42.

Lippman, W. (1943), *US Foreign Policy*, Boston, MA: Little, Brown and Company.

Little, R. (1995), 'Neorealism and the English School: A Methodological, Ontological and Theoretical Reassessment', *European Journal of International Relations*, Vol. 1, No. 1, pp. 9–34.

Machiavelli, N. (1988), *The Prince* (ed. by Q. Skinner), Cambridge: Cambridge University Press.

Morgenthau, H. (1964), 'The Four Paradoxes of Nuclear Strategy', *The American Political Science Review*, Vol. 58, No. 1, pp. 23–35.

Morgenthau, H. (1978), *Politics Among Nations: The Struggle for Power and Peace*, New York: Knopf.

Niebuhr, R. (1932), *Moral Man and Immoral Society*, New York: Charles Scribner's Sons.

Niebuhr, R. (1953), *Christian Realism and Political Problems*, New York: Charles Scribner's Sons.

Schelling, T. (1960), *The Strategy of Conflict*, Cambridge, MA: Harvard University Press.

Spykman, N. (1942), *America's Strategy in World Politics: The United States and the Balance of Power*, New York: Harcourt, Brace and Company.

Thucydides (1998), *The Peloponnesian War* (new transl. W. Blanco, ed. W. Blanco and J. Tolbert Roberts), New York: Norton.

Waltz, K. (1959), *Man, the State and War: A Theoretical Analysis*, New York: Colombia University Press.

Waltz, K. (1979), *Theory of International Politics*, Reading, MA: Addison-Wesley.

Wight, M. (1979), *Power Politics*, Harmondsworth: Pelican.

Williams, M. (1993), 'Neo-Realism and the Future of Strategy', *Review of International Studies*, Vol. 19, No. 2, pp. 103–21.

Wolfers, A. (1962), *Discord and Collaboration: Essays on International Politics*, Baltimore, MD: Johns Hopkins Press.

The IPE texts cited are:

Gilpin, R. (1987), *Political Economy of International Relations*, Princeton, NJ: Princeton University Press.

Keohane, R. (1984), *After Hegemony*, Princeton, NJ: Princeton University Press.

Kindleberger, C. (2000), *Comparative Political Economy: A Retrospective*, Cambridge, MA; London: MIT Press.

The English School text cited is:

Bull, H. (1977), *The Anarchical Society: A Study of World Order in Politics*, Basingstoke: Macmillan.

Structuralism

Amin, S. (1974), *Accumulation on a World Scale: A Critique of the Theory of Underdevelopment* (2 Volumes), London: Monthly Review Press.

Amin, S. (1990), *Maldevelopment: Anatomy of a Global Failure*, London: Zed Books.

Arrighi, G. and Sliver, B.J. (2001), 'Capitalism and World (Dis)Order', *Review of International Studies*, Vol. 27, Special Issue, pp. 257–79.

Baran, P. (1957), *The Political Economy of Growth*, New York: Monthly Review Press.

Cardoso, F. and Faletto, E. (1979), *Dependency and Development in Latin America*, Berkeley, CA: University of California Press.

Chase-Dunn, C. (1989), *Global Formation: Structures of the World Economy*, Oxford: Blackwell.

Escobar, A. (1995), *Encountering Development: The Making and Unmaking of the Third World*, Princeton, NJ: Princeton University Press.

Galtung, J. (1971), 'A Structural Theory of Imperialism', *The Journal of Peace Research*, Vol. 8, No. 1, pp. 81–117.

Gamble, A. (1999), 'Marxism After Communism: Beyond Realism and Historicism', *Review of International Studies*, Vol. 25, Special Issue, pp. 127–44.

George, S. (1994), *A Fate Worse Than Debt*, London: Penguin.

Gunder Frank, A. (1979), *Dependent Accumulation and Underdevelopment*, New York: Monthly Review Press.

Harris, N. (1990), *The End of the Third World*, London: Penguin.

Harvey, D. (2003), *The New Imperialism*, Oxford: Oxford University Press.

Kamrava, M. (1993), *Politics and Society in the Third World*, London: Routledge.

Kolko, J. (1988), *Restructuring the World Economy*, London: Random House.

Marx, K. and Engels, F. (1965), *The Communist Manifesto*, New York: Washington Square Press.

McLellan, D. (1977), *Karl Marx: Selected Writings*, Oxford: Oxford University Press.

Mies, M. (1986), *Patriarchy and Accumulation on a World Scale*, London: Zed Books.

Prebisch, R. (1964), *Towards a New Trade Policy for Development*, New York: United Nations.

Rodney, W. (1972), *How Europe Underdeveloped Africa*, London: Bogle l'Ouverture.

Rostow, W.W. (1960), *The Stages of Economic Growth: A Non-Communist Manifesto*, Cambridge: Cambridge University Press.

Said, E. (1993), *Culture and Imperialism*, New York: Knopf.

South Commission (1990), *The Challenge to the South: The Report of the South Commission*, Oxford: Oxford University Press.

Van der Wee, H. (1986), *Prosperity and Upheaval: The World Economy 1945–1980*, London: Viking Books.

Wallerstein, I. (1974, 1980, 1989), *The Modern World-System* (Vols 1–3), San Diego, CA: Academy Press.

Wallerstein, I. (2000), 'From Sociology to Historical Social Science: Prospects and Obstacles', *The British Journal of Sociology*, Vol. 51, No. 1.

Wilber, C. (ed.) (1973), *The Political Economy of Underdevelopment*, New York: Random House.

Critical Theory

Ashley, R. K. (1981), 'Political Realism and Human Interests', *International Studies Quarterly*, Vol. 25, No. 2, pp. 204–36.

Ashley, R. K. (1986), 'The Poverty of Neorealism', in R. Keohane (ed.), *Neorealism and its Critics*, New York: Columbia University Press, pp. 255–300.

Barnett, M. (ed.) (1998), *Security Communities*, Cambridge: Cambridge University Press.

Baylis, J. (1997), 'International security in the post-Cold War era', in J. Baylis and S. Smith (eds) (1997), *The Globalization of World Politics: An Introduction to International Relations*, Oxford: Oxford University Press, pp. 193–211.

Brown, C. (1992), *International Relations Theory: New Normative Approaches*, Harlow: Prentice Hall.

Buzan, B., Wæver, O. and de Wilde, J. (1998), *Security: A New Framework for Analysis*, Boulder, CO: Lynne Rienner.

Cox, R. W. (1986), 'Social forces, states and world order', *Millennium: Journal of International Studies*, Vol. 10, No. 2, pp. 126–55, reprinted as 'Social forces, states and world orders: Beyond international relations theory', in R. Keohane (ed.), *Neorealism and its Critics*, New York: Columbia University Press, pp. 204–54.

Cox, R. W. (1987), *Production, Power and World Order: Social Forces in the Making of History*, New York: Columbia University Press.

Croft, S. and Terriff, T. (eds) (2000), *Critical Reflections on Security and Change*, London: Frank Cass.

Dallmayr, F. (2001), 'Conversation across boundaries: political theory and global diversity', *Millennium: Journal of International Studies*, Vol. 30, No. 2, pp. 331–47.

Denzin, N.K. (1995), *The Cinematic Society: the Voyeur's Gaze*, London: Sage.

Devetak, R. (1996), 'Critical Theory', in S. Burchill and A. Linklater (eds), *Theories of International Relations*, Basingstoke: Macmillan, pp. 145–78.

Gill, S. (ed.) (1993), *Gramsci, Historical Materialism and International Relations*, Cambridge: Cambridge University Press.

Gill, S. and Law, D. (1988), *The Global Political Economy: Perspectives, Problems and Policies*, Harlow: Prentice Hall.

Gramsci, A. (1971), *Selections from Prison Notebooks*, London: Lawrence and Wishart.

Habermas, J. (1972), *Knowledge and Human Interests*, London: Heinemann.

Held, D. (1990), *Introduction to Critical Theory: Horkheimer to Habermas*, Cambridge: Polity Press.

Hoffman, M. (1987), 'Critical Theory and the inter-paradigm debate', *Millennium: Journal of International Studies*, Vol. 16, No. 2, pp. 231–49.

Hoffman, M. (1988), 'Conversations on critical international relations theory', *Millennium: Journal of International Studies*, Vol. 17, No. 1, pp. 91–5.

Horkheimer, M. (1972), *Critical Theory: Selected Essays*, New York: Seabury Press.

Katzenstein, P. J. (ed.) (1996), *The Culture of National Security: Norms and Identity in World Politics*, New York: Columbia University Press.

Krause, K. and Williams, M. C. (eds) (1997), *Critical Security Studies*, Minneapolis, MN: University of Minnesota Press.

Linklater, A. (1988), *The Transformation of Political Community*, Oxford: Polity Press.

Linklater, A. (1990), *Beyond Realism and Marxism: Critical Theory and International Relations*, London: Macmillan.

Linklater, A. (1992), 'The question of the next stage in international relations theory: a critical-theoretical point of view', *Millennium: Journal of International Studies*, Vol. 22, No. 2, pp. 77–98.

Linklater, A. (1996), 'The Achievements of Critical Theory', in K. Booth and M. Zalewski (eds), *International Theory: Positivism and Beyond*, Cambridge: Cambridge University Press, pp. 279–98.

Rengger, N. J. (1988), 'Going critical? A response to Hoffman', *Millennium: Journal of International Studies*, Vol. 17, No. 2, pp. 81–9.

Rengger, N. J. (1990), 'The fearful sphere of international relations', *Review of International Studies*, Vol. 16, No. 4, pp. 361–68.

Rengger, N. J. (2001), 'The boundaries of conversation: a response to Dallmayr', *Millennium: Journal of International Studies*, Vol. 30, No. 2, pp. 357–64.

Rengger, N. J. and Hoffman, M. (1992), 'Modernity, postmodernity and international relations', in: J. Doherty, E. Graham and M. Malek (eds), *Post-modernism and the Social Sciences*, London: Macmillan, pp. 127–47.

Shultz, R. H. *et al.* (eds) (1997), *Security Studies for the Twenty-first Century*, Washington, DC: Brassey's.

Teriff, T. *et al.* (1999), *Security Studies Today*, Oxford: Polity.

Wyn Jones, R. (1999), *Security, Strategy, and Critical Theory*, Boulder, CO: Lynne Rienner.

Postmodernism

Ashley, R. K. (1988), 'Untying the sovereign state: a double reading of the anarchy problematique', *Millennium: Journal of International Studies*, Vol. 17, No. 2, pp. 227–62.

Ashley, R. K. (1989), 'Imposing international purpose: notes on a problematic of governance', in E.-O. Czempiel and J.N. Rosenau (eds), *Global Changes and Theoretical Challenges: Approaches to World Politics for the 1990s*, Lexington, MA: Lexington Books, pp. 251–90.

Ashley, R. K. (1995), 'The power of anarchy: theory, sovereignty, and the domestication of global life', in J. Der Derian (ed.), *International Theory: Critical Investigations*, Manchester: Manchester University Press, pp. 94–128.

Ashley, R. K. (1996), 'The achievements of post-structuralism', in S. Smith, K. Booth and M. Zalewski (eds), *International Theory: Positivism and Beyond*, Cambridge: Cambridge University Press, pp. 240–53.

Ashley, R. K. and Walker, R. B. J. (1990), 'Speaking the Language of Exile', *International Studies Quarterly*, Vol. 34, No. 3, p. 259.

Bartelson, J. (1995), *A Genealogy of Sovereignty*, Cambridge: Cambridge University Press.

Brown, C. (1992), *International Relations Theory: New Normative Approaches*, Hemel Hempstead: Harvester Wheatsheaf.

Campbell, D. (1993), *Politics without Principle: Sovereignty, Ethics, and the Narratives of the Gulf War*, Boulder, CO: Lynne Rienner.

Campbell, D. (1998), *National Deconstruction: Violence, Identity, and Justice in Bosnia*, Minneapolis, MN: University of Minnesota Press.

Campbell, D. (1998), *Writing Security: United States Foreign Policy and the Politics of Identity* **(rev. edn), Manchester: University of Manchester Press.**

Connolly, W. (1991), *Identity/Difference: Democratic Negotiations of Political Paradox*, Ithaca, NY: Cornell University Press.

Connolly, W. (1993), *Political Theory and Modernity* (2nd edn), Ithaca, NY: Cornell University Press.

Der Derian, J. (1989), 'The boundaries of knowledge and power in International Relations', in J. Der Derian and M. J. Shapiro (eds), *International/Intertextual Relations: Postmodern Readings of World Politics*, Lexington, MA: Lexington Books, pp. 3–10.

Der Derian, J. and Shapiro, M. (eds) (1989), *International/Intertextual Relations: Postmodern Readings of World Politics***, Lexington, MA: Lexington Books.**

Derrida, J. (1978), *Writing and Difference*, London: Routledge and Kegan Paul.

Devetak, R. (1996), 'Postmodernism', in S. Burchill and A. Linklater (eds), *Theories of International Relations*, London: Macmillan.

Edkins, J. (1999), *Poststructuralism and International Relations: Bringing the Political Back In*, Boulder, CO: Lynne Rienner.

Foucault, M. (1970), *The Order of Things*, London: Tavistock.

Foucault, M. (1979), *Discipline and Punish: The Birth of the Prison*, Harmondsworth: Penguin.

Foucault, M. (1980), *Power/Knowledge: Selected Interviews and Other Writings, 1972–1977* (ed. C. Gordon), Brighton: Harvester Wheatsheaf.

Foucault, M. (1989), *The Archaeology of Knowledge*, London: Routledge.

George, J. (1994), *Discourses of Global Politics: A Critical (Re)Introduction to International Relations*, Boulder, CO: Lynne Rienner.

George, J. (1994), 'Thinking Beyond International Relations: Postmodernism – Reconceptualizing Theory as Practice', in J. George, *Discourses of Global Politics*, Boulder, CO: Lynne Rienner, pp. 191–217.

Hansen, L. (1997), 'A Case for Seduction? Evaluating the Poststructuralist Conceptualization of Security', *Cooperation and Conflict*, Vol. 32, No. 4, pp. 369–97.

Heidegger, M. (1969), *Identity and Difference*, New York: Harper & Row.

Heidegger, M. (1993), *Basic Concepts*, Bloomington, IN: Indiana University Press.

Neumann, I. B. (1996), 'Self and other in international relations', *European Journal of International Relations*, Vol. 2, No. 2, pp. 139–74.

Nietzsche, F. (1954), *The Portable Nietzsche*, New York: Viking Press.

Nietzsche, F. (1990), *Unmodern Observations*, New Haven, CT: Yale University Press.

Rengger, N. and Hoffman, M. (1992), 'Modernity, postmodernism and international relations', in J. Doherty, (eds), *Postmodernism in the Social Sciences*, London: Macmillan, pp. 127–47.

Rosenau, P. (1991), *Postmodernism and the Social Sciences: Insights, Inroads and Intrusions*, Princeton, NJ: Princeton University Press.

Smith, S. (1995), 'The self-images of a discipline: a genealogy of international relations theory', in K. Booth and S. Smith (eds), *International Relations Theory Today*, Oxford: Polity, pp. 1–37.

Smith, S. (1999), 'Is the Truth Out There? Eight Questions about International Order', in T.V. Paul and J.A. Hall (eds), *International Order and the Future of World Politics*, Cambridge: Cambridge University Press, pp. 99–119.

Walker, R. B. J. (1987), *One World, Many Worlds: Struggles for a Just World Peace*, London: Zed Books.

Walker, R. B. J. (1993), *Inside/Outside: International Relations as Political Theory***, Cambridge: Cambridge University Press.**

Weber, C. (1995), *Simulating Sovereignty: Intervention, the State and Symbolic Exchange*, Cambridge: Cambridge University Press.

Feminist perspectives

Butler, J. (1990), *Gender Trouble: Feminism and the Subversion of Identity*, London: Routledge.

Carver, T., Cochran, M. and Squires, J. (1998), 'Gendering Jones', *Review of International Studies*, Vol. 24, No. 2, pp. 283–98.

Chatterjee, P. (1991), 'Whose imagined communities', *Millennium: Journal of International Studies*, Vol. 20, No. 3, pp. 625–60.

Chinkin, C. (1999), 'Gender, inequality and International Human Rights Law', in A. Hurrell and N. Woods, *Inequality, Globalization and World Politics*, Oxford: Oxford University Press.

Chowdhry, G. and Nair, S. (2002) (eds), *Postcolonialism and International Relations: Race, Gender and Class*, London: Routledge.

Connell, R. W. (1995), *Masculinities*, Cambridge: Cambridge University Press.

Cooke, M. and Woollacott, A. (1993), *Gendering War Talk*, Princeton, NJ: Princeton University Press.

Elshtain, J. B. (1987), *Women and War*, New York: Basic Books.

Enloe, C. (1989), *Bananas, Beaches and Bases; Making Feminist Sense of International Relations*, London: Pandora.

Enloe, C. (1993), *The Morning After: Sexual Politics after the Cold War*, Berkeley, CA: University of California Press.

Enloe, C. (2000), *Maneuvers: The International Politics of Militarizing Women's Lives*, Berkeley, CA: University of California Press.

Fukuyama, F. (1998), 'Women and the Evolution of World Politics', *Foreign Affairs*, Vol. 77, No. 5, pp. 24–40.

Grant, R. and Newland, K. (1990), *Gender and International Relations*, Milton Keynes: Open University Press.

Harcourt, W. (ed.) (1999), *Women@Internet*, London: Zed Books.

Hoffman, J. (2001), *Gender and Sovereignty*, Basingstoke: Palgrave.

Hooper, C. (2000), 'Hegemonic masculinity in transition: the case of globalization', in M. Marchand and A. Runyan, *Gender and Global Restructuring: Sitings, Sites and Resistances*, London: Routledge.

Hooper, C. (2001), *Masculinities, International Relations and Gender Politics*, New York: Columbia University Press.

Hutchins, K. (2000), 'Towards a Feminist International Ethics', *Review of International Studies*, Vol. 26, Special Issue, pp. 111–30.

Jones, A. (1996), 'Does "gender" make the world go around? Feminist critiques of International Relations', *Review of International Studies*, Vol. 22, No. 4, pp. 405–29.

Jones, A. (1998), 'Engendering Debate', *Review of International Studies*, Vol. 24, No. 2, pp. 299–303.

Keohane, R. (1989), 'International Relations theory: Contributions of a feminist standpoint', *Millennium: Journal of International Studies*, Vol. 18, No. 2, pp. 245–54.

Keohane, R. (1998), 'Beyond dichotomy: Conversations between International Relations and Feminist Theory', *International Studies Quarterly*, Vol. 42, No. 1, pp. 193–8.

Krause, J. (1995), 'The international dimensions of gender inequality and feminist politics', in J. MacMillan and A. Linklater (eds), *Boundaries in Question: New Directions in International Relations*, London: Pinter, pp. 128–43.

Marchand, M. (1996), 'Reconceptualizing gender and development in an era of globalization', *Millennium: Journal of International Studies*, Vol. 25, No. 3, pp. 577–603.

Marchand, M. and Runyan, A. S. (2000), *Gender and Global Restructuring: Sitings, Sites and Resistances*, London: Routledge.

McGlen, N. and Sarkees, M. R. (1993), *Women in Foreign Policy*, London: Routledge.

Mernisi, F. (1987), *The Veil and the Male Elite: A Feminist Interpretation of Women's Rights in Islam*, New York: Addison Wesley.

Meyer, M. and Prugl, E. (1999), *Gender Issues in Global Governance*, Oxford: Rowman and Littlefield.

Murphy, C. (1996), 'Seeing women, recognizing gender, recasting International Relations', *International Organisation*, Vol. 3, No. 5, pp. 513–38.

Myerson, M. and Northcott, S. (1994), 'The question of gender: An examination of selected textbooks in International Relations', *International Studies Notes*, Vol. 19, No. 1, Winter.

Peterson, V. S. (1990), 'Whose rights? Challenging the discourse', *Alternatives*, Vol. 15, No. 3, pp. 303–44.

Peterson, V. S. (1992), 'Transgressing boundaries: Theories of knowledge, gender and International Relations', *Millennium: Journal of International Studies*, Vol. 21, No. 2, pp. 183–206.

Peterson, V. S. (1992) (ed.), *Gendered States; Feminist (Re)Visions of International Theory*, Boulder, CO: Lynne Rienner.

Peterson, V. S. and Parisi, L. (1998), 'Are women human? This is not an academic question', in T. Evans (ed.), *Human Rights Fifty Years On: A Reappraisal*, Manchester: Manchester University Press.

Peterson, V. S. and Runyan, A. (1993), *Global Gender Issues*, Boulder, CO: Westview Press.

Pettman, J. J. (1996), *Worlding Women: A Feminist International Politics*, London: Routledge.

Robinson, F. (1999), *Globalizing Care: Ethics, Feminist Theory and International Relations*, Oxford: Westview Press.

Schneir, M. (1972), *Feminism: The Essential Historical Writings*, London: Vintage.

Special Issue: 'Women in International Relations', *Millennium: Journal of International Studies*, Vol. 17, No. 3.

Steans, J. (1998), *Gender and International Relations*, Oxford: Polity Press.

Steans, J. (2003), 'Conflicting loyalties: Women's human rights and the politics of identity', in M. Waller and A. Linklater (eds), *Loyalty and the Post-National State*, London: Routledge.

Steans, J. (2003), 'Engaging from the margins: Feminist encounters with the mainstream of International Relations', *British Journal of Politics and International Relations*, Vol. 5, No. 3, pp. 428–54.

Sylvester, C. (1994), 'Empathetic cooperation: A feminist method for IR', *Millennium: Journal of International Studies*, Vol. 23, No. 3, pp. 315–34.

Sylvester, C. (1994), *Feminist Theory and International Relations in a Postmodern Era*, Cambridge: Cambridge University Press.

Tickner, J. A. (1992), *Gender in International Relations: Feminist Perspectives on Achieving Global Security*, New York: Columbia University Press.

Tickner, J. A. (1997), 'You just don't understand: Troubled engagements between feminists and IR theorists', *International Studies Quarterly*, Vol. 41, No. 4, pp. 611–32.

Tickner, J. A. (1998), 'Continuing the conversation', *International Studies Quarterly*, Vol. 42, No. 1, pp. 205–10.

Tickner, J. A. (1999), 'Why women can't run the world: International politics according to Francis Fukuyama', *International Studies Review*, Vol. 3, No., pp. 3–12.

Tickner, J. A. (2001), *Gendering World Politics*, New York: Columbia University Press.

True, J. (1996), 'Feminism', in S. Burchill and A. Linklater (eds), *Theories of International Relations*, London: Macmillan.

Walker, R.B.J. (1992), 'Gender and critique in the theory of International Relations', in V.S. Peterson (ed.), *Gendered States: Feminist (Re)Visions of International Relations Theory*, Boulder, CO: Lynne Rienner.

Weber, C. (1994), 'Good girls, bad girls and little girls: Male paranoia in Robert Keohane's critique of feminist International Relations', *Millennium: Journal of International Studies*, Vol. 23, No. 2, pp. 337–49.

Weber, C. (2001), '*Gender*', in *International Relations Theory: A Critical Introduction*, London: Routledge.

Whitworth, S. (1989), 'Gender in the interparadigm debate', *Millennium: Journal of International Studies*, Vol. 18, No. 2, pp. 265–72.

Whitworth, S. (1994), *Feminism and International Relations: Towards a Political Economy of Gender in Interstate and Non-Governmental Institutions*, Basingstoke: Macmillan.

Whitworth, S. (1994), 'Theory as exclusion: Gender and international political economy', in R. Stubbs and G. Underhill, *Political Economy and the Changing Global Order*, London: Macmillan.

Zalewski, M. (1993), 'Feminist standpoint meets International Relations theory: A feminist version of David and Goliath', *The Fletcher Forum of World Affairs*, Vol. 17, No. 2, pp. 221–9.

Zalewski, M. (1993), 'Feminist Theory and International Relations', in M. Bowker and R. Brown (eds), *From Cold War to Collapse: Theory and World Politics in the 1980s*, Cambridge: Cambridge University Press.

Zalewski, M. (1994), 'The woman/"women" question in International Relations', *Millennium: Journal of International Studies*, Vol. 23, No. 3, pp. 407–23.

Zalewski, M. (1995), 'Well, what is the feminist perspective on Bosnia?', *International Affairs*, Vol. 71, No. 2, pp. 339–56.

Zalewski, M. and Enloe, C. (1995), 'Questions about identity', in K. Booth and S. Smith (eds), *International Relations Theory Today*, Cambridge: Polity Press.

Zalewski, M. and Parpart, J. (1998), *The Man Question in IR*, Oxford: Westview Press.

Social constructivism

Adler, E. (1997), 'Seizing the middle ground: constructivism in world politics', *European Journal of International Relations*, Vol. 3, No. 3, pp. 319–63.

Adler, E. (2002), 'Constructivism and International Relations', in W. Carlsnaes, B. Simmons and T. Risse (eds), *Handbook of International Relations*, London: Sage, pp. 95–118.

Adler, E. and Barnett, M. (eds) (1998), *Security Communities*, Cambridge: Cambridge University Press.

Biersteker, T. and Weber, C. (eds) (1996), *State Sovereignty as Social Construct*, Cambridge: Cambridge University Press.

Bull, H. (1966), 'International theory: the case for a classical approach', *World Politics*, Vol. 18, No. 3, pp. 361–77.

Bull, H. (1977), *The Anarchical Society: A Study of Order in World Politics*, Basingstoke: Macmillan.

Buzan, B. (1991), *People, States, and Fear: An Agenda for International Security Studies in the Post-Cold War Era*, Hemel Hempstead: Harvester Wheatsheaf.

Buzan B. (2004), *From International to World Society? English School Theory and the Social Structure of Globalisation*, Cambridge: Cambridge University Press.

Buzan, B., Wæver, O. and de Wilde, J. (1998), *Security: A New Framework for Analysis*, Boulder, CO: Lynne Rienner.

Checkel, J. (1998), 'The constructivist turn in international relations theory', *World Politics*, Vol. 20, No. 2, pp. 324–48.

Christiansen, T., Jørgensen, K. E. and Wiener, A. (eds) (2001), *The Social Construction of Europe*, London: Sage.

David, P. (1985), 'Clio and the economics of QWERTY', *American Economic Review*, Vol. 75, No. 2, pp. 332–7.

Der Derian, J. (1987), *On Diplomacy: A Genealogy of Western Estrangement*, Oxford: Basil Blackwell.

Dunne, T. (1998), *Inventing International Society: A History of the English School*, Basingstoke: Macmillan.

Fierke, K. M. and Jørgensen, K.E. (eds) (2001), *Constructing International Relations: The Next Generation*, Armonk, NJ: M.E. Sharpe.

Finnemore, M. (1996), *National Interests in International Society*, Ithaca, NY: Cornell University Press.

Giddens, A. (1984), *The Constitution of Society*, Berkeley, CA: University of California Press.

Habermas, J. (1985), *Theory of Communicative Action: Reason and the Rationalisation of Society*, London: Heinemann.

Jachtenfuchs, M., Diez, T. and Jung, S. (1998), 'Which Europe? Conflicting models of a legitimate European political order', *European Journal of International Relations*, Vol. 4, No. 4, pp. 409–45.

Katzenstein, P. (ed.) (1996), *The Culture of National Security: Norms and Identity in World Politics*, New York: Columbia University Press.

Kratochwil, F. (1989), *Rules, Norms and Decisions: On the Conditions of Practical and Legal Reasoning in International Relations and Domestic Affairs*, Cambridge: Cambridge University Press.

Kubálková, V., Onuf, N. and Kowert, P. (eds) (1998), *International Relations in a Constructed World*, Armonk, NJ: M.E. Sharpe.

Lapid, Y. (1989), 'The third debate: on the prospects of international theory in a post-positivist era', *International Studies Quarterly*, Vol. 33, No. 3, pp. 235–54.

March, J. G. and Olsen, J. P. (1989), *Rediscovering Institutions: The Organizational Basis of Politics*, New York: Free Press.

Neumann, I. (1999), *Uses of the Other: 'The East' in European Identity Formation*, Minneapolis, MN: University of Minnesota Press.

Øhrgaard, J. C. (1997), ' "Less than supranational, more than intergovernmental": European political cooperation and the dynamics of intergovernmental integration', *Millennium: Journal of International Studies*, Vol. 26, No. 1, pp. 1–29.

Onuf, N.G. (1989), ***World of Our Making: Rules and Rule in Social Theory and International Relations,*** **New York: Columbia University Press.**

Risse, T. (2000), '"Let's argue!" Communicative action in world politics', *International Organization*, Vol. 54, No. 1, pp. 1–39.

Risse, T., Ropp, S. and Sikkink, K. (eds) (1999), ***The Power of Human Rights: International Norms and Domestic Change,*** **Cambridge: Cambridge University Press.**

Ruggie, J. G. (1998), *Constructing the World Polity: Essays on International Institutionalization*, London: Routledge.

Schimmelfennig, F. (2003), *The EU, NATO and the Integration of Europe: Rules and Rhetoric*, Cambridge: Cambridge University Press.

Vincent, J. (1986), *Human Rights and International Relations : Issues and Responses*, Cambridge: Cambridge University Press.

Wæver, O. (1998), 'Figures of international thought: introducing persons instead of paradigms', in I. Neumann and O. Wæver (eds), *The Future of International Relations: Masters in the Making*, London: Routledge, pp. 1–37.

Weldes, J. (1996), 'Constructing national interests', *European Journal of International Relations*, Vol. 2, No. 3, pp. 275–318.

Wendt, A. (1992), 'Anarchy is what states make of it', *International Organization*, Vol. 46, No. 2, pp. 391–425.

Wendt, A. (1999), ***Social Theory of International Politics,*** **Cambridge: Cambridge University Press.**

Zehfuss, M. (2002), *Constructivism in International Relations: The Politics of Reality*, Cambridge: Cambridge University Press.

Green perspectives

Adams, W. M. (1990), ***Green Development: Environment and Sustainability in the Third World,*** **London: Routledge.**

Barnett, J. (2001), *The Meaning of Environmental Security: Ecological Politics and Policy in the New Security Era*, London: Zed.

Brundtland, G. (1987), *Our Common Future*, Oxford: Oxford University Press (World Commission on Environment and Development, The Brundtland Report).

Carson, R. (1962), ***Silent Spring,*** **Harmondsworth: Penguin.**

Conca, K., Alberty, M. and Dabelkoa, G. (eds) (1995), *Green Planet Blues*, Boulder, CO: Westview Press.

Dobson, A. (1995), *Green Political Thought* (2nd edn), London: Routledge.

Dobson, A. (ed.) (1999), *Fairness and Futurity: Essays on Environmental Sustainability and Social Justice*, Oxford: Oxford University Press.

Eckersley, R. (1992), *Environmentalism and Political Theory: Towards an Ecocentric Approach*, London: UCL Press.

Elliot, J. (1994), *An Introduction to Sustainable Development: The Developing World*, London: Routledge.

Hayward, T. (1994), *Ecological Thought: An Introduction*, Oxford: Polity Press.

Homer-Dixon, T. and Blitt, J. (eds) (1998), *EcoViolence: Links Among Environment, Population and Security*, London: Rowman and Littlefield.

Hurrell, A. and Kingsbury, B. (eds) (1992), *The International Politics of the Environment*, Oxford: Oxford University Press.

Imber, M. (1994), *Environment, Security and UN Reform*, Basingstoke: Macmillan.

Litfin, K. (ed.) (1998), *The Greening of Sovereignty in World Politics*, Cambridge, MA: MIT Press.

Lomborg, B. (2001), ***The Skeptical Environmentalist: Measuring the Real State of the World,*** **Cambridge: Cambridge University Press.**

Matthews, F. (1991), *The Ecological Self*, London: Routledge.

McCormick, J. (1989), *Reclaiming Paradise: The Global Environmental Movement*, Indiana: Indiana University Press.

Meadows, D., Meadows, D.L., Randers, J. and Behrens, W.W. (1972), *The Limits to Growth*, Washington, DC: Potomac Associates.

Mellor, M. (1997), *Feminism and Ecology*, Oxford: Polity Press.

Merchant, C. (1992), *Radical Ecology: The Search for a Liveable World*, London: Routledge.

Paterson, M. (1996), *Global Warming and Global Politics*, London: Routledge.

Paterson, M. (1996), 'Green politics', in S. Burchil and A. Linklater (eds), *Theories of International Relations*, Basingstoke: Macmillan, pp. 252–74.

Paterson, M. (2000), *Understanding Global Environmental Politics. Domination, Accumulation, Resistance*, Basingstoke: Macmillan.

Pepper, D. (1996), *Modern Environmentalism: An Introduction*, London: Routledge.

Porritt, J. (1984), *Seeing Green*, Oxford: Blackwell.

Sessions, G. (ed.) (1995), *Deep Ecology for the Twenty-first Century*, London: Shambhala.

Shiva, V. (2002), *Water Wars: Privatization, Pollution, and Profit*, London: Pluto Press.

Susskind, L. (1994), *Environmental Diplomacy: Negotiating More Effective Global Agreements*, Oxford: Oxford University Press.

Thomas, C. (1992), *The Environment in International Relations*, London: Royal Institute of International Affairs.

Vogler, J. and Imber, F. (1996), *The Environment and International Relations*, London: Routledge.

Werksman, J. (ed.) (1996), *The Greening of International Institutions*, London: Earthscan.

Conclusions

Ashley, R. (1981), 'Political realism and human interests', *International Studies Quarterly*, Vol. 25, No. 2, pp. 204–36.

Ashley, R. (1986), 'The poverty of neorealism', in R. Keohane (ed.), *Neorealism and Its Critics*, Princeton, NJ: Princeton University Press, pp. 255–301.

Banks, M. (1985), 'The inter-paradigm debate', in A.J.R. Groom and M. Light (eds), *International Relations: A Handbook of Current Theory*, London: Pinter, pp. 7–26.

Barrett, M. and Phillips, A. (1992), *Destabilising Theory: Contemporary Feminist Debates*, Oxford: Polity Press.

Booth, K. (1997), 'Discussion: A reply to Wallace', *Review of International Studies*, Vol. 23, No. 3, pp. 371–7.

Booth, K. and Smith, S. (eds) (1995), *International Relations Theory Today*, Cambridge: Polity Press.

Brown, C. (1992), *International Relations Theory: New Normative Approaches*, Harlow: Prentice Hall.

Brown, S. (1988), 'Feminism, International Theory and International Relations of gender inequality', *Millennium: Journal of International Studies*, Vol. 17, No. 3, pp. 461–76.

Carver, T., Cochran, M. and Squires, J. (1998), 'Gendering Jones', *Review of International Studies*, Vol. 24, No. 2, pp. 283–98.

Connolly, William E. (2001), 'Cross-state citizen networks: a response to Dallmayr', *Millennium: Journal of International Studies*, Vol. 30, No. 2, pp. 348–55.

Cox, R. (1986), 'States, social forces and world order', in R. Keohane (ed.), *Neorealism and Its Critics*, Princeton, NJ: Princeton University Press.

Dallmayr, F. (2001), 'Conversation across boundaries: political theory and global diversity', *Millennium: Journal of International Studies*, Vol. 30, No. 2, pp. 331–47.

Enloe, C. (1989), *Bananas, Beaches and Bases; Making Feminist Sense of International Politics*, Berkeley, CA: University of California Press.

Enloe, C. (1993), *The Morning After: Sexual Politics at the End of the Cold War*, Berkeley, CA: University of California Press.

Enloe, C. (2000), *Maneuvers: The International Politics of Militarizing Women's Lives*, Berkeley, CA: University of California Press.

'Interview with Professor Cynthia Enloe', (2001), carried out at the February 2001 Annual Convention of the ISA in Chicago in *Review of International Studies*, Vol. 27, pp. 649–66.

Fearon, J. and Wendt, A. (2002), 'Rationalism v. Constructivism: A skeptical view', in: W. Carlsnaes, T. Risse and B. Simmonds, *Handbook of International Relations*, London: Sage.

Foucault, M. (1980), *Power/Knowledge: Selected Interviews and Other Writings, 1972–1977* (ed. by C. Gordon), Harlow: Prentice Hall.

Fraser, N. (1985), 'What's critical about Critical Theory? The case of Habermas and gender', *New German Critique*, Vol. 35, pp. 97–131.

Frost, M. (1998), 'A turn not taken: Ethics in IR at the millennium', *Review of International Studies*, Vol. 24, Special Issue, pp. 119–32.

Fukuyama, F. (1998), 'Women and the evolution of world politics', *Foreign Affairs*, Vol. 77, No. 5, pp. 24–40.

Gadamar, H. (1977), *Critical Hermeneutics*, Berkeley, CA: University of California Press.

George, J. (1994), *Discourses of Global Politics: A Critical (Re)Introduction to International Relations*, Boulder, CO: Lynne Rienner.

Grant, R. and Newland, K. (1990), *Gender and International Relations*, Milton Keynes: Open University Press.

Haacke, J. (1996), 'Theory and praxis in international relations: Habermas, self-reflection, rational argumentation', *Millennium: Journal of International Studies*, Vol. 25, No. 2, pp. 255–89.

Habermas, J. (1972), *Knowledge and Human Interests*, London: Heinemann.

Halliday, F. (1988), 'Hidden from International Relations: Women and the international arena', in *Millennium: Journal of International Studies*, Vol. 17, No. 3, pp. 419–28.

Harding, S. (1987), 'Is there a Feminist Method?', in S. Harding (ed.), *Feminism and Methodology*, Milton Keynes: Open University Press.

Harding, S. (1990), 'Feminism, science and the anti-Enlightenment critiques', in L. Nicholson (ed.), *Feminism/Postmodernism*, London: Routledge, pp. 83–106.

Harding, S. (1991), *Whose Science? Whose Knowledge?*, Milton Keynes: Open University Press.

Held, D. (1990), *Introduction to Critical Theory: Horkheimer to Habermas*, Cambridge: Polity Press.

Hoffman, M. (1987), 'Critical Theory and the inter-paradigm debate', *Millennium: Journal of International Studies*, Vol. 16, No. 2, pp. 231–50.

Hoffman, M. (1988), 'Conversations on critical international relations theory', *Millennium: Journal of International Studies*, Vol. 17, No. 1, pp. 91–5.

Hollis, M. and Smith, S. (1994), 'Two stories about structure and agency', *Review of International Studies*, Vol. 20, No. 3, pp. 241–52.

Jones, A. (1996), 'Does gender make the world go around? Feminist critiques of International Relations', *Review of International Studies*, Vol. 22, No. 4, pp. 405–29.

Jones, A. (1998), 'Engendering debate', *Review of International Studies*, Vol. 24, No. 2, pp. 299–303.

Keohane, R. (1989), 'International Relations theory: Contributions of a feminist standpoint', *Millennium: Journal of International Studies*, Vol. 18, No. 2, pp. 245–54.

Keohane, R. (1998), 'Beyond dichotomy: Conversations between International Relations and Feminist Theory', *International Studies Quarterly*, Vol. 42, No. 1, pp. 193–8.

Kourany, J., Sterba, J.P. and Tong, R. (eds) (1993), *Feminist Philosophies*, Harlow: Prentice Hall.

Lapid, Y. (1989), 'The Third Debate: On the prospects of International Theory in a post-positivist era', *International Studies Quarterly*, Vol. 33, No. 3, pp. 235–54.

Linklater, A. (1992), 'The question of the next stage: A critical theoretical point of view', *Millennium: Journal of International Studies*, Vol. 21, No. 1, pp. 77–98.

Maclean, J. (1981), 'Political theory, international theory and problems of ideology', *Millennium: Journal of International Studies*, Vol. 10, No. 2, pp. 102–25.

Nicholson, L. (1990), *Feminism/Postmodernism*, London: Routledge.

Peterson, V.S. (1992), 'Transgressing boundaries: Theories of knowledge, gender and International Relations', *Millennium: Journal of International Studies*, Vol. 21, No. 2, pp. 183–206.

Peterson, V. S. (1992) (ed.), *Gendered States; Feminist (Re)Visions of International Theory*, Boulder, CO: Lynne Rienner.

Rengger, N. J. (1990), 'The fearful sphere of international relations', *Review of International Studies*, Vol. 16, No. 4, pp. 361–8.

Rengger, N. J. (1991), 'Going critical? A response to Hoffman', *Millennium: Journal of International Studies*, Vol. 17, No. 1, 81–9.

Rengger, N. J. (2001), 'The boundaries of conversation: a response to Dallmayr', *Millennium: Journal of International Studies*, Vol. 30, No. 2, pp. 357–64.

Rengger, N. and Hoffman, M. (1992), 'Modernity, postmodernity and international relations', in J. Doherty, E. Graham and M. Malek (eds), *Postmodernism and the Social Sciences*, London: Macmillan, pp. 127–47.

Risse, T. (2000), 'Let's argue!: Communicative action in world politics', *International Organization*, Vol. 54, No. 1, pp. 1–39.

Smith, S. (1996), 'Positivism and beyond', in S. Smith, K. Booth and M. Zalewski (eds), *International Theory: Positivism and Beyond*, Cambridge: Cambridge University Press, pp. 1–5.

Smith, S. (1996b), 'Power and truth: A reply to William Wallace', *Review of International Studies*, Vol. 23, No. 4, pp. 507–16.

Smith, S. and Hollis, M. (1996), 'A response: Why epistemology matters in International Theory', *Review of International Studies*, Vol. 22, No. 1, January, pp. 111–16.

Smith, S., Booth, K. and Zalewski, M. (eds) (1996), *International Theory: Positivism and Beyond*, Cambridge: Cambridge University Press.

Special Issue: (1987), 'Women in International Relations', *Millennium: Journal of International Studies*, Vol. 17, No. 3.

Special Section on 'Habermas and International Relations: A useful dialogue?' (2005 forthcoming), in *Review of International Studies*.

Steans, J. (1998), *Gender and International Relations*, Oxford: Polity.

Steans, J. (2003), 'Engaging from the margins: Feminist encounters with the mainstream of International Relations', *British Journal of Politics and International Relations*, Vol. 5, No. 3, pp. 428–54.

Sylvester, C. (1994), *Feminist Theory and International Relations in a Postmodern Era*, Cambridge: Cambridge University Press.

Sylvester, C. (1994), 'Empathetic cooperation: A feminist method for IR', *Millennium: Journal of International Studies*, Vol. 23, No. 3, pp. 315–34.

Tickner, J. A. (1992), *Gender in International Relations: Feminist Perspectives on Achieving Global Security*, New York: Columbia University Press.

Tickner, J. A. (1997), 'You just don't understand: Troubled engagements between feminists and IR theorists', *International Studies Quarterly*, Vol. 41, No. 4, pp. 611–32.

Tickner, J. A. (1998), 'Continuing the conversation', *International Studies Quarterly*, Vol. 42, No. 1, pp. 205–10.

Tickner, J. A. (1999), 'Why women can't run the world: International politics according to Francis Fukuyama', *International Studies Review*, No. 3, pp. 3–12.

Tickner, J. A. (2001), *Gendering World Politics*, New York: Columbia University Press.

Tooze, R. and Murphy, C. (1993), 'Getting beyond the "common sense" in the IPE orthodoxy', in R. Tooze and C. Murphy (eds), *The New International Political Economy*, Boulder, CO: Lynne Rienner.

Vasquez, J. (1983), *The Power of Power Politics*, London: Pinter.

Vasquez, J. (1995), 'The post-positivist debate: Reconstructing scientific enquiry and International Relations theory after Enlightenment's fall', in K. Booth and S. Smith (eds), *International Relations Theory Today*, Cambridge: Polity Press.

Wallace, W. (1996), 'Truth and power, monks and technocrats: Theory and practice in International Relations', *Review of International Studies*, Vol. 22, No. 3, pp. 301–21.

Waltz, K. (1979), *Theory of International Politics*, Reading, MA: Addison-Wesley.

Weber, C. (1994), 'Good girls, bad girls and little girls: Male paranoia in Robert Keohane's critique of feminist International Relations', *Millennium: Journal of International Studies*, Vol. 23, No. 2, pp. 337–49.

Weber, C. (2001), *International Relations Theory: A Critical Introduction*, London: Routledge.

Wendt, A. (1992), 'Anarchy is what states make it: The social construction of power politics', *International Organisation*, Vol. 6, No. 2.

Wendt, A. (1999), *A Social Theory of International Politics*, Cambridge: Cambridge University Press.

Whitworth, S. (1989), 'Gender in the inter-paradigm debate', *Millennium: Journal of International Studies*, Vol. 18, No. 2, pp. 265–72.

Whitworth, S. (1994), 'Theory as exclusion; Gender and international political economy', in R. Stubbs and G. Underhill, *Political Economy and the Changing Global Order*, London: Macmillan.

Zalewski, M. (1994), 'The women/"women" question in International Relations', *Millennium: Journal of International Studies*, Vol. 23, No. 3, pp. 407–23.

Zalewski, M. (1995), 'Well, what is the feminist perspective on Bosnia?', *International Affairs*, Vol. 71, No. 2, pp. 339–56.

Zalewski, M. and Parpart, J. (1997) (eds), *The 'Man' Question in International Relations*, Oxford: Westview.

Index

acquis communautaire 194
actors 14, 234
Adler, Emanuel 185, 199
Africa 4, 130
agency 15
   see also structure
Agenda *21* 206, 221, 222, 223
aggression 11, 32
aid given as percentage of GDP 105
AIDS pandemic 4
Algeria 80–1
alienation 76
alliances 59, 61
Althusser, Louis 79, 87
Amnesty International 36, 121
anarchy 27, 35, 53–4, 68, 133, 213, 245
   and English School 74
   influences on Green Thought 218
   realism on 53–4, 55, 57
   types of 194–5
Anderson, Benedict 144
Animal Aid 215
animal rights discourse 215, 216, 226–7
anthropocentrism 210, 212, 214, 215,
   221, 226, 228
Arab-Israeli war 45, 64
argumentative behaviour 190–1, 200
Ashley, Richard 113, 150–1
asylum, gender-based claims 167–8
atomic bomb 2–3
autarky 42, 43
authoritarian regimes 36

Bartelsen, Hans 53
behaviourist school 237
Bentham, Jeremy 26, 27, 213, 216
billiard ball model 53, 70
binary oppositions 131
Bolsheviks 131
bourgeoisie 80, 84, 103
Brandt Report 25–6
Brazier, Chris 216
Brazil 83, 218
Bretton Woods System 28–30, 68–9,
   120–1
Britishness 145, 148, 169, 197
Brown, Gordon 118–19, 208
Brundtland Commission 221
Bull, Hedley 66, 184, 193, 201
Butler, Judith 163, 164
Buzan, Barry 194, 199, 200

Cambodia 46
Campbell, David 125, 147
capitalism 14, 75, 108, 112–13, 119
   and class system 106–7
   and conflict 86–7, 123–4

crisis of 79–80, 86, 111
   and environment 223, 224
   as exploitative 77, 86, 99
   future collapse of 207
   global 75, 88–9, 107
      core-periphery model 92–3
   search for markets 80, 81, 113, 116
Cardoso, Henrique 83, 88
Carr, Edward Hallet 54, 237
Carson, Rachel *Silent Spring* 205, 212
child labour in Victoria era 104
China 3, 59, 143, 208
Chomsky, Noam 18, 87
civil society 36
class 75, 79–80, 99, 100–1, 123, 127
class consciousness 112
class struggle 97, 117
climate change 207, 208–9, 222, 226–7
cobweb model 38
Cold War 28, 55, 62–3, 206, 210
   and neo-realism 239, 240
colonialism 80–1, 116
common sense 10, 138–9, 238–9
communicative rationality 114, 115
community 147–9, 168–71, 226–7
   non-human beings 215, 226
conflict 48, 98–9, 150, 219–20
   and capitalism 98, 123–4
   Critical Theory on 113, 123–4
   environmental damage 223
   and realism 57, 62–4
   as structural 75
   and women 178–9
   see also violence
Connolly, William 133
constructivists 7–8
consumerism 113, 215, 228
cooperation 31, 42, 49, 66, 68, 72
Copenhagen School of security studies
   200
core-periphery model 76, 84–5, 89–90,
   92–3, 94–5
counter-hegemonic forces 112, 118, 121,
   126
Cox, Robert 8, 115, 120, 124, 139, 239,
   242, 245
critical security studies 124–5, 199
Critical Theory 8, 14, 15, 103–28, 240,
   242, 245
   core assumptions 115
   criticisms 126–7
   origins 107–15
   and scientific analysis 236
   summary 126
Cuba 43, 94–5
culture and ideology 105, 107
cyberspace *see* Internet

Davies, Nick: *Dark Heart* 100
Davison, Emily 166–7
de Beauvoir, Simone 139, 163, 164
deconstruction 131, 132–3
democracy 24, 31
democratic peace theory 32–3
Dependencia School 83, 99
dependency theory 76, 81–4, 91, 94, 99
depression (1930s) 111
Derrida, Jacques 131, 134, 140–1, 146,
   152
Descartes, René 214, 227
deterrence theory 245
developing countries *see* Third World
development theory 49
dialogic politics 123, 126
dialogue 139
diplomatic community 196
discourse 3, 138–9, 140, 142, 188, 191,
   201, 233–4, 241, 244
   of danger 6, 147
   ethics 115, 190
discrimination 96, 97, 123, 126, 127
domestic violence 158
Doyle, Michael 32–3

earth from space 211
East Timor 98
Easter Island 209
eco-feminism 227, 229
ecocentrism 210, 214, 216, 226, 229
ecological self 227
economic crisis (1980s) 25
economic crisis (2007–9) 4, 5, 41,
   118–19
economic determinism 83
economic liberalism 27, 30, 35, 103
economic power 67
economy as exploitative 80, 83
ecosystems 211, 226
El Salvador 87, 179
elites 36, 40, 93
emancipation 106, 107, 108, 109, 113,
   116, 122–3, 131, 135, 136, 154,
   242
   and knowledge 114, 115
   and state system 121
Engels, Friedrich 66, 76, 80, 101, 161
English School 66, 70, 184, 192–3, 236
   and anarchy 74
Enlightenment 110, 213, 214, 215
Enloe, Cynthia 155, 168, 242
environment 205, 206–11, 222, 223
   degradation 224, 225, 228
   disasters 212, 223
   and social organisation 222
   see also Green perspectives

environmentalism, deep and shallow 221, 222–3, 228
epistemic communities 218
epistemological approach 6, 233, 234
   criticisms of realism 71, 125
   feminism 163
   social constructivism 200
EPS project 218, 219–20
ethnocentric perspective 72
European Union 3, 40, 42, 66, 193
   enlargement 147, 199
   legislation 194–5
   as normative power 142

Falk, Richard 43–4
false consciousness 96
feminist perspectives 7, 9, 13, 15, 107, 155–82, 233, 235, 236, 244, 245
   CEDAW 174–5
   common misunderstandings 181
   core assumptions 165
   critical 242–3
   criticisms 180–1
   historical materialism 157, 160–2
   liberal 155, 157–60, 165–8, 243
   and married life 160–1, 162
   origins 157–65
   poststructuralist 155, 163–5, 242
   power relations 164–5
   standpoint 155, 162–3, 243
   summary of 180
films 17–18, 63, 70, 81
   and human rights 45
   postmodernism 137
   Weimar Republic 111–12
First World War 1–2, 17–18, 23
food security 177, 207
Ford car production 37
foreign policy 72, 144, 147, 183–4
Foucault, Michel 134, 138–9, 140–1, 152, 163, 241
foundationalism 233
fourth debate 113, 184, 232
France 80–1
Frankfurt School 107, 109–13, 126, 237
   origins of 136
free market 27, 28, 30, 46
Free Trade Agreement 26
Friends of the Earth 39
Fukuyama, Francis 28, 177
functionalism 39–40, 48
future of IR theory 245–6

Gaia beliefs 216
Galtung, Johan 99
GATT (General Agreement on Tariffs and Trade) 29, 69
GDP, shares of world 90
gender 156–7, 164

discrimination 96, 97
   division of labour 161, 171
gender inequality 126, 162, 167
   by country 173
   and cultural difference 170–1
   and Sharia Law 170–1
gender-based persecution 167–8
Germany 62–3, 89, 90
Giddens, Anthony 195
Gilpin, Robert 68
global warming 5, 10, 207, 208–9, 217, 219, 225, 226
   since 1860 222
globalisation 10, 24
   and humane governance 43–4
   hybrid identities 148
GONGOs (governmental non-governmental organisations) 38
Gorbachev, Mikhail 223
governance 43, 151, 171–2
   humane 43–4
government, liberalism on 31
Gramsci, Antonio 14, 105, 107, 112–13, 114, 115, 116, 117, 118, 121, 124, 126
Greek city states 194
Green perspectives 205–30, 240
   criticisms of 228–9
   decentralisation of power 218, 219
   origins of 212–16
   relationship with nature 243, 244
   spirituality 206
   summary of 228
green theory of value 212
Green Thought 15, 49, 210, 211, 212
green-wash 206
Greenpeace 30, 36, 37, 38–9, 50, 121, 230, 231
Guantanamo Bay 72
Guatemala 95
Gulf war (1991) 98

Habermas, Jurgen 107, 113–14, 116, 123, 124, 126, 188, 190, 242, 245
Haeckl, Ernst 213
Hamilton, Alexander 66
Harding, Sandra 236
Hegemonic Stability Theory 67, 68, 113
hegemony 42, 67, 112–13, 117–18, 121
historical materialism 77
   feminism 157, 160–2, 167
history 71, 205
Hitler, Adolf 34, 136, 152
Hobbes, Thomas 55, 56, 70, 213
Hoffman, Mark 115, 245
human nature 14, 76, 115, 242
   and aggression 11
   liberalism on 31, 48, 50
   postmodernism on 138, 142

realism on 57, 64, 72
   structuralism on 85
human rights 3, 24, 44, 72, 122
   abuses 3, 4, 45
   defining 194
   and film 45
   and liberalism 32, 47–8, 49
   and multiculturalism 47–8
   as norm 193, 194
   spiral model 198
   UN Declaration on 44, 45
   women's 172–3
human-nature relationship 211, 228, 243
   influence of religion 213
humane governance 43–4
humanism 135
Huntington, Samuel: thesis 5, 6
hybridity 148

IBRD see World Bank
ideal speech situation 114–15, 127, 190
idealism 23–4, 48
identity 69, 196–9
   Critical Theory on 121–3
   and external shocks 197–8
   feminism on 168–71
   Green Thought 226–7
   liberalism on 47–8
   postmodernism on 144–5, 146–9
   structuralism on 96–7
ideology 7, 8, 86, 105, 107
   rule by 108, 112, 117
IGOs (intergovernmental organisations) 24
imagined communities 144–5
IMF (International Monetary Fund) 29, 30, 68, 88, 89, 93, 99
   and neo-liberal agenda 151
imperialism 80–1, 142
income, global distribution 106
India 208
Indonesian deforestation 218, 224
inequality 109, 123
   gender 173–5
   Green Thought 225–6
   liberalism on 44–7
   postmodernism on 149–50
   realism on 69–70
   structuralism on 94–6
institutionalism 189–90
institutions 39–43, 120–1
   domination by elites 93
   forming superstructure 77
   and gender relations 171–3
   Green perspectives 220–3
   and interests of states 124
   as neo-liberal 151
   realism on 57, 65–9

social constructivism on 187, 192–6
supporting capitalism 107
interdependence 32, 41–2, 47, 48
and financial crisis 41
sensitivity costs 42–3
vulnerability costs 43
interdependence theory 24, 40
interests 126, 188
see also national interest
International Criminal Court 194
International Labour Organisation 120,
174
International Political Economy 66–7
International Politics 20, 66, 86
Internet 148–9
women's use of 170
intersubjectivity 124, 127, 139, 175, 188,
246
Iran, government of 27
Iraq war 3, 35, 70, 98, 197
Islamophobia 5

Japan 3, 60, 89, 90
Jordan 88
justice
and feminism 173–5
Green Thought 225–6
structuralism on 75, 94–6

Kant, I. 23, 26–7, 28, 31, 48, 195, 237
Kaplan, Morton 193
Keohane, Robert 68, 233
Keynes, John Maynard 26, 28, 48
Kindleberger, Charles 67
knowledge 8, 105, 200, 244
and common sense 138–9
constructed 191
as ideology 126
inter-subjective 114
scientific 243
types of 115
Korean War 62
Kosovo 194
Kuhn, Thomas 239–40

labour theory of value 77
Lang, Fritz: *Metropolis* 112
language 8, 114, 139, 201
Lapid, Yosef 184
Latin America 3, 4, 83, 130
Le Corbusier 111
League of Nations 23, 33–4, 53, 54, 65
Lenin, V.I. 80, 81, 96, 98
liberal economics 28, 83–4
liberal feminism 155, 157–60, 165–6,
242
liberal idealism 26
liberal internationalism 24, 35
liberal peace theory 24

liberal pluralism 24, 25, 31, 37–8, 40–1,
47, 48, 49, 210
liberalism 15, 23–51, 66
core assumptions 31–2
critique of realism 71
development strategies 49
and environment 220
left-leaning 46, 49
legitimising exploitation 104
origins of 26–31
right-leaning 46, 49
summary of 48–9
Limits to Growth 205, 212, 213, 220
Linklater, Andrew 113, 115, 121, 122–3,
190
Locke, John 107, 195
logic of appropriateness 188, 190, 191,
198, 200
logic of consequentiality 188, 190, 200

Machiavelli, N. 55–6, 74
March, James 188
marginalised groups 9, 244
markets 27, 28, 30, 46
de and re-regulation of 118–19
Marx, Karl/Marxism 7, 66, 76–7,
108–10
on capitalism 130–1
on communism 28
and Critical Theory 104–5
on liberalism 103–4
on pluralism 50
on women 161
see also structuralism
mass media 77, 112
meanings 139, 140, 142
social 6, 7
Medecins Sans Frontières 5
Mellor, Mary 227
Merchant, Carolyn 214
meta-narratives 132, 140, 152
methodologies 6, 233, 237
Mexico 89
Michigan Project 32
Middle East 3, 64, 142
Midgley, Mary 227
Mies, Maria 97
migration and environmental scarcity
220
militarism 223
military power 60, 61
Mill, John Stuart 26, 30
mind/body dualism 227
MNCs (multinational corporations) 15,
24, 37, 39, 49, 59
modernisation theory 83
modernity 110–11, 117, 213–14
dark side of 110–11, 126, 137
and Enlightenment project 134–5

modes of production 76–7, 78, 108
Monbiot, George 219, 229
moral autonomy 24, 135
moral reason 35
Morgenthau, Hans 61, 237
multiculturalism 24, 47–8
Muslim Laws 170–1, 175

Nair, Sheila 165
national identity 144–5
national interest 54, 55, 144, 145, 196,
231
criticisms of realism 72
gender lens on 166
primacy of 65
national security 237
nationalism 96–7, 121
and male privilege 169
and modern states 116
post-Cold War 125
NATO 197
Nazi regime 135, 136, 137, 237
neo-colonialism 83, 94
neo-Gramscianism 242
neo-imperialism 83
neo-institutionalism 189
neo-liberal economics 30, 44
neo-liberal institutionalism 8, 24, 30, 39,
42–3, 48, 50, 237–40
and cooperation 68
neo-liberalism 49, 100, 118, 151, 184,
185
and gender inequality 171
and international regimes 195–6
neo-neo debate 184–5, 186, 187
neo-realism 8, 42, 43, 53, 55, 57, 66, 67,
71, 73, 125, 184, 185, 192, 233,
236, 237–40
on international system 183
as orthodoxy 238–40
Neumann, Iver 193
new medievalism 193
newly industrialising countries 3, 92
NGOs (non-governmental organisations)
15, 37, 38, 40, 49, 218
criticisms of SAPs 30
and gender inequality 171–2, 175
Nicaragua 169
Nicholson, Michael 236
NIEO (new international economic
order) 96
non-intervention 192, 193, 194
normative entrapment 198
normative theory 8, 44
norms 32, 195, 241
and external shocks 197–8
human rights 70, 198
non-intervention 192, 193, 194
role of 187, 193

social constructivism on 188, 189, 190, 200, 201
and state behaviour 201
Northern Ireland 59
Norway 39
nuclear deterrence strategies 245
nuclear weapons 2–3, 17–18, 41

Obama, Barack 4, 106
OECD 89
oil crisis (1973) 19, 62, 82, 88
oil prices, future 207
Okin, Susan Moller 170
Olsen, Johan 188
ontology 6, 184, 200, 233
criticisms of realism 71, 125
feminism 163, 164
OPEC 62, 88
oppression 126
origins of IR 1–2, 18
other 141–2
othering 197
temporal 147
Oxfam 30, 231
ozone depletion 209, 219

Palestine 45, 59, 64
Pankhurst, Emmeline 166
paradigms, nature of 239–40
Parpart, Jane 155
patriarchal state 167
peace 27
Critical Theory on 124–5
and feminism 175–8
Green perspectives 223–4
liberalism and 32–3
realism on 64–5
structural analysis 99
Peace Studies 99
peace theory 32–3, 34
peak oil 207, 208
Pearce, Jenny 179
Peterson, V. Spike 155, 164
pluralism 24, 25, 31, 36, 38–9, 50, 244
ethos of 133
liberal 40–1
political liberalism 30
political pluralism 25, 31
population
growth across history 229
size and national power 62
positivism 6, 8, 234–5, 237, 246
post-Marxism 103, 107
postcolonial feminism 164–5
postmodernism 127, 129–54
criticisms of 152–3
and discourse 191
and oppression 136

origins 134–42
summary of 151–2
postpositivism 6, 7, 8, 232–7, 240–5, 246
feminism 158
poststructuralism 8, 115, 130, 153, 240, 241, 244
and discourse 233–4
poststructuralist feminism 155, 163–5, 180, 242
poverty 93, 95, 220
power 61, 192
Critical Theory on 116–19
in democracies 38
distribution of 32
economic 67
feminist perspectives 165–8
Green perspectives 217–19
happy slave 90
liberal pluralists view 39
military and economic by state 60
postmodernism and 144–6, 150, 153
pursuit of 54, 55
realism on 57, 59–62
structuralist view 86–90
power politics 32, 34, 35, 70, 71, 124, 210
legitimisation of 239
power/knowledge 8, 136, 138–40, 149
pressure groups 24
problem-solving approach 8, 124, 245
to environment 228
problematising 234
proletariat 80, 84, 104
protectionism, economic 28

racial discrimination 96, 97, 123
radicalism 76, 130
Ragged Trousered Philanthropists 77, 78
rationalism 244, 246
rationality 24, 27, 31, 49, 237–8
of foreign policy 72
realism 11, 15, 23, 36, 37, 53–74, 125, 132–3, 210, 237
as agency-centred 58
classical 53, 57
conflict and violence 62–4
core assumptions 57
criticisms of 71–3
origins of 54, 55–6, 71
on pluralism 50
two approaches 53
realpolitik 57, 237
recognition 58
reflectivists 185, 186, 201
refugees 3, 167–8, 177
regimes 36, 195–6
religious influences 213–14
republics 26–7
research methodologies 233, 237

resources 208, 213
scarcity 207, 208, 210, 218
squandering of 49, 124, 216
Ricardo, David 17, 26, 27, 35, 48, 66
Rio Conference (1992) 206, 221
Risse, Thomas 190, 198
Ropp, Stephen 198
Rostow, Walt 82
Rousseau, Jean-Jacques 213
Runyan, Ann Sisson 155
Russett, B. 25, 85, 87, 229

science 234–6, 243
security 32–5, 99, 146–7, 175–8, 245
communities 199–200
Critical Theory on 124–5
cultures of 199–200
food 177, 207
Green perspectives 223–4
realism on 64–5, 69
self 227
ecological 243
and other 141–2, 147
self-determination 130
separation of powers 31, 37
September 11th attacks 5, 72, 197, 234
Sikkink, Kathryn 198
Simpson, Homer J. 235, 246
Singer, Peter 216
slave labour 44–5
Smith, Adam 26, 27, 35, 48, 66
social classes *see* class
social constructivism 13, 125, 139, 183–203, 240, 241, 244, 246
assumptions 187–91
common misunderstandings 202
criticisms of 201–2
methodology 200
origins 184–6
summary of 200
social movements 112, 126, 148–9
socialisation 187, 188, 190, 200
Solzhenitsyn, Alexander 111, 131
Somalia 194
sovereignty 33, 37, 65
and environmental practices 217–18
external 59
internal 59, 69
and liberalism 36–7
postmodernism on 144, 145, 146
realism on 57, 69–70
Soviet Union, collapse of 3, 125
spice trade 117
spiral model 198
stag/hare analogy 65
Stalin, J. 96, 110, 111, 131
Stanton, Elizabeth Cady 157
Starr, H. 25, 85, 87, 229
state intervention 27–8, 46, 49

state of nature 26, 56, 131, 133
state-centric approach 72, 73, 144, 201,
    234, 236
state/s 14, 58, 86–90, 99, 144–6, 192
    and capitalism 117
    and Critical Theory 116–19
    as exclusionary 122
    feminist perspectives 165–8
    financial management role 118–19
    and global threats 149–50, 217–18
    Green perspectives 217–19
    interests of 237
    power creating enemies 147
    realism on 57, 58–9
    reflecting class interests 86
    society of 193, 194
    violence embedded in 150, 178
statecraft 144, 147
structural adjustment programmes 30
structural realism 74
structuralism 66, 75–102, 210, 239
    core assumptions 85–6
    criticisms of 100–1
    critique of realism 71
    and justice 75
    origins of 76–85
    as reductionist 100
    summary 99–100
structure and agency 58, 85, 109, 185–6
    social constructivism on 183, 184,
        187, 191, 201
suffragettes 166–7
superpowers: post-WWII 2, 3, 63
superstructure and base 77, 78
surplus value 77, 99
survivalist discourse 213
sustainable development 206, 221, 225,
    228

Tarantino, Quentin: *Pulp Fiction* 137
technological innovation
    and identity 47
    and networking 148–9
teleology 79, 100, 101
terrorism

Algeria 81
    war on terror 5–6, 72
Thatcher, Margaret 100
theory 10, 14–16, 107, 108, 231, 244
    deconstructing 132–3
    next stage in IR 245–6
    and practice 11, 106, 126, 244–5
thinking green 210–11
Third World 82, 84, 90, 95–6
    debt burden 87, 88–9
Thucydides 55
Tickner, J.A. 155, 156, 163, 177, 233
toxic waste dumping 39
trade
    historically 116
    and liberalism 27, 28
transnationalism 24, 47
Tressell, Robert 77, 78
truth/s 8, 109, 131, 138, 244
    realism and 71
    universal 135

ulema 27
United Nations 33, 35, 42, 93
    Declaration on Human Rights 44, 45
    and environment 205, 206, 220
    food security 177
    foundation of 34–5
    UNCED 206, 225
    UNCHE 205, 220
    and women 172–3, 174–5, 177
United States 60, 62, 89, 90, 119, 142
    hegemonic decline 42, 68
    human rights and security 72
    invasion of Iraq 35, 70, 98, 197
universalism 49
utilitarianism 27

Vietnam war 17–18, 62
Vincent, John 194
violence 48, 62–4, 98–9, 150, 219–20
    Critical Theory on 123–4
    systemic 100
    and women 178–9
    see also conflict

Wæver, Ole 147, 185, 200
Walker, R.B.J. 149
Wallerstein, I. 84, 89, 92–3, 96–7, 100,
    101, 207
Waltz, Kenneth 58, 64, 74, 237
war 1–3, 5, 35, 64, 235
    and oil resources 98
    and peace theory 34
    realism on 54, 64
    war on terror 5–6, 72
water resources 210, 219
Weber, Cynthia 146, 158
Weber, Max 107, 110, 150, 187
Weimar Republic 111–12
welfarism 49
Wendt, Alexander 193, 195, 200, 201,
    233, 241
Whitworth, Sandra 162
Wilson, Woodrow 34
Wollstonecraft, Mary 157, 160
women 159, 174
    male roles 178, 179
    public/private sphere 157, 161–2, 166,
        180
    as refugees 167–8, 177
    see also feminist perspectives
World Bank 29, 30, 68, 88, 89, 99
    domination by elites 93
    and gender 172
    and neo-liberal agenda 151
world order 116–17, 120–1, 133
    and gender relations 171–3
    Green perspectives 221–2
    and institutions 39–43, 65–9
    social constructivism on 192–6
    structuralism on 91–3
world politics 11, 134, 156
world society 24, 32, 48
World War II 1–3, 23, 67
world-systems theory 15, 75, 76, 82,
    84–5, 91, 92–3, 94–7, 99
WTO (World Trade Organisation) 29,
    151

Zalewski, Marysia 155, 164